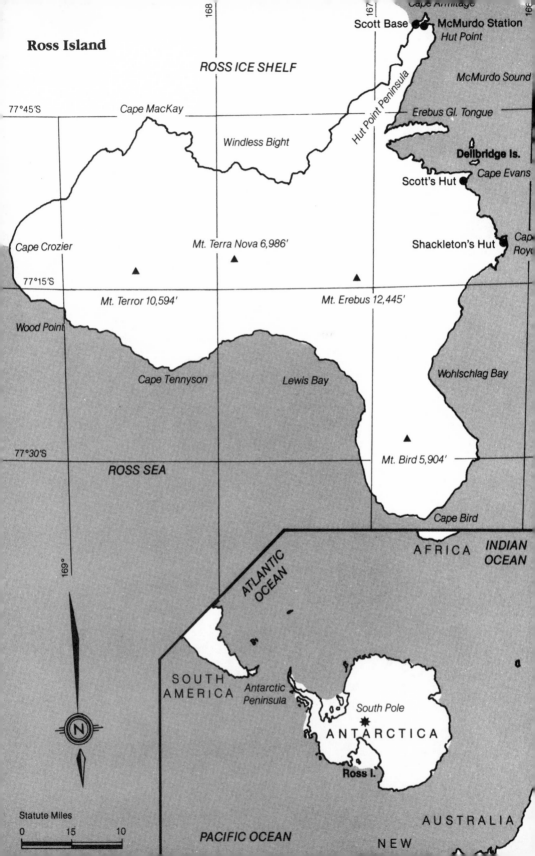

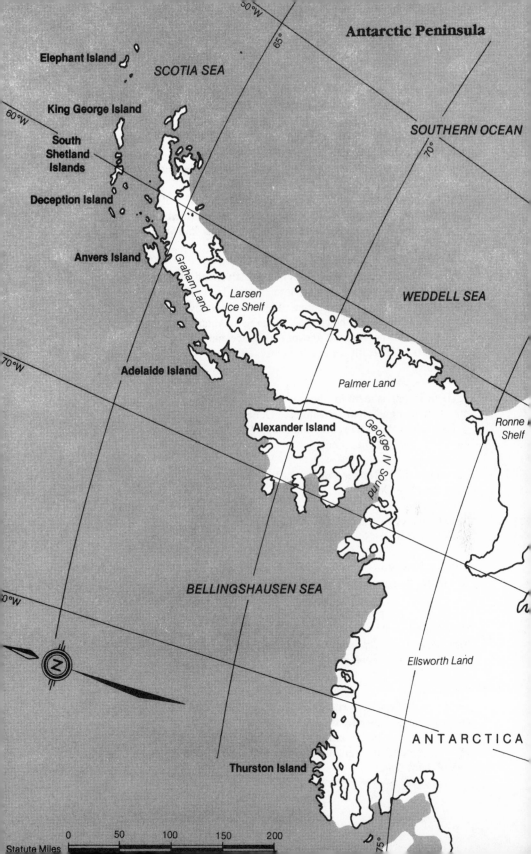

Praise for Beyond Cape Horn

"Anyone who believes that the planet Earth is fully charted and that no vast areas of wonder and beauty remain would be well advised to read this book. . . . It is nothing short of a public service to the human race." —NORMAN COUSINS, author of *Anatomy of an Illness as Perceived by the Patient*

"Neider's Antarctic adventures include the bizarre dance of the killer whales and observations of amazing weathers and skies unseen elsewhere on earth. The book is an excellent introduction to the earth's least-known continent." —*San Francisco Chronicle*

"Neider's knowledge of the region is exhaustive, and he delights in displaying believe-it-or-not nuggets of polar lore. . . . Neider's primary purpose is neither factual nor polemical. He is a man of letters who knows that for the vast majority of his readers the chances of going to Antarctica are nil. For this reason, he feels duty-bound to evoke the place and the journey for us. . . . The frigid ends of the earth are brought closer to home." —*St. Louis Post-Dispatch* (Missouri)

"Scientific data is there for those who wish it, but [this book] is also first-rate entertainment and often amusing. . . . Delightful reading." —KENHELM W. STOTT, JR., *San Diego Union*, explorer, zoologist, and former curator of the San Diego Zoo

"Fascinating. . . . Neider paints a startling portrait of the vast ice-covered wasteland." —*Dallas News*

"Neider packs a great deal of information into his *Beyond Cape Horn*." —*Denver Post*

"Neider conveys a sense of the awesome beauty and terror of Antarctica, and a feeling for those who love it." —*Library Journal*

"Neider's eye is a precision instrument. His descriptions are not impressions, but verbal equivalents of scintillating color photographs. . . . Excellent." —CLIVE SINCLAIR, *Times Literary Supplement* (London), critic and author of *Cosmetic Effects* and *Augustus Rex*

"[*Beyond Cape Horn*] is enlivened by interviews with three key explorers of past eras: Sir Charles Wright, who was with those who found the bodies of Scott and his companions after their fatal attempt at the South Pole; Sir Vivian Fuchs, who led the first land crossing of Antarctica; and Laurence McKinley Gould, who was second in command of Admiral Robert Byrd's Antarctic expedition." —*New York Times*

Beyond Cape Horn

BOOKS BY CHARLES NEIDER

Editor:
Antarctica
The Autobiography of Mark Twain
The Complete Essays of Mark Twain
The Complete Short Stories of Robert Louis Stevenson
The Complete Tales of Washington Irving
Essays of the Masters
Man Against Nature
George Washington: A Biography
Great Shipwrecks and Castaways
Great Short Stories: Fiction from the Masters of World Literature
The Great West: A Treasury of Firsthand Accounts
The Fabulous Insects, The Travels of Mark Twain
Life as I Find It: A Treasury of Mark Twain Rarities
Mark Twain: Plymouth Rock & the Pilgrims and Other Speeches
Plymouth Rock and the Pilgrims
Short Novels of the Masters
Stature of Thomas Mann
The Travels of Mark Twain

Author:
Adam's Burden: An Explorer's Personal Odyssey through Prostate Cancer
Edge of the World: Ross Island, Antarctica
The Grotto Berg

CHARLES NEIDER

❋ BEYOND CAPE HORN

Travels in the Antarctic

Cooper Square Press

First Cooper Square Press edition 2002

This Cooper Square Press paperback edition of *Beyond Cape Horn* is an unabridged republication of the edition first published in San Francisco, California in 1980, with the deletion of twelve photographs. It is reprinted by arrangement with the Estate of Charles Neider.

Designed by Anita Walker Scott
Map Design by Charles Neider
Cartography by Jon Goodchild

Published by Cooper Square Press
A Member of the Rowman & Littlefield Publishing Group
200 Park Avenue South, Suite 1109
New York, New York 10003-1503
www.coopersquarepress.com

Distributed by National Book Network

The Library of Congress has cataloged the hardcover edition of this book as follows:

Neider, Charles, 1915–
  Beyond Cape Horn.
  Bibliography: p.
  Includes index.
  1. Antarctic regions. 2. Neider, Charles, 1915– 3. Travelers—United States—Biography. I. Title.

  G860.N39   919.8'904   80-13220
  ISBN 0-8154-1235-5

⊖™ The paper used in this publication meets the minimum requirements of American National Standard for Information Sciences—Permanence of Paper for Printed Library Materials, ANSI/NISO Z39.48–1992.
Manufactured in the United States of America.

✸ Contents

List of Illustrations

Acknowledgments

THE MAKING OF A WORK such as the present one depends in great measure on the active good will and support of many organizations and people. My debts in this respect are incalculable. Nevertheless I should like to thank, however inadequately, the following institutions and persons. It goes without saying that I alone am responsible for the views and shortcomings of this volume.

The Division of Polar Programs of the National Science Foundation; the United States Antarctic Research Program (Grant No. 76-24096/S-301B); the United States Coast Guard; the United States Navy; the British Antarctic Survey; and the Scott Polar Research Institute.

Officers and crew, USCGC *Burton Island*, RRS *Bransfield*, RRS *John Biscoe* and R/V *Hero*, and the personnel of the following stations: McMurdo and Palmer (United States), Scott Base (New Zealand), Adelaide Island, Rothera Point and Argentine Islands (United Kingdom), Bellingshausen (U.S.S.R.), Presidente Frei (Chile), Arctowski (Poland) and Almirante Brown (Argentina).

The Center for Advanced Study in the Behavioral Sciences in Stanford, California, of which I was a Fellow; the National Endowment for the Humanities, Washington, by which I was designated a Fellow (Grant No. FC-26278-76-1030); the John Simon Guggenheim Memorial Foundation, New York, of which I was a Fellow; the University of California at Santa Cruz, of which I was Research Associate in Literature for a calendar year; the MacDowell Colony of Peterborough, New Hampshire; the Department of Politics of Princeton University; the Henry L. and Grace Doherty Charitable Foundation, New York.

The libraries of: the Center for Advanced Study in the Behavioral Sciences; Princeton University; Stanford University; the University of California at Berkeley, Los Angeles and Santa Cruz; the National Center for Atmospheric Research in Boulder, Colorado; the National Climatic Center in Asheville, North Carolina; the Scott Polar Research Institute in Cambridge, England; the British Antarctic Survey in Cambridge, England; and the Division of Polar Programs in Washington, D.C.

Grant Barnes, Leigh Bienen, David Bresnahan, Peter Christopoulos, George Cody, C. Michael Curtis, William Dalton, Richard Falk, Robert Flint, Jr., Sir Vivian and Lady Fuchs, Laurence M. and Margaret Gould, William Gregory, Jerry Huffman, Jeanie Jordan, Harold Kuebler, Pieter Lenie, Leopold Levy, John Lohr, John Lowrance, Frank Mahncke, Nicki Marx, Lyle McGinnis, Robert Murphy, Samuel and Tessie Noble, Edward Olsen, Donald Osby, Patricia Perkins, David Rubinfine, Conrad Spohnholz, Marshall Sylvan, James Westwater and Shane Williams.

Gardner Lindzey (director), Preston Cutler (associate director), Kay Jenks (assistant director), Margaret Amara (librarian) and Yaron Ezrahi, Thomas H. Hunter, Carolyn Merchant and Eugene Roberts (colleagues) of the Center for Advanced Study in the Behavioral Sciences. James F. Mathias (vice president) of the John Simon Guggenheim Memorial Foundation. Eugene Cota-Robles (academic vice chancellor), Helene Moglen (dean of the Division of Humanities and Arts), Joseph Silverman (provost of Stevenson College) and Paul Spriggs (bursar of Stevenson College) of the University of California at Santa Cruz.

I wish especially to thank:

Senator Harrison Williams, Jr., of New Jersey; Guy Guthridge and Robert Rutford of the Division of Polar Programs; Stuart Lawrence, William O. Sloman, Ron Lewis Smith and Charles Swithinbank of the British Antarctic Survey; Henry

Acknowledgments

Bienen of the Department of Politics and Robert A. Axtmann of the Department of Chemical Engineering, Princeton University. I am indebted to Jon Beckmann and James Cohee of Sierra Club Books for excellent editorial advice. My gratitude to James Cohee for fine and precise editorial suggestions of many kinds is very considerable.

My debt to Joan Merrick Neider, my wife, for her tolerance of my long absences, for her supportiveness of my Antarctic activities and for her invaluable comments on the manuscript of the present work is so great that I recognize the futility of trying to convey it.

1 ❈ Prologue

IT IS NOT TOO EARLY to speak up on behalf of a continent that has a reputation for being fiercely hostile to life and yet which, when the weather is quiet, impresses one with its gentleness, peacefulness, innocence—a place remote from other great landmasses, different because so extreme, the sole continent that never harbored man.

Jesus said, "The poor ye shall always have with ye," and one has to agree, sadly, that he has not been proved wrong. Now it seems likely that we will have overpopulation with us for a long time, and the increasingly rapid depletion of the earth's fossil-fuel resources that will be an inevitable result.

The present oil crisis has dramatized the pressure to exploit such reserves, and it is not surprising that the eyes of certain nations, our own among them, have turned to Antarctica, for Antarctica comprises one-tenth of the earth's landmass, and there are many reasons to believe, if we are to trust geological research and extrapolation, that the continent and its continental shelves may contain great oil and gas resources. It is only a question of a decade or two before the advanced nations possess the technology for exploiting them.

The harm that can be done by unchecked commercial activity in Antarctica was witnessed early in the last century when freewheeling, often secretive sealers decimated the fur seals to a point close to extinction and slaughtered vast numbers of penguins for a pittance of blubber. It may be observed today in

1

the frightful depredations being committed by Japanese and Soviet whaling vessels outfitted with the latest apparatus for killing and processing great whales, whose like, if they are not soon protected by international outcry, mankind may never see again. The management of Antarctica is in a state of confusion despite the claims of the Antarctic Treaty signatories that the continent and its sea are safeguarded by human reason and enlightened disinterest.

The treaty has reserved certain regions for the protection of special fauna and flora but the areas are small, isolated and scattered, and the provisions covering them are limited in scope and do not envision the desirability of selection and protection of sites for aesthetic as well as ecological reasons. Furthermore, their life is limited to that of the treaty, and their effect is possibly limited to the treaty signatories.

The heart of the matter was touched in a little-publicized resolution of the second World Conference on National Parks, held in Wyoming in September 1972. More than four hundred delegations from seventy-five countries urged (unanimously, it was reported) that a world park be established in the Antarctic region, under the direction of the United Nations, to "further protect the unaltered natural ecosystem of the Antarctic continent and the areas surrounding it."

In Antarctica man can view a truly primeval wilderness. It is essential to his psychic well-being that his feelings of awe, wonder, mystery, humility, his appreciation of incredible and unspoiled natural beauty on a tremendous scale, not be taken from him. But what will protect this so-called savage place against the coming ravages of man if it is not a concordance of international opinion? Antarctica is an everyman's land, and any nation, however small, or any private firm, for that matter, if it has the capabilities, can go there to do its commercial will.

Those who have experienced Antarctica and have fallen under its great spell imagine a time of the continent's commercial exploitation, of hostile international rivalry, perhaps even of physical conflict in a huge landmass where, as far as is known, no murder has ever been committed. But one does not need to know Antarctica personally to be profoundly saddened by the prospect.

What more appropriate place for an international park than

Antarctica where, although a number of nations claim sovereignty over various slices of the Antarctic pie, all such claims were shelved for the duration of the treaty, which went into effect in June 1961 and whose life-span, without counting possible renewals, is thirty years.

It should be agreed that no exploitation of any sort may take place in the proposed park. We owe it to our descendants, near and remote, to undertake this task before it is too late.

Why is Antarctica so important? It has a commanding influence on the weather of the southern hemisphere and a considerable influence on the weather of the entire planet. It is the only continent that pulses or fluctuates. In winter it spawns masses of dense sea ice that spread out for hundreds of miles, and at that time it is about twice as large as it is during the austral summer. It has its own kind of ocean. The Antarctic waters are colder and less saline than the other oceans. With their rich supply of nutrients, both phytoplankton and zooplankton, they provide a major grazing area for the great whales. And there is another kind of ecology—political ecology, so to speak—that makes Antarctica more important than ever. I refer again to the Antarctic Treaty, under which nineteen nations (including the United States and the Soviet Union) have agreed to respect the continent as a demilitarized zone and preserve it for scientific research. Thus far, the signatories have avoided any major violation and the treaty stands as a remarkable prototype of international cooperation. But the stress of international competition is bound to increase, and the treaty has no teeth except moral ones. Any tearing of its fabric will be a loss not only to contemporary man but to our posterity.

I do not think I have to belabor Antarctica's current importance, but let me stress one resource which is not often spoken of and which in our utilitarian and pragmatic age is insufficiently valued. And that is Antarctica's remarkable beauty. It is of first importance to remember the value of beauty and aesthetics for man's psychic health. It would be tragic if humanity were no longer able to view a primordial and unbelievably beautiful wilderness that far predates man. I make a plea for the distinction between humanizing a continent and manhandling it.

The Arctic Ocean is a basin within large landmasses: Eurasia,

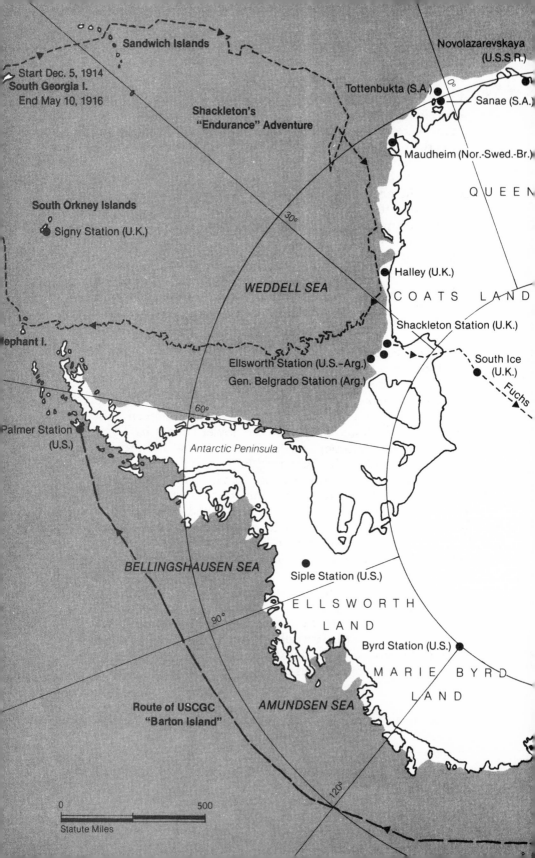

Sandwich Islands

Novolazarevskaya (U.S.S.R.)

Start Dec. 5, 1914
South Georgia I.
End May 10, 1916

Tottenbukta (S.A.)

Sanae (S.A.)

Shackleton's "Endurance" Adventure

Maudheim (Nor.-Swed.-Br.)

QUEEN

30°

South Orkney Islands

Signy Station (U.K.)

Halley (U.K.)

WEDDELL SEA

COATS LAND

Shackleton Station (U.K.)

Elephant I.

Ellsworth Station (U.S.-Arg.)

Gen. Belgrado Station (Arg.)

South Ice (U.K.)

Fuchs

60°

Palmer Station (U.S.)

Antarctic Peninsula

BELLINGSHAUSEN SEA

Siple Station (U.S.)

90°

ELLSWORTH LAND

Byrd Station (U.S.)

MARIE BYRD LAND

AMUNDSEN SEA

Route of USCGC "Barton Island"

120°

0   500
Statute Miles

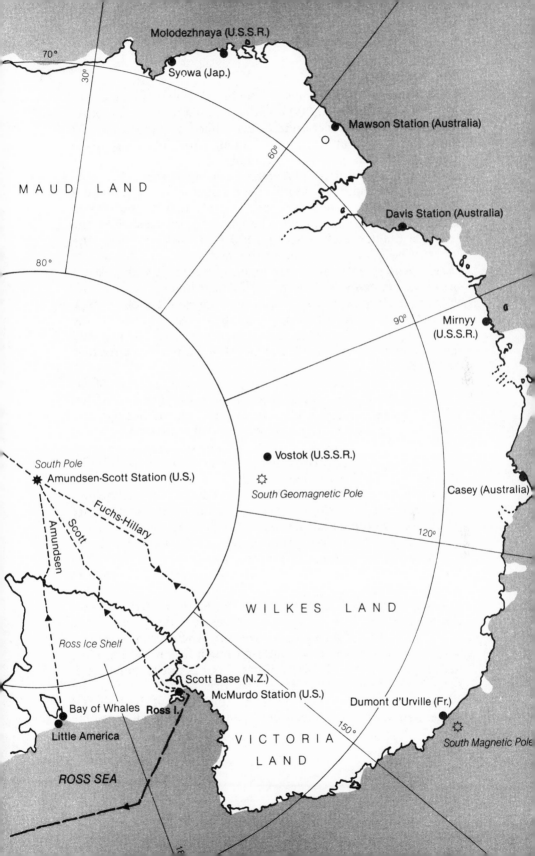

North America and Greenland. The North Pole is an imaginary point on a sea about 10,000 feet deep. Antarctica, on the other hand, is a circumpolar continent surrounded by a great sea. The South Pole, with an elevation of about 9200 feet, is approximately at the center of the continent.

To give a sense of scale: Antarctica occupies more than one-quarter of the landmass south of the Equator. Its area is about 5,500,000 square miles, or approximately that of the United States and Mexico combined. The largest of its ice shelves, the Ross Ice Shelf, which is some 1400 feet thick and is mostly afloat, although it is attached to the land, is roughly the size of France. Antarctica is by far the highest continent, with an average elevation of some 7000 feet. The next highest is Asia, with an average altitude of about 3000 feet. There are mountains in Antarctica, such as Mt. Tyree and the Vinson Massif of the Ellsworth Mountains, whose elevation exceeds 16,000 feet, and several peaks of the Transantarctic Mountains are higher than 14,000 feet.

The Antarctic icecap, which covers about 92 percent of the continent, is roughly conical in form, always in motion, and has a depth of as much as 15,000 feet. It is so vast and heavy that it has been surmised it has depressed the Antarctic land by about 1950 feet. It contains around 90 percent of the world's fresh water. It has been calculated that if this icecap were to melt, the level of the world ocean would rise 200 to 250 feet, with obvious disastrous effects on the world's port cities. No earthquakes have been recorded in Antarctica, possibly because they are suppressed by the icecap's weight. But there is volcanic activity in the huge iceland. Deception Island, off the northwest coast of the Antarctic Peninsula, erupted about a decade ago. And Mt. Erebus on Ross Island is continuously active, although in varying degrees.

The lowest recorded temperature on earth occurred at Vostok Station, the Russian Antarctic base near the geomagnetic pole: minus 126.9° F. As for its dryness: Antarctica is the great white desert. It is too cold to permit much free moisture. During the fierce blizzards, what blows about is not so much new-fallen stuff as old matter that is very dry, hard and harsh. The average annual fall in terms of water equivalent at the Pole is 2 inches as against 7 1/2 inches in Phoenix, Arizona. The extreme dryness can create physiological problems. Dehydration can lead to spasms of large muscles such as the hamstring. And as for winds: there are places where you can experience gales of up to 200 miles an hour.

Another example of scale. Antarctic icebergs, in contrast with Arctic ones, are tabular because they calve off the tabular ice shelves. A tabular berg is a berg that's like a table. Some years ago such a berg was encountered that was roughly the size of Connecticut.

In addition to being the highest, driest, coldest and windiest continent, it is also by far the most remote. In 1969 a fossil was found there, Lystrasaurus, that nailed down the theory of continental drift from the point of view of paleontology. The tectonic and oceanographic evidence for the theory had been developing over a period of many years but it was still possible to be an anti-drifter, so called. But here was a freshwater amphibian, largely reptilian, with some mammalian characteristics, that was separated from the nearest other landmass in which you find its counterpart by at least 600 miles of open, salt sea, across which it could not possibly have migrated.

Antarctica was once the hub of a southern supercontinent called Gondwanaland after a region in India, and was attached to South Africa, southern South America, the Indian peninsula and Australia, and it is obvious by extrapolation that this continent and its continental shelves should have resources similar to those found in the previously contiguous areas, such as minerals and fossil fuels. Nations are developing the technology for drilling for gas and oil in polar regions, not only in the northern hemisphere but in the southern as well. Recently a multinational scientific group penetrated the Ross Ice Shelf down to waters of primeval darkness, which had not seen light for centuries and perhaps millenia. After a season of failure, corrections were made and the new drilling was successful. Such progress in basic science cannot be divorced from progress in applied science. The days of "little" science, of individuals and small teams, are giving way to those of "big" science, including multinational operations such as the Dry Valley Drilling Project and the Ross Ice Shelf Project. The multinational oil companies are watching the developments closely. One of the things that's keeping them from pouring large sums of money into attempts to exploit the continental shelves is the fact they can't yet be guaranteed their investment will be safe, and the reason is the problem of territorial sovereignty claims.

Antarctica's ecosystems are fragile, almost marginal, and great and irreparable damage could be done. As for oilspills, the waters are so cold that oil is not readily biodegradable. And the currents would spread the spills into the temperate regions. The hazards of working in the Antarctic weather and in the teeth of the tabular bergs which are known to be able to scour the ocean bottom because of their great thickness are extreme. If the North Slope and the Alaska oil line presented problems, with the environmental degradation that ensued, not to mention the improper work such as the bad welds, consider what might happen in the Antarctic, where the arena is international in scope.

The ancient Greeks postulated that because there was a landmass in the high northern latitudes, to balance things out there had to be a landmass in the high southern ones. They turned out to be correct although not for the right reason: the landmass of the northern hemisphere is more than twice as large as that of the southern one. For centuries it was believed the southern continent was huge and even torrid. Antarctica exists, linguistically, by sufferance. It means "opposite the Arctic." The word "arctic" is from a Greek root meaning "bear" and refers to a northern constellation known as the Great Bear.

For a long time it was believed that beyond the tropics (if one were ever able to cross them; they were imagined to be devastatingly hot) there was a great continent to be discovered, claimed and exploited. Then came the age of sea exploration. Perhaps the world's greatest navigator, Captain James Cook of the British Royal Navy, made three great voyages between 1772 and 1775 specifically to determine if such a continent existed. In 1773 and again in 1774 his was the first ship to cross the Antarctic Circle. He reached a latitude of 71°S. And because he was able almost completely to circumnavigate the globe at a high latitude he disproved forever the possibility of the existence of a continent that was thought to stretch from the Pole all the way up to the Drake Passage. It was Cook's published reports of the prodigious numbers of fur seals on Antarctic islands like South Georgia that started the fur seal trade and eventually the fur seal madness. Cook was a marvelous navigator and a very admirable person, but as a prophet of Antarctica's future he was mistaken. He doubted that anyone would find it profitable to proceed southward beyond him into the great and beautiful and deadly icy wastes.

Then there was the age of commerce, with its harvesting of fur seals for their fur, and penguins and whales for their blubber. The United States and Great Britain were the chief sealers. In the early decades of the last century the United States needed a balance of trade and got it by shipping fur seals to China. Around the middle of that century, when whaling profits in the Arctic grew marginal, there came the destruction of the great whales. And now there's a unilateral and unchecked harvesting of krill. All this is sad to have to report, for Antarctica is remarkable in many ways, among them the fact that it's the only large landmass on earth that you can visit without a colonialistic sense of guilt—there was no native class there to be expropriated and dishonored, if not destroyed.

We are all becoming aware of krill, *Euphausia superba*, a small, shrimplike crustacean that's a very significant point in the Southern Ocean food chain and that has a high protein yield. You often see parts of snowy hillsides in Antarctica tinted pink because the penguins feed on the reddish krill. The Southern Ocean, which is the confluence of the Pacific, Indian and Atlantic oceans at a high latitude, has its own characteristics. It encircles a roughly circumpolar continent, is the coldest and least saline great sea on earth, and is very rich in nutrients, most of which are formed in the so-called Antarctic bottom water, particularly that of the Weddell Sea, and many of which nourish the world ocean. The rich Humboldt Current on the western shore of South America is part of that water. The Southern Ocean has lots of phytoplankton and zooplankton, and the chief zooplankton that processes the phytoplankton is krill. Although the Southern Ocean has few species as compared with other oceans, it has extremely large numbers of individuals.

It has been said you can annually harvest more krill than the whole of the world's annual catches of fish, and you can supply this high-protein substance to undernourished populations. Unfortunately such populations are mostly to be found in the Third World, which doesn't yet possess the technology required for harvesting krill successfully. Among other problems involved in harvesting krill is that the crustacean spoils rapidly. Chile, Japan, Poland, the Soviet Union, Taiwan and West Germany are currently harvesting krill, and with the modern sonar and other sophisticated devices it's startling how much they can dredge up. The krill is turned into a powder and later made, among other things, into a sort of anchovy paste. It is also sold as a meal or directly as a seafood.

Few if any of the harvesting nations have been willing to heed a simple question: Has the depletion of the great whales been balanced by increasing numbers of seals, penguins and other animals that feed off the krill? We don't know very much about krill and its relation to the rest of the Southern Ocean biomass, yet we are very busy doing our will there, which historically is about what is to be expected of any common. By "we" I mean mankind in general, and I exclude the United States, whose fisheries in modern times have not been active in the Antarctic.

After the age of commerce, there followed the heroic age which began around the turn of the present century, when the first deep land explorations were made under the direction of a remarkable member of the Royal Navy—Robert Falcon Scott, who died with four companions on his return from the Pole after learning at the Pole that he had been bested as its discoverer by the Norwegian, Roald Amundsen, but who nevertheless in his dying left a much greater mark on western civilization than Amundsen in his triumph. The reason for this is complex but is certainly to be found in the manner in which he died, the grace with which he died and, most remarkable of all, the documents he wrote while dying. By the way, readers interested in twentieth-century works of great literature should not overlook Scott's last diaries, letters and journals in a volume called *Scott's Last Expedition*. Nor should they fail to read Apsley Cherry-Garrard's *The Worst Journey in the World*, which is an extremely well-written and authentic account. It is debatable when the heroic age ended, whether it was with the death of Ernest Shackleton on South Georgia in 1921, or with the completion of one of Richard E. Byrd's expeditions.

In 1957 came the age of science. The continent's chief current exported product is scientific information, as it has been for some time. I am not antagonistic to science. I have a science degree and I find the world most fascinating to me when I deal with it in terms of scientific concepts. But I do not like the idea of a monopoly in the Antarctic, and one that is supported by the federal treasury and tends to exclude people like myself.

Despite this caveat, the monopoly of science has been one of the most intelligent, far-seeing and benevolent of monopolies. Men of good will, with a large sense of things, and concerned with ideals of conservation, have done much to protect the continent despite their relative political innocence. They have had an important influence on national and international policies in the Antarctic, although admittedly in varying degrees. And the role of the United States in the Antarctic in modern times has on the whole been admirable. The nation has been a leader in exploration, in science, in conservation, in political enlightenment (including the employment of women both in science and logistics). Under its guidance and laws, numerous environmental impact studies and statements have been drafted and implemented, and significant efforts have been and are being made to protect the unique environment. The mistakes of the past, such as the dumpground at McMurdo Station and the pollution of the floor of McMurdo Sound near it, are recognized and regretted. I was impressed by what I saw of the attempts to respect the environment.

I think I can understand why people like me are not begged to go to the Antarctic. In the first place, the channels have been set up by Congress to send scientists there via the National Science Foundation. The National Endowment for the Humanities does not have direct access to Antarctica. In the second place, I am not a team member, I am not "controllable" in the normal sense, I have loyalties that possibly seem nebulous and threatening, I don't feel that my first allegiance is necessarily to the National Science Foundation or to the British Antarctic Survey or even to the United States or to the United Kingdom. In writing the present work I have an allegiance to what I call the general public, or my own conscience. I don't know precisely what that is but certainly it has something to do with trying to portray the truth as accurately as one's talents and psychic limitations and defenses permit. I hope the present book will help broaden the United States program to make it a less hostile one toward humanists.

Antarctica was included in the great global scientific study known as the International Geophysical Year (1957–58). As a result of the remarkable international scientific cooperation, twelve nations that were involved in Antarctic research decided it was in the best interests of science and its internationalizing influence to continue the excellent work there. The result was the Antarctic Treaty, of which the United States was a leading advocate and architect. The treaty was signed in Washington in December 1959. The twelve original signatories (the claimants are asterisked) are Argentina*, Australia*, Belgium, Chile*, France*, Japan, New Zealand*, Norway*, South Africa, the United Kingdom*, the United States and the Soviet Union. The acceding powers are Brazil, Czechoslovakia, Denmark, the German Democratic Republic, the Netherlands, Poland and Romania.

It is generally understood that science has a benevolent internationalizing effect. Perhaps the most monumental work of science, in the sociological and diplomatic senses, was the creation of the treaty, which was put together so there would be free scientific use of the demilitarized continent, free international exchange of scientists and scientific information, and above all free access. Nuclear explosions and the deposit of nuclear wastes were banned and open inspection of stations permitted. It is the sole international treaty set up primarily in the interest of science. It has already served as a prototype for two important international treaties, the Treaty for Outer Space and the Nonproliferation Treaty.

The treaty came into being through secret diplomatic means. It was believed that this was the only way in which it could be born. But unfortunately the secrecy, which amounts to a distrust of the public that foots the bill, or to disbelief that the people who pay to flesh out such ideas are capable of being large-minded and reasonable, has continued in the all-important consultative meetings of the treaty powers that are held regularly around the world. This is a disservice to the public and to Antarctica itself. We need open discussions of the issues, and we need to introduce into the Antarctic new kinds of people, such as the social scientists, who can help broaden the area of understanding and can help bring the public to a greater awareness of the Antarctic and of its importance to the health of mankind and the globe.

One of the most nettlesome problems in the Antarctic politically is: Just how are the territorial claims to be resolved? It's not so much a question of whether they have a solid basis in fact (many and possibly all of them do not), for logic is not the principal force to contend with. Much more important are nationalistic emotions and interests, and whether the claimants will resort to the use of force if hard pressed. Under contemporary international law it is not enough to raise a standard, or nail a brass plaque to a tree, or make an oral proclamation, as in the old days, to secure a territory for one's country. Nowadays you must have what is known as effective occupation. But how do you effectively occupy Antarctica, which is so very hostile to life? To date no one has effectively occupied any part of the continent, yet the territorial sovereignty claims are felt nevertheless, even though they have supposedly been shelved for the life of the treaty.

When consultative meetings of the treaty powers are held and someone raises the issue of keeping the treaty viable by being realistic and dealing openly with problems of possible exploitation of mineral resources and fossil-fuel reserves (otherwise the outside world will step in; it isn't going to be patient with the treaty powers forever; it will move in with its own ships, either unilaterally or under the aegis of the United Nations, and do what it wishes, as some nations are doing now with krill), everything comes to a standstill because the claimants in certain respects refuse to act as though they've actually shelved their claims. I should add that the two superpowers make no claims to sovereignty in the Antarctic. However, both reserve the right to make such claims based on geographical discovery and scientific research while disclaiming the right of other nations to make sovereignty claims.

Another very difficult question arises in connection with the treaty: Is the treaty too utopian in banning the use of force? When you have a treaty whose ideal is the non-use of force, what do you do about mavericks? What do you do about a contracting party, or an acceding party, or a nation that does not belong to the treaty, or a private consortium, or an extremely wealthy individual, that says, "I'm going to go down there and do my will"? What do you do, for example, about Prince Faisal of Saudi Arabia, who has publicly announced his intention of harvesting Antarctic icebergs and hauling them to Saudi Arabia to supply fresh water to his country at a much cheaper price than by desalinization processes? And who has also announced he's going to offer such bergs for profitable sale to anyone who cares to buy them?

Many people think it's a great joke, and Prince Faisal goes on TV and is written about widely. Or people say, "Terrific. How wonderful. We do need fresh water." But it's not likely to be a joke or terrific to southern hemisphere nations, particularly the more temperamental and nationalistic ones like Chile and Argentina, whose climate and the ecology of whose waters may be disturbed by large-scale movement of tabular bergs to the northern hemisphere.

Harvesting icebergs may well involve problems of the Law of the Sea as well as those connected with Antarctic sovereignty claims. The claims are not limited to the Antarctic continent. They include great portions of the Southern Ocean and its islands. For eons the bergs have moved northward until they melted, and they have affected the temperature and salinity of the austral waters and no doubt have had their effect on the Antarctic atmosphere as well. Are the austral nations to be expected to watch placidly while their environment is changed by northern ones? Or can one foresee, while peering dimly into the future, North–South confrontations?

And what of the effects of the huge bergs if they're parked in the northern low and middle latitudes? What would happen, for example, to the weather of the San Francisco Bay area, not to mention to the ecology of the bay itself, if one were placed in San Francisco Bay?

Saudi Arabia is neither an original signatory of the Antarctic Treaty nor an acceding nation, and yet who is to exclude it from the Antarctic, and on what legal grounds? For that matter, on what legal grounds is the Third World to be excluded, or any agency of the United Nations such as the FAO (Food and Agriculture Organization), which has shown much recent interest in the Antarctic, to the considerable nervousness of the treaty club nations? At present the Third World lacks the technology required for harvesting Antarctic riches, the riches presumed to be there, but what of the future? And what of the Third World's claim to a share of the riches in any event, based on their reasoning of "the common heritage of mankind"?

As an example of the complexity of the politics of the Antarc-

14

tic, let us briefly examine the Antarctic Conservation Act of 1978, which the United States Congress created in October of that year, which circumscribes various activities of American citizens in the Antarctic and which makes it a criminal offense to do certain things there.

The act (95–541), which was initiated by the State Department, is described as intended "to implement the Agreed Measures for the Conservation of Antarctic Fauna and Flora, and for other purposes." The term "Antarctica" (note that this term usually refers to the continent) is defined as "the area south of 60 degrees south latitude," and so it includes large portions of the Southern Ocean and their islands. The act begins: "The Congress finds that (1) the Antarctic Treaty and the Agreed Measures for the Conservation of Antarctic Fauna and Flora, adopted at the Third Antarctic Treaty Consultative Meeting, have established a firm foundation for the continuation of international cooperation and the freedom of scientific investigation in Antarctica; and (2) the study of Antarctic fauna and flora, their adaptation to their rigorous environment, and their interrelationships with that environment has special scientific importance for all mankind."

The purpose of the act is "to provide for the conservation and protection of the fauna and flora of Antarctica, and of the ecosystem upon which such fauna and flora depend, consistent with the Antarctic Treaty, the Agreed Measures for the Conservation of Antarctic Fauna and Flora, and Recommendation VII-3 of the Eighth Antarctic Treaty Consultative Meeting."

The act makes it unlawful for any United States citizen, unless authorized by regulation or permit prescribed under the act, "to take within Antarctica any native mammal or native bird, to collect within any specially protected area any native plant, to introduce into Antarctica any animal or plant that is not indigenous to Antarctica, to enter any specially protected area or site of special scientific interest, or to discharge, or otherwise dispose of, any pollutant within Antarctica." It further makes it unlawful "for any United States citizen wherever located . . . to possess, sell, offer for sale, deliver, receive, carry, transport, or ship by any means whatsoever, or to import into the United States, to export from the United States, or to attempt to so import or export, any native mammal or native bird taken in Antarctica or any native plant collected in any specially protected area." The act excepts actions committed "under emergency circumstances to prevent the loss of human life."

The act prescribes civil penalties (fines of up to $10,000 per prohibited act) and criminal ones (a fine of $10,000 or imprisonment for not more than one year, or both, for each offense). It empowers certain authorized officers to *"search without warrant* any person, place, or conveyance where there is reasonable grounds to believe that a person has committed or is attempting to commit an act prohibited by section 4 (a); *seize without warrant* any evidentiary item where there is reasonable grounds to believe that a person has committed or is attempting to commit any such act" and to "make an arrest with or *without a warrant* with respect to any act prohibited by section 4(a) if such officer has reasonable grounds to believe that the person to be arrested is committing such act in his presence or view, or has committed such act." The italics are mine.

Regarding large-scale commercial activity in the Antarctic, the act is not as rigorous as it might seem at first glance, for section 13, near the end of the act, states: "Nothing in this Act shall be construed as contravening or superseding the provisions of any international treaty, convention, or agreement, if such treaty, convention, or agreement is in force with respect to the United States on the date of the enactment of this Act, or of any statute which implements any such treaty, convention, or agreement."

It is a curious act. Under it, I, as a United States citizen, would be committing an unlawful offense if, while living alone on an uninhabited Antarctic island, I carried a penguin from one place to another, or if I did so while a guest of the British Antarctic Survey or any other foreign Antarctic organization. There is no question but that the intent of the act is idealistic. However, good intentions do not justify bad means. In the first place, one wonders about the right of Congress to circumscribe the behavior of American citizens "wherever located." Is this a case of Big Brother reaching out too long an arm? Of course, Congress has the right to legislate the behavior of its citizens when they are bearing arms overseas, as well as to control their behavior in commerce with other nations. But does it have the right to legislate their behavior while they are within the bor-

16   BEYOND CAPE HORN

ders of other sovereign states? Surely if I am in Moscow or London I must obey the laws of Moscow or London rather than those of Washington. If I am a guest of the British Antarctic Survey in Antarctic waters or at an Antarctic station, in a territory claimed by the United Kingdom, Chile and Argentina but not by the United States, and in many senses in a territory to which no nation has authentic claims, is my behavior to be legislated by Congress or by the United Kingdom or by Chile or by Argentina? Realistically and diplomatically it would require that it be legislated by the United Kingdom, yet the fact is I would be subject to the act wherever I was located. To make the point: Precisely where in the Constitution does Congress derive the right to pass and enforce such an act?

There are other important questions. Is it wise of Congress to pass legislation that possibly it cannot enforce? What specific quid pro quos do we have with other Antarctic Treaty powers for preserving the Antarctic in this connection and in this manner? And what about the clauses of the act that provide for search and seizure without a warrant, on suspicion only? Do they violate one's constitutional right to due process?

The Antarctic Conservation Act of 1978 bases itself prominently upon certain recommendations of the Antarctic Treaty powers. As a matter of fact, the chief purpose of the act is to have the nation abide by its treaty commitments. But is this not very self-serving? Does it not help to legitimize a treaty created by self-appointed Antarctic landlords? And does it not also possibly legitimize the exclusion of the Third World from the Antarctic, not to mention other non-acceding nations?

In order to have a more complete understanding of the political basis of the act, one needs to know something about the clubs-within-clubs structure of the group of nations adhering to the Antarctic Treaty. Article XIII of the treaty states in part that the treaty shall be open to accession by any state which is a member of the United Nations or by any other state which may be invited to accede to the treaty with the consent of all the signatories who have consultative power, that is, the power to attend and to vote at the consultative meetings. Article IX of the treaty states in part that each acceding nation shall be granted consultative status "during such time as that Contracting Party demonstrates its interest in Antarctica by conducting substantial scientific research activity there, such as the establishment of a scientific station or the dispatch of a scientific expedition."

In short, the original signatory powers have the self-granted right to attend and vote at the important consultative meetings regardless of whether they continue to demonstrate their interest in Antarctica "by conducting substantial scientific research activity there." Among the twelve original signatories, Belgium and Norway have been inactive in Antarctica for varying periods without damaging their consultative power. Nations that merely accede to the treaty are not granted a similar right. It was not until July 1977 that an acceding nation was given consultative status, which Poland received after two years of conducting regular Antarctic research expeditions and after building ArctowskiStation on King George Island. Technically, Poland may lose this right, which she enjoys only "during such time as that Contracting Party demonstrates its interests in Antarctica by conducting substantial scientific research activity there," whereas Norway and Belgium do not have to fear the loss of the right.

And so we have the original signatories, which have this important right without restrictions, and acceding nations that do not have the right or vote, and the unique acceding nation that has been granted the right but on condition she continues to be active in Antarctica. This is what I mean by clubs within clubs. Not to forget the claimant nations, which hope to have their territorial sovereignty claims ratified by the rest of the chief club and by the world at large, as against the nonclaimant ones, which recognize no territorial claims and make no claims in Antarctica, yet reserve the right to make them.

I have no wish to belabor the point. Political matters with regard to the Antarctic are difficult and complex.

Antarctica is in some respects intermediate between terrestrial places and those in outer space. If we hope to find reasonable solutions to coming political problems in deep space and on the moon (for example, the willful international destruction of satellites, or territorial sovereignty claims to parts of the moon), we had better reach intelligent precedents for them in the Antarctic while there is still time.

Before I close this Prologue I should like to say a few words about myself in relation to the Antarctic and about the present book. I have been absorbed in the study of the Antarctic region for the past decade and I have visited Antarctica three times. My first trip was made in 1969 under the auspices of the United States Navy, my second in 1970 under the sponsorship of the National Science Foundation (an independent United States federal agency) and my third once again with NSF. During the last trip I was for a while a guest of the British Antarctic Survey, so it may be said that the third visit was partly sponsored, although perhaps unofficially, by that organization.

The first trip gave me a rapid, overall view of American activities in a major part (the Ross Island Dependency sector) of the continent. The second was a working residence, made for the purpose of gathering materials for a book. The product of this trip was *Edge of the World: Ross Island, Antarctica*, a large, illustrated book published in April 1974. In it I described the life, the scientific research, the history of exploration, and the beauty of the sector containing the chief American base, McMurdo Station. I also described a visit to the Russian base, Vostok Station, and life at Scott Base, the New Zealand station on Ross Island, where I lived for a time.

Prior to the beginning of my last trip the National Science Foundation and I jointly selected the Southern Ocean and the Antarctic Peninsula as my new focus of Antarctic interest, the Southern Ocean because I was unacquainted with it, and the Peninsula, in addition to my being unfamiliar with it, because it is the most international of all sectors of the continent in the sense that it contains, within a relatively small area, bases owned by six nations: Argentina, Chile, Poland, the United Kingdom, the United States and the Soviet Union. Also, it is the richest part of the continent historically. It is here the sealers and whalers operated in the early decades of the last century. Finally, the Peninsula is the scene of three overlapping sovereignty claims (made by Argentina, Chile and the United Kingdom), and is most likely to be the place of international contention should mineral or other valuable resources be discovered there. In visiting this sector it was my hope to fill out my understanding of the continent, of its ecological problems, of its scientific work and goals, of the relationship between science and the increasing encroachment of technology, of the use of science and technology by national states as part of their geopolitical strategy, and of the problems of international relations, the latter very likely to come under considerable strain in the Peninsula sector (if not in the entire Antarctic region) during the next decade or two.

Let me end this prologue by saying what the present work is not. It is not an Antarctic primer. Nor is it an extended fact sheet. Attempts to sum up the Antarctic in terms of "hard" facts are at present still doomed to be dated rapidly. In the first place, many of the so-called hard facts turn out on intensive examination to be quite soft. In the second, some of the most exotic facts have surfaced in just the last several years. Examples of the latter come readily to mind: perhaps the most remarkable meteorite finds in history, in terms of number, weight and possibly also kind of meteorites; the discovery that there are benthic life forms in the great darkness under the Ross Ice Shelf; the discovery of microecosystems a few millimeters beneath the surface of certain rocks, particularly Beacon sandstone, in the Dry Valleys; and the discovery that algae flourish deep under the ice of certain Dry Valleys freshwater lakes.

The present volume is not didactic by intent or nature; that is, it is not primarily interested in making moral observations or with unburdening itself of a shipload of facts. However, it attempts, especially in this Prologue, to orient the reader unsophisticated in the subject of the Antarctic.

What then are its hope and intention? They are no more nor less than to be a narrative of one person's second reunion with the Antarctic, and an attempt to humanize the place, so far as this can be done, by capturing the texture of human existence there, not the least task of which involves an effort to describe the Antarctic's remarkable and haunting beauty, and not simply impressionalistically, to use the word as the painters used it, but with as much precision as possible, the belief being that aesthetic, psychological and emotional facts are just as authentic and valuable as scientific ones, and possibly more so. The book may be described as evocative insofar as it tries to avoid the abstract and to suggest instead the quality of human existence in the Antarctic, including human work and human relationships, and the strange relationship between humans and the haunting continent together with its equally haunting and remarkable ocean.

It attempts, among other things, to present the first literary narrative of an extended voyage on the Southern Ocean at an extremely high latitude, two degrees south of the Antarctic Circle. Similarly, the book tries to offer the first literary narrative of the crossing of the Drake Passage from Antarctica to Tierra del Fuego, and on a relatively small vessel, a 125-foot motor sailer.

The present book is also an attempt to describe certain regions of the Antarctic for the first time in literary ways and to give an interior, an emotional, a psychological equivalent to the exterior places I have seen. The latter do have their human counterparts. It would take a dull human being indeed to go to the Antarctic and just look and say, "So what? There's a mountain, there's ice, there are a lot of actinic rays and cosmic rays, and now I'll go home." That's not the way it works. There are deprivations you experience in the Antarctic—sensory, perceptual, emotional, sexual—and there are fascinating interior consequences, which the present work will try to explore.

There are things in the Antarctic that no human imagination can dream up. They're unearthly. As a matter of fact, one of the haunting things about the place is that you look at pictures you yourself have taken, and you do not believe you actually saw such scenes of surpassing nobility, mystery and beauty, and it's part of the Antarctic addiction to have a voice in you that says with increasing intensity and persistence, "I *must* go back to check out that I truly did see them."

It does not often happen, in a contemporary lifetime, that one has the visible opportunity, in one's chosen medium, to confront the challenges of an absolutely fresh frontier. I was well aware of the opportunities that presented themselves. They were part of the reason I urgently wanted to visit the Antarctic again. I trust I was equally aware of the responsibilities that came interwoven with them.

2 ✸ Ross Island Revisited

THERE IS ONLY ONE United States base (Palmer Station) in the entire Peninsula region of Antarctica. Access to it is by a relatively small motor sailer, R/V (Research Vessel) *Hero*, owned by the National Science Foundation and operated for the Foundation by a private contractor, Holmes & Narver of Southern California. In any single austral summer season the vessel could make only a limited number of trips across the Drake Passage between Argentine Tierra del Fuego and the American base on Anvers Island, and the maximum number of passengers it could carry, for safety reasons, was thirteen.

My visit to the Peninsula did not have the priority of those of most scientists, and even scientists were having special trouble reaching the Peninsula at the beginning of 1977. Earlier in the season the *Hero* had been disabled in trying to shove an iceberg, and had to retreat to South America for repairs, and this narrowed the bottleneck even further. It was out of the question for me to fly directly to Tierra del Fuego and to cross the Drake Passage on the vessel.

Consequently I would fly to Christchurch, New Zealand, where I would receive polar clothes, would fly from there to McMurdo Station almost due south of New Zealand, and the United States Coast Guard icebreaker *Burton Island* would take me across a vast stretch of the Southern Ocean to Palmer Station. I would depart the United States on January 3, 1977, from Pt. Mugu in Southern California.

22

From my journal: "Landed at Hickam Air Force Base near Honolulu at 10:30 P.M. California time (8:30 Hawaii) for a two-hour refuel stop. We had been fed a TV dinner at 6:30— steak like charred wood. Now we ate papaya in the cafeteria. Temperature outside: 70° F."

I went out for a long solitary walk. Although I was familiar with Hickam and Honolulu, I was already feeling that loosening of emotional connections that occurred as one stretched the umbilical cord between home and Antarctica. I could sense the gravitational force of my normal life begin to diminish and I imagined briefly that I was in a space ship moving steadily away from earth. Somewhere between Christchurch and McMurdo that cord would be effectively severed, as a consequence of which one would begin, in the Antarctic, the process of rebirth and would return to one's home a strangely seachanged figure, however hidden from external scrutiny that change might be. The field stretched away, spacious, flat and dark.

4 JANUARY. "We landed at Pago Pago, Samoa at 6:15 A.M. California time. I think it was 3:15 A.M. local time. Balmy, fruity, humid night. 81° F. The familiar small terminal building. Natives and Americans sleeping on mats, benches and pebbles. Sweating heavily, I stretched out on a bench in the terminal."

In Pago Pago we were in the Southern Hemisphere, almost fifteen degrees below the Equator, and we were very close to the International Dateline. We were not only tired, we were disoriented as well. All we wanted now was the solace of landing at Christchurch and ridding ourselves of the plane's noise and of our sweat and our crowded condition. As we strolled on the tarmac to the great plane whose wings at rest drooped like those of a tired or injured bird (they straightened in flight), breathing the solid, perfumed air, taking in the backdrop of green and very rank mountains and the tropical flowers and hearing the lulling sough of combers, Samoa seemed romantic enough despite our weariness.

Above all it spoke to us of the very great climatic change we would soon experience. We had left winter and entered summer, and in Christchurch we would be at a latitude of almost 45°, farther south than Australia and even Tasmania and a good deal south of the Cape of Good Hope. The South Island, of which Christchurch was the largest city, was the latitudinal equivalent, approximately, of Nova Scotia, South Dakota and Oregon. We would feel the fullness of early summer in Christchurch, only to leave it for the perennial winter of Antarctica. And 45° would seem a low latitude indeed to those of us who voyaged to 90°, the Pole itself. If Samoa seemed romantic with all its associations of tropical languor, our destination seemed even more so at the spectrum's other end: the paucity of warmth and warm colors and of life itself.

5 JANUARY, WEDNESDAY. "Arrived in Christchurch at 10:15 A.M. New Zealand (daylight saving) time. Shared a room at the Town Hall Motel on Peterborough Street with Don Osby, a young geology graduate student at Northern Illinois University, going to the Dry Valleys for work to be used in his doctoral dissertation: logging gamma rays in boreholes."

7 JANUARY, FRIDAY. "Arrived at CDC (Clothes Distribution Center) at the U.S. Navy depot at 8:45. Tried on clothes and separated my hold luggage from my survival gear. Asked for and got an anorak, which had not been issued me. It will make a good windbreaker on the *Burton Island*. New mukluks, which I'll probably not use.

"Osby and I took a cab back to the motel, where we received this message: we will fly to the ice Monday morning at the latest. The motel is on Peterborough Street, which reminds me constantly of Peterborough, New Hampshire and of the MacDowell Colony there."

The MacDowell Colony is an artists' colony at which I had spent much time. Thoughts of it brought back memories of Peterborough town, of Mt. Monadnock and Pack Monadnock, of long evenings playing cowboy pool (a combination of pool and billiards), of poker games, of long swims in the Y pool in Keene twenty-two miles to the west, of Dublin Lake, of endless bike rides to Jaffrey and Hancock and beyond, of people I had grown very close to, and above all of the glories of solitude devoted to doing exactly what one wanted or hoped to do in terms of work, solitude mixed with fireplace smoke, bright meadows hot and redolent of early fall, the sounds of an ax on a fallen tree, the scratching and racing sounds of small squirrels living in my roof.

10 JANUARY. "10:25 P.M. Osby and I have checked out of the motel. The last couple of evenings he has been staying up very

24   BEYOND CAPE HORN

late trying to reduce rocking play in a 35mm *f*/2.8 lens, using a set of tiny screwdrivers I brought with me. He's charming, of medium height, with dark curly hair and a full beard, quiet, respectful and serious but with a good sense of humor."

The C-130 Hercules, which had a silvery pylon tank under each wing, was a large, four-engine turboprop plane capable of carrying troops and equipment. The present one, owned by NSF and operated by the U.S. Navy, had skis as well as wheels. We would land on skis when we reached McMurdo.

It was mid-January, the equivalent of mid-July in the northern hemisphere, a full-blown summer's day, yet here we were, dressed in polar clothes, for this afternoon we would debark onto a great floating ice sheet, the world's greatest, the Ross Ice Shelf, the size of France and 1400 feet thick. This Christchurch day would be followed by night, for here the world still behaved diurnally, rationally, whereas tonight at McMurdo the sun would not set but would go round and round counterclockwise, a little higher over the horizon at noon than at midnight.

I remembered how, during my second Antarctic trip, I had yearned for the sun to quit stabbing and bristling for just a while, to stop bouncing off all the ice and sunburning me at three and four in the morning when I was camping out, and how I would sometimes think, "Please, sun, go away. Go to sleep." And I recalled how marvelous it had felt on my return to Christchurch when, standing in the middle of the night on a motel balcony, I had stared up through willows past a church-yard and steeple at the wondrous stars and the sky's sweet, dark, soothing blanket, and how grateful my facial skin, which at times had come off in shreds because of Antarctic sunburn, had felt.

We had hung around Christchurch and New Brighton Beach and now we were hanging around Harewood Airport. Hanging around felt like an essential part of getting to Antarctica. And after you entered the Herc and found a seat and dumped your survival bag and parka wherever you could, you hung around some more, only now you were chatting and laughing and your spirits were very high, for you had made it to the inside of the C-130 and there was a good prospect of your leaving this town at last. We waited about an hour before takeoff.

We headed 2400 statute miles almost due south. The craft's

noise was terrific and eventually exhausting, and although you tried not to talk against it, to content yourself with plugged ears and plugged privacy, the need to communicate with something other than gestures (in a situation better suited to deaf mutes) occasionally was too strong to resist, and so you unplugged yourself and shouted and strained to hear until you were rewarded with a sore throat and throbbing eardrums. Still, one was grateful for the incessant sound and the powerful vibrations. If they had suddenly stopped, the effect would have been great and instantaneous alarm. The plane was too crowded for much moving about. The general feeling, at least for me on this third flight down, was compounded of excitement, disorientation, physical irritability and a strong desire to get the flight over with. The midday meal, which you balanced on your lap, because it broke the flight's monotony had some of the glamour of a banquet and all the careful tiny gestures of openheart surgery.

The C-130 did not have a round-trip capability between Christchurch and McMurdo Station, therefore there was a PSF, a Point of Safe Return, past which the craft had to continue toward McMurdo. There had never been an instance of a C-130 going down on this flight. I thought how lucky this was, for there was little rescue possibility in the high-latitude southern waters, and a large loss of life would be a severe blow to the American Antarctic program. The C-130 was a remarkable workhorse. It could take a great deal of punishment. In many significant ways it had transformed the American program. When one first took this flight there was a tendency to think about the PSF, and I had noticed several persons quietly crossing themselves, but later one was as fatalistic about this aspect of Antarctic travel as any other.

Ross Island is one of the most fascinating places in Antarctica. Of volcanic origin, situated at a latitude of almost 78°, roughly triangular in shape and some forty-five miles wide and an equal distance long, it is the site of the continent's largest and most active volcano, Mt. Erebus, 12,450 feet high. On its western side, at Cape Royds, it harbors a group of Adélie penguins in the world's southernmost penguin rookery.

Above all, Ross Island is famous for the historical events

which have occurred there and for the remarkable stature of the men who participated in them. In this respect it surpasses any other place on the continent. Both Robert Falcon Scott (1868–1912) and Ernest Shackleton (1874–1922) used the island as the base for their polar explorations. Scott's two huts at Hut Point and Cape Evans and Shackleton's hut at Cape Royds are still intact. All three are protected as historic sites under the Antarctic Treaty.

The island was discovered by James Clark Ross (1800–1862), a British explorer who also discovered the Ross Sea and the Ross Ice Shelf and who named many of the most conspicuous features of the island and its vicinity: Mt. Erebus, Mt. Terror, Cape Crozier, Cape Bird, McMurdo Bay (renamed McMurdo Sound by Scott's first expedition), Victoria Land, Beaufort Island and Franklin Island. On January 21, 1902, Scott, in the ship *Discovery* (of about 700 tons and specially built for Antarctic work), with a crew of some fifty men, became the first explorer since Ross to make his way into McMurdo Sound.

Scott devoted almost his entire life to the service of the Royal Navy. He had become a naval cadet at thirteen, a midshipman at fifteen and a full lieutenant at twenty-three. He was reticent, sensitive and moody. His intelligence and admirable personal style marked him as a leader. He was a naval commander when he was selected to head the Discovery Expedition. During the expedition he introduced a number of Fridjof Nansen's Arctic techniques into Antarctic work and opened the era of full-scale land exploration of the continent, using sledging traverses. He made many geographical discoveries, among them Edward VII Land, which much later was found to be a peninsula and was renamed accordingly. He also discovered and named Mt. Discovery, the Royal Society Range and many important landmarks among the "Western Mountains." The Western Mountains was the name often used by him for the chain of mountains (part of the Transantarctic Range), beautifully visible from McMurdo Station, on the western side of McMurdo Sound. He, Ernest Shackleton and Edward A. Wilson sledged to a new farthest south of 82°17' on December 30, 1902.

On the return trek from the new southing Shackleton came down with scurvy complicated by the coughing of blood, and Wilson, a doctor, had fears for his life. Scott seemed to feel that

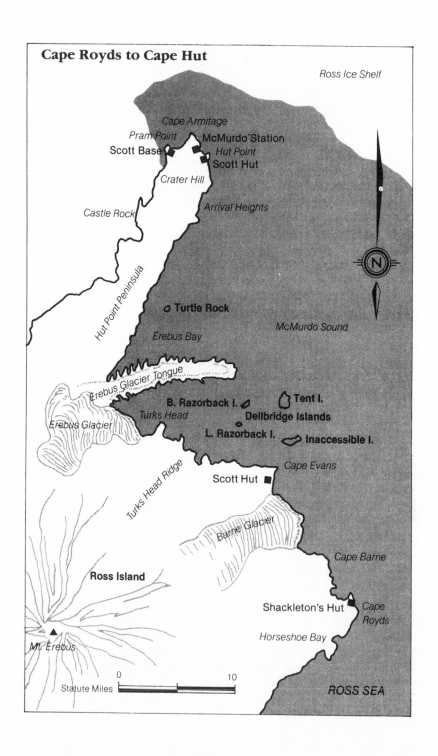

Cape Royds to Cape Hut

Ross Ice Shelf

Cape Armitage

Pram Point

McMurdo Station

Scott Base

Hut Point

Scott Hut

Crater Hill

Castle Rock

Arrival Heights

Hut Point Peninsula

Turtle Rock

McMurdo Sound

Erebus Bay

Erebus Glacier Tongue

B. Razorback I.

Tent I.

Turks Head

Dellbridge Islands

Erebus Glacier

L. Razorback I.

Inaccessible I.

Cape Evans

Scott Hut

Barne Glacier

Turks Head Ridge

Cape Barne

Ross Island

Shackleton's Hut

Cape Royds

Mt. Erebus

Horseshoe Bay

0   10

Statute Miles

ROSS SEA

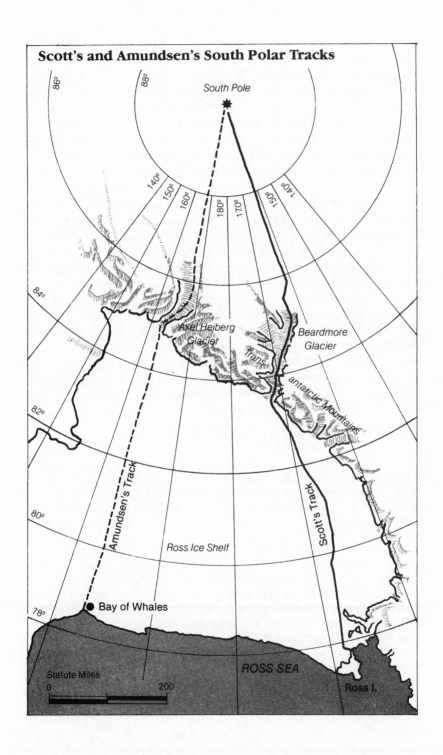

Scott's and Amundsen's South Polar Tracks

South Pole

86° 88°

140° 150° 160° 180° 170° 150° 140°

84°

Axel Heiberg Glacier

Beardmore Glacier

Trans

antarctic Mountains

82°

Amundsen's Track

Scott's Track

80°

Ross Ice Shelf

78°

● Bay of Whales

Statute Miles

0   200

ROSS SEA

Ross I.

Shackleton had let the party down, even though he realized that Shackleton's illness was as disappointing and disagreeable to Shackleton as to himself. Shackleton was invalided home in March 1903 with a taint of disgrace. After his recovery he mounted his own expedition, although he had difficulty in getting it financed. When he asked Scott if he could use the latter's Discovery Hut as his base, Scott declined, explaining that he himself hoped to use it in the not distant future.

Shackleton's British Antarctic Expedition left England on the *Nimrod* in 1907. Shackleton hoped to base himself on the Ross Ice Shelf off the Bay of Whales but on examining the ice there decided it was too dangerous. He thereupon sailed to Ross Island, where he found he could penetrate the sea ice only as far south as Cape Royds, some twenty-two miles north of Hut Point. He settled on this cape, where he built his now famous hut, in which I had the honor to live during my second Antarctic trip. On January 9, 1909, he and three companions made a southing to within 97 geographical miles (almost 112 statute miles) of the Pole, in the process pioneering the Beardmore Glacier route over the Transantarctic Mountains. The party barely made it back to Ross Island. In his work of laying depots and at the beginning and end of the great traverse Shackleton made use of the Discovery Hut. He first revisited the hut August 14, 1908. In *The Heart of the Antarctic* he recalled:

It was very interesting to me to revisit the old scenes. There was the place where, years before, when the *Discovery* was lying fast in the ice close to shore, we used to dig for the ice that was required for the supply of fresh water. The marks of the picks and shovels were still to be seen. I noticed an old case bedded in the ice, and remembered the day when it had been thrown away. Round the hut was collected a very large amount of *débris*, including seal-skins and skeletons of seals and penguins. Some of the seal-skins had still blubber attached, though the skuas [a polar bird which preys on Adélie eggs and chicks] had evidently been at work on them. . . . The old hut had never been a cheerful place, even when we were camped alongside it in the *Discovery*, and it looked doubly inhospitable now, after having stood empty and neglected for six years. One side was filled with cases of biscuit and tinned meat and the snow that had found its way in was lying in great piles around the walls. There was no stove, for this had been taken away with the *Discovery*, and coal was scattered about the floor with other *débris* and rubbish.

Shackleton's expedition accomplished important work in addition to the new southing. For example, it made the first ascent of Mt. Erebus and it reached the south magnetic pole. At that time the latter was some 375 statute air miles northwest of Cape Royds.

Scott's second and last expedition (the British Antarctic Expedition, 1910–13) left England in June 1910 on the *Terra Nova* and reached McMurdo Sound in the first week of January 1911. Unable because of ice conditions that year to base himself again at Hut Point, Scott chose a cape known as "The Skuary," some fifteen miles to the north, for his base. He renamed the cape Cape Evans in honor of his second in command, Lt. E. R. G. R. Evans. Like the great eighteenth-century English explorer and navigator James Cook, Scott was much interested in the scientific work of his expeditions, to such an extent that he often tempered the fevers of geographical exploration in order to gather and retain the materials for scientific investigation. But always his and the British nation's prime hope for this expedition was the discovery of the South Pole.

The Discovery Hut was again destined to be used as a staging post for depot-laying parties and as a jumping-off base in an attempt to reach the Pole. Scott revisited it January 15, 1911. He was appalled by its condition. He wrote in his journal:

Shackleton reported that the door had been forced by the wind, but that he had made an entrance by the window and found shelter inside—other members of his party used it for shelter. But they actually went away and left the window (which they had forced) open; as a result, nearly the whole of the interior of the hut is filled with hard icy snow, and it is now impossible to find shelter inside. . . . There was something too depressing in finding the old hut in such a desolate condition. . . . To camp outside and feel that all the old comfort and cheer had departed, was dreadfully heart-rending. I went to bed thoroughly depressed. It seems a fundamental expression of civilised human sentiment that men who come to such places as this should leave what comfort they can to welcome those who follow, and finding that such a simple duty had been neglected by our immediate predecessors oppressed me horribly.

By March 7, after some hard work, the hut had been put into good condition again. On November 3, 1911, Scott and four companions—Edward A. Wilson, Henry R. Bowers, Lawrence E. G. Oates and Edgar Evans—left the hut for the last time. They reached the Pole on January 18, 1912, only to find they had been bested by Roald Amundsen, the Norwegian explorer. Their return journey was beset by illness, hunger and blizzards. Evans died February 17 at the foot of the Beardmore Glacier. On March 16 Oates walked out of the tent into a blizzard in the hope of saving those more physically fit. Scott, Wilson and Bowers pitched their final camp only some eleven miles from One Ton Depot on the Ross Ice Shelf (about 150 miles from Hut Point) but were hopelessly blizzarded in. In a great naval tradition of keeping logs under the most adverse conditions, Scott kept writing his journal until close to the end. Also, he wrote several letters to friends and colleagues explaining what had gone wrong and crediting his sledging companions with noble behavior under heartbreaking circumstances. He referred to himself and his companions as dead men but there was no self-pity and little self-concern in either the journals or the letters. His outlook remained broad to the end.

On November 12, 1912, a search party discovered the tent, containing his body and those of Wilson and Bowers, as well as his records, letters and journals. On the sledge were thirty-five pounds of geological specimens, gathered on the Beardmore Glacier, that the party had declined to abandon despite the fact that for a long time they had been exhausting themselves in manhauling.

The Discovery Hut was to play still other important roles during the heroic era of exploration of the continent. After hearing that Amundsen had reached the Pole, Shackleton concluded that "there remained but one great main object of Antarctic journeyings—the crossing of the South Polar continent from sea to sea." The route he chose was from the Weddell Sea to McMurdo Sound. In 1914 he commanded the British Imperial Trans-Antarctic Expedition in the hope of achieving this goal. He failed to reach it, but as with Scott the failure was in some respects a glorious one: a triumph of the human spirit over great adversities. His ship *Endurance* was trapped by ice in the Weddell Sea, drifted ten months and was eventually crushed. The crew thereupon lived on an ice floe for almost five months, drifting northward. Finally escaping by whaleboats which they had saved from the *Endurance*, they reached deserted Elephant Island. Shackleton and five companions then set out in an open boat to seek help, crossing 800 miles of Antarctic waters to South Georgia, where they became the first men to traverse the island's high, dangerous mountains in their journey to the Norwegian whaling station on the opposite side of the island. The men stranded on Elephant Island were rescued, but only on the fourth attempt. One of the extraordinary facts of the Weddell Sea part of the expedition is that not one life was lost.

In February 1947, members of the U.S. Navy's Operation High Jump, a task force that had already established Little America IV at the Bay of Whales, landed at Hut Point to survey the possibility of setting up an auxiliary base there. They also landed at Cape Evans. A year later members of Operation Windmill toured the historic huts briefly, after which Ross Island was not visited by man until late in December 1955, when Operation Deep Freeze I established a base in preparation for the extensive and continent-wide scientific activities of the International Geophysical Year of 1957–58. Hut Point was selected as the site in January, and the base was called Naval Air Facility McMurdo, McMurdo being Archibald McMurdo, a lieutenant on the *Terror*, in honor of whom Ross named McMurdo Bay.

Suddenly we landed, with a few heavy bumps on the skis. The aft platform was lowered, bluish polar light streamed in. We disembarked by the front door and there one was, on the ice of Williams Field, with plow trucks and huts all around, and Mt. Erebus looming like an unbelievable hill. I say hill because that's the impression Erebus gives despite its great altitude. It's a shield volcano, with gently sloping sides, as compared with a cone volcano like Mt. Fuji, which is to say that the lava that formed it was relatively thick. Erebus is one of the great active volcanos of the world and is larger than Vesuvius, Fuji or Etna. It is one of two or three volcanos that contain a red-hot lava lake, and I believe it's the only white volcano in the world. In Greek mythology Erebus was the son of Chaos. It was also the dark nether place through which souls passed on their way to Hades. Shakespeare used the phrase "as dark as Erebus," and

Homer in *The Odyssey* described souls gathering and stirring in Erebus.

I had a special and personal reason for being moved by the sight of it now, for near the end of my second Antarctic trip I had been one of four men who crashed in a Coast Guard helicopter close to its crater. The story is a complex one which I have no desire to tell again, having detailed it in *Edge of the World*. But for reasons that will become clear later, the reader of the present work needs to know about this special relationship I had with the volcano, and the fact that my companions and I were for a time believed to be dead and that I regarded myself as a dead man during much of the episode.

Williams Field is roughly half a dozen miles from McMurdo by bus. It comprises a large airfield complex that includes a skiway, the adjacent camp, and ice runways for wheeled aircraft on the sea ice. It is the focal point of aerial support provided to inland stations. Through it Antarctic Development Squadron Six (VXE-6) maintains air links between the interior of the continent and the outside world. The field was named for Richard T. Williams, a Seabee tractor driver who drowned off Cape Royds when his Caterpillar D-8 tractor broke through the sea ice on January 6, 1956. Williams went down about two miles west of Royds while he was en route to Cape Evans. His tractor crossed a bridge over a crack in the bay ice and was twenty feet beyond when a section of ice broke and the vehicle fell through. The tractor weighed more than thirty tons. Its escape hatch and side door were locked open but the machine went down so rapidly Williams was unable to escape. It was after this tragedy that the Navy decided to use a sea-ice runway at Hut Point for its aircraft rather than one that was planned for Cape Evans. When the McMurdo base became known as McMurdo Station, the station's unusual airfield was named Williams Field.

McMurdo is the center of American logistic and scientific activity in Antarctica. Its winter population of about two hundred and summer population of almost a thousand make it the largest base on the continent. Perched on volcanic hills on the southern tip of Ross Island, it has a severe climate, with an all-time recorded low of $-59°$ F and with winds clocked as high as 155 miles an hour. Its black hills and roads give it the look of a mining camp.

The base looked as I had described it in *Edge of the World*.

The station, dark, its background hills dark also despite their mantle of snow, was much uglier than I remembered it to be, for now it lacked a benign covering of snow and ice. Porous volcanic rock was everywhere, crushed to gritty dust in the main roads. There were no streets, only lanes, unpaved, without sidewalks, gray, uneven. Littered as it was with much equipment, some of it on pallets—crates, cases, gas cylinders, sledges, huge fuel tires, generators, bulldozers, reels of heavy wire—the station suggested a wartime supply dump. One saw telephone poles, power lines and large silvery tubing on wooden trestles. The place was not without some color. In addition to green Jamesway huts there were rust structures, wine-colored ones and crimson boxlike plywood shacks. Towering over the station was the brown-gray heap of Observation Hill, a trail snaking up to the crest, on which stood the Polar Party Cross. At times you wanted to spread something over the hill's embarrassing, ugly nakedness.

Building 166 was a large, blue, two-story prefabricated metal building with buff stripes and was set on heavy wooden timbers so that drift snow wouldn't pile against it but would blow under and past it, and because it was cheaper and quicker to build in this manner than to drill into volcanic permafrost. There were eighteen separate rooms on the first floor and single rooms and a couple of dormitory rooms on the second, together with a lounge. A simple wooden stairway of six steps, with a wooden balustrade, stood at the main entrance. The Lodge was luxurious by comparison with most of the continent's structures. At its main entrance were heavy, foyered double doors.

My room was spacious, had two closets, two single beds, a Formica-topped desk, an overhead light, a floor lamp, bed lamps, two red armchairs, red curtains to match, a coffee table, a linoleum floor and steam heat. One view out of the windows was of a row of red Nodwells (a large, heavy, tracked vehicle) parked on the southern side of the USARP garage across the road.

The Lodge (Building 166) was situated on the station's eastern extremity. A little way south of it was the USARP administration building, known as the Chalet. The Chalet was a rare structure in Antarctica because it had a bit of style, even though it was imitation-Swiss. It sat on a hill above the helo pads and hangar. As you approached it from the Lodge you saw beyond it

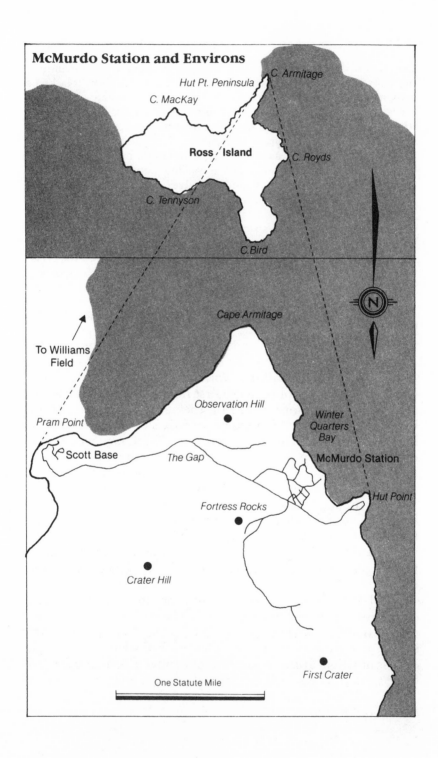

McMurdo Station and Environs

Hut Pt. Peninsula

C. Armitage

C. MacKay

Ross / Island

C. Royds

C. Tennyson

C. Bird

Cape Armitage

To Williams Field

Observation Hill

Winter Quarters Bay

Pram Point

McMurdo Station

Scott Base

The Gap

Hut Point

Fortress Rocks

Crater Hill

First Crater

One Statute Mile

N

the sea ice of McMurdo Sound and the beautiful white cone of Mt. Discovery. To the right of the entrance door, in silver letters, was the legend: NATIONAL SCIENCE FOUNDATION.

Standing on the Chalet's small open porch, I noticed that the Richard E. Byrd Memorial, a bronze bust of Byrd on a polished black Norwegian marble pedestal, had been moved from the close vicinity of the chapel to an open space closer to the Chalet. It was donated by the National Geographic Society and was originally erected in October 1965. Byrd (1888–1957) was one of Antarctica's greatest explorers. More than any other person, he was responsible for the introduction into and wide use of aircraft on the continent. He led five successive Antarctic expeditions, beginning with the expedition of 1928–30. During this expedition he constructed the station Little America on the Ross Ice Shelf near the site of Amundsen's old base off the Bay of Whales, and made numerous geographical discoveries, including the Rockefeller Mountains, Marie Byrd Land (named in honor of his wife), and the Edsel Ford Mountains (now called the Ford Ranges). It was on November 29, 1929, that he first flew over the South Pole and became the first person to fly over both geographic poles.

Returning to Antarctica in 1934, he made other significant geographical discoveries. It was during this second expedition that he wintered over alone at Bolling Advance Weather Station on the ice shelf some 125 miles south of Little America. It appears from his narrative that he not only wanted to take weather readings of the continent's interior but to experience the extreme solitude of a solitary winter-over. This was the kind of human exploration reminiscent of Scott's insistent desire to see how far the human body could be pushed short of disaster during manhauled traverses. An aloof, reserved member of an old Virginia family, Byrd was reluctant to publish the personal details of the near-tragedy that overtook him at Bolling station but was persuaded by friends and colleagues to do so. He came close to dying from carbon monoxide poisoning at Bolling station but tried to keep his condition a secret from Little America because he feared that men would risk their lives in a midwinter rescue attempt if his true state became known. His increasingly erratic and irrational radio messages during the scheduled radio contacts gave him away and a successful rescue attempt was made. His narrative, *Alone,* is one of the finest to come out of the continent. He belongs to that select group of well-educated, intelligent, gifted and imaginative naval officers (beginning with Cook and including Scott and Shackleton) who produced first-rate narratives out of their Antarctic experiences.

I had no trouble, after an absence of six years, in finding my way. The greatest change probably was that Nukey Poo, the nuclear power plant which had been located halfway up Observation Hill and had been the sole such plant on the continent, had been dismantled and carted away. It had provided electrical power and desalinated water for the base, which was now back on diesel fuel and generators, whose smell and roar were greatly in evidence. I said the station itself had not changed much. The personnel had greatly changed. Although no doubt there were people here from my time, there was no one, to my knowledge, whom I had known at all well. And so walking the roads and lanes had some of the feeling of a stroll through a ghost town.

Sauntering back from the chow hall to my room, I stared at Observation Hill, familiarly known as Ob Hill. On top of the hill stands a great cross, made of Australian jarrah wood, in memory of Scott and his four companions in tragedy. It was erected by members of Scott's last expedition, who took two days to carry it to the hill's crest.

There was such a degree of comfort in the Lodge and increasingly in the station that at times it was difficult to remember that nothing lived or grew here that we readily recognized. There were no mosquitoes or flies, no spiders spinning webs, no scratching sounds of mice: all those things that, whether pleasant or not, once one was without them one realized were part of one's "reality," upon which one depended for one's normal orientation and in a sense even, at times, for one's survival.

3 ❈ McMurdo Station and Environs

I COULD NOT APPROACH the dispensary without being strongly reminded of the last two times I had been inside it. The first was immediately after my rescue from the crash site on Mt. Erebus. This was how I described the scene in *Edge of the World*:

How warm and bright it felt at McMurdo when we stepped off the helos!

The crowd that approached and surrounded us seemed to be observing us closely, as if we were ghosts. I wondered if all survivors of a taste of death felt for a time like ghosts.

In 1415 [a helo], on the way down from Erebus, sensing the possibility of a loss of face by a too strong show of emotion, I had cast about for a way to defend myself. Humor, I had decided: the mask of comedy.

"You all right?" Dave Murphy asked, frowning despite his smile, and studying me searchingly.

"I *told* you I'm rugged," I replied.

We laughed.

The medic who escorted us to the ambulance drove us up the hill not to the front of the dispensary but the rear, and ushered us in, and didn't request us to remove our boots to spare the linoleum the ravages of volcanic grit.

"Any injuries?" he inquired.

Palmer said. "Chuck, tell about your hands."

I spoke briefly about them.

"We can use some aspirin," Palmer said.

The medic countered, "Not without the doctor's orders."

But the medical officer wasn't on duty at this hour [about 3 A.M.].

Drawling in his Georgia accent, Palmer said, "We've had headaches all night and we need some *aspirin*."

There was a pause.

"You probably have altitude headaches," the medic said.

"Yes, indeed we have altitude headaches and we don't need to be told what's perfectly obvious. What we need is some *aspirin*."

There was a bite in Palmer's voice.

The medic gave each of us two tablets of aspirin.

On Erebus, after 1377 had found us, Palmer had said, "Hell, they'll open the wardroom for us. *They'll* get us a bottle."

"Any chance of getting a shot of scotch?" I asked the medic. "We could use it."

The medic went to a storeroom and returned with eight miniature bottles of blended whisky. He gave each of us two.

Dave Murphy, who was waiting outside the dispensary, walked with me toward my room.

"Van looked *bad* when he got off the helo," he said.

"Bad?"

"He looked real *bad*. We all thought so."

I had caught glimpses of Enderby and he had looked fine to me: tall, straight, like a young lumberjack.

"What do you mean? Was he pale?"

"He looked very *bad*. He kept smiling too much."

I thought, "Great God, don't they realize where Van has been?"

"I don't agree," I said. "He looked good to me."

I heard my voice quivering. Its pitch was lower than normal. And my hands felt strange. There was no sensation in the finger ends. The skin there felt as if it was half an inch from the flesh.

"Did he look any different from the rest of us?"

"You all looked bad. You were joking and smiling too much."

I thought, "Don't you understand that at least part of it is due to our being, suddenly, strangers to ourselves? We flew into a new dimension."

For a moment the bridge of communication was down. I felt alone and very tired. He came into my room and sat on my bed while I sipped the whisky.

He said, "I was *so pissed off* because I couldn't go with you on the flight. Then I realized it could have been me instead of Van who was dead."

When he left I shut the door, pulled the drapes and removed my clothes, wondering if it was really true my family and friends would hear from me again. I fell asleep.

There were two icebreakers working in McMurdo Sound. The present companion of the USCGC (United States Coast Guard Cutter) *Burton Island* was the *Northwind*. The icebreakers do not cut ice. They ride up onto it and their weight cracks it. Then they back off down the lane they have cut, reverse direction, gather speed, and ram again. The ships have rounded sides and are capable, by means of a ballast system, of rolling to help the ice crack. When the bow meets and climbs the ice there's a great growling, snarling and hissing, and the metal hull roars as the larger ice chunks scrape against it. Momentarily you're unsure of your footing. Then the ship slides back, or settles through the newly formed cracks. There are a few moments of quiet and stability before it backs off. The ships usually work side by side and ram the ice about one and a half ship's lengths before coming to a halt with grinding, rending, cracking sounds. They make huge cracks in the ice between them. Each ship cuts its own channel but the strategy is to chop up the cracked ice between the channels, forming a broader lane that hopefully the wind will clear of brash. If the wind fails, the brash often freezes and the ships have their work to do over again.

13 JANUARY. "Yesterday Jim Westwater invited me to be his 'buddy' on a flight today to Upper Wright Valley. We landed on the valley's southern side on a slope of a weird, high mesa overlooking icefalls spilling wildly off the continental ice sheet. Westwater and the American pilot and I left the helo and wandered around. The three other crewmembers stayed in the craft to keep warm. Once again I knew what it was like to be very cold, but now I was also threatened by a powerful, relentless, disorienting westerly that buffeted the helo and made the pilot wonder aloud if it was going to overturn it. Soon I had the feeling the wind had begun to dehumanize me. My left hand grew numb in its double glove [black leather shell and khaki woolen liner]. My eyes ran copiously and my footing was uncertain.

"We walked under a ringing blue sky on a chocolate

Ross Island, McMurdo Sound and Victoria Land

Minna Bluff

Disc

Black Island

78°15'S

Ross Ice Shelf

White Island

Brown Per

77°45'S

Ross Island

McM

77°15'S

170°

168°

166°

ROSS SEA

0   15   30

Statute Miles

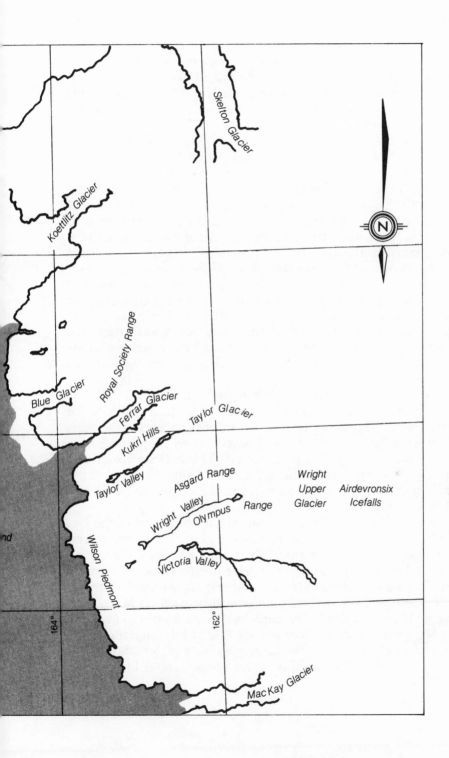

moonscape, lifeless, rock-littered, a high northern slope of the Asgard Range close to the broad Airdevronsix Icefalls spilling off the plateau and feeding Wright Upper Glacier.

"Everywhere around us were chocolate or near-black pitted rocks of many sizes, all highly wind-polished [and therefore called ventifacts]. So smooth were the surfaces worked over by the wind that they looked freshly oiled. The nether parts were pale gray and appeared to have fine crystals of some salt attached to them. What persistent winds, at what velocities, managed with the aid of ice specks, a scarcity of rock particles, the chemistry of salts and low temperatures and the absence of water, together with the help of centuries if not millentia, to carve these strange, attractive objects that at times struck me as being like miniature modern scuptures? Most were rust-colored or rich brown or blackish with tiny red flecks and looked as if they had been annealed and stained into a hard oiled mass. But some were pale-ivory sandstone four or five inches long, in which fractured individual sand grains sparkled like zircon facets. The most beautiful of the small rocks were dark and deeply pitted, suggesting blobs of molten metal suddenly cooled. Some of the pits disappeared from view as tortuous tunnels."

I was embarrassed at Upper Wright Valley. I felt bumbling, old, because my eyes kept filling with tears, making it hard for me to see, and when I bent down to observe rocks, the tears grew pear-shaped and distorted objects even more. I hoped I wasn't making a spectacle of myself. The rocks were strewn thickly. This and the buffeting I took from the wind made walking hazardous. I felt like an interloper on the privacy of geologic time.

In 1971 Taylor Valley, probably the most famous of the Dry Valleys, was considered by scientists to be an excellent terrestrial analogue to Mars in that, like much if not all of Mars, it is a cold and largely lifeless desert. Consequently it was used by the Jet Propulsion Laboratory of Pasadena, California, in the development of a life detection system to be used on Mars. During my hike in Taylor Valley early in 1971, just prior to my crash on Mt. Erebus, neither I nor anyone else had the slightest suspicion of an extraordinary fact: that, relatively lifeless though the valleys are, they contain tiny forms of indigenous life just beneath the surface of certain rocks, chiefly Beacon sandstone. Nor was I aware of this fact during my visit to the Dry Valleys in January 1977.

E. Imre Friedmann of the Department of Biological Science of Florida State University at Tallahassee had written in the September 1976 issue of the *Antarctic Journal of the United States:*

Recent study of rock samples from the dry valleys of southern Victoria Land revealed the presence of endolithic [living within rock] blue-green algae under the surface of some samples. Both the organisms and the type of growth are similar to those we have found in hot deserts. This is the first evidence of primary producers in the cold antarctic desert ecosystem.

Later, in the October 1977 issue of the *Antarctic Journal,* Friedmann reported on some of his findings made during the 1976–77 austral summer.

In this preliminary report only a few general and rather incomplete statements can be made about the varied endolithic microbial flora of the Antarctic deserts. In friable Beacon sandstone the dominant organism is an unusual type of lichen: it is cryptoendolithic, growing inside the porous rock and forming a thin layer a few millimeters below the surface. Sexual fruiting bodies were not seen and are probably absent, although formation of conidia has occasionally been observed. This lichen is often (but not always) associated with a characteristic exfoliating weathering pattern of the rock.

14 JANUARY. "Westwater invited me to fly a mission with him at 1 P.M. today: to look at Erebus crevasses. Set down among sponges near Brown Peninsula. Crevasses startling."

Great raw slabs of purple snow wrenched open deeply into vertical slices showing the striations of annual snowfalls. The purples in many hues, from some approaching white to others suggesting the cobalts of very deep crevasses. These we now observed were naked crevasses, the safer kind. The really bad ones are the snowbridged variety, whose presence often is discovered only when a man or animal or machine disappears into one. The kinesthetic excitement of banking and receiving constantly changing forms, light, colors. Serrated areas like knife slashes. Wonderfully swooping blue and ivory lines. In places the crevasse field had crumbled under pressure and you saw thousands of small chunks lying around. Views of the Western Mountains and of two tiny dashes in the sea ice of McMurdo Sound to the southwest of us, which on a careful look turned out to be the two icebreakers.

"Then we turned around and headed toward McMurdo above the frozen Sound, and Westwater, who wore an intercom helmet, told me we had been ordered back to the station because of a 'simulated emergency.' The helo was doing 120 knots."

One had had to be careful about the use of water even in the days of the nuclear plant. Now one was a good deal more conscious of how precious fresh water was, of how much diesel fuel it took to desalinate water and how costly such fuel could be by the time it reached McMurdo. The nuclear plant at McMurdo proved to be not at all economical to operate, and questions have been raised as to how safely it was constructed and run. Readers interested in the details are referred to "The Story of Nukey Poo," by Owen Wilkes and Robert Mann, which appeared in the October 1978 issue of *The Bulletin of the Atomic Scientists*.

From my journal. "To bed about 11:30, very sleepy as Westwater talked about minor things. I wish I had more control over events, but who down here doesn't? Fear I'm throwing a chunk of my life away. I have a long way to go before I return to the States."

15 JANUARY. "Up about 8 and after breakfast set out on a hike to Scott Base. Erebus magnificent, white smoke pouring out of the crater in a high column. Yesterday only a faint wisp showed. On the sea ice many huskies howling various notes and creating a strange music, with a background of pressure ice, islands, Cape Armitage, ice shelf. Something hauntingly primeval in their doing that in a prolonged way."

I remembered a solitary night walk I had taken to Scott Base during my previous Antarctic trip. I had started out at nine o'clock. Later I had described the hike.

The evening was extraordinarily warm. I removed my cap and left my parka unzipped. The road through the Gap, gravelly, gray, in spots soft, was well-traveled now that the sea-ice route was too rotten to be trusted. It was the main way to Williams Field: over the Gap; a brief distance northward of Scott Base; east past pressure ice and onto the ice shelf; and several miles east on the shelf to the field. A truck, coming downhill toward McMurdo, stirred a cloud of dust resembling steam. On my left the southern slope of Crater Heights still held much snow. Pools of meltwater marked the road shoulders. Those in the shadow of Observation Hill had ice skim forming on them. In the sun my ungloved hands were warm; in the shadow of the hill they turned painfully cold. A rivulet was scurrying across the road on its way to the Sound. The road was pockmarked as if by small explosives. Each hole contained milky water.

I reached the Gap's crest. Pressure ice on the left of silhouetted Cape Armitage rose in jagged masses, its crevices showing cobalt blue. On my right the lower portion of Observation Hill swooped down in a black plane. Beyond the hill lay the mottled, pale blue annual or sea ice, which, in the evening sun, had a faint, lilac, pearly cast. Directly ahead of me, some miles away on the ice shelf, the gray of White Island's cliffs and hilltops peeped through embayments of creamy snow. The little island looked almost idyllic, it rose so gently out of the shelf. I made out a faint, ribbonlike white line on the icescape, running approximately north and south. This was where the shelf and the sea ice met. At this point the shelf was barely ten feet higher than the Sound. The low-hanging sun illumined hills, ice and snow in a subtly dramatic, at times beautifully nostalgic way with a gentle ivory light. The sky was smoky except at the zenith, where it was deep blue.

I heard hillside snow and ice melting and occasionally a tinkle as of metal when a piece of ice broke loose and skittered down. The sun was lower at night than by day, so there was more glare during the night hours. At night it was painful to observe the Royal Society Range without sunglasses. My hands were atingle with warmth, yet earlier in the day they had felt like frozen claws, and the fingertips and nails had been very white.

I spotted Scott Base below me, with its handful of pale green huts on Pram Point. It seemed very strange to find a human settlement there. The sudden green of the base struck me as extraordinary, suggesting as it did young grass or spring leaves. I was surrounded by a black wasteland that seemed to have been blasted into infertility. All around me were porous volcanic rocks, most of them black but some with a reddish hue. Yet the visual beauty was what one was chiefly aware of: the terrific contrasts between sweeping black shapes and the faintly blue ice, or between the rose-tinted powderpuff clouds and the sky's azure.

In the south Mt. Discovery was tall, large, majestic, its cone suggesting a bald white head. In the north, beyond the great white stretch of Windless Bay, Mt. Terror, a contemplative-looking mountain sweeping eastwardly into a cape, or so it seemed from where I stood, its bayside cliffs resembling chalk because of the way the snow was catching the light directly opposite them, its luminous gentle shadows the palest blue-grays, was thrillingly opalescent. It was a fairy world over there of pale blues, dappled grays and gleaming, glowing nacres. In the bay itself—this was the bay well known to Wilson, Bowers and Cherry-Garrard from their midwinter traverse between Capes Evans and Crozier—the shelf ice looked subdued, a twilight blue, but nothing was flat or dead there, everything was textured, even if only faintly, and was therefore alive.

When one turned one's head one experienced a tremendous sweep of space, and within the framework of this relatively monochromatic world there was the excitement of color: the sweet blue of the zenith, the lime above the horizon, the lavender, lilac and prune in the iceshelf, the slate blues of islands and mountains. The sea ice was a fiery mirror. The water rushing down the hillside gleamed like a stream of mercury. The unspoiled silence, the uncluttered views, the aloofness of the Royal Society Range, and the scene's incredible expanse worked profoundly on me. I felt in love with something or someone. Also, I felt loved, blessed, graced. 'Lord, Lord,' I kept saying to myself, 'how lucky I am to be here,' and my eyes filled with tears.

The site of Scott Base, which is about two miles by road from McMurdo Station, was chosen by Edmund Hillary of New Zealand, one of the two men (the other was Tenzing Norkay) to make the first ascent of Mt. Everest (May 1953). He selected it for two reasons: as a scientific station for the International Geophysical Year, and as the Ross Island base of the British Commonwealth Transantarctic Expedition, whose goal was Shackleton's old one of traversing the continent from the Weddell Sea to the Ross Sea via the Pole. Hillary led his nation's section of the expedition. His main task was to set up depots from Ross Island to the Pole to support Vivian Fuchs's party, which would make the full traverse. Hillary reached the Pole in a tractor January 4, 1953, becoming, after Scott, the first man to attain it overland. At the time there was some question as to the propriety of his having gone to it before Fuchs, who was commander and originator of the expedition. Later, in the interview with Sir Vivian Fuchs in Chapter 13, we shall see Fuchs's response to his loss of priority in the matter.

Scott Base was constructed in 1957. Hillary was a member of its first wintering-over team. During the IGY the base conducted almost all the scientific research in the McMurdo area. It was not until after the conclusion of the IGY that McMurdo Station began its scientific program. Scott Base was planning to celebrate its twentieth anniversary on January 20, five days from my present visit, and there were active plans to expand the station by fifty percent, with completion expected by the early 1980s. The foundation for the first new building had recently been lain.

Named for Robert Falcon Scott, the base is located on Pram Point, a low, rocky projection on the eastern side of Hut Point Peninsula. During the time I lived there at the end of 1970 and now during my present visit it consisted chiefly of nine prefabricated huts linked by corrugated iron tunnels or ways. The ways permitted movement around the station regardless of the weather and without the loss of time that would be involved in changing clothes. Auxiliary buildings included two magnetic huts, two seismology huts and a large former hangar, now a garage and work space. The main reason for the present existence of the station was its scientific work. It conducted experiments in seismology, geomagnetism, ionospheric physics, auroral and air glow, VLF (very low frequency) radio propagation, satellite tracking and meteorology. Its post office was the world's most southerly one to provide all postal and communications facilities, and it had its own set of stamps, known as the Ross Dependency Series.

My quarters had been the tiny hospital room in D Hut. (The station handled minor medical problems. More serious ones were treated at McMurdo.) It felt like a freighter cabin and was quite cold even though I wore thermal underwear and a heavy wool shirt. To save on laundry (water was made by melting ice cut and transported from the ice shelf's pressure ridges) I had been asked to use a sleeping bag instead of sheets. To my amusement the thin, zipperless khaki bag on the bed was narrower than a mummy bag. It was tricky to slip into it. You mounted the high bed, braced your behind against the wall, set your feet into the bag and slowly snaked your way down. Once you were inside it was difficult to move about. A friend of mine compared it with a body bag, the kind used to contain battlefield corpses.

Few nations in the Antarctic nowadays keep dogs. The trend for some time has been all to motor toboggans, which don't run off without you, don't fight each other and aren't carnivorous. Scott Base legitimately feeds its dogs seals under the Antarctic Treaty but occasionally I heard grumbling at McMurdo about the misuse of Weddell seals in order to hold to a tradition now anachronistic. Whether the Kiwis (New Zealanders) continue to use huskies in addition to motor toboggans more out of a sense of tradition and romance than for other reasons, I do not know. No doubt they get good work out of the dogs in the field. Sometimes the huskies and sledges are airlifted to distant work sites by the United States Navy. But it seems to me in keeping with New Zealand's slower and more nostalgic pace in the world for Scott Base to continue to use dogs.

I remembered sledging on the ice shelf with them, racing madly while leaving a trail of blood because of a general fight that had occurred while they were being harnessed, and flying over narrow crevasses (called slots by the Kiwis), and I recalled the Siberians and Greenlanders (huskies) with eyes suggestive of an oriental look, and the name of the lead dog, Osman, because an Osman was also a leader on Scott's last expedition, and the dog driver's virtuosity in swearing at the animals. I had never heard four-letter words used with such art before, even if they had little effect.

From my journal. "Immediately on entering the station I saw a tall, gray-haired and gray-bearded handsome figure I thought I recognized, standing against a wall and speaking with another man. I kept going, then turned and inquired if he had been at the base in 1970. He asked, 'Are you Mr. Neider?' When I said yes he introduced himself as Jim Rankin and said he was pretty sure, on first seeing me, that my face was familiar but he couldn't believe I'd be back here. When he showed me around the station he referred to me as 'the famous Mr. Neider, a notorious character here,' and he mentioned 'the Neider memorial at the Fang Glacier,' meaning, I think, the helicopter still on Mt. Erebus, and he remembered my first name and called me Charley and all the others did too. Someone asked if I had ridden with Osman when I lived at the base. I said yes, I had. Then I was told that Osman, nine years old, died last night after vomiting and excreting blood. When I inquired about the cause of death I was informed by a young man with a tense, humorless gaze and a very red nose shaped like a triangle that the problem had been deterioration of the intestinal walls caused by bacteria and that it was not uncommon for huskies to die by the age of nine."

While I was being shown around the garage, Osman was carried in on a stretcher. He would be opened up in an effort to better understand the cause of death. He looked fast asleep. Large, heavy paws, gray fur. Three five-month-old pups, dark in coat and weighing about 55 pounds each, were moaning and howling outside at the doorway. I went over and patted them. One licked my hand. Their coats felt greasy, as if they had been treated with water repellent, and were very thick. They had delightful faces.

My journal. "At times, especially at night, am greatly concerned about my long delay here, with consequent shortening of my peninsula stay. The icebreakers are still having serious trouble with wind and ice. The wind is a northerly, which means that it blows the brash back into the newly cut channel, where it refreezes. After supper I walked alone to the Discovery Hut."

The hut is spacious (some thirty-six feet square) and has a pyramidal roof and overhanging eaves. It was brought from Austrialia and was the kind of bungalow used by Australian frontier settlers of the time. Inasmuch as the ship *Discovery* was iced in and available as living quarters, the hut was not lived in during Scott's first expedition. It was used for such purposes as drying furs, skinning birds, refitting awnings and for the rehearsal and performance of various theatrical entertainments, complete with scenery and footlights. It was also used for gravity observations made by the swinging of pendulums.

Both Hut Point and Hut Point Peninsula derive their names from the famous hut which stands here, overlooking Winter Quarters Bay, McMurdo Station, Observation Hill, Cape Armitage, McMurdo Sound and the Western Mountains. During Scott's first expedition the hut had no formal name, but when Scott returned for his second expedition he always referred to the structure as the Discovery Hut. The hut is probably the most important single historic site on the continent. Over the years it became filled with ice and compacted snow. It was restored in 1963 and 1964 by members of the New Zealand Antarctic Society, with the help of the United States Navy. Scott wrote in *The Voyage of the "Discovery"*:

It was obvious that some sort of shelter must be made on shore before exploring parties could be sent away with safety, as we felt that at any time a heavy gale might drive the ship off her station for several days, if not altogether. With the hut erected and provisioned, there need be no anxiety for a detached party in such circumstances. . . . We found, however, that its construction was no light task, as all the main and verandah supports were designed to be sunk three or four feet in the ground. We soon found a convenient site close to the ship on a small bare plateau of volcanic rubble, but an inch or two below the surface the soil was frozen hard, and many an hour was spent with pick, shovel, and crowbar before the solid supports were erected and our able carpenter could get to work on the frame.

In addition to the main hut, and of greater importance, were the two small huts which we had brought for our magnetic instruments. These consisted of a light skeleton framework of wood covered with sheets of asbestos.

The smaller huts are no longer extant.

16 JANUARY, SUNDAY. "Noise and smell of diesel power plant going night and day. Smell of DFA [Diesel Fuel Arctic]. Smell, taste and feel of volcanic grit everywhere. Intensely dry air. Intensely dry hands. Cracked, painful fingertips, lips, intense thirst, painful cheeks after shaving. Clouds of earth dust from passing trucks. Sounds of heavy trucks. Sounds of helos. Winds. Voices and door slams in the night. Sunlit bathroom all night. Unkempt bearded faces at all hours. Dirty fingernails."

I treasured the times I spent writing in the lounge. The room was spacious and usually quite empty, it was free of bustle and interruption, and I could always find a little desk in a corner up against a wall, where I felt tidy and comfortable, and return to my island of serenity, which essentially was my focus on my work. After a session there I always felt more sane, more philosophic and somehow more cleansed, as if I had just come out of a sauna or long hot shower. Things came together then, making my mood as sweet as brown-sugared sourcream apple pie. It was there too I would come upon solitary men reading long letters from home.

I was about to fly to the so-called "dirty ice" section in the mouth of the Koettlitz Glacier; to Butter Point on the Bowers Piedmont Glacier; to Marble Point to refuel; to the edge of the McMurdo Sound sea ice in the hope of seeing some killer whales; and to an ice cave in some Ross Island ice cliffs on the island's western shore.

I loved flying in helicopters and I enjoyed all the details that went with it: the fuss of getting your gear ready (cameras, film, notebooks, survival bag), suiting up properly, lugging your stuff down to the helo pad, boarding the craft, chatting with the crew, lifting off, suddenly banking, your head buzzing with the noise, your nostrils filled with the smells of fuel, cabin, cockpit. And I delighted in being out in the field despite any physical discomforts: embracing Antarctica and being bearhugged by it in the way I had been bearhugged by barrel-chested Jim Brandau, the Navy helicopter pilot to whom I had dedicated *Edge of the World.* And, to be entirely confessional, I enjoyed the sense of possibly being killed, and that sunburned, windburned and wonderfully tired feeling you had after a large excursion, when you were dragging yourself and your gear from the helo pad back to your room, only now you were reborn, you had spent time in a state of special grace, you had in a way been removed from this planet, from yourself, and released into a remarkable world whose music was as powerful as that of the Sirens. And now you were bringing home precious data: memories, latent images on film, scrawls in notebooks, inspirations for work to be done.

Westwater was on the verge of leaving the Antarctic and I avoided talking to him about it, for I didn't want to make leaving the more difficult for him by bringing the matter up, or possibly I thought that any knowledge in this direction I might receive would be more valuable if it came from him spontaneously. He was methodical in his work habits and meticulous about little things, such as the way in which he had attached a lens cap to a lens with a bit of fishing line, or had made for himself a canvas pouch that he strapped around his waist and which contained photographic odds and ends. But I was perplexed by the fact I rarely if ever saw him make notes, either photographic ones or journal entries. Now, on his last day here, he seemed quite remote and, at moments, almost a little bitter. Perhaps he *was* having a bit of a separation problem, or possibly he was profoundly disappointed because he had not experienced as much of Antarctica as he had hoped. We never got to talking about his personal life back in the States. A good listener, I let him talk for long stretches, which I enjoyed, for I was fond of him.

The Navy pilot of the helicopter, a twin-engine Huey with

the white numerals 14 on its brilliant red sides (its official des-
ignation was Gentle 14), was Randy Graham. The copilot and
crewman were Kiwis from Scott Base, whose names I did not
learn. The reason for having a Kiwi copilot and crewman was to
provide them with experience in flying in the Ross Island environs. They were not needed by the U.S. Navy in the Antarctic.
It was simply a goodwill gesture on the part of McMurdo towards its neighbor, Scott Base, on the eastern side of Cape
Armitage. The Kiwis did not have their own helicopter in the
Antarctic. It made the flight particularly pleasant for me to have
them aboard and, in the quiet moments, to hear their speech,
for I had only yesterday had a most pleasant reception at Scott
Base, where I had once lived, and I was partial to New Zealand
and its citizens.

We flew southwest from McMurdo across the McMurdo Ice
Shelf, which is west of and adjacent to the Ross Ice Shelf and
which faces McMurdo Sound, and headed for a landing just
northeast of Brown Peninsula. I was familiar with this remarkable terrain, but only from the air. I had overflown it at a low
altitude in a helo while en route in a roundabout way to Taylor
Valley on January 7, 1971. I had no sense of scale in the fantastic icescape below me then, which I described in *Edge of the
World.*

As we drew near to Brown Peninsula—the tip of the peninsula is
about twenty miles southwest of Hut Point—we flew low over vast
fields of chaotic ice, much of which, mixed with morainic deposits,
resembled mudflats. Dark silt lay between the morainic ridges. We
encountered a few patches of dirty snow. Water was visible in the
form of pools and rivulets but none was blue. We had a cloud cover
now and the water, failing to catch a blue sky, showed black. It was a
black-and-white scene, for both ice and snow were entirely and unusually white, although a dirty, messy white. I was totally unprepared
for such a wild wasteland, which was unlike anything I had ever seen.
At times we crossed great furrows and ridges, like plowed black land
that had been snowed upon long ago. At others we viewed mazes of
ruts and crisscrosses that suggested an alluvial delta. It was impossible,
from the helicopter, to judge the depths of the streams or whether the
ice surface would support a human body but the area looked
thoroughly untraversable. Everything was a stark black and white except for a bit of thin blue sky far, far to the west.

We swung north and crossed the mouth of the Koettlitz Glacier, which is some twelve miles wide. The Koettlitz, about forty miles long, flows between Brown Peninsula and the mainland to the McMurdo Ice Shelf at the head of McMurdo Sound. With the exception of the piedmont glaciers it is the largest glacier west of the Sound. Its eastern side is full of ridges, icefalls, gullies and undulations; its western half is marked by deep thaw streams, bastions of pinnacled ice, silt, and ridges of moraine materials. Discovered by Scott's first expedition, it was named by Scott for Dr. Reginald Koettlitz, physician and botanist of the expedition.

In the glacier's mouth we saw fantastic blue ice forms, some of which must have been a hundred feet high. Blue? Not the subtle glacial pastel. I mean a blue bluer than the desert sky; a riotous candy blue. What we saw was as unbelievable and pleasurable as fairy tales: snow and ice forms looming out of fields of ice: teahouse kiosks, turrets, battlements, cliffed islands, Swiss lake dwellings. And blue ice streams snaking along in a stupendous nightmare of slow motion. The blue showed despite the cloud cover, so I assumed it was in the ice itself. What a scene it was: the glacier so spacious, we flying quite low, and all these varied shapes against the powder blues of the basic glacial ice. The exotic formations were caused by erosion, by sublimation of ice and by variations in the tempo of melting, the latter being due to the debris the glacier was carrying, the darker portions, absorbing more heat, melting more rapidly than the lighter ones. The ice river was moving and depositing a vast amount of material and was exerting pressure against the land and against the sea ice. It caused the sea ice adjacent to its mouth to look utterly chaotic. Meltwater ponds were as fascinating as the ice shapes. Observing them, I imagined I was seeing non-objective paintings, or cross-sections of agate, moonstone, coral, pearl.

As we drew closer, lovely blues began to appear in the rivulets: pale but electric in their intensity, probably coming from submerged ice chunks. And what had seemed for a while flat now revealed itself as strikingly three-dimensional. Much visual excitement: patches of pure white snow, pale blues of ice towers, the near-jet shades of rich earth. A controlled chaos. More and more blues. And then the earth was long, longitudinal mounds, very high ones, actually small hills, and the heavy, pearl-gray sky included touches of serene blue that contained much less green than the ice blues, and the latter showed more green by the split-second. And then the snowcapped round dome of Mt. Discovery was seen sunlit in the distance. Also, but farther away, was a part of the Royal Society Range. And then there were textured icefields backed by stark, blackish earth mounds.

We set down beside a huge, long, dark mound, a moraine feature that probably looked like a line from the air, and among patches of snow and ice and meltwater pools. The crew, Pat Perkins and Captain Westbrook stayed near the helicopter while Westwater and I used ice axes to probe our way across undulating and broken and heavy ice-snow to some large, light-weight, pale-tan sponges of many shapes, brought up from the sea floor by slowly ablating glacial ice, and to small seashells so thin they crumbled when you fingered them.

I let the place possess me. I thought of Robert Falcon Scott and of members of his Discovery Expedition at the turn of the century who had first discovered such sponges and shells, and I remembered Brandau, who had flown me over this terrain, and I felt an inner distance, a distance engendered by reverberations of historic and nostalgic time, between me and my present companions.

I had profound personal connections with the Antarctic past through my meeting with Richard E. Byrd when I was a very young man and through my friendship with Sir Charles Wright, who had led the search party in November 1912 that had found the bodies of Scott, Bowers and Wilson in a tent on the Ross Ice Shelf, and through my close friendship with Larry Gould. And I had solid emotional memories of my second Antarctic trip. Human features and the sound of voices rambled through my mind now. Also, strong autobiographical tentacles connected me with that day six years ago when I had overflown this terrain and hiked in Taylor Valley, for two days later I had considered my life forfeited when I had crashed on Mt. Erebus.

When we were on the surface now I had no idea of precisely where we were. Aside from Mt. Discovery there were no landmarks familiar to me, and inasmuch as the sun was mostly obscured, I couldn't use its position and my watch to determine directions, my attention was preoccupied with the relative minutiae of my surroundings: free water, thin ice shelves dripping audibly, sponges, thick snow mantles. Intensely blue sky patches, and the contrast between these and the somber, almost

56   BEYOND CAPE HORN

grim, gray-brown, naked, longitudinal earth mounds. Dead-gray pools of water. Ablated snow turrets like furry asbestos. The feeling of being inside a maze. But you did not feel threatened or menaced. There was no wind, the day felt benign and mild.

Much soft, spongy, dirty snow. Snow speckled by blown dirt as if sprayed by an airgun. The way dirty snow ablates: the brown earth particles reflect back less light and heat, melt more rapidly, leaving snow spicules. Mt. Discovery a bit higher than 8800 feet. We stayed only briefly. We had come for a look, not an exploration.

My journal. "Psychologically this part of the flight was important because it aroused in me a kind of bewildered awe that verged on a strange, exotic kind of fear. We flew over these features so long, the overcast was so considerable as to disorient me regarding the positions of Ross Island or the Western Mountains or directions in general, and the terrain began to seem so endless that I felt for a moment or two that I was growing dizzy with disbelief, in the way one does when the helo banks suddenly, tilting the horizon, and continues to bank until the world seems to be spinning slowly and madly, causing the beginnings of seasickness unless one firmly stares at the horizon and imagines it to be level—that is, horizontal.

"At times we passed over brown earth completely lacking in snow, ice or water and looking plowed or harrowed on some gigantic scale: vast moraines that kept stretching away from us despite our speed of about 100 knots. And then there was ice that seemed to contain hieroglyphic messages: only frost patterns, but one tried vainly to decipher them and felt foolish for it. Decipher what? No humans here, and no mammals either. The enormity of these deposits, indicating the vastness of the glacier and of geologic forces, and the smallness of ourselves in our puny helicopter, humbled and in some new way frightened one.

"The immensity of scale in Antarctica. And the disbelief that I'm really privileged to be here again. And missing old friends like Brandau and feeling a bit strange to have returned here without them, as if the reality or poetry of this place in part depends on their simultaneous presence. And feeling quite alone with one's thoughts in the helo that isolates one because of the tremendous noise and vibrations the engine and rotors create. The hatch door shaking almost violently, and if your head by accident presses against the window or its frame you feel your brains getting a good scrambling and you draw away quickly to protect your sanity. And the eeriness of this small craft and its occupants daring to venture above this mad scape."

And then we flew over snaking blue lines and blue flats and over huge blue ice fields with highway-like markings, a terrific sweep, all in the mouth of the Blue Glacier. Bands of dappling light far away on our port side, streaking across the horizon. And then we were over a vast ice plain, the Bowers Piedmont Glacier, where earth and sky blended so well you could barely make out the horizon line. Horizontal bands of light across the milky grayness.

We landed at Butter Point in order to have a look at one of Sir Edmund Hillary's depots, a series of which he established between Ross Island and the Pole and the purpose of which was to enable Vivian Fuchs, who would start at the head of the Weddell Sea, to complete the first transcontinental traverse. I shall discuss some of the details of the traverse in Chapter 13.

Fifteen or twenty crates and three or four fuel drums half-buried in snow. Graham the dark-bearded pilot in Navy greens. The Kiwi pilot and his crewman in khaki greens. Pat Perkins looking like Captain Westbrook, both being dressed in red parkas, black trousers and white bunny boots. Westwater tall, bearded, wearing a khaki wool hat, red parka, bunny boots and using a Topcon 35mm SLR camera. The helo red, long and sleek. Its main rotor blades looked particularly long. Its landing gear was of the simplest kind, just some metal tubing. Seen at a distance from the rear, the craft suggested a fat squat insect.

Later Westwater photographed a solitary emperor penguin anxiously tobogganing in his fear of the helicopter's noise and size and hoverings above and beside him. The bird looked large, heavy, like a big egg, and seemed ineffectual at tobogganing, in this respect being very different from the Adélies, who are good at it. His wings, short in relation to his body, seemed to give him little thrust. He aided them with his feet but his efforts looked pathetic and I wondered at the value or even good taste of shooting a poor animal in a panic that you yourself have caused.

My journal. "We set down near some ice cliffs. Using an ice ax, I probed my way to two Weddell seals north of us. Pressed seal forms in the ice where seals had been basking. Clear tail forms impressed. Seal tracks. Good to be alone, quiet, ears subsiding from the helo roar, on one's booted feet (I didn't use mukluks as some others did), enjoying the windless, warm area. I was aware I had to be careful to avoid sunburn (the sun now was very sharp). The larger of the two seals (the other was a sizable pup) was asleep and didn't hear me approach. I awoke her with a greeting. She lay on her back, opened her large soulful eyes at me and took to scratching parts of herself with a clawed flipper that, when spread, vaguely resembled fingers. Occasionally she seemed to lapse into sleep. Now and then she yawned, showing a pink mouth with surprisingly large teeth, some of them fangs. She opened her mouth very wide when yawning but made no sound.

"The second seal was dark brownish, the first was grayish. The second never awoke until the Kiwi pilot and crewman and Westwater joined me and advanced close and spoke loudly. Then Seal One made a mooing sound and Seal Two quickly turned its head to look at One. Seal One began wiggling away toward the shore. Seal Two followed."

We flew south to Erebus Glacier Tongue to see the well-known ice cave there. This is how I described the place in *Edge of the World:*

The Tongue cliffs, massive although from the air they seemed insignificant, resembled chalk. The Tongue, afloat but attached to Ross Island, thrust into the Sound with the appearance of a serrated knife from above. From our landing spot we could see Hut Point Peninsula, Castle Rock jutting black out of it, black islands on the snow-ice expanse of the Sound, the crisp Royal Society Range, and lovely, thin cloud formations in an azure sky. The day was utterly brilliant: cold if you were in shadow, warm if you weren't. We walked on patches of thick snow in which we descended to our shanks, and on gleaming, hard, uneven, treacherous, beautiful bluish and greenish ice.

The cave entrance was like a pelvic slit, gorgeously and startlingly blue. We climbed and clambered into the cave. The glowing light inside was an eerie, electric lavender. Strange ice formations clung like frozen whipped cream to the ceiling, and glistening ice crystals were encrusted high on the walls. I was the only member of the party not wearing gloves. Occasionally, in a narrow passageway on the rolling, slippery floor, I had to lean a hand against an ice hummock to avoid falling. My hand screamed immediately as though burned. The ice inside the cave was probably at close to mean temperature, many degrees below zero. The view toward the cave entrance showed patches of light, burning through long, thick icicles, that made both walls and ceiling dance.

Now, in January 1977, when I stood just inside the cave I looked out at an exotic world framed by great, gleaming, translucent icicles, a world of blues and violets, with a touch of volcanic black here and there informing you where a couple of the island's naked capes were. In the north were snow hills as sensuous as sand dunes. The snow-ice in the cave's immediate vicinity lay in tumultuous pressure hummocks and ridges. Broken icicle chunks lay scattered near the cave's door like tubular glass. Parts of the cave's ceiling reminded me of the wonderful ceiling forms in the Alhambra in Grenada, Spain. It was dazzling to see how the thick icicles captured the brilliant sunlight. From inside the cave they seemed to be the sole source of light in an otherwise purple world.

Long before I composed the present chapter in March 1979, I wrote a vignette about what happened next on this remarkable day.

We're cruising in a small, twin-engine helicopter along the northern ice edge of frozen McMurdo Sound, scanning the blue waters of the Ross Sea for signs of whales: spouts, dorsal fins, an arching back, crinkling water, flukes. Nothing in sight except the textured, pale-violet sea ice and the sea that sometimes looks like obsidian. So we head southward, land on the salt ice, explore a very cold and beautiful freshwater ice cave, then fly south toward McMurdo Station on Ross Island over the freezing resupply channel cut by the twin U.S. Coast Guard icebreakers.

It's hard times for the icebreaker crews. Almost no liberty ashore, for the ships have been struggling night and day to cut the channel and keep it clear. But the ice is unseasonably thick and the expected, needed south wind which would blow the channel brash out to sea has been replaced by a persistent northerly that clogs the channel and lets it refreeze.

Some ten miles north of the base we spot a whale, then two, breaching and blowing in a channel pool. Strange to see them down there, seemingly surrounded by miles and miles of sea ice. We circle a couple of times to make sure of our luck. It's almost 6 P.M. and the sun, hovering over the Western Mountains and alpine or tongue glaciers and valley glaciers and precipitous icefalls and huge, broad piedmont glaciers, is due west now. To avoid having sun and mirrored sun like spotlights in our eyes as we observe the creatures, we land to the west of the channel, then approach them on foot across the hard-crusted snow that caps the sea ice, occasionally breaking loudly through to our calves.

They're killer whales, about twenty-five feet long and weighing some eight tons, a mammal of considerable intelligence, legendary ferocity and great grace and beauty. In packs, on occasion, they takeon the blue whale itself, earth's largest creature, ripping away great chunks of lip and tongue. The killer is king: There is nothing in all the sea that it needs to fear. There's no mistaking the prominent dorsal fin, blunt snout, compact muscular body, glossy dark back and tawny underside.

The two whales have metamorphosed to five. And we have them at our convenience, in a sense. In the Ross Sea they might suddenly leave our vicinity for whatever reason, whereas here they're penned in by the pool shores. Of course, they can dive and swim away to the sea from which they came, or to some other part of the channel. But they can't swim far under the firm sea ice, for, being mammals, they must surface to breathe. Obviously they're confident they can find air holes. We're some twenty miles south of the Sound's northern ice edge now, and so they made their way through and under the clogged, refreezing channel.

Our latitude is almost 78° and we're some 850 statute miles from the Pole. You can't go very much farther south by water here, or elsewhere for that matter. The station is pretty close to man's southern seagoing limit.

Camera in hand, I leave the firm ice, which is some five feet thick, jump across a lead onto a floe so I can be as close to them as possible, kneel on my left knee for better composition, and begin to shoot. I have only a 50mm lens with me and I want to fill my 35mm frame. I am not unaware the killers have the capacity, working as a group, of ramming a floe from beneath and tipping seals and penguins into the water, where they can get at them when hungry. I have heard stories told by otherwise sensible men that killers will not attack a human. I consider such tales to be foolishly anthropocentric and I have no need to be a test case.

I recall how a pack of killers pursued Herbert Ponting, the remarkable photographer of Robert Falcon Scott's last expedition, and how he barely escaped, leaping from floe to floe. That incident occurred in January 1911 off Cape Evans some five miles north of here, and Scott himself witnessed it and described it in his journal.

It's awesome to watch these huge gleaming creatures rise slowly, snout-first, like nightmare bullets or cigars, showing their smoky-sulfur ventral side. They look around before submerging. Not one opens its mouth to reveal peglike teeth. I'm not particularly aware of their eyes—the organ is relatively small, the large action lively—great streamlined beautiful glistening oceanic masses enthrall me—but I sense them closely studying me and—is it possible?—observing me with irony.

The whales pause briefly at the crest, then slowly descend. At first only one or two do this, while others breach in graceful slow arcs, blow, dive. But actually, despite their seeming dreamlike slowness, the scenes happen rather quickly, and for the most part the water is unbroken, looking innocent, empty, unsuggestive of the life and potential death it contains. At 30°F it would kill a human rapidly even if the whales spared him. For the most part nothing happens, leaving you thirsty with suspense, burning with rare visual memories and apprehensive that the show is over.

Then, seeming to catch the spirit of this rare event, this remarkable meeting between land creatures and oceangoing ones in a vast expanse of salty ice, three rise together and I disbelieve my eyes. The salt water is not mine, yet I stand above it. It is theirs, yet they are denied access to it, and are here this far south, now, at this season, only because of human work, work of the icebreakers. Then four rise up and it seems much too wonderful and rare to be true, my luck can't be this fabulous, and I almost forget to shoot, photographs seem beside the point, the thing that matters is to let these scenes engrave themselves on my memory. Most of their breasts are the color of rich or old ivory that has undergone a tanning process, but a couple have darker ventral sides, suggesting deep meerschaum, and one has a ragged front that looks tattered in color and deeper in hue than all the others.

The whales rise higher, higher, as if stretching upward for us. It takes a solid burst of speed to perform like that. Splendid dream creatures rising, sinking, counterpointing, arching, making visual music in their innocence, beautifully submerging in a waking dream enhanced with the possibility of nightmare. Threat palpable in the cold air fishy with their hot moist noisy spouting. A series of inventions, surprises, enabling one to stretch with them to dimensions only glimpsed till now.

Are they playing, showing off? It would seem so. As far as I can gather they're entirely uninterested in the solitary Weddell seal sleeping on the ice beside another, long, narrow, rectangular pool about 150 feet north of them. What an icescape, what a theater, what a midsummer's gambol!

And now I realize that the pool is crammed with bodies and I count nine in all, and half a dozen stand poised together in a fantastic water ballet. And I notice with admiration, almost with awe, that so delicate is their tactile sense and so superb their bodily control that not once do they touch the pool's ice edges or each other. Observing them, I glow with a tremendous sense of vitality even when they come quite close. And then I wonder if they're mocking me with a display of superior strength and agility while spurning me as food, and I have the uncanny sense that something mysterious and about which they know more than I is occurring between us, that perhaps they're ironically amused by me, the puny figure with the fiercely red top, my parka. And, analogous to reverberations of remembered sound, I sense that these burning images of sleek giant bodies rising and falling—now three, now five, and at one immense moment seven—will remain in my inner sight for along, inspired time.

Turning around for some reason, I see a single Adélie penguin, which has appeared from nowhere, apparently, standing very still on the ice, observing all of us quizzically. Its breast is immaculate, so it probably hasn't been tobogganing on the ice recently but has swum in the channel and walked on the ice to this point. The Kiwi crewman goes up close and speaks to it.

The penguin observes him cooly. But when the crewman draws even closer the bird quack-squawks in warning and irritation and shambles off southward.

At this moment I notice a whale breaching in the rectangular pool beside which the Weddell seal still lies. I hurry to have a close look. The whale is so tremendous it almost fills the pool. Rearing up snout-first diagonally northward to spout and breathe, it scatters showers of seawater and creates a temporary fog with its moist, warm, fishy exhalation. It breaches and sinks with watery explosions. Standing close to the edge of the firm ice and peering down, I can see him lying like a submarine there, and I brace myself as I watch him coming upward. I'm so close to him that my shadow at times falls upon him.

Wham! goes his double spout loudly. His dorsal or upper side is dark gray, his ventral is pale gray, his snout is long, tapering, and his under jaw protrudes beyond his upper. He turns out to be a fin—or, as an older term had it, a finback—second only to the blue whale in size. He's about seventy-five feet long, three times as long and perhaps ten times as heavy as the killer, and is a baleen whale, which is to say he is untoothed, has whalebone depending from his upper jaw, with which he strains krill and other small varieties of food in great daily masses.

The Weddell watches him as if half-asleep, then they study each other during the intervals when the fin's snout pauses in the air, so high the blow holes are clearly visible. The Weddell, some ten feet long, looks unafraid. Does he know that the fin, being a baleen, won't attack him? And then, to my amazement, the seal slips into the water.

BEYOND CAPE HORN

4 ❧ *Wright and Victoria Valleys*

THE CONTINUATION OF THE Transantarctic Mountains fringes the coast of Victoria Land on the western side of McMurdo Sound. It contains scores of glaciers and valleys. Some of the names in this region are: Killer Ridge, Purgatory Peak, The Pimple, Mt. Dromedary, Obelisk Mountain. Many of the valleys, large and small, are free of ice as a result of deglaciation and are therefore known as the Dry Valleys, although in the austral summer they may be rich in meltwater flowing from the receding glaciers. They are strange, rare and rather sterile oases in a continent of ice and have fascinated explorers and scientists since their discovery by Scott's first expedition.

They reveal extensive outcrops of bedrock, consequently they offer scientists an opportunity to glimpse the geology of the continental margins. In a number of instances their surface-frozen lakes act as solar heat traps. The waters of the lake bottoms may be as warm as the middle seventies Fahrenheit. Such lakes provide material for wonder as well as study. The valleys are characterized by low mean temperatures, very low humidity and frequent and high winds. They are earth deserts within the vast ice desert of the continent, and contain ventifacts, sand dunes and mushroom rocks. Evidence that postglacial processes have begun is not lacking. Soils have begun to form, and algae, mosses and lichens are to be found. It is not surprising that since the International Geophysical Year the Dry Valleys of the so-called McMurdo Oasis (there are several other, lesser oases in Antarctica) have received the special attention of geologists, geomorphologists, glaciologists and botanists. The deglaciation of the McMurdo Oasis is not well understood. It does not necessarily suggest an ebbing of the Antarctic icecap in general. The question of whether the cap is increasing or decreasing, known as the Antarctic budget, is still unresolved.

The most famous and one of the largest of the Dry Valleys is Taylor Valley, first explored by Scott during the Discovery Expedition. In *The Voyage of the "Discovery"* Scott used the plural form, referring to the valleys. But Shackleton, in *The Heart of the Antarctic,* referred only to "the Dry Valley," meaning the still unnamed valley that Scott had found. And Griffith Taylor, the geologist on Scott's last, Terra Nova Expedition, who was the first to understand that the Ferrar Glacier is really two glaciers in apposition (the two are Siamese twins, in a sense), adhered to Shackleton's usage. Scott later named both the Taylor Glacier, formerly the northern arm of the Ferrar, and Taylor Valley in honor of the geologist. Historically, Taylor Valley was the original Dry Valley. Extending from the Antarctic ice plateau on the west to McMurdo Sound on the east, and lying just north of the Kukri Hills, it was once entirely occupied by Taylor Glacier. The glacier has receded toward the plateau from much of the valley and has diminished both in depth and width, but what is left of it still constitutes a mighty ice river, more than sufficient to plug up the valley's western end.

Lyle McGinnis, whom I took to be in his forties, was a professor of geology at Northern Illinois University at Dekalb. He had all his hair (gray), a carefully clipped gray beard and mustache, and wore spectacles. He had a keen look about him and was in very good shape physically. This present trip to Antarctica was his ninth. Most of his visits had been for periods of two or three months. In 1957–59 he had wintered over during a thirteen-month stay. His current research, aside from his borehole probes, involved study of the tectonics of the Transantarctic Mountains. He had been prominently connected with the trinational (Japan, New Zealand and the United States) Dry Valley Drilling Project (DVDP), which had drilled fifteen boreholes, including three at McMurdo Station and one in McMurdo Sound, and he had been a member of the committee which had prepared the DVDP environmental impact statement. The statement noted:

Antarctica is truly an underdeveloped continent, and its main use is in the realm of diverse scientific investigations undertaken in an atmosphere of international cooperation. Scientific information is the only presently exploitable resource of the continent. It is agreed that the Antarctic must not be endangered in regard to future scientific endeavors. . . .

Traditional surface or near-surface measurements used to reconstruct Antarctic prehistory often are limited and contradictory. Most clues to Antarctica's past have been skimmed from easily accessible surficial materials. The first deep, or intermediate depth, boreholes in sedimentary and igneous rock will permit earth scientists to view the long but poorly known Cenozoic era immediately preceding our historical period. It was during Cenozoic time that Antarctica became established as earth's most extensive, ice-covered region. . . .

DVDP was planned to take advantage of the diverse geological framework of the McMurdo Sound region, which contains rocks and sediments ranging in age from the Precambrian to Recent. The unique setting of glacial, volcanic, terrestrial, and marine environments will permit a series of independent analyses of Antarctic geochronology, paleoclimatology, and paleomagnetism. Because of the diverse geological record, and the fact that the region straddles the ancient suture between east and west Antarctica, the retrieval of continuous, hard rock, and sedimentary rock core will permit a detailed reconstruction of an unknown period of Antarctic history, which in turn played a critical role in global history.

McGinnis told me the Dry Valleys were still an enigma but that we now knew the fiord valleys were cut before ten million years ago and afterward were invaded by a temperate arm of the sea. Taylor Valley had been open to the sea longer than Wright Valley and had some 400 meters (about 1300 feet) of marine sediment on its floor. Wright Valley had shallow pockets of marine sediment and contained the most interesting hydrology, associated with groundwater brines in Don Juan Pond. Victoria Valley had no marine sediment.

While at work on the final stages of *Edge of the World*, I published a condensed version of Chapter 23, "A Walk in Taylor Valley," in the November–December 1972 issue of the *Antarctic Journal*. As far as I'm aware, this is the sole purely literary contribution to the *Journal* to date. As a consequence of the publication I received only one fan letter but it was the most astonishing such letter I could possibly have imagined getting. It was from Sir Charles Wright, the only survivor of Griffith Taylor's geological party of Scott's last or Terra Nova Expedition, the sole survivor of the Pole parties of 1911 and 1912, and one of the two survivors of the search party that had found Scott's tent on the Ross Ice Shelf some 150 statute miles from Hut Point, Ross Island. (Tryggve Gran, a Norwegian, was the other.) As a matter of fact, according to Apsley Cherry-Garrard in his classic book, *The Worst Journey in the World,* Wright had been the first to spot the tent. Wright was leading the party and was its navigator, so Cherry-Garrard was probably correct, at least in the opinion of Sir Charles, as I was to learn.

Before I received his letter I was not even aware that Wright was still alive, but I knew well that at the age of twenty-five he had led the search party for Scott and the others of the polar party in November 1912. I was startled to realize that at his advanced age he was still actively interested in Antarctica, as was proven by the fact that he received and read the *Antarctic Journal.* What a leap across a great age gap that letter was!

Early in May 1973 I visited the remarkable man who was a living link between the so-called heroic era of Antarctic exploration and the modern one. Although I included a lengthy chapter, "Conversations with Sir Charles Wright," in *Edge of the World,* I did not have room enough to publish all the talks, and I was obliged to omit most of the interesting details of my visit. I shall present both the details and the rest of the talks in the next chapter. Meanwhile I hope the reader will understand why I had complex and rich memories and emotions on flying to the north fork of Wright Valley now with McGinnis and Don Osby, his assistant.

It was a dreary looking place on this overcast day: gray Dais (a long, mesa-like formation dividing the valley into two forks), gray mountains, gray-tan empty valley floor, an arid wasteland in which you could seemingly hike for miles and see little. The only thing that recommended it to me at the moment, in addition to its being named for Wright, was that it was ice-free. Nothing moved, so you didn't visually sense the nasty wind we had that day. But you heard it whistling past your ears and flapping parts of your clothes and you felt it pushing you around, both physically and emotionally. Geologic litter of countless gray rocks. The sweeping north side, like sand dunes, of the Dais. But our site was by no means typical of the valley. East of us were Lake Vanda about five miles away and then the Onyx River, which flowed up the valley and fed the lake, and there were some eight hanging or alpine glaciers on the valley's southern ramp. The floor terrain was more varied there.

While McGinnis and Osby worked at gamma-ray logging the borehole, I observed their work for a while, then idly studied the rocks in the vicinity, which were not interesting looking, not ventifacts, not colored, just angular gray chips. McGinnis said the Dry Valleys were cut at least as long ago as eight million years and have been deglaciated for a couple of hundred thousand. The piercing, acrid, smell of DFA (Diesel Fuel Arctic). DFA oozing out of the borehole, staining the ground, being sprayed westward by the wind. DFA staining my companions' clothes.

When they finished with their work we flew eastward, climbed over Bull Pass and landed in Victoria Valley near the northwestern corner of Lake Vida. The borehole pipe rose conspicuously about hip-high out of the ground. We hauled only the essential gear over to it, leaving tent, sleeping bags, food, radio, generator and survival bags at the helo's landing spot. Using a huge wrench, McGinnis unscrewed and removed the pipe's cap. Osby reeled out a long line of black cable and stretched it on the ground away from the pipe. They began logging the gamma rays.

Drill penetration was 306 meters (about 1000 feet), core recovery was 303 meters. The hole was 96 mm (about 3.8 inches) wide. Drilling had occurred in December 1973.

My journal. "This is what they were doing. They had a black electric cable on a small drum, contained in a blue metal box. At one end of the cable they attached a long (about 24 inches) metal-covered probe that could detect gamma rays. The cable was marked at 1-meter intervals. The other end of the cable was connected to a gamma-ray logging machine, and the machine to a 12-volt car battery. The machine had a clock that counted seconds and a gauge that counted gamma rays. You started the clock, and when the machine registered 100 gamma rays it automatically shut the clock down. (The clicking stopped.) You knew then how many seconds it took the machine to register 100 gamma rays at a particular level in the borehole.

"McGinnis had camped at Vida some years ago. He said he had never seen this lake with an unfrozen surface, as it was today. The color was green. Some miniature bergs floated on the wavy water. A powerful easterly blew steadily, unrelentingly through this naked valley all the time we were there—some six hours. I was not about to take the punishing cold here, so put on parka liner and windpants without their liner and was quite comfortable for a while. But as the wind grew stronger and colder we secured our parkas with cords and snaps and put the hoods up. Still the wind found its way to undergarments and naked skin. Osby got his anorak out of his survival bag, which he put on under his parka. He said it cut down the wind a lot. My eyes kept watering heavily. The light was too subdued for sunglasses. The sky was overcast."

A heavy wooden yellow tripod standing astride the borehole. A heavy metal pulley suspended from the tripod's apex. A fuel drum. A wooden pyramid with a red flag marking the borehole site. The prevailing winter westerly had eaten away the soft portions of the marker's grain and had sandblasted away the red paint on its western side. A large khaki wooden tool box. Two blue metal cases. My companions red-parka'd, hooded, black-trousered, yellow-gloved. New black windpants, new black-and-white mukluks. New leather gloves already soaked with DFA. New parkas smelling pungently. McGinnis sitting with his back against the fuel drum, face hidden inside the long parka-hood tunnel. Osby standing, facing him, face equally hidden. Two red figures backed by the green slash of Lake Vida and the faulted mountains of the Olympus Range showing strata of dolerite alternating with sandstone. Endless valley rocks.

Getting restless, and feeling I had nothing to contribute to what McGinnis and Osby were doing and nothing useful further to observe in their immediate activities, and believing I ought to take this opportunity to have a look around on my own, to do my own thing, as it were, to open myself to this strange landscape in the hope of getting some impressions that would be of later use to me, I went off to take a look at the delta with its rapid brooks, whose varied glitter pleased me with an illusion of life. Here was something I felt I could relate to in some way, although certainly these brooks were unlike any I had ever seen in the temperate world. I hiked northward, slowly ascending.

I was far from the Antarctic sea now and its rich life. Thinking of penguins and other birds, I realized that I had never seen one in the Dry Valleys. I wondered about the skua's willingness to adapt to such a life-hostile place as Antarctica and was reminded that when I flew over the glacial wasteland near Brown Peninsula yesterday I saw a solitary skua flying below and that I thought then of the occasional skua sighted close to the Pole itself. What were those south-wandering birds looking for, I asked myself now. Were they explorers among their kind, Scotts and Shackletons of their world?

Looking at the gray mountains in the west, I experienced certain thoughts I had had before on this continent, but so powerful was Antarctica for my emotions, mind and imagination that they struck me as freshly as though they were new-minted. No Maori, no Bushman, no Tierra del Fuegan, no aborigine could suddenly appear, searching for game. For there were no humans indigenous to this place. No giraffe could show itself, no horse, no lion, no wolf, no dog. They had never lived on this continent that occupied one-tenth of the earth's landmass. Nor could any insect or arachnid, familiar or strange, show itself: no tsetse fly, no bumblebee, no mosquito, no safari ant, no black widow, no hay-colored scorpion. And no leaf, whether fresh or sere, no frond, no blade of grass, no bit of heather. This valley was almost lifeless. One would need a microscope in order to detect life here. It was not only the low temperatures and winds that were hostile to life. The extremely low humidity was perhaps even more inimical. I recalled that this is the sole continent that has never harbored man, for it broke away from Gondwanaland, the southern supercontinent, long before man's advent and has been the remotest place on earth for a very long time.

I rejoined McGinnis and Osby, who soon finished their task. We walked westward along beaches and saw fast-running streams heading for the lake. Osby bent down and drank. The easterly was still blowing hard. McGinnis and I returned to our mound of gear and sat on some, our backs propped against the wind. Osby went eastward to climb a large sand dune about a mile and a half away. Looking for him later, we saw him as a tiny upright mark on top of the dune. I spotted the helo as a dot in the eastern sky. We were relieved to see it, for the weather had turned increasingly thick and scuddy.

19 JANUARY."Went onto the ice pier and photographed the Discovery Hut from a new angle, then took pictures of a lone skua perched on the black cindery hill near Vince's Cross."

The ice pier was anything but smooth. Winds, tides and pressure had scarred it. The last time I was at McMurdo there had been no ice pier at the station and therefore no way except from a boat to get such photographs. The hut, the interior of which I knew well, looked as fresh and solid as ever in spite of the fact it had been constructed during February and the early part of March 1902 and so was just about a month short of being seventy-five years old.

I climbed the hill to Vince's Cross, made of wood and erected in 1902 to commemorate Seaman George T. Vince, the first man to lose his life in McMurdo Sound. One of a party of nine that got caught in a blizzard and decided to make their way back to the ship instead of lying low, Vince, unfortunately wearing fur-soled boots, with little traction, slid down what was later to be called Danger Slope and plunged off its cliff into the Sound. His body was never recovered.

Scott wrote in his journal:

Tuesday, March 11, was to be one of our blackest days in the Antarctic. . . . From the moment when he joined us at the Cape of Good Hope, Vince had been popular with all; always obliging and always cheerful, I learnt that he had never shown these qualities more markedly than during the short sledge journey which brought him to his untimely end. His pleasant face and ready wit served to dispel the thought of hardship and difficulty to the end. Life was a bright thing to him, and it is something to think that death must have come quickly in the grip of that icy sea.

Almost miraculously, no other member of the group was permanently injured, although a seaman of eighteen named Hare fell asleep and lay under the snow for about thirty-six hours, yet was free of frostbite. He went forty hours without food and sixty without warm food.

72   BEYOND CAPE HORN

From the cross I saw the blue tidal crack below. The icebroken channel was a piece of rough white string lying lengthwise on the frozen Sound.

20 JANUARY. In the afternoon, at about 4:30, I strolled up to the Earth Sciences Lab on the hill above the Field Center, meaning to look up Osby there, where he and McGinnis had a cubicle office for storing, studying and partially processing their data. I ran into an exciting story: the largest single meteorite find in Antarctica in terms of weight, made by Ed Olsen of the Field Museum of Natural History in Chicago, Bill Cassidy of the University of Pittsburgh, and a Japanese colleague (Keizo Yanai). Their find comes to about 900 pounds.

"Some Japanese scientists made an important meteorite find last year in the region of Showa Station on the other side of the continent. The Americans decided to follow up this discovery with a search in the Ross Island sector and found two meteorites as soon as they began looking, but then camped and hiked fruitlessly for six weeks and decided they had failed. The team was preparing to leave McMurdo in a state of semidepression.

"Cassidy ran into helo pilot Ken Kraper at the O'Club and got to talking. Kraper said he had seen some rocks on blue ice near Allan Hills, and why didn't Cassidy have a look? At first Cassidy was skeptical. The point is you're not supposed to find earth rocks on blue ice on the continental ice sheet. Such ice does not ordinarily, if ever, carry morainic materials. Consequently if you see 'rocks' in it you have good reason to suspect them of being of extraterrestrial origin.

"The meteorite team's helicopter time had been used up, I gathered from Olsen. Special extra time had to be requested from the Chalet. It was granted. So off the team flew to Allan Hills and indeed there were rocks on the blue ice. The find was largely serendipitous, as was the Japanese find of 1969. The Cassidy team looked, found four, then took another flight, found five, and among these was a large stony meteorite, according to Olsen perhaps one of the five largest in the world.

"Olsen, whom I had met in Scottsdale, Arizona, in September, where he had asked me to autograph his copy of *Edge of the World,* was tremendously elated, enthusiastic, charming, childlike, full of meteorite lore. For now there was a great silver lining in the team's cloud. Cassidy was cool by comparison and seemed to prefer to stay in the background, although he was the team's principal investigator. I was fascinated, listened to both for some time. The Japanese colleague, who seemed to speak little English, was mostly silent."

I saw the meteorites about two hours after they were brought in from the field. There was already much fussing with measuring and weighing them and deciding how to divide them up. I gathered that Japan would get half the find. Olsen said the helo pilot would be given a small piece for his services. The Navy crewman from the flight was hanging around the lab room, observing and listening with fascination. Olsen said he and his colleagues were debating whether to look for more meteorites in the brief time they had left, or to call it a day. He asked for my opinion about this. I suggested they quit while they were ahead, while it was quite obvious they would have no trouble getting funded for more searching next season. Why be pressured by time, and risk experiencing the kind of failure they had so recently had in full measure? He said he agreed with me.

One of the meteorites was a small iron one, which I was certain I would have recognized for what it was, but I would not have known the true nature of the large, broken stony meteorite if I had stumbled upon its pieces. They looked very much like broken chunks of fine-grained granite, and the brown fusion crust that had beenformed by heat during the entry into the earth's atmosphere was thin and unobtrusive looking. I didn't notice it until Olsen pointed it out to me. I would have assumed it was due to earthly weathering. The Chalet was strangely silent about the meteorites. It was not publicizing them at the moment, and I probably would not have learned about them soon enough to see them (for they would soon be crated and shipped) if I hadn't gone up to the Earth Sciences Lab looking for Osby.

Later this same year of the spectacular American find, 1977, Cassidy reported in the October *Antarctic Journal*:

Before 1969 only four meteorites had been found in all of Antarctica. In 1969, members of the Tenth Japanese Antarctic Research Expedition discovered nine meteorites lying on the ice near the Queen Fabiola Mountains (Japanese workers refer to this range as the Yamato Mountains and to the meteorites discovered there as the Yamato meteorites). The intriguing feature of their find was that these meteorites did not come from a single shower—five or six different meteorite types were represented among them.

Searches have been made at the same locality during three succeeding field seasons, and the Japanese collection from that site now totals an incredible 992 specimens. Many of these probably are members of a number of showers, and the meteorites found so far may represent only 30 to 300 individual falls. It is abundantly clear, however, that an abnormal concentration of meteorites exists in that part of Antarctica.

During the field season 1976–1977, I was principal investigator on a search for meteorites in areas accessible by helicopter from McMurdo Station. My co-investigator was Edward Olsen of the Field Museum of Natural History, Chicago. We were joined by Keizo Yanai, of the Japan National Institute of Polar Research, who had been associated with some of the Yamato meteorite searches and had led one of them. We planned to try to find meteorite concentrations similar to the one at the Queen Fabiola Mountains, 3,200 kilometers [about 1985 miles] away. . . .

We had almost immediately found two meteorites on the ice; each was first sighted by Dr. Yanai. They apparently were different types of chondrite, lying about 700 meters [about 2300 feet] apart. Thus, we could say that we had found two meteorites during our first 20 minutes in the field. Unfortunately, we did not find any more for the next 6 weeks.

In a final endeavor, we flew to an extensive blue ice field on the plateau side of the Allan Hills and almost immediately began finding meteorites. Because we now had time limitations, we asked the pilot to set up a search pattern and taxi slowly over the ice at about 10 meters [about 32.8 feet] altitude. We found that under those conditions he could see pebbles as small as 2 centimeters [0.79 inches] in diameter lying on the ice. The area of this ice patch is about 100 square kilometers [about 38.6 square miles], and in 4 hours of aerial searching over this exposure we found what may be as many as nine meteorites. The last one, a hypersthene chondrite, was found as 33 fragments scattered over an area of about 4,500 square meters [about 5380 square yards]. The largest fragment weighed 114 kilograms [about 251 pounds], and the parts summed to 407 kilograms [about 897 pounds].

21 JANUARY. "Osby dropped by in the late afternoon to give me two volcanic bombs he found on the way to Castle Rock."

The bombs were lava that had probably been ejected by Erebus. Originally molten, they had solidified while falling, and gravity caused them to be pear-shaped. You could see the point of impact where the bottom of the pear had flattened. They were gray rocks and heavy. In places they showed a salt deposit of some sort. It was very good of Osby to give them to me. One of the reasons he and McGinnis had hiked to Castle Rock was to look for such bombs, for it was well known they could be found in the vicinity of the Rock. I was touched by Osby's affection for me. I had liked him very much ever since we first met at the airport in Christchurch.

"At the end of dinner Bresnahan came to my table to tell me the *Burton Island* will definitely leave at 3 P.M. tomorrow. More information will follow. Walked with Osby to Hut Point, where he had his first look at the exterior of Scott's Discovery Hut and where we saw the *Northwind,* the *Burton Island* and the *Bland* come into harbor. The *Bland* looking very large."

The *Burton Island* and the *Northwind,* sister ships, were quite far apart as they preceded the *Bland,* moving slowly through the ice channel toward McMurdo. They seemed to be gliding on top of the light-bristling ice. Piedmont glaciers were agleam in Victoria Land across the Sound. The *Burton Island,* which I could distinguish from the *Northwind* by its number (283) painted in white on its bow, was almost gaudy with its bright red hull, white superstructure and colorful mast-strung flags flying high. It looked to be not quite half as long as the *Bland.* The latter was a strange-looking vessel because of its five two-columned vertical crane towers, which stood astride the ship in a row from bow to stern.

I had complex and mixed feelings about the *Burton Island,* which reminded me of its sister ship the *Staten Island,* on which I had lived for a little while during my second Antarctic trip. I had a small proprietary sense about the *Burton Island,* the way you have about a cruise ship you're about to board.

5 ❦ Conversation with Sir Charles Wright

IN MAY 1973 I HAD FLOWN to Vancouver after a stopover in Boulder, Colorado, to visit my Antarctic friend Dale Vance, who had wintered over with the Russians at Vostok Station and about whom I had devoted part of a chapter in *Edge of the World.* I spent a night in Vancouver and early the next morning took a crowded bus to Tsawwassen (pronounced without the first "s"), where I boarded the ferry for Saltspring Island, on which, in Ganges, Sir Charles Wright lived.

As a working scientist Wright had made three trips to Antarctica. At the time of my visit he had recently turned eighty-six (he was born on April 7, 1887) but, as I would soon discover, he was still energetic, witty and full of enthusiasm regarding Antarctica. Living with him and his mementos of those early days, it was eerie to think he had known Scott and those other now legendary figures of the Terra Nova Expedition. He had had a long and distinguished career as a scientist and a scientific administrator and had been knighted for his work as an administrator in the Admiralty during the Second World War. Far from being formidable, which I feared he might be, he proved to be a delight to live and work with, as well as an adequate drinker who plied us both with various liquids in order to keep our voices well oiled, as he explained.

77

In his first letter to me, dated early February 1973, he said he found my article on Taylor Valley "extremely interesting" and hoped I would let him know when my book came out, for he wanted to get a copy. He explained that he was the only survivor now of Taylor's geological party and of several other parties, including the Pole Party of 1912 that returned from the top of the Beardmore Glacier. He said he still tried to keep in touch with what went on in the Dry Valleys and especially in his namesake valley and added he was almost sure it was Brandau in a 1965 visit to Wright Valley, "who put the wind up me" (meaning scared him) when he seemed about to land on one of the sharpest of ridges, which fell away on each side at about 70 degrees.

I replied on February 25.

"What a marvelous surprise to have a letter from you. Of course, I know about your work with Scott's last expedition and about Wright Valley. Although I was scheduled to visit Wright Valley during my last trip to Antarctica, I was prevented from doing so because I was involved in a helicopter crash close to the summit of Mount Erebus, as a result of which my hands were not very good for field work for a time.

"My book is being dedicated to Brandau, whom I admire extremely. It will be my pleasure and honor to send you a copy as soon as one is available. For your interest I enclose a copy of the Table of Contents. I also enclose a booklet about Ross Island that I wrote at the request of the National Science Foundation."

I sent another letter to Wright on the 27th.

"You have been much on my mind since I wrote to you the other day. I hope you won't mind hearing from me again so soon. I'd like to ask you several questions. Did you publish an account of your experiences as a member of the party that found Scott, Bowers and Wilson in November 1912? Do you have any theories or hunches regarding the Scott tragedy that differ from those of Cherry-Garrard, Atkinson, Debenham and Amundsen? Had you returned to Antarctica between the time of the Terra Nova Expedition and 1965? If not, you must have had some striking impressions in 1965, given the contrast between the sledging days and the days of aircraft, and given all the changes that had taken place at what had become McMurdo

Station. Did you stay long in Antarctica in '65? Have you published your impressions of the '65 visit?

"I have other questions that come to mind and would very much like to interview you for my book. Will you kindly tell me if the idea of an interview appeals to you?"

Wright responded on March 2, saying he had published nothing about his early Antarctic experiences but that he was now, with the help of his daughter Pat, trying to interpret the pencil diaries he had kept in the old days and which had become difficult to decipher as well as to interpret. The Scott Polar Research Institute in Cambridge, England, had offered to copy them, but Wright preferred to keep things in his own hands. At any rate, the diaries were not intended for publication. As for a taped interview by telephone, he was definitely interested. He expressed the wish to be helpful so far as he could. I wrote to him again on March 30.

"I'm increasingly inclined to believe that the best and perhaps the only way to conduct a really productive interview is in person. If you wish, it could be held in successive days if we found we had a great deal to talk about."

I phoned him the evening of April 18 and had a pleasant and productive conversation. And so I went to Saltspring Island.

Exiting from the ferry's car deck, I ascended a slope and saw Wright standing beside his daughter, recognizing him from the two photos Dale Vance had given me. He was thinner than in the photos, possibly more bent, had spectacles, and in general I had no trouble spotting him because of his great age. I walked up to them, introduced myself, and to my amusement had to decline their determined offers to take my heavy blue airline bag. Even Wright really tried to take it from me. He directed me to sit on the front seat of the car and he got in the back seat and we drove not through a hamlet or settlement as I had expected—where and what was Long Harbour?—but on a narrow asphalt road through heavy woods, seeing cyclists starting up hills from the ferry slip, some families at a picnic ground, then only road and trees.

When we arrived at Wright's property at around 1 P.M., he got out to open and shut a long wire gate to keep out a neighbor's geese. His place was indeed quite rustic—and attractive—simple, informal, with views of saltwater inlets. Pat Wright showed me to a room, which, as it turned out, was her own, and said I could use the top drawer of the chest of drawers (which had been left partly open for guidance), but I said I preferred to live out of my bag, which I was used to doing.

One of my first and most vivid impressions was of a large sepia print, framed, of the famous photo by Ponting of Scott seated at his collapsible desk in his cubicle in the Terra Nova Hut on Cape Evans. Herbert G. Ponting was a great photographer of the Antarctic. I guess the negative was 8×10. The print in Wright's house was a good deal larger than that and very effective. Above and to the left of it was a large print of young Wright on his knees, peering upwards through a theodolite. This too appears, as I seem to recall, in *Scott's Last Expedition*. I became vividly aware of other memorabilia: rare first editions, even rarer photographic scrapbooks, a bookcase made of a Nansen polar sledge cut in half, a large, wood-cased thermometer, a wooden 4×5 camera, a theodolite, a penguin-shaped menu from the last midwinter's feast of the Terra Nova Expedition signed by many of the expedition members.

Without delay, after lunch I set up my equipment in Sir Charles's room. He wore a tie and a sports jacket with a white handkerchief in the breast pocket. He was lean and had almost all his hair, now white and cut very short. The fingers of his darkened hands were gnarled. I wondered if he had arthritis pain. He had a habit of stroking his hands lengthwise, one above the other. Brown, age-darkened hands, with much extra, paperlike skin that he sometimes absently pursed into mountain ranges, then, catching himself, smoothed out. His habit of saying, during pauses, "Hm-hm," the first on a higher note than the second. Once he said to me he remembered only poorly events of last week but recalled very well what had happened fifty years ago.

So we taped a good deal. We took a lunch break when his voice began to fade. His fading voice was a problem Pat had warned me about. He corrected it by drinking plenty of rye while insisting that I drink also. I chose scotch and soda with ice. The rye did seem to improve his voice considerably.

Neider: Let me just read to you what Cherry-Garrard says. "That scene can never leave my memory. We with the dogs had seen Wright turn away from the course by himself and the mule party swerve right-handed ahead of us. He had seen what he thought was a cairn and then something looking black by its side. A vague kind of wonder gradually gave way to a real alarm. We came up to them. All halted. Wright came across to us. 'It is the tent.' I do not know how he knew." You don't take exception to that?

Wright: No, not at all. It's very precise and very correct.

Neider: The reason I'm interested, as somebody who's trying to get the facts straight about the history of Ross Island, is that by an irony of history that I think is well justified Scott in his great tragedy made a more lasting mark on Western civilization than Amundsen in his great triumph.

Wright: It's very interesting.

Neider: And I think it's for two reasons. One, Scott's style as a man, and two, his style as a writer. Therefore I think that any revelation that we have of this primal, terrible scene is important to our society, increasingly important because of the difference in moral values that we are experiencing today. To think back on Scott, for all his possible errors of judgment, is to think back on a time and a man when a certain nobility of conduct was to be taken for granted.

Wright: Yes, I agree with you entirely.

Neider: Cherry-Garrard seems to be certain that Scott died last. Do you share his opinion?

Wright: I'm not prepared to be certain about that. He bases it on the fact that Scott was sort of half out of his bag, leaning over with his diary toward Dr. Bill [Edward A. Wilson].

Neider: To your knowledge did Wilson or Bowers also write final messages?

Wright: I don't think so. Otherwise it would appear in Dr. Bills's diary.

Neider: I was fascinated by a little anecdote you mentioned at breakfast, and that is that going up the Beardmore you had a sleepless—

Wright: I felt sleepless, shall I say. I lay awake the whole night.

Neider: This was only at around 3000 feet.

Wright: Yes, it was about that, I should think.

Neider: The idea of being sleepless on a sledging traverse, is that something to be concerned about?

Wright: I wasn't concerned about it in the least. It was an interesting thing and I thought back and I remembered—I was quite a youngster—people talking about sleeplessness at elevation.

Neider: But Atkinson [Edward L.] then reported it to Scott, did he?

Wright: Oh, it got through to Scott.

Neider: But in what sense? Do you think Atkinson was actually worried about you because you hadn't slept well that night?

Wright: I don't know. I never spoke about it to Atch.

Neider: What interests me here is that Atkinson reported to Scott that perhaps one of the people in his group was not feeling too well on the basis of this, and that may have affected Scott's decision in sending you back.

Wright: Might be, I don't know.

Neider: If that indeed was the case, then how extraordinary an event that was for your life, as it turned out.

Wright: Yes, I would have liked to have gone further, but I never had any expectation of being one of the party going right to the Pole. I knew who I thought it should be.

Neider: You went to the top of the Beardmore. How far is that from the Pole?

Wright: We must have been 250 or 300 miles from the Pole.

Neider: One of the men, when told off to go back, burst into tears, according to Scott. I forget who it was, it's in Scott's diary. Apparently everyone wanted to go.

Wright: Scott would certainly go, one knew this. Scott always had Wilson in his train, and Birdie Bowers and Wilson and Cherry-Garrard had done a wonderful job with the winter journey, you see. You could almost put your finger on the people who were almost certain to go. And they had all proven themselves very fit for this sort of thing.

Neider: One of the things that is never mentioned by the early explorers, and it seems to me to be rather vitally important for a complete understanding of life in the Antarctic, is toilet habits in the field. For example, Cherry-Garrard never talks about the fact that it's sometimes necessary to leave the tent at minus seventy [Fahrenheit].

Wright: Yes, well that's insane, of course. But we did it. We all did it. Scott wanted it that way and we all went out of the tent if we had to. Well! It's quite a business, because the first thing

82   BEYOND CAPE HORN

that happens if you go outside in that sort of temperature, everything freezes solid. You see, you've come from your sleeping bag, you've taken into the sleeping bag all the frozen sweat of the previous day, and the previous day and the previous day and the previous day. There's a lot of it at the end. And during the night you first melt that frozen sweat. And very often it freezes at the bottom of the bag, where your feet are. And if you're going to have a decent night you've got to melt all that before you have a chance. And even then it's not comfortable because whatever is next door is wet and cold, and every breath you take brings some of the cold stuff into the small of your back. So a winter's night when you're sledging is not a comfortable thing at all. But you've got to, before you get anywhere, you've got to melt the ice. And sometimes there's fifteen pounds of ice or something like that that's got to be turned into water before you begin to sleep. But that's not what you were thinking of when you asked that.

Neider: No. But when you leave the tent you're wet, actually.

Wright: Oh yes. You freeze straightaway. You manage to get in again and you tie it up again and hope that you get to sleep again before you have to get out. It's not comfortable. But in summer it's quite different. Your sleeping bag loses its condensed water vapor and you have a relatively dry bag. And there's all the difference in heat conductivity between a wet bag and a dry bag, as you can imagine. Worst of all is the frozen bag.

Neider: You were very pleased that Scott wanted you, as he calls it, to saturate your mind with ice problems?

Wright: Yes, yes indeed. It was not very respectable but I dearly wanted the opportunity of seeing some of the country, you see, and if I hadn't taken on glaciology I'd have spent my time, I'm afraid, in headquarters. And I couldn't bear to think of that.

Neider: I gather that you have fallen into many a crevasse. There are not many people in modern times who fall into crevasses. What was it like?

Wright: The unpleasant part is the jerk that comes at the end of your fall. You've got a harness, you see, with a rope. In crevasse country there's usually at least one man well ahead, an extended line ahead. And there *is* an art in walking, something like walking on slippery ice. You walk from your knees and not from your toes. You walk flatfooted, and it helps enormously, if you're not to fall into a crevasse, if that's the way you do it.

Neider: I gather that there were times when one just accepted the notion of falling into crevasses and was very cool about it.

Wright: I can remember Scott, about opposite the Cloud-maker [a mountain], up the Beardmore. He stopped just before we got to some rough level stuff and said, "Well, here are the crevasses. Somebody's got to fall into them." He was the first one in. [Both laugh.] That pleased us all immensely.

Neider: Did you fall very far?

Wright: Not as a rule. You haven't got a very long stretch between yourself and the sledge. You lengthen the distance at least for one man so that the whole outfit doesn't go down at once. But the thing that surprised me was to find out how much more difficult it is to see what's ahead of you coming down than going up. Extraordinary. I went badly astray coming down to the Mid-Glacier Depot. Got to a tangle of crevasses. Not crevasses so much as separate seracs, spikes filled up on the surface with snow. And I was very ashamed of myself that time, almost as ashamed as the time when, later on, I led our party in a complete circle to meet our own sledge tracks again.

Neider: When was this?

Wright: On the way back from the Beardmore. And the funny thing—it's really quite interesting. Normally I had no real difficulty in navigating. Something went wrong this day. I don't know what it could have been. But it was a bad day. Couldn't see the horizon, couldn't see the sky, couldn't see anything. Nothing to look at. No wind. Just a sheer white wall. But the interesting thing was that once I'd done this I lost my confidence in the ability to keep a straight line and I had to tell Atch, "'I can't go on, I can't trust myself any more." It was very curious.

Neider: And what did he say?

Wright: He said, "Yes, right-o." It's the most interesting phenomenon. Having made a muck of it, I didn't trust my ability any more—till we camped next day. [Laughs.]

Neider: And then it was over.

Wright: Oh yes. Yes, yes. No trouble after that.

Neider: When Shackleton was coming back down the

Beardmore after his farthest south the party developed dysentery.

Wright: One of our own people picked that up—Keohane [Patrick]. We'd had our Christmas dinner at the Mid-Glacier Depot, and we put it down to the cubic inch of Christmas pudding that was too much for his tender stomach. That was spartan fare. *He* got it then. What sort of confirmed our idea was that we all ate enormously when we came into One Ton Depot—rations of everything, you know, and I remember eating three days' meal at one whack. It was not very much. That didn't affect me but it started Atkinson off and he had quite an unpleasant time of it for three or four days. By that time Keohane had recovered.

Neider: That's a disaster in itself, to have something like dysentery when you're manhauling sledges.

Wright: Oh, it is. You're not there all the time and you have to catch up.

Neider: Did you ever have any signs of scurvy?

Wright: No. When I saw my legs on getting back, saw them for the first time—you don't take your clothes off—I was surprised. They were really swollen up. Which I put down to having stopped marching. I don't know whether it was incipient scurvy or not. I never went into it. I never mentioned it to anybody except to Priestley [Raymond], who said, "Oh yes, I had the same when *we* came in." And then he said [whispers], "I put on ten pounds in three weeks after I got back."

Neider: It occurs to me that being out in the field for so long in those conditions you have a very unusual relationship with your own body. You don't see parts of your body for a long time.

Wright: You wear windproof trousers, and puttees over them.

Neider: At night did you undress to get into the sleeping bag?

Wright: Oh no. I put another pair of socks on, maybe. You see, our allowance of personal stuff was eleven pounds apiece, and I should say that three pounds of that went for tobacco, and another two pounds for reading matter, and a sledging diary (just a few ounces)—but it didn't leave much room for spare clothing. We all had a pair of spare socks but they were really wet. A woolly thing gets really wet and there's quite a weight in them. In that abortive attempt to relieve the northern party—that would be the autumn of 1912, I guess—I weighed the sweater I had on, when I came back, and it was thirteen pounds overweight.

Neider: Scott and Cherry-Garrard often said there was never any bad feeling among the men. As a matter of fact, Cherry-Garrard says that during the entire winter journey he almost cannot remember one swear word despite the desperation that they felt. Do you think this is romanticizing?

Wright: Yes. It's impossible when we're with seamen to go along with the kind of things happening, you see, and not to have a few words, seamen's language. I just don't believe it. It wasn't meant in any special sense.

Neider: Did Scott react to seamen's language?

Wright: He was used to it. Of course, so was Dr. Bill, he'd been from before.

Neider: But you do feel that the reports that have come out, of really good behavior under very trying circumstances, are true?

Wright: Absolutely. Yes, there was nothing in it. If a few unpleasant words were used it just meant nothing at all. It was normal seamen's language or normal Londoner's language.

Neider: But under desperate circumstances men did behave very well?

Wright: Extraordinarily well.

Neider: So this was not an exaggerated report?

Wright: Not a bit.

Neider: Now you mentioned at lunch today that you felt—it came out quite naturally—that in some ways Cherry-Garrard is not appreciated. I'd like to hear you talk about that.

Wright: I feel it quite strongly because, first of all, Cherry was one of the nicest people. He was a real gentleman of the nicest kind you find in England. Although he was educated in Oxford he didn't have any Oxford accent, it didn't stick out at all. And he was one of the nicest of the party. Now, he also had a stake in every really sticky journey. The depot journey, where they lost some of the ponies to killer whales. The winter journey, which was a terrible thing, terrible. The Pole journey, although he was with us all the time when I was there—that was the only easy time. And then this awful journey with Dmitri [a dog and pony handler] and the dogs to help Scott and the party get back quickly to catch the ship at Hut Point, you see, a quick journey to catch the ship, and then keep remembering, when you're inclined to think that things needn't to have gone wrong. I dare say Scott's orders to be at a certain place by a certain time were arranged by him in order to catch the ship on the way back, he didn't want to stay another winter if it wasn't necessary. Well, there we are. What I started to say was Cherry had a stake in all these difficult things. The only not difficult part was on the polar journey and the return journey. On the return journey we came through without any trouble at all except for dysentery for a short time on the part of Keohane and a little bit on the part of Atkinson. When we met all the food in the world and all the oil that anyone could use we took our proper share of that and a bit more, I think. So Cherry had a hard time. He stuck it extraordinarily well. Mind you, he rowed when he was at Oxford, he was a tougher guy than he looked, much tougher, but he wasn't as tough on that winter journey as Wilson and Birdie Bowers. He was not in quite such good shape when he got back, at any rate. I'd say asleep on his feet.

Neider: Why do you feel he's not appreciated? In what sense?

Wright: Well, he's written a book, and like most Englishmen in similar cases he understates everything in which he's involved, and I think that people reading his book don't realize, because he understates something he really knows, don't appreciate that he had really, really difficult times. And I know that many other people who were down there feel the same as I do.

Neider: Did you feel a distinction being made between the civilians and the noncivilians of the expedition, let's say at winter quarters? Did you feel that you and Cherry-Garrard had a great deal more in common because you were civilians?

Wright: No, they didn't come the naval officer over us. We were really part of the gang, and as a matter of fact what welded us into the right position very firmly was when we had to take over bailing the ship out, two hours on and two hours off. About a day and a half. [Chuckles.] On deck, trying to keep the dogs and the ponies alive.

Neider: This was during the storm.

Conversations with Sir Charles Wright   87

Wright: This was during the storm about four days after we left New Zealand. And we did a pretty good job, if you ask me. Man the buckets. [Laughs.]

Neider: Somebody I read recently—I don't know if it was Atkinson or Taylor—remarked on your awareness of beauty in Antarctica and as an example they said that during a field trip studying ice crystals in crevasses you were the only one who was fascinated by and remarked on the beauty of the crystals. This convinces me that you were very much aware of the beauty in Antarctica.

Wright: It wasn't so much the beauty of it as the geometrical designs and the reasons for it. It's the reasons for it that are really interesting. You see some funny shape and you wonder, "Now how did that come about? Did this part of it get made at night, and this part in the daytime?" All that business, you see. It's fascinating, really, if you don't *know.*

Neider: And you became very adept at photographing ice crystals. Some of your photographs are reproduced in *Scott's Last Expedition,* volume two. They're beautiful against a black background. Ponting says that he gave you some tips on that. The grotto by Ponting, by the way, is very beautiful.

Wright: I'll never forget that. That was an iceberg that tilted over, and there were killer whales in the open water. When we were told officially, Griff [Griffith Taylor] and I, to go with Pont—naval people were scared of him, he had the reputation of a Jonah—things didn't happen to him, they happened to people *with* him. [I laugh. Wright joins me.] At any rate he said, "I'll take several pictures of you going up," and I said, "Look here, that's rather too steep, we'll have to cut steps to get up." He said, "Oh that's all right, you go and cut the steps first and then you go up and pretend to cut the steps." And we did that. Griff and I had sense enough to rope ourselves together. Up I went [chuckles] and at the top, at an unguarded blow, a great bit of ice fell down amongst the killer whales. And Ponting said [shouting]: "That's wonderful! Do it again!" [Both laugh.] You'd see these darn killer whales, waiting for you, hoping.

Neider: When you returned to Antarctica was it always in connection with scientific work or did you ever embark on what they used to call a sentimental journey?

Wright: Well, it's very difficult, you know, to answer a question like that because you go, ostensibly anyway, you make an excuse, possibly, to go, but when you get there then you find, or at least I found, that one is regarded as one of the old gang. They used to talk of the heroic age. I've heard that word several times.Heroic age. The Americans *make* it so. They *make* it so. By their attitude and by what they say and so on. But the sentimental part, as far as I was concerned, was an inescapable thing over which I had no control.

Neider: You wouldn't disagree with the fact that it's referred to as the heroic age of Antarctic exploration?

Wright: I don't know, it's very difficult to say. It depends on how one's brought up. I spent most of my life in England, and the British attitude is quite different from the American, you know.

Neider: Can we go into that briefly, that difference?

Wright: I don't know what it's based on, this is the trouble. The U.S. of A. no doubt is a frightful mixture of people, races. And so is England. But the mixture had been formed umpteen years ago in England—the Angles and the Saxons and all the other people. And we've come to expect this difference, but why it comes about, unless it's a mixture of races that does it, I don't know.

Neider: Is it also partly a difference in what was happening in the Anglo-Saxon world in the years just before the first war? Wasn't Britain undergoing a kind of inspirational surge of patriotism in preparation for the contest with Germany?

Wright: Yes, that's true enough.

Neider: Let me read you this from Scott, who says, "One of the greatest successes is Wright. He is very thorough and absolutely for anything. Like Bowers, he has taken to sledging like a duck to water, and although he hasn't had such severe testing I believe he would stand it pretty nearly as well. Nothing ever seems to worry him, and I can't imagine that he ever complained of anything in his life."

Wright: [Chuckles.] Well, on the last thing he's certainly gone astray. What does he mean by complain? I think you can complain to yourself, very often, without complaining to anybody else. With these glasses, which I had to wear, and another pair of glasses, snowglasses, goggles, as well—it was quite a burden. When the weather was cold you couldn't see where you were going and I used to complain to myself, "What a silly ass. Why didn't I get some special lenses made of snow goggle glass?"

Because with two of these things, you see, you have four surfaces on which you can either have condensation of ice or water vapor or actual stuff sticking to the outside lens. So that it was a dreadfully stupid thing not to have got some special glasses made. That's what I call complaining. I was complaining to myself.

Neider: Scott of course had something else in mind, and what he had in mind was your willingness and eagerness—

Wright: It was all very interesting, you see.

Neider: And your optimism and your enthusiasm. Have you enjoyed your life, on the whole?

Wright: Until a little while ago I was thinking very seriously of writing a memoir, and the title I had was "Diary of a Fortunate Man."

Neider: How do you account for your extraordinary longevity and vigor?

Wright: Well, I can't account for it now, it's gone. [Laughs.] I don't know. I said I was odd, a long time ago. I think I was odd even when I was a youngster at school, because I remember that for some incredible reason I thought it was a good thing—I was living in Toronto at the time—to toughen oneself a bit, so I wore the same clothes in summer and winter. Not a sensible thing at all to do. [Chuckles.] I don't know what would account for it. My mother didn't last very long. My father only lasted until about 80. Nothing in heredity, anyway.

Neider: Scott said how fit you were. You were very fit, weren't you?

Wright: I was, of course.

Neider: Can you tell me something about your early years? Were they happy ones?

Wright: Oh, very. Although they weren't very happy after my father married again. I had a stepmother and I didn't entirely approve of her, shall we say.

Neider: How old were you then?

Wright: About ten. Not that one was unhappy but, like every youngster, I was very ready to fly elsewhere, to get away from home. Every youngster with any guts wants to clear out.

When in February 1974 I sent Wright a copy of the dust jacket of my forthcoming *Edge of the World,* he remarked that he was sorry to see I was a flat-earth believer. The book was published in April. Early in May he wrote to me, "I am not qualified as a critic in your field of effort, but I think you have written a very fine book." At the end of May he wrote me saying he had been very busy as the result of an "event" at Victoria University, where he was the recipient of an honorary degree of Doctor of Laws. In a footnote he added that this reminded him of the Royal Navy admiral who already was a Knight of the Order of the British Empire (K.B.E.) and who was then made a Knight Commander of the Bath (K.C.B.), and that a message received by the admiral read, "Congratulations. Twice a knight at your age."

He died November 1, 1976, at the age of eighty-nine.

6 ❁ *Glimpses of My Life on the "Burton Island"*

22 JANUARY, SATURDAY. "Mike of the Chalet came to my room to tell me it was time to go to the *Burton Island.* This was at 12:50 P.M. Gave him my room key. Was driven in a truck to the pier, led aboard the ship with other civilians. Had to climb a high gangplank ladder from the pier to the *Bland,* cross the *Bland,* climb down a steep frail ladder from the *Bland* to the *Burton Island.* Netting beneath the second ladder but I had an unpleasant sensation.

"There are seven guests besides me on the *Burton Island:* two young ornithologists, the three members of the Antarctic inspection team, Bob Murphy and Joe Warburton. We signed in on reaching the *Burton Island* and I was immediately shown to my rack (bunk) in CPO (Chief Petty Officers) quarters—an upper bunk on the deck below the wardroom, on the port side."

I seemed almost able—but not quite, it was tantalizing—to identify a man on shore, watching the ship as if wistfully. Was it Osby? Or was it someone who felt stuck at McMurdo and daydreamed about leaving it? The figure turned away and climbed the hill road back to the station's center.

Standing on the helicopter deck in the aft part of the vessel as we maneuvered in Winter Quarters Bay, I had views of McMurdo new to me. Beyond the deck nets which served as gunnels you could see Ob Hill and halfway up it the green buildings of the former nuclear power plant; then, farther down, various structures, a number of them also green against the oxford-gray terrain (the station was free of snow and ice now). The most startling thing to see was the great garbage dump at the station's end just east of the bay, with the dark sweep of Cape Armitage beyond it. The dump seemed to contain mostly rusty metal. When the ice on which it rested melted, the materials would sink to the bottom of the bay. Meanwhile what an unsightly mess it was. McMurdo and the waters near it had been thoroughly ruined scientifically through pollution. As for aesthetics, the station had never been pretty.

Erebus was smoking as I said my silent farewells to it. I busied myself with photographic work to prevent tears. And farewell to the exquisite Western Mountains. But what a luxury it was to have this moving platform under me, this new home, from which to view the great polar world. I was both sad and tremendously happy. And I felt very lucky to have, at my age, a socially useful function, the feeling that I was still needed, that I was not yet being shunted aside into retirement. I was determined to work very hard to gather the materials for my new book. I had many great psychological debts to pay off.

We spotted a killer whale on our port side, sticking its snout above the channel. The Western Mountains showed sharply, their piedmont glaciers agleam. Skuas soared past us occasionally and we saw the dark prone forms of Weddell seals on the ice. It was a gloriously clear day. Very soon I would learn how rare such crystal days are in the maritime Antarctic: the Southern Ocean and the Peninsula area. At times we passed open pools in the sea ice, water so still it seemed to reflect Erebus perfectly. But mostly we were aware of the jagged gleaming of ice, and of sunlight bristling nakedly, and of ice waves called sastrugi, and of the helter-skelter knives and swords and ax heads of those parts of the icebroken channel that had partially refrozen. I was particularly moved when the northwestern side of Mt. Erebus, with the Fang and the Fang Glacier, came into view, for it was on that side, near the summit, that I had crashed.

Cape Bird came into view, profiling the pack ice and small bergs with chalky whites. Erebus was blowing smoke puffs now, columns of white perhaps a thousand feet high. Only music could hope to suggest the beauty, strength and delicacy of the rich blues of sky and water, the pale blues of land ice shadows, and the life-surging joy afforded by the gleaming, chalky ice cliffs. The most haunting form I saw today, visually more lasting even than Erebus, was a stranded tabular berg just beyond the cape, the sidelit white cliffs of which made me think of a series of brilliant trills.

Awaking in the middle of the night to go to the head by the faint red door light and my own tiny flashlight, and climbing down the vertical rack ladder, and passing sleeping bodies and being assaulted by the comparatively brilliant light inside the head, light that was never turned off, I felt the throb of the ship's engines and the uncertain footing and heard the loud scraping sounds of the breaking of ice, and I sensed too the vessel's pulsing life and my unfamiliarity with everything, and I felt extremely happy, for at least inaction had turned to action, there was no longer any possibility of my missing the ice-breaker, either through my own cause or someone else's. I was *onboard*.

23 JANUARY, SUNDAY. Noon position: 75°00′S, 174°00′E.

At times the sea was green. There was almost no wind. Then we got some swells, and the tan-orange wardroom drapes began to pendulate and we heard tales of forty- and fifty-degree rolls the ship had taken coming down from New Zealand, and of people unable to sleep and eat. We wondered when our sea luck would suddenly run out.

After leaving the sea ice of McMurdo Sound we came to the richly blue waters of the Ross Sea. Our traverse of a significant stretch of the Southern Ocean was also for me a journey through time, for whenever we crossed the track of a leading explorer I tended to think of him and his narrative. Thus now I thought of the man after whom the sea was named. Of the discovery of his namesake sea Ross had written:

In approaching the pack we had passed a great many bergs, but after midnight comparatively few were seen. The wind freshened to a strong breeze from the northwestward, and carried us rapidly to the southward. At 8 A.M. [January 5, 1841] we again came in sight of the main pack, and ran several miles along the edge of it to examine it. From the masthead it seemed sufficiently open to admit of our penetrating as far as we could see to the southward; and although other circumstances were not so favourable for taking the pack as I could have wished, owing to the unsettled state of the weather and the wind blowing so directly upon the ice as to preclude our regaining the open water if thought desirable, I nevertheless determined to make the attempt, and push the ships as far into it as we could get them. The signal was made to the Terror, and we bore away before the wind, selecting the most favourable point to break through the outer edge of the pack, which, as usual, was formed of much heavier ice than the rest, and which we accomplished without sustaining any serious injury, although necessarily receiving some very heavy blows.

After about an hour's hard thumping, we forced our way into some small holes of water, connected by narrow lanes, for which we had purposely steered; and, closely followed by the Terror, we found the ice much lighter and more scattered than it appeared to be when viewed from the distance. . . .

At noon we were in latitude 66°55'S, and longitude 174°34'E. The clear sea was no longer discernible from the masthead; with nothing but ice around, and fortunately a clear sky above us, we pursued our way through the pack, choosing the clearest 'leads,' and forcing the interposing barriers as they occurred; the way continued, if not to open before us, still sufficiently so to enable us to navigate freely amongst the ice, without danger or difficulty as we proceeded, at times sustaining violent shocks, which nothing but ships so strengthened could have withstood. . . .

The wind gradually moderated as we got farther into the pack, and had declined to quite a gentle air at midnight, by which time we were between sixty and seventy miles from the pack edge; there was, however, still so much motion amongst the ice, that I have no doubt it was blowing a strong gale in the open sea to the northward; the clouds drifted swiftly over our heads, and thick showers of snow fell, but we had, at intervals, an extensive view from the crow's nest, which enabled us to pursue our southerly course with confidence, though under diminished sail, throughout the night.

Early the next morning the ice became much closer, compelling a more varying course, and greatly retarding our progress; a strongly marked 'water-sky,' which was seen to the southeastward, raised our hopes of being able to reach an open sea at no great distance, and all our means were employed to force the ships onward through the ice in that direction; but early in the afternoon we found it so close as to baffle all our exertions, and we were obliged to heave to in a small hole of water, out of which we could find no way to the southward, and wait until the ice opened. . . .

At noon we were in lat. 68°17'S, long. 175°21'E, and found we had been driven by a current twenty-six miles to the S.E. during the last two days; another proof to us that there must be open space in that direction. But the ice remained so close until the afternoon of the following day, that we could not make any way through it; and whilst thus detained we tried for soundings, but without reaching the ground with 600 fathoms. . . . At 11 P.M. a thick fog came on, and the ice being much too compact for us, we were obliged to heave to for several hours. At 4 A.M. we recommenced our labour, aided by a light south-westerly wind, and succeeded in forcing the ships several miles through the pack by noon, when it fell perfectly calm. . . . A great change in the ice was produced by the calm opening it out in all directions, as we always found to be the case in the Arctic Seas; and a breeze springing up from the northward at 8:00 P.M. we made some way through the pack, pressing forward under all sail towards the southeast water. . . . At 5 A.M. the next day we had accomplished the object of our exertions, and found ourselves again in a clear sea. . . . At noon we were in lat. 69°15′S, and long. 176°15′E.

The wind veered round gradually to the eastward, so that we continued to make some progress to the southward notwithstanding the fog and snow being so thick that we could seldom see more than half a mile before us, and sometimes not so far; but as we met with no icebergs, and only a few straggling pieces of ice and a heavy sea having arisen, we felt assured that we had gained an open space of great extent.

The storm blew with great violence from the eastward until 2 A.M. the next day, when it began to abate, and by nine o'clock had moderated so much as to admit of our setting reefed courses. The fog also began to disperse about that time, and at noon we had a most cheering and extensive view; not a particle of ice could be seen in any direction from the masthead. Our observations gave us a lat. 70°23′S, long. 174°50′E and the magnetic dip had increased to 85°.

We were leaving behind us the nostalgic southern light. Strange counterpoint: vast somber winecolored cloudbanks, spotlight remnants of light in the south, milky wake of the ship, ship life, and the busyness of Antarctic petrels as twilight deepened. What beautiful, bright, intense fliers they were, with a clean, white, hull-like body and dark head and wings. Feeding, they dipped one wing and seemed to graze the water as they skimmed it. We could make out now a line of mountains far to the west.

I was becoming acquainted with the ship. I already knew

some salient facts about her. Overall length: 269 feet. Beam (width): 64 feet. Draft: 29 feet. Displacement: 6515 tons. Cruising range: approximately 38,000 nautical miles at a speed of 10.5 knots. Maximum speed: 16 knots, with a range of 16,000 nautical miles at this speed. She was propelled by two 5,000-horsepower electric motors driving two propellers which measured 17 feet each in diameter. Electricity for the motors was provided by six 2,000-horsepower diesel engines. She was capable of carrying 676,000 gallons of diesel fuel for her main engines and an additional 17,000 gallons of aviation fuel to support the two helicopters carried onboard.

Many of her features were keyed to the demands of frozen seas. The hull was red for vivid contrast with ice. There was a conning bridge or station above the pilot house (main bridge), from which one could better seek out leads in the ice. She was heavily insulated against the cold. Her relatively short length increased maneuverability, her wide beam provided a channel through which merchantmen could be escorted and her deep draft afforded a place for people, stores and fuel. She was named for a small island off the coast of Delaware.

Homeported in Long Beach, California, she was one of seven major Coast Guard icebreakers then in commission. She was built for the U.S. Navy in San Pedro, California, in 1946 and was turned over to the Coast Guard in 1966. She carried two HH52A helicopters, which were used as airborne conning towers in looking for leads in the ice and for ship-to-shore transportation over ice or water. When the ship was on a long and rough sea voyage the helos were wired down in their telescopic hangar in the aft part of the vessel and the pilots had little or nothing to do.

Icebreakers are notorious for their poor riding qualities in an open sea. According to a Navy report, she had rolled as much as 65 degrees during winter storms in the Gulf of Alaska and in the Roaring Forties enroute to Antarctica. The reason she rode poorly in open seas was that, in order to break ice, she was relatively keel-less. She was built roughly like a football, as one of the officers described her for me. She was excellent for breaking ice, which she did by riding onto ice masses with her special bow, and she could roll by means of ballast tanks to help her weight break through.

She had taken part in numerous Arctic and Antarctic expeditions and had been part of the search and rescue related to my crash on Erebus. During the latter she served as a platform for refueling helicopters, and many men with binoculars on her searched the western shore of Ross Island in the hope of spotting the lost helicopter or its wreckage.

A Navy release dated 1957 said:

Duty aboard an icebreaker is like serving on every type of ship in the Navy at once. She does the work of a Service Force vessel, has the flight deck of an aircraft carrier, the draft and armor of a battle ship, the handling characteristics of a motor launch, the power of a seagoing tug, the roll of a destroyer, the battering power of the old *Monitor*.

In order to serve south of 60° south latitude, in accordance with the requirements of the Antarctic Treaty her large weapons had been removed.

A leaflet given to me by the Coast Guard read:

The ship is one of a very special type that calls the polar regions of the Arctic and Antarctic their natural habitat. *Burton Island* does many things. She provides support for scientific expeditions, escorts merchantmen through ice to keep trade moving when otherwise it might stop, performs search and rescue in areas where other ships cannot go and, through the scientists and laboratories aboard, does various types of research. During the Arctic summer she frequently visits remote Indian villages in Alaska to provide those communities with medical and dental services.

The Coast Guard, founded in 1790, is one of the Armed Forces of the United States and is its oldest sea-going service. The U.S. Coast Guard is a unique organization, with no exact counterpart anywhere in the world. Almost 40,000 strong, it is charged with a number of roles—the safety of life and property at sea, the enforcement of the laws of the United States, the operation and maintenance of aids to navigation, polar and domestic icebreaking, oceanography, and a distinct military role as one of the five Armed Forces. In peacetime the Coast Guard functions within the Department of Transportation.

I soon knew quite naturally how to move from my rack to the door leading to the steep steel stairs that went up to the wardroom deck, and how to get from the wardroom to the ship's prow on the same deck, and how to go to the hangar deck, where one could jog or walk, or to the forward deck between bridge and wardroom deck. One was aware of how low the gunnels were, of how easy it would be, when the ship was rolling or the decks were icy, to pitch overboard, and of how little hope there would be of a rescue if that happened. Often, later when the weather was rough, I was alone on deck for varying periods of time, and if I had been swept overboard I would not have been missed for hours. And one was aware of how much steel there was in the form of hatches, decks, stairways and stanchions, and of how injurious a fall could be. You were most likely to feel the bite of the polar air in the prow. It was wonderful to be alone there, with no human artifact to spoil your view, with the illusion of being solitary in this very remote place, yet with the comforting sense of the ship's power beneath and behind you.

23 JANUARY, SUNDAY. Noon position: 71°00′S, 176°00′W. Because we crossed the International Dateline we had a second Sunday, 23 January, and Sunday holiday hours and routines were repeated. It was now 24 January at McMurdo.

We had entered the extended belt of pack ice that rides between the Ross Sea and the Southern Ocean. It was such ice fields as these that Ross was the first to penetrate in his hope to discover the south magnetic pole. He was already then prominent for being the discoverer of the north magnetic pole. He was to be frustrated in his new ambition because the south magnetic pole was inland and he had no capability for land journeys or for wintering over. But because of his daring and persistence he was rewarded when he suddenly broke through the fields to encounter the great and completely unexpected southern sea later named for him. I was well aware of his story, as I was of the fact that the fields were now summer-thin, and of the fact that Antarctica is the sole continent on earth which pulses or fluctuates. During the austral winter the continent greatly expands in size because the seas freeze for hundreds of miles outward from its coastline. No ship can penetrate the ice then. Those frozen seas profoundly affect the earth's albedo—its power to reflect sunlight and other extraterrestrial radiation—and are consequently an important element of world climate.

The vacation warmth of our first day out was definitely and permanently gone. There were fields of pack as far as one could see. We were embraced by pack. At first the ice was thin, flat—pancakes—but soon it grew so heavy we had trouble making our way. The probing ship, seeking leads, shoving floes aside, sometimes mounted the heavier ice in the hope of cracking it with its weight, but at times the ice was too strong and the ship, forced to leave its course, had to try another tack. At times the leads were spacious, resembling small ponds or lakes. Sometimes a dark lead snaked away from us like a quiet river and we would see a Weddell's cigar-shaped body on the shore, head raised in an effort to comprehend us, or we would startle three or four into humping wildly in an effort to escape what they no doubt expected to be disaster. A troop of Adélies on a large floe stared wonderingly as we drew close, then tobogganed madly toward the water and dove in, and madly breached and dove to get out of our monstrous way as we shoved their floe aside. The stretches of open water were as somber as the sky.

Standing alone in the prow, you felt very strong, as if you yourself were moving ice islands, probing for leads, shattering floes. You were free of the funnel exhaust, felt the wind most keenly and were in greater motion than elsewhere on the ship. You had kinesthetic thrills as the bow rode up onto a floe and slowly cracked and split it and moved through and beyond it, or as it silently or with just a faint swishing sound knifed its way through gently heaving pack. You felt closer to the Southern Ocean and its inhabitants. You glimpsed electric turquoises when submerged ice was turned over. It felt like a voyage through a fairy tale. I was on deck as often and as long as I could stand the cold.

For a while the world had been colorless, bland, milky. Then with twilight the lower part of the brooding sky turned indigo, and upheaved floes were faint yellow with plankton, and pressure ridges showed elusive pale blues, so we had color again although in a restrained way. The ice grew thicker, or at least wore a heavier snow crust, and we seemed stronger, able to split whole islands. Lightning spears of electric blues showed in the snow cracks. Brash was thick in the murky leads. Occasionally we rode up onto an island without cracking it, and finally veered away, leaving some of our red paint on the small inlet we had created. We sounded harsh and metallic as our bow struck ice, and I had to look to my footing and to grip something in order not to be thrown down or against a stanchion. At times the sky ahead of us was polluted by our smoke.

Gorgeous and crinkled gray-blue, as of old elephant hide, an ice island's submerged part. Softness of snow and water. The ice islands were now thicker and more extensive but always there were leads, some very blue when you looked straight down at them. Wilson's storm petrel, small, dark, fast, with a white rump, fluttered as restlessly as a swallow, hugging the water. The snow petrels were shy, ghostly, and hauntingly beautiful with their softly white bodies and black eyes. And they were fast and very hard to see against snow and ice. At times I thought they were an illusion. The presence of birds helped humanize these very high latitudes. We were in an indigo world now: sky, ice and water suggested a requiem mass, and the world seemed ready to cry.

About forty-five species of birds live south of the Antarctic Convergence, and of these only three are indigenous residents of the continent in that they breed exclusively on it: the skua, the Antarctic petrel and the emperor penguin. Only the emperor penguin nests in winter, consequently it is the sole true avian resident of the winterized continent. As for fish, only some 100 species out of the roughly 20,000 species of modern times are found south of the Antarctic Convergence.

Sometimes an Antarctic petrel, a beautiful glider with its large wings, would soar by us with wings tilted in a steep bank and give the eerie impression of being a black cross against the moody sky. Birds rarely came close to the ship, yet they were obviously attracted by it. Although I was well aware of the exotic life of penguins, having lived near the southernmost penguin (Adélie) colony in the world at Cape Royds on Ross Island, my imagination was startled when I saw a solitary Adélie on a large ice floe ahead of us. What a strange existence, I thought, spent partly in this water (the world's coldest), partly on the pack and partly on the continent's fringes. The hardihood of life was very impressive in the world's most extreme places. The penguins made me think of sky and sea, of flying birds and sea mammals simultaneously.

I was fascinated by the flying birds, almost mesmerized by them. Aside from the spectacle of movement they provided, there were two other reasons for this: They were the sole form of life, aside from human life, that I could observe steadily (seals and penguins were increasingly rare events and I had not seen whales in this sea yet). Their way of life struck me as remarkable and I could not get enough of observing them, or rather trying to do so. I found them difficult to photograph, for they were usually in very rapid motion, motion compounded by the ship's rolling. Still, despite their strangeness for me I sensed I knew them in some mysterious way, as if I had an exotic bird life of my own or as though they were human in some respects. On this voyage I was never to lose my intense curiosity about them and often I would get very badly chilled through watching them. At moments they seemed as mysterious and as fascinating as beings from another planet. In the Antarctic there was so much to excite one that you had little need to believe in UFO's and Martians. There was an inevitable sense of anti-climax when, being so chilled that I was shivering, and having temporarily run out of film, I left these marvelous creatures, whom I saw soaring at a distance or with great rapidity whipping by me, and returned to my own form of life in the wardroom.

The two ornithologists (or birdwatchers, as they were referred to by everyone in the wardroom) were David G. Ainley, the principal investigator, and his assistant, Robert J. Boekelheide, both from the Point Reyes Bird Observatory at Stinson Beach, California. They were making bird counts, noting species and taking note of other inhabitants of the Southern Ocean along our track. I can best give an idea of what they were doing by quoting from an article they contributed to the October 1977 issue of the *Antarctic Journal of the United States* titled "Seabirds in Antarctic Marine Ecosystems."

In the face of disappearing whales and human exploitation of krill stocks, much needs to be learned about the ecological structure of marine communities in the Antarctic and the Subantarctic. One need is for information on the biomass of organisms so that their ecological importance in these communities can be established relative to competitor and prey stocks. Birds are one group of organisms, among several, for which ecological data are lacking. This may come as a surprise in that so much is known about the social behavior and nesting biology of antarctic avian species. Birds, however, spend most of their lives at sea, where in the Antarctic ornithologists have not often ventured.

The purpose of our work was to assess the biomass of birds in various pelagic habitats of antarctic seas, to compare their biomass simultaneously to that of mammals, thereby providing more complete data for analyses such as those recently attempted by Laws and Green, and to describe the ecological structure of avian communities. By ecological structure we mean species composition (based on density and biomass), habitat partitioning, and division of food resources through behavior and prey selection. We also sought to compare the biomass per unit area, species diversity, and other factors of polar and tropical bird communities. . . .

Preliminary analysis shows a marked increase in bird biomass as one passes from subtropic into subpolar waters. Avian biomass in the tropics and the subtropics averaged slightly less than 1 kilogram per square kilometer but jumped to an average of about 4 kilograms per square kilometer in the Subantarctic and the Antarctic. Species diversity, calculated by the Shannon–Weaver formula, remained about the same, regardless of latitude, at a level well below that measured for any terrestrial bird community. Why one or a few seabird species dominate their respective communities, rather than there being broader representation of several species, is a question we will pursue.

Throughout our South Pacific cruise we were impressed by the occurrence of densest bird concentrations at oceanographic fronts, or at least in areas where water temperatures changed rapidly within short distances (indicating the meeting of ocean currents, water masses, etc.). . . .

A cursory view of our Ross Sea data indicates that birds, at an average 11.3 per square kilometer, outnumber seals (0.2 per square kilometer) and cetaceans (0.03 per square kilometer). Based on these density figures, and a general conception of relative weights of animals in each group (the largest whales were minke whales), one can project that the three groups are about equal in biomass. Most of the bird biomass was contributed by penguins, but we were impressed by the large numbers of petrels present. The Ross Sea petrel populations alone must number in the millions. If the Ross Sea is representative of seas elsewhere in the Antarctic, then their numbers, derived largely from counts at the few known breeding sites, have been underestimated in the past.

The icebreaker was a military ship and I was informally classed as an officer. There was a definite class structure on board. A couple of times a young crewman approached me on a weather deck about the use of a camera and the kind of film I was using and gave me a clear sense that I was avuncular. For the most part the enlisted men kept their distance on the weather decks, and they were not permitted in the wardroom unless they served in the pantry or as waiters.

In the times when there were no leftovers in the wardroom we went down to an enlisted men's galley for the midrats (midnight rations), picked up a tray, a plate, a glass and cutlery and were served in cafeteria style. You could ask for anything available there, including soft drinks and ice cream. As a matter of fact you could gorge yourself on a full meal if you wished. You paid nothing. That was one of the few times I had a sense of the lower-deck life. It appeared to be easy-going, a bit rowdy and on the sloppy side.

At Ross Island and in its vicinity the sun had not set. Now we were beginning to experience not real night but a profound twilight that excited me, and it was this perhaps, as much as the pleasures of chatting and the disinclination to go to one's narrow, dark rack, that lured me into staying up very late and going out to the weather decks even when the hour was an overcast one. You had an acute sense of the earth's roundness, of its spinning eastward on its southern axis (a spin that had a good deal to do with the prevailing westerlies and certain Southern Ocean currents), of our position still fairly close to the Pole and of our slowly pushing northward. I had not stayed long enough on Ross Island during this current visit to feel night deprivation, as I had in the past, to yearn for stars in a black sky, to wish the sun would go away for awhile, but I had sharp enough memories of endless sunlight reflecting off everything and seeming to bite at me to cause me to enjoy the changing, softening light now.

24 JANUARY. Noon position: 68°40′S, 171°00′W.

Without direct sunlight the world seemed psychologically frozen. All was extremely still. It was not a brooding stillness, nor was it menacing. It was simply stillness: mixed with whiteness and indigo washes. The snow-ice was softer now. Our bow pushed through it with a swishing sound. We made no sound in open water, at least not where I was, in the prow. Indigo sky and water set off snow-ice figures extremely well.

And then we encountered massive skies with some light in them, and ice islands whose "continental shelves" showed vivid green under water, and oddly formed small bergs, and more clear water, the latter lake-calm.

We were now north of the Bay of Whales, that indentation of the Ross Ice Shelf where Amundsen had based himself during his race for the Pole. His expedition of 1910–12, originally intended as a North Polar voyage, dramatically changed character when he reversed course at sea and sailed to Madeira, from which he cabled Scott in Melbourne, Australia, the terse news that he was heading south. This could mean only one thing to Scott: Amundsen intended to be first at the Pole. Thus the race between the Norwegian and the English parties began.

Amundsen sailed from Madeira to the Ross Sea without calling at any port, and established his base at the Bay of Whales in an area which Shackleton a few years earlier had rejected as too hazardous because it was in danger of calving off from the shelf and floating out to sea as a tabular berg. The advantage of this position was that it placed Amundsen some sixty miles closer to the Pole than Scott, who, as we know, was based at Cape Evans on Ross Island. In later years Cherry-Garrard wrote that the Scott party had badly underestimated Amundsen's abilities.

By 1910 Amundsen had had considerable polar experience. He was not a newcomer to the Antarctic. He had been a mate on the *Belgica* expedition of 1897, which was the first to winter over on the continent. He knew skiing, sledging and huskies well and was able to make brilliant decisions based on limited information. Instead of depending, as Scott did, on the Beardmore Glacier route over the Transantarctic Mountains, which had been pioneered by Shackleton, he used the still unexplored Axel Heiberg Glacier, and the glacier served him well. Amundsen relied heavily on dogs. He did not mistrust them in polar work as Scott did, and he did not believe in the value of manhauling sledges, in which Scott seemed at times to have an almost mystical faith.

Amundsen landed on the ice shelf with 116 dogs and erected a hut some two miles inland. He started for the Pole October 20, 1911, with four companions, four sledges and fifty-two dogs and reached the Pole December 14, beating the Scott party by a little more than a month. His journey to the Pole was fast and easy in contrast with that of the ill-fated Scott. To some extent Scott's tragedy had a national cause rather than a personal one, in that his country was strongly prejudiced against the use of dogs as work animals. The sensitive Scott could not bear the beating of dogs to make them work in polar conditions. He had a horror of shooting them when it was merciful to do so at a time when they were fatally exhausted. Nor did he relish eating dog cutlets, a practice Amundsen found absolutely necessary for the success of his polar journey. Parenthetically it may be added that the Scott party would probably have survived if they had been willing to eat the remains of Petty Officer Edgar Evans. But their survival in that event would have been physical only. Socially they would not have been acceptable in Edwardian society after such an expedient.

Amundsen and the Italian explorer, Umberto Nobile, crossed the North Pole by dirigible in 1926. In 1928, when Nobile's airship, *Italia,* was wrecked on his return from the North Pole, Amundsen went to search for him. He was lost over the Arctic seas and no trace of him was found.

In *The South Pole* Amundsen wrote a vivid, modest and admirably simple account of his great adventure. This is how he described the supreme moments of nearing and then reaching the Pole.

December 7 began like the 6th, with absolutely thick weather, but, as they say, you never know what the day is like before sunset. Possibly I might have chosen a better expression than this last—one more in agreement with the natural conditions—but I will let it stand. Though for several weeks now the sun had not set, my readers will not be so critical as to reproach me with inaccuracy. With a light wind from the northeast, we now went southward at a good speed over the perfectly level plain, with excellent going. The uphill work had taken it out of our dogs, though not to any serious extent. They had turned greedy—there is no denying that—and the half kilo of pemmican they got each day was not enough to fill their stomachs. Early and late they were looking for something—no matter what—to devour. To begin with they contented themselves with such loose objects as ski bindings, whips, boots, and the like; but as we came to know their proclivities, we took such care of everything that they found no extra meals lying about. But that was not the end of the matter. They then went for the fixed lashings of the sledges, and—if we had allowed it—

BEYOND CAPE HORN

would very quickly have resolved the various sledges into their component parts. But we found a way of stopping that: every evening, on halting, the sledges were buried in the snow, so as to hide all the lashings. That was successful; curiously enough, they never tried to force the 'snow rampart.' . . .

The curtain of cloud was rent more and more, and before we had finished our work—that is to say, caught the sun at its highest, and convinced ourselves that it was descending again—it was shining in all its glory. . . . We had a great piece of work before us that day: nothing less than carrying our flag farther south than the foot of man had trod. We had our silk flag ready; it was made fast to two ski sticks and laid on Hanssen's sledge. I had given him orders that as soon as we had covered the distance to 88°23'S, which was Shackleton's farthest south, the flag was to be hoisted on its sledge. It was my turn as forerunner, and I pushed on. There was no longer any difficulty in holding one's course; I had the grandest cloud formations to steer by, and everything now went like a machine. First came the forerunner for the time being, then Hanssen, then Wisting, and finally Bjaaland. The forerunner who was not on duty went where he liked; as a rule he accompanied one or other of the sledges. I had long ago fallen into a reverie—far removed from the scene in which I was moving; what I thought about I do not remember now, but I was so preoccupied that I had entirely forgotten my surroundings. Then suddenly I was roused from my dreaming by a jubilant shout, followed by ringing cheers. I turned round quickly to discover the reason of this unwonted occurrence, and stood speechless and overcome.

I find it impossible to express the feelings that possessed me at this moment. All the sledges had stopped, and from the foremost of them the Norwegian flag was flying. It shook itself out, waved and flapped so that the silk rustled; it looked wonderfully well in the pure, clear air and the shining white surroundings. 88°23' was past; we were farther south than any human being had been. No other moment of the whole trip affected me like this. The tears forced their way to my eyes; by no effort of will could I keep them back. It was the flag yonder that conquered me and my will. Luckily I was some way in advance of the others, so that I had time to pull myself together and master my feelings before reaching my comrades. We all shook hands, with mutual congratulations; we had won our way far by holding together, and we would go farther yet—to the end.

We did not pass that spot without according our highest tribute of admiration to the man who—together with his gallant companions—had planted his country's flag so infinitely nearer to the goal than any of his precursors. Sir Ernest Shackleton's name will always be written in the annals of Antarctic exploration in letters of fire. Pluck and grit can work wonders, and I know of no better example of this than what that man has accomplished. . . .

On the morning of December 14 the weather was of the finest, just as if it had been made for arriving at the Pole. I am not quite sure, but I believe we dispatched our breakfast rather more quickly than usual and were out of the tent sooner, though I must admit that we always accomplished this with all reasonable haste. We went in the usual order—the forerunner, Hanssen, Wisting, Bjaaland, and the reserve forerunner. By noon we had reached 89°53' by dead reckoning, and made ready to take the rest in one stage. At 10 A.M. a light breeze had sprung up from the southeast, and it had clouded over, so that we got no noon altitude; but the clouds were not thick, and from time to time we had a glimpse of the sun through them. The going on that day was rather different from what it had been; sometimes the ski went over it well, but at others it was pretty bad. We advanced that day in the same mechanical way as before; not much was said, but eyes were used all the more. Hanssen's neck grew twice as long as before in his endeavor to see a few inches farther. I had asked him before we started to spy out ahead for all he was worth, and he did so with a vengeance. But, however keenly he stared, he could not descry anything but the endless flat plain ahead of us. The dogs had dropped their scenting, and appeared to have lost their interest in the regions about the earth's axis.

At three in the afternoon, a simultaneous "Halt" rang out from the drivers. They had carefully examined their sledge meters, and they all showed the full distance—our Pole by reckoning. The goal was reached, the journey ended. I cannot say—though I know it would sound much more effective—that the object of my life was attained. That would be romancing rather too barefacedly. I had better be honest and admit straight out that I have never known any man to be placed in such a diametrically opposite position to the goal of his desire as I was at that moment. The regions around the North Pole—well, yes, the North Pole itself—had attracted me from childhood, and here I was at the South Pole. Can anything more topsy-turvy be imagined?

7 ❄ *The Southern Ocean: One*

IT DID NOT TAKE LONG before one settled into clearly defined routines: getting up in the morning, with all it entailed in terms of washing and shaving in the head; having breakfast, which you began at the wardroom sideboard by pouring yourself coffee and which you continued at the table by ordering from the pantry some staple like ham and eggs, served by a crewman; going outside if the weather permitted in order to fill your lungs with sea air, stretch your legs and observe anything interesting that might be available; having lunch; writing or reading a bit; perhaps napping; taking some photos outside (I never took any indoors); "taking the air" again; chatting; waiting for dinner; looking forward to the nightly movie; watching the ship's TV program on the set in the wardroom (the program, almost invariably run by crewmen, presented news, interviews and at times skits and usually elicited ironic or sarcastic comments among the officers watching it); playing cards; and so on. You beat a simple path from CPO or TOQ quarters to the head, to the wardroom, to the weather decks, and at day's end you returned to your rack. We all needed and throve on events and consequently we created them. Each meal was an event, a movie was an event, as was an excursion to the ship's prow or to the helo deck, or having midrats whether you were properly hungry or not. And chewing the fat with the helo pilots, at least for me, was an event, and I relished it.

One sensed one was filling time, or even serving it. And

Time, with a capital T, was a character whose presence you felt strongly: in the daily routines, the slippage of days, the frequent advancing of clocks. These too were events. In addition, there was something paradoxical and vaguely disturbing in the passage of Time. On the one hand Time seemed to drag its heels, otherwise there would have been less need to create events. On the other it raced by, probably just because it was routinized, and the speed with which it was moving worried me because I felt I was not gathering many materials for my book.

25 JANUARY. Noon position: 68°25'S, 158°00'W.

The weather turned markedly rougher as we came into contact with the westerlies. The air was exhilarating and bitter, and there was no large landmass to shelter us. All that was due west of us some thousand miles away was the relatively insignificant mass of the Balleny Islands. Due south and also very distant from us was the eastern edge of the Ross Ice Shelf. One of our engines was out for a while. This fact together with the heavy ice that had slowed us meant we were making poor time. Normally the voyage was a nine- or a ten-day one. Ours was to take thirteen. It felt as if we were moving slowly from nowhere to nowhere.

My journal: "We've managed to avoid two low pressure areas and are hugging the ice pack to the south of us, which dampens swells and subsides bad seas. Have heard that the captain gets sick, tries to avoid rough water. Have been grossly overeating, and exercising not at all. Boredom among us. With the weather cold, wet (hail, snow driving into your face), the decks slippery, the hatch doors heavy and ready to slam against your hands, you tend to stay inside, where there is little to do and no privacy."

We took ten-degree and fifteen-degree rolls and at times pitched quite heavily. Occasionally we rolled as much as twenty or twenty-five degrees. One nice thing about being on a keelless ship was that the rolls were predictable. If you rolled heavily to starboard you could prepare yourself for the roll to port. I heard it said a number of times that the ship had the capability of doing a complete somersault without foundering. I took this statement with a generous grain of salt. The wardroom's main, long, rectangular table was bolted into place, the chairs were wired down. Behind the orange-tan drapes on the starboard side was a metal wall, and if the chairs on that side had been free to move about, a person sitting in one might have gone careening backwards against it. The table had a fiddle (a low railing around its perimeter to keep plates from tumbling into your lap) but despite it you had to be careful about navigating food.

The effects of the new weather on one's nerves became readily apparent. People were tiring and growing irritable more rapidly. There were a couple of inclinometers in the general neighborhood of the wardroom by which we could check our rolling, but the wardroom drapes were fairly good indicators and were sufficiently inaccurate to generate a variety of opinions, some of them dogmatic. This was useful in that it provided a timely subject of conversation to interrupt the growing boredom, even though it also increased your awareness of what was happening to your inner ear.

Whenever possible I would venture out onto wet, tilting decks or decks partially littered with snow or hail, where if you didn't hang onto something with a solid grip you might head for the gunnels and possibly be unable to stop yourself from going overboard. I wondered why the rails had been built so low and why there was a good measure of space between the top and the bottom of them, through which a human body could roll. Of course, the water was so cold you would not have felt much before drowning. If you went overboard there was little chance of your being spotted, even if someone saw you leave the ship. I did not consider that I was being foolhardy to be outside. It was part of my job, as I understood it, to get a sense of the Southern Ocean through as many of its moods and as intimately as possible. I had not come all this way to be comfortable.

You could not stand outside long before beginning to feel frozen and mesmerized. When you returned to the warm wardroom you felt sleepy, relieved and—strange combination—vaguely irritable, as if (as indeed was the case) unusual demands were being made on you. Your nerves were losing some of their protective fat.

It was important to keep one's mind off the ship's movements if one was to resist seasickness, and it was equally or more important to avoid realizing that our situation was likely to continue for a long time and probably to grow a good deal worse. You got very tired physically doing nothing. The hatches were heavy, and the ship's rolling seemed to make them intent on amputating a hand or leg. You fought with them. Many times it was questionable as to who was shoving whom. Descending steep, steel, often slightly oily stairs while the ship pitched and rolled was something you did with as much precision as possible.

It was odd how the ship routines seemed to brainwash you, caused you to do things you normally wouldn't, such as sit through movies that were a complete waste of time and which now seemed like large events simply because they were ordained in some way. Was a crowd psychology overtaking you, or was any kind of distraction a relief from the realities of ship and Southern Ocean? Uniformed men gathered each evening as if for a serious colloquium. Chairs were arranged just so, one chair always reserved for the captain. The latter made his formal appearance, all rose in obedient acknowledgment, the film was spun through the projector in the little projection booth, and somehow, temporarily, you believed this was a significant event, even though for the most part you knew it was nonsense, for on the whole the films weren't worth making to begin with, much less spending time seeing. Of course, if the weather was very raw, that is to say, typical of the Southern Ocean, and the wardroom was filled by men and darkened for a movie, where else could you go? Nowhere except to your rack, where it was dark because men were sleeping.

Nothing interesting seemed to be happening out there, and you felt that nothing interesting was happening anywhere, including inside you. The need for events took you to the ship's store during the hours when it was open. Finding your way there, standing around with the odd feeling of being in a shop, studying things, spending money: These were events to be treasured. I had been to the Navy PX in Christchurch and to the Navy PX at McMurdo but the very same items when viewed in the ship's store looked magical because they were displaced in some profound way. Had there been a ship's store on Captain James Cook's vessels when they circumnavigated the globe at a very high latitude and crossed the Antarctic Circle for the first time in history in 1773–74? I very much doubted it. Cameras, film, sheath knives, shaving cream, toothpaste, candy, stationery, ship T-shirts and plaques, shirt patches: such items seemed to create a world apart, an illusion aided by the store's being below waterline and therefore without portholes, a pleasant world, far from the Southern Ocean.

27 JANUARY. Noon position: 68°20'S, 132°30'W.

Fog, endless fog and endless heavy rolling. Our speed was down to ten and sometimes eight knots. We were in the center of a low. Visibility was often a mile at most. Although the helo deck with its relatively large open stretch lured you because you were feeling claustrophobic, it was no place to try in ugly weather. The weather hit you fully on it and there was nothing to hang on to.

The outside decks were eerily silent except for our engine sounds and an occasional bird cry. Antarctic petrels and southern fulmars glided in pairs high above us. The fulmars in particular soared high. No signs of bergs or ice. Much spray. Time passed slowly. The weather had slowed down our time sense.

We took rolls of thirty-five and sometimes forty degrees. They were easiest to handle lying down. If you stood, they took your breath away after centrifuging your stomach, then suddenly reversed direction. You learned to walk while leaning like the Tower of Pisa. When you sat, the wired-down chairs and your body had an unceasing and unpleasant confrontation, and parts of you ached afterwards. There was a great desire to sleep, caused not only because you wanted to blot the rolling out but because you were experiencing a derangement. Some of us now slept through mealtime or were too sick to eat. I was among those who stayed well. I ascribed my luck to the fact I was highly motivated, that I could not afford to be ill. We had come a long way from McMurdo's meridian, 166°39'E. We were due north of Marie Byrd Land now, named by Rear Admiral Richard E. Byrd for his wife.

Our rolls were not always steady-state. Now and then, through some strange combination of waves or because of exceptionally large swells, we would start keeling over and keep going beyond the point where I expected we'd stop. And then we would go still further and I would think, "Surely this is enough."

But it wasn't, and I would wonder when we *would* stop and if we were going to go right around, and the suspense inside me by now would be considerable, and I would find myself holding my breath, or as much of it as was left to me, and I would think, "All right, now it *has* to stop, this is getting to be silly." And yet the roll would continue, and everything, including me, seemed about to lie on its side, and I would think, "Enough! This is now dangerous!" At last the vessel would pause, hover, tremble, then change roll direction, and all my muscles and organs would scramble.

Crewmen such as CPO Bob Burton had given me tips about how to stay in my rack during very bad rolling. Mostly they advised me to shore up the edges of my mattress in such a way as to secure me in the middle. For shoring materials I would have to use my clothes, for I had no others. I had not taken their advice, for I had not yet experienced the severe rolling they had in mind. They talked of times when it was impossible to sleep no matter how you fixed your rack, for you had to hang on in order not to go flying out onto the floor. I had no way of knowing to what extent, if any, they were exaggerating, but my guess was that they weren't. They were talking of coming down from New Zealand, when they crossed the Roaring Forties and the Screaming Fifties, seas in which there were no ice fields to hug.

Afterwards, when the icebreaker resumed its normal rolls, which were heavy enough, I would wonder just how large that particular roll had been. A couple of times I phoned the bridge from the wardroom, identified myself and inquired. The replies were always courteous and prompt. I would be disappointed, for what I had thought had been a fifty-degree roll turned out to have been "just" a forty or a forty-two. But coming suddenly after a long series of twenties and twenty-fives, its effect had been extraordinary.

If I needed comic relief from the weather's severity I could readily find it in my bedtime conditions. The CPO quarters were almost invariably in darkness, for there were always crewmen sleeping, some of whom had not bothered to draw their rack curtain and others of whom lacked one, and I did not care to ingratiate myself by flicking on the overhead light, the only general light available. At times you could vaguely grope your way by the single red wall light but often this light too was off. I was helped by a tiny French-made flashlight whose rays just barely showed me the way and which I always carried in my travels.

I was located at the end of a narrow corridor between rows of racks, so narrow I often navigated it sideways to avoid brushing against curtains, or, God forbid, portions of human bodies. I had nowhere to put the clothes I took off. Nor did I have anything to sit on when I removed my boots and socks. I should have sat down on the floor but it took a unique experience to teach me that simple lesson.

I was bending over and untying my laces. Then I was standing on one foot while removing a boot. The deck felt perfectly stable. Suddenly the ship lurched severely and I was flung into the curtained rack on my right. It turned out to my intense embarrassment that the rack was occupied, and by CPO Bob Burton, whose rack I knew it was. (He usually kept his curtain drawn, whether he was in the rack or not.) He bolted upright, glared at me as I disentangled myself, and angrily growled, "What the hell's going on?" He looked as if he was ready to clobber me. I mumbled an apology and an explanation. He slowly, angrily and skeptically disappeared behind his curtain. I sat down to remove my boots.

When I was seated on the bed I would proceed to stash my clothes wherever I could: under my pillow mostly, or across my feet. Luckily the top of a metal cabinet was directly on the left of my pillow. Much of its space was already preempted by odds and ends belonging to the occupants of the next corridor but I managed to sneak a bit here and there. I worked either in darkness or with the aid of my flashlight, whose batteries were showing signs of depletion. My rack light was out of order.

It was quite hazardous for me to sit upright, for much of the ship's complex plumbing—massive pipes, some insulated, some bare—threaded its way in many levels just above the length of my bed. Occasionally I used it as a clothes rack until I slammed my forehead against metal, which disoriented me for a couple of hours, and realized I had better leave it clearly visible. I always turned in with the self-admonition that never was I to come awake bolt upright.

As for the temperature, there were times when I was reminded of McMurdo's sauna, and I understood then why some of the crewmen, not one of whom I ever saw wearing pajamas (they slept in their underwear), didn't draw their rack curtain. You felt you were in the tropics except for the times when you half froze.

This evening I made my way down to the ham radio "shack" in the bowels of the ship and waited in line for my turn to get a phone patch. CPO Bob Burton was the ham operator. After putting in a normal full day's work on the ship, he donated his services as an operator.

I called home and had a fine patch with a good signal. The Stateside ham operator was in California. I spoke with Joan, my wife, and Susy, my daughter. They were excited to be talking with someone in the middle of the Southern Ocean. I explained to Joan that because of fog I'd be late getting into Palmer. She asked if that meant I might be delayed in leaving Palmer. I said no, but I was taking the *Hero's* last trip out of Palmer for the austral summer season, that the sea ice would be beginning to form then (mid-March) and that if anything happened to the *Hero* I would face the possibility of an involuntary winter-over.

"None of that," she said.

Things seemed to be heaving and moving all the time. You wished the ship would stop rolling for a little while so you could remember what life was like when the world was stable underfoot. We were running out of things to talk about, were feeling trapped, were getting bored with each other, were counting the days and hours, serving time, asking ourselves how a whole day could slip by with nothing happening, were increasingly hoping something pleasantly unusual would occur to end the monotony. We had become sea-mesmerized.

All my fine resolve to exercise on the ship went by the board, as did my intention to eat moderately. With such rolling it was not possible to walk about outdoors, even when the decks were unsecured, and even to walk up and down some of the ship's corridors was too hazardous. You could hardly call it walking, nor could you call it dancing. It was a sort of wild weaving, in which you tried not to slam into objects.

Standing on the fantail alone, I could make out nothing except the water close to the ship, for there was much fog and sea mist. The world was closed in, a claustrophobe's nightmare. Garbage tube slanting toward the sea; capstans; an orange life preserver; four vertical brooms in a series of metal broom holders; the wood-planked aft deck; and the senseless shooting with a camera when there was almost nothing to see, not even one bird. A desire to record even boredom and nothingness. But precisely because of the boredom and because of the ocean's ability to mesmerize and soothe one, I stood staring.

29 JANUARY, SATURDAY. Noon position: 68°31'S, 109°30'W.

It was on this day that we crossed 106°54' west longitude, on which Captain James Cook had reached 71°10'S on January 30, 1774, a bit more than two centuries earlier. Thus at noon we were less than 3° north of his farthest southing. This is how he described that important moment in his voyages.

At four o'clock in the morning of the 29th, the fog began to clear away; and the day becoming clear and serene, we again steered to the South with a gentle gale at N.E. and N.N.E. The variation [in the compass] was found to be 22°41'E. This was in the latitude of 69°45' South, longitude 108°5' West; and, in the afternoon, being in the same longitude, and in the latitude of 70°23' South, it was 24°31' East. Soon after, the sky became clouded, and the air very cold. We continued our course to the South, and passed a piece of weed covered with barnacles, which a brown albatross was picking off. At ten o'clock, we passed a very large ice island; it was not less than three or four miles in circuit. Several more being seen ahead, and the weather becoming foggy, we hauled the wind to the Northward; but in less than two hours, the weather cleared up, and we again stood South.

On the 30th, at four o'clock in the morning, we perceived the clouds, over the horizon to the South, to be of an unusual snow-white brightness, which we knew announced our approach to field-ice. Soon after, it was seen from the top-masthead; and at eight o'clock, we were close to its edge. It extended East and West, far beyond the reach of our sight. In the situation we were in, just the southern half of our horizon was illuminated, by the rays of light reflected from the ice, to a considerable height. Ninety-seven ice hills were distinctly seen within the field, besides those on the outside; many of them very large, and looking like a ridge of mountains, rising one above another until they were lost in the clouds. The outer, or northern edge of this immense field, was composed of loose or broken ice close packed together; so that it was not possible for any thing to enter it. This was about a mile broad; within which was solid ice in one continued compact body. It was rather low and flat (except the hills), but seemed to increase in height, as you traced it to the South; in which direction it extended beyond our sight. Such mountains of ice as these, were, I believe, never seen in the Greenland Seas; at least, not that I ever heard or read of; so that we cannot draw a comparison between the ice here, and there. It must be allowed that these prodigious ice mountains must add such additional weight to the ice fields which inclose them, as cannot but make a great difference between the navigating this icy sea and that of Greenland.

I will not say it was impossible any where to get farther to the South; but the attempting it would have been a dangerous and rash enterprise, and what, I believe, no man in my situation would have thought of. It was, indeed, *my* opinion, as well as the opinion of most on board, that this ice extended quite to the pole, or perhaps joined to some land, to which it had been fixed from the earliest time; and that it is here, that is to the South of this parallel, where all the ice we find scattered up and down to the North, is first formed, and afterwards broken off by gales of wind, or other causes, and brought to the North by the currents, which we always found to set in that direction in the high latitudes. As we drew near this ice some penguins were heard, but none seen; and but few other birds, or any other thing that could induce us to think any land was near. And yet I think there must be some to the South behind this ice; but if there is, it can afford no better retreat for birds, or any other animals, than the ice itself, with which it must be wholly covered. I, who had ambition not only to go farther than any one had been before, but as far as it was possible for man to go, was not sorry at meeting with this interruption; as it, in some measure, relieved us; at least, shortened the dangers and hardships inseparable from the navigation of the southern polar regions. Since therefore we could not proceed one inch farther to the South, no other reason need be assigned for my tacking, and standing back to the North; being at this time in the latitude of 71°10′ South, longitude 106°54′ West.

It is interesting to compare Cook's style and perspective with those of George Forster (1754–1794). It has been said that George (Johann George Adam) Forster had some influence on the creation by Goethe, Heine and other German literary masters of a style of travel literature in which natural scenes and objects are lovingly presented, yet correctly detailed. His father, Johann Reinhold Forster, was a clergyman and a talented amateur scientist. Both father and son were born in Germany and both emigrated to England in 1766, where George, through translation work, mastered English prose. The Forsters were scientific members of Cook's second voyage around the world, one which was to be the turning point of the son's life. The son wrote, "On the 11th of June, 1772, my father and myself were appointed to embark in this expedition, in order to collect, describe, and draw the objects of natural history which we might expect to meet with in our course." His masterly two-volume history of the voyage, based on his father's journals, made him famous.

He was twelve when he emigrated to England, eighteen when he went on the expedition and twenty-three when his book was published. He died at forty. His interests were wide-ranging and humanitarian, with a modern skeptical cast. The following, in which he describes Cook's farthest southing, is an example of his style and perspective. It also affords an extraordinarily vivid and authentic sense of Antarctic ship conditions of his time, so tremendously different from those I experienced on the ice-breaker.

At nine o'clock a huge mountainous wave struck the ship on the beam, and filled the decks with a deluge of water. It poured through the sky-light over our heads, and extinguished the candle, leaving us for a moment in doubt, whether we were not entirely overwhelmed and sinking into the abyss. Every thing was afloat in my father's cabin, and his bed was thoroughly soaked. His rheumatism, which had now afflicted him above a fortnight, was still so violent as to have almost deprived him of the use of his legs, and his pains redoubled in the morning. Our situation at present was indeed very dismal, even to those who preserved the blessing of health; to the sick, whose crippled limbs were tortured with excessive pain, it was insupportable. The ocean about us had a furious aspect, and seemed incensed at the presumption of a few intruding mortals. A gloomy melancholy air loured on the brows of our shipmates, and a dreadful silence reigned amongst us. Salt meat, our constant diet, was become loathsome to all, and even to those who had been bred to a nautical life from their tender years; the hour of dinner was hateful to us, for the well known smell of the victuals had no sooner reached our nose, than we found it impossible to partake of them with a hearty appetite.

It will appear from hence that this voyage was not to be compared to any preceding one, for the multitude of hardships and distresses which attended it. Our predecessors in the South Sea had always navigated within the tropic, or at least in the best parts of the temperate zone; they had almost constantly enjoyed mild easy weather, and sailed in sight of lands, which were never so wretchedly destitute as not to afford them refreshments from time to time. Such a voyage would have been merely a party of pleasure to us; continually entertained with new and often agreeable objects, our minds would have been at ease, our conversation cheerful, our bodies healthy, and our whole situation desirable and happy. Ours was just the reverse of this; our southern cruizes were uniform and tedious in the highest degree; the ice, the fogs, the storms and ruffled surface of the sea formed a disagreeable scene, which was seldom cheered by the reviving beams of the sun; the climate was rigorous and our food detestable. In short, we rather vegetated than lived; we withered, and became indifferent to all that animates the soul at other times. We sacrificed our health, our feelings, our enjoyments, to the honour of pursuing a track unattempted before.

The crew were as much distressed as the officers, from another cause. Their biscuit, which had been sorted at New Zealand, baked over again, and then packed up, was now in the same decayed state as before. This was owing partly to the revisal, which had been so rigorous, that many a bad biscuit was preserved among those that were eatable, and partly to the neglect of the casks, which had not been sufficiently fumigated and dried. Of this rotten bread the people only received two thirds of their usual allowance, from economical principles; but, as that portion is hardly sufficient, supposing it to be all eatable, it was far from being so when nearly one half of it was rotten. However, they continued in that distressful situation till this day when the first mate came to the captain and complained bitterly that he and the people had not wherewith to satisfy the cravings of the stomach, producing, at the same time, the rotten and stinking remains of his biscuit. Upon this the crew were put to full allowance. The captain seemed to recover again as we advanced to the southward, but all those who were afflicted with rheumatisms continued as much indisposed as ever. . . .

On the 28th [January 1774], in the afternoon, we passed a large bed of broken ice, hoisted out the boats, and took up a great quantity, which afforded a seasonable supply of fresh water. At midnight the thermometer was not lower than 34°, and the next morning we enjoyed the mildest sunshine we had ever experienced in the frigid zone. My father therefore ventured upon deck for the first time after a month's confinement.

We now entertained hopes of penetrating to the south as far as other navigators have done towards the north pole; but on the 30th, about seven o'clock in the morning, we discovered a solid ice-field of immense extent before us, which bore from E. to W. A bed of fragments floated all round this field, which seemed to be raised several feet high above the level of the water. A vast number of icy masses, some of a very great height, were irregularly piled up upon it, as far as the eye could reach. Our latitude was at this time 71°10' south, consequently less than 19 deg. from the pole; but as it was impossible to proceed farther, we put the ship about, well satisfied with our perilous expedition, and almost persuaded that no navigator will care to come after, and much less attempt to pass beyond us. Our longitude at this time was nearly 106°W. The thermometer here was at 32°, and a great many penguins were heard croaking round us, but could not be seen on account of the foggy weather which immediately succeeded.

A phone patch is a combination of short-wave radio and a normal telephone line. The Antarctic ham operator gets in touch with a ham operator in the States, who patches his short-wave gear into his telephone line and dials your party collect. Your party is informed by the phone company operator that a call from Antarctica is about to be received. The Stateside ham operator explains to your party that a ham patch call is one-way at a time and that the signal for indicating that you're ready to stop talking is to say "Over." Both ham operators listen in on the call in order to be able to switch their gear over at the appropriate moments and both monitor their gear for strength, clarity and persistence of signal. Other ham operators around the world may be listening in. When you're making a phone patch you have a clear sense of lack of privacy and of the existence of certain taboos, such as the use of profanity.

This evening as I waited in line for a patch I heard a young enlisted man pleading with his young wife not to leave him. I could only surmise what she was saying. He had not had mail from her for a long time, and that which he had received had been very negative. He assured her he was going to chapel regularly and placing his faith in God, and praying to God to save his marriage. We were standing in semidarkness in the bowels of a ship designed primarily to ride up onto and break ice, a ship that seemed perfectly made to give the human body fits in open water, a ship that now rolled very heavily somewhere north of the Amundsen Sea, in the world's most forsaken waters.

Someone whom I didn't know whispered to me, "He's not the only one. I've heard that shit many times. I heard a guy once say, 'What? What? What'd you say, honey?' And the ham operator had to tell him, 'She said she's *leaving* you, Mac.'"

I heard another young enlisted man talking with a psychiatrist about his daughter, who had cracked up, turned schizophrenic—I wasn't sure of the details. He spoke earnestly, soberly, prayerfully, and thanked the psychiatrist effusively for being willing to talk to him at a very odd hour—I forget, if I ever knew, what the time differential was.

But I glowed after my patch, as did many other men who had gotten through. A happy patch had an incredible effect in the Antarctic. Suddenly you were in touch with somebody meaningful and close to you, and were lifted in spirit out of your present remoteness and frigidity and showered with human warmth.

I thanked Big John, the California ham operator who gave so much of his time to make patches from the Antarctic to the States possible, and CPO Bob Burton, who had worked at least eight hours of patches yesterday during his free time after his regular day's chores.

While out on deck I tried touching my toes in order to stretch my hamstring muscles. I almost fell on my face because of a heavy roll. I remembered that when I was in the head this morning and put tooth powder on my palm and reached out to wet my toothbrush at the faucet, the next thing I knew I was in the shower stall.

Bob Murphy and Joe Warburton joined me outside. Murphy was an Antarctic representative of Holmes & Narver, a California-based private contractor that provided logistic services to various American installations in the Antarctic, including Palmer Station and the research vessel *Hero*. He was having a first look at some of the installations. He was a strong, straight-postured, bearded, handsome, taciturn, serious man who did not often smile, laugh or chew the fat. He invariably wore a Buck knife on his belt. It was as if he always used the knife while camping back in California and was so accustomed to it that he preferred not to be without it even on the sophisticated icebreaker. He was an avid reader of currently popular novels and yet I got the sense that he was highly factual. I imagined him to be a good deal more complex than he gave the impression of being. I remember him standing alone in the prow or on the fantail, or being absorbed in a thick paperback in the crowded, noisy wardroom, perhaps sitting on a corner of the aft couch, where civilian parkas were often piled. If one were roughly to categorize the civilians among us, he would probably have represented the practical man.

Joe Warburton, our professor, of middle height, with a carefully trimmed brown mustache and beard and clipped Aussie accent, frowned often as though lost in abstruse thinking, often played solitaire on the heaving wardroom table, or cannily and with the help of scientific formulas gauged the degree of the drapes' pendulation. He had a good, crisp laugh and sharp eyes that looked wittily at the world. He was our academic.

30 JANUARY, SUNDAY. Noon position: 68°30'S, 97°00'W.

We were about 225 statute miles north of Thurston Island and had come some 2500 miles from McMurdo, but that was not reckoning the unknown miles we had lost in having to move off course. Overcast. Water like obsidian. Milky curds (air bubbles) alongside the ship. Heavy swells. The weather began to lighten. An occasional berg on the horizon. Wilson's storm petrels skimming the water. Antarctic petrels. Cape pigeons with bright dark and white feather markings sailing around us. Bergs, soft glassy swells. A spectral light. Grottoed tabular berg at a distance. Land beyond it: Peter I Island to the south of us. Slate sky and sea, band of light along the horizon. Herringbone sky, restless waves. Minke whale blowing at a distance. Three minkes breaching far away. Our wake like curdled milk. In the foreground: spray caused by our bow. In the middle ground: inky textured sea. On the horizon: a tall berg the southern side of which caught the pure chalky light. The sky a harmony of pale blues, with a band of ineluctable rose.

During the evening we crossed the track of the United States Exploring Expedition, a fact which, together with the beauty of these bergs, reminded me of an early American explorer who had appreciated such sights with much sensitivity. And my recent close encounter with killer whales recalled for me also that this same explorer had described a battle between killers and a great whale.

A vast part of Antarctica south of Australia, from approximately 100° to 140° east longitude and including Knox Coast, Budd Coast, Sabrina Coast, Banzare Coast, Clarie Coast and Adélie Coast, is now known as Wilkes Land in honor of Charles Wilkes (1798–1877), the American who claimed the discovery of Antarctica as a landmass of continental proportions. His claim was challenged by some contemporary explorers but posterity has proved him correct.

Wilkes's father, a successful businessman, provided Wilkes with a good education, a fact which comes through in Wilkes's account, *Narrative of the United States Exploring Expedition,* written with intelligence, vividness, simplicity and sensitivity. Wilkes entered the United States Navy as a midshipman in 1818. In 1826 he became a lieutenant. He was chosen to command a wide-ranging United States exploring expedition (proposed by the Navy as early as 1828) although he was still only a lieutenant. This was the first voyage to the Southern Ocean sponsored by the United States Congress, which authorized it in May 1836. The expedition's purpose was to aid navigation and commerce and to advance science.

The expedition, consisting of the flagship *Vincennes* and five other vessels (the *Flying Fish, Peacock, Porpoise, Relief* and *Sea Gull*) left the United States in August 1838 and returned in July 1842. Prominent among its goals was the exploration of the high southern latitudes. It reached the South Shetland Islands in March 1839 but because of stormy weather and heavy pack ice was unable to penetrate the Weddell Sea. An attempt to exceed Cook's farthest southing failed in the same month when the *Flying Fish* reached only 70°S at 102°W. Wilkes's "Chart of the Antarctic Continent," much criticized in his time, especially by foreign explorers, today is considered to be a very good piece of work. After the expedition's return to the United States, Wilkes was court-martialed for excessive strictness with his men but the charges did not stand.

This day [January 20, 1840], on board the *Peacock* they witnessed a sea-fight between a whale and one of its many enemies. The sea was quite smooth, and offered the best possible view of the whole combat. First, at a distance from the ship, a whale was seen floundering in a most extraordinary way, lashing the smooth sea into a perfect foam, and endeavouring apparently to extricate himself from some annoyance. As he approached the ship, the struggle continuing and becoming more violent, it was perceived that a fish, apparently about twenty feet long, held him by the jaw, his contortions, spouting, and throes all betokening the agony of the huge monster. The whale now threw himself at full length from the water with open mouth, his pursuer still hanging to the jaw, the blood issuing from the wound and dyeing the sea to a distance around; but all his flounderings were of no avail; his pertinacious enemy still maintained his hold, and was evidently getting the advantage of him. Much alarm seemed to be felt by the many other whales around. These 'killers,' as they are called, are of a brownish colour on the back, and white on the belly, with a long dorsal fin. Such was the turbulence with which they passed, that a good view could not be had of them to make out more nearly the description. These fish attack a whale in the same way as dogs bait a bull, and worry him to death. They are armed with strong sharp teeth, and generally seize the whale by the lower jaw. It is said that the only part of them they eat is the tongue. The whalers give some marvellous accounts of these killers and of their immense strength; among them, that they have been known to drag a whale away from several boats which were towing it to the ship. . . .

The last two days we had very many beautiful snow-white petrels about. The character of the ice had now become entirely changed. The tabular-formed icebergs prevailed, and there was comparatively little field-ice. Some of the bergs were of magnificent dimensions, one-third of a mile in length, and from one hundred and fifty to two hundred feet in height, with sides perfectly smooth, as though they had been chiselled. Others, again, exhibited lofty arches of many-coloured tints, leading into deep caverns, open to the swell of the sea, which rushing in, produced loud and distant thunderings. The flight of birds passing in and out of these caverns, recalled the recollection of ruined abbeys, castles, and caves, while here and there a bold project-ing bluff, crowned with pinnacles and turrets, resembled some Gothic keep. A little farther onwards would be seen a vast fissure, as if some powerful force had rent in twain these mighty masses. Every noise on board, even our own voices, reverberated from the massive and pure white walls. These tabular bergs are like masses of beautiful alabaster: a verbal description of them can do little to convey the reality to the imagination of one who has not been among them. If an immense city of ruined alabaster palaces can be imagined, of every variety of shape and tint, and composed of huge piles of buildings grouped together, with long lanes or streets winding irregularly through them, some faint idea may be formed of the grandeur and beauty of the spectacle. The time and circumstances under which we were viewing them, threading our way through these vast bergs, we knew not to what end, left an impression upon me of these icy and desolate regions that can never be forgotten.

8 ✾ *The Southern Ocean: Two*

31 JANUARY. Noon position: 68°29′S, 82°00′W.

The ship felt like a prison when the weather kept you inside or was too boring (fog with heavy swells) to make it worth staying outdoors. The helo pilots were more bored than ever. Now that we were nearing the end of our voyage we expected to encounter pack ice again soon. We spotted a couple of snow petrels. They were a sign that pack was nearby, for they spend much of their life in the pack. We had come some 400 statute miles since yesterday's noon reading. We were now due north of the Bellingshausen Sea (named for Thaddeus Bellingshausen, the great Russian explorer who went to the Antarctic early in the last century), where the curving neck of the Antarctic Peninsula begins to stretch northward and northeastward away from the continent proper.

Of this sea, *Sailing Directions for Antarctica* states,

Ice is ever present in these waters and no vessel has been able to reach the continental shores. The limit of the pack varies from season to season. The sea lies within the 'Westerlies' and also within the continental winds, and is the site of a definite 'low.' The currents are variable in direction and velocity. These factors produce ice conditions which are impossible to foretell . . . . The pack is often heavy, reaching 15 feet in height, with few large open water areas. In view of the density of the pack, it is probable that it extends to the continental coast.

It was in this sea that the *Belgica*, under Adrien de Gerlache

126

and of which Roald Amundsen was first mate, was trapped in the pack ice in 1898. Drifting involuntarily with the ice for more than a year, it became the first scientific expedition to winter in the Antarctic. The expedition's medical doctor was Frederick Cook, who later challenged Robert Peary's claim as the discoverer of the North Pole and who ended up in a Federal penitentiary on charges of mail fraud, as I seem to recall. A very interesting point and one indicative of Amundsen's unconventionality and courage is that when many people were contemptuous of Cook and treated him as a criminal, Amundsen, on the basis of Cook's behavior on the *Belgica*, spoke and wrote highly of him and visited him in prison.

Bellinghausen (1779–1852) entered the Russian navy at the age of ten. By eighteen he had graduated from the naval academy at Kronstadt to become a naval officer. In 1819 he was given command of two sloops, each of about 500 tons, with the assignment to circumnavigate Antarctica, which he fulfilled. His primary goal was exploration, his secondary one the gathering of scientific information. The vessels were *Mirnyy*, meaning "peace," and *Vostok*, meaning "east." They are commemorated by two present-day Russian Antarctic stations, Mirnyy on the coast at approximately 90° east and Vostok on a high inland plateau near the geomagnetic pole.

Bellingshausen greatly admired Cook. It was his hope to supplement Cook's findings, not to compete with him. Thus he undertook to sail in seas which Cook had not had the opportunity to explore. He made the first sightings of land within the Antarctic Circle, discovering and naming Peter I Island and Alexander Island. He made charts of the South Sandwich and South Shetland Islands and was the first to map the southern coast of South Georgia. In January and February 1820 he was close enough to Queen Maud Land to have sighted mainland mountains. In mid-January 1821 he became the first explorer to enter the sea named for him.

Some seven years after the conclusion of the expedition of 1819–21 he distinguished himself in naval operations against the Turks. At his death he was an admiral and the governor of Kronstadt.

Often when I thought of Bellingshausen I thought of another explorer after whom a great Antarctic sea is named. The Weddell Sea is on the Peninsula's eastern side and roughly opposite the Bellingshausen. The eastern shore of the Peninsula, like the shore of the Bellingshausen, is poorly known because great masses of pack ice guard it. Shackleton's ship *Endurance* was crushed by the ice pack there.

James Weddell (1787–1834) was one of the rare early British sealers to write an account of his explorations: *A Voyage Towards the South Pole.* His father, an upholsterer, died when Weddell was very young. The youthful Weddell educated himself by reading. At an early age, with only a meager schooling, he was bound to the master of a coastal vessel. He made several voyages to the West Indies and became a capable navigator.

In 1819 he was given command of the sealing brig *Jane of Leith*, in which he made three voyages to the Antarctic. During the last of these (1822–24), accompanied by the cutter *Beaufoy*, while persistently searching for a large tract of land in very high latitudes, he penetrated pack ice until he broke out and discovered the large sea named in his honor. Here on February 20, 1822, he reached a new farthest southing of 74°15'.

His style is unpolished and nautical, as one can see from the following extracts taken from the high point of his narrative.

I had offered a gratuity of 10£ to the man who should first discover land. This proved the cause of many a sore disappointment; for many of the seamen, of lively and sanguine imaginations, were never at a loss for an island. In short, fog banks out of number were reported for land; and many, in fact, had so much that appearance, that nothing short of standing towards them till they vanished could satisfy us as to their real nature . . . .

By the evening of the 4th [February 1822] we were within 100 miles of Sandwich Land, and within such a distance of the track of Captain Cook, as convinced me that no land lay between.

Our pursuit of land here, therefore, was now at an end, but I conceived it probable that a large tract might be found a little farther south than we had yet been. I accordingly informed Mr. Brisbane of my intention of standing to the southward, and he, with a boldness which greatly enhanced the respect I bore him, expressed his willingness to push our research in that direction, though we had been hitherto so unsuccessful . . . .

At daylight in the morning of the 10th the chief mate reported land within sight, in the shape of a sugar loaf; as soon as I saw it I believed it to be a rock, and fully expected to find *terra firma* a short distance to the southward.

It was 2 o'clock in the afternoon before we reached it; and not till then, when passing within 300 yards, could we satisfy ourselves that it was not land, but black ice. We found an island of clear ice lying close, and detached above water, though connected below, which made a contrast of colour that had favoured or rather completed the deception. In short, its north side was so thickly incorporated with black earth, that hardly any person at a distance would have hesitated to pronounce it a rock. This was a new disappointment, and seriously felt by several of our crew, whose hopes of having an immediate reward for their patience and perseverance were again frustrated.

The wind was at south and blowing a fresh gale, with which we might have gone rapidly to the northward; but the circumstance of having seen this ice island so loaded with earth, encouraged me to expect that it had disengaged itself from land possessing a considerable quantity of soil; and that our arrival at that very desirable object might, perhaps, not be very distant. These impressions induced me to keep our wind, and we stood to the S.W. . . . .

In the morning of the 17th the water appearing discoloured, we hove a cast of the lead, but found no bottom. A great number of birds of the blue peterel kind were about us, and many hump and finned back whales . . . . On the 18th the weather was remarkably fine, and the wind in the S.E. Having unfortunately broken my two thermometers, I could not exactly ascertain the temperature, but it was certainly not colder than we had found it in December (summer) in the latitude of 61° . . . .

In the evening we had many whales about the ship, and the sea was literally covered with birds of the blue peterel kind. NOT A PARTICLE OF ICE OF ANY DESCRIPTION WAS TO BE SEEN. The evening was mild and serene, and had it not been for the reflection that probably we should have obstacles to contend with in our passage northward, through the ice, our situation might have been envied. The wind was light and easterly during the night, and we carried all sail . . . .

In the morning of the 20th the wind shifted to S. by W. and blew a fresh breeze, and seeing a clouded horizon, and a great number of birds in the S.E., we stood in that direction . . . . The atmosphere now became very clear, and nothing like land was to be seen. Three ice islands were in sight from the deck, and one other from the mast-head. On one we perceived a great number of penguins roosted. Our latitude at this time, 20th February, 1822, was 74°15', and longitude 34°16'45"; the wind blowing fresh at south, prevented, what I most desired, our making farther progress in that direction. I would willingly have explored the S.W. quarter, but taking into consideration the lateness of the season, and that we had to pass homewards through 1000 miles of sea strewed with ice islands, with long nights, and probably attended with fogs, I could not determine otherwise than to take advantage of this favourable wind for returning.

I much regretted that circumstances had not allowed me to proceed to the southward, when in the latitude of 65°, on the 27th of January, as I should then have had sufficient time to examine this sea to my satisfaction.

As we now rapidly approached the Antarctic Peninsula I thought increasingly of its history. I said in the Prologue that the Peninsula is the richest part of the continent historically. This statement needs now to be qualified. I mean it is richest in time. It was the first part of the continent to be explored and exploited, which is due to two reasons: It is the lowest latitude portion of the continent and it is the part (I include the offshore islands and waters when I speak of the Peninsula) that had something commercially desirable: fur seals, elephant seals, penguins and whales.

Richest in historical drama is the Ross Island sector, or the Ross Island Dependency, as it is called by New Zealand, its claimant. It is in this region that so many heroic events occurred: the race for the Pole, the first flight over it, the earliest probes of the continent for science and the first transcontinental traverse. Some of the leading actors (in alphabetical order) were Amundsen, Byrd, Fuchs, Hillary, Shackleton and Scott. Of the three greatest of these, Amundsen, Shackleton and Scott, only Amundsen and Shackleton visited the Peninsula area: Amundsen briefly making landfalls in the Belgica Expedition, and Shackleton in his ill-fated but extraordinary adventure, the Endurance Expedition, in which he never set foot on the mainland. The only island Shackleton visited was Elephant Island. He eventually reached South Georgia, but this island is north of 60°S and is not part of the Peninsula sector. I have already indicated the nature of his Endurance Expedition to the Weddell Sea.

James Eights (1798–1882) of Albany, New York, who had been trained as a physician and who became a competent geologist and naturalist, was the first American scientist to enter the Antarctic region. He did this in the combined sealing and exploring expedition of 1829–31, composed of the brigs *Annawan* and *Seraph* and the schooner *Penguin*, under the command of Captains Nathaniel B. Palmer and Benjamin Pendleton, both of Stonington, Connecticut. Eights worked aboard Palmer's *Annawan*. This privately financed American expedition was a forerunner of Charles Wilkes's government-sponsored exploring expedition.

Because of the rapidly depleting stock of fur seals due to the great harvest of the animals, the expedition hoped to discover reported new land and hopefully more seals in its exploratory cruise west of the Peninsula, but no such land was found. Eights surmised that it existed south of the ships' tracks. In an account titled, "Description of a New Crustaceous Animal Found on the Shores of the South Shetland Islands, with Remarks on their Natural History," communicated to the Albany Institute July 10, 1833, and published in the *Transactions of the Albany Institute*, he noted:

The existence of a southern continent within the Antarctic Circle is, I conceive, a matter of much doubt and uncertainty, but that there are extensive groups, or chains of islands yet unknown, I think we have many indications to prove, and were I to express an opinion, I would say that our course from the South Shetlands to the southwest, until we reached the 101° of west longitude, was at no great distance along the northern shores of one of these chains. The heavy clouds of mist which encircled us so often could arise from no other cause than that of the influence of large quantities of snow and ice on the temperature of the atmosphere; the hills of floating ice we encountered, could not form elsewhere than on land. The drifting fuci [brown algae] we daily saw, grow only in the vicinity of rocky shores, and the penguins and terns, that were almost at all times about us, from my observations of their habits, I am satisfied never leave the land at any great distance. During our cruise to the southwest above the 60° of south latitude, we found the current setting continually at a considerable rate towards the northeast, bearing the plants and ice along in its course, some of the latter embracing fragments of rock, the existence of which we could discover no where on the islands we visited. When the westerly winds drew well toward the south, we were most generally enveloped in banks of fog, so dense it was with difficulty we could distinguish objects at the distance of the vessel's length. When Palmer's Land becomes properly explored, together with the known islands situated between the longitude of Cape Horn and that of Good Hope, I think they will prove to be the northeastern termination of an extensive chain, passing near where Capt. Cook's progress was arrested by the firm fields of ice in latitude 71°10'S. and west longitude about 105°;

had that skillful navigator succeeded in penetrating this mass of ice, he would unquestionably in a short time have made the land upon which it was formed.

In the same article, one of seven which Eights published on the Antarctic, he was the first discoverer of an Antarctic fossil.

The only appearance of an organized [organic] remain that I anywhere saw [on the shores of the South Shetlands] was a fragment of carbonized wood imbedded in this conglomerate. It was in a vertical position, about two and a half feet in length and four inches in diameter; its color is black, exhibiting a fine ligneous structure, the concentric circles are distinctly visible on its superior end, it occasionally gives sparks with steel, and effervesces slightly in nitric acid.

It may be noted that although the still young Charles Darwin published a very perceptive observation on the importance of erratic boulders in Antarctic bergs, as indicating the type of bedrock one might expect to find on the Antarctic continent, Eights published a similar view six years earlier. Unfortunately Eight's Antarctic work was long neglected and he is said to have died, after a lengthy and anonymous life, "a broken and disappointed man."

I was bracing myself to part from Frank Mahncke, the observation team member who had made himself accessible to me and whom I had gotten to know and like best. He had a deep, resonant voice and spoke in a manner that suggested he was projecting it to a large audience. He enunciated precisely yet without giving the impression of being in the least pedantic. He was for me the most easy-going member of the inspection team. He was an intelligent man and well read, as was his colleague, Alex Akalovsky. He had been a member of an Antarctic observation team twice before: in the austral summers of 1970–71 and 1974–75. He was thirty-eight, married and had two children. He considered himself to be "a middle American" and a "civil servant" and sometimes referred to himself ironically and with a laugh as a "bureaucrat." At college he had majored in mathematics, but he was not a practicing mathematician.

United States inspections of foreign Antarctic stations had

also been made during the austral summers of 1963–64 and 1966–67. Argentina, Australia, New Zealand and the United Kingdom had also conducted inspections under the Antarctic Treaty's provisions. In 1975 the United States had chosen to inspect Antarctic Peninsula stations because it had not inspected such stations since 1963–64. The team of which Mahncke had been a member had sailed from McMurdo to Palmer on the Coast Guard icebreaker *Glacier* and had visited and inspected Argentine Islands (United Kingdom), Almirante Brown (Argentina), Bellingshausen (Soviet Union) and Presidente Frei (Chile).

He told me now, after lunch, that back in Christchurch he and his two colleagues had been greatly amused and impressed by the fact that although they were soon going to represent the United States in an international arena, not one of their names looked or sounded "American," that is, Anglo-Saxon, and that two of the team had been born abroad, Akalovsky of White Russian parents in Yugoslavia and Combemale in France. His own name was of German origin. He reminded me that there was a *c* in his surname, that Combemale's real first name was not John but Jean, that the latter's middle name was Loup, and that his last name was pronounced Kom-buh-moll. He thought it particularly funny that the foreign-born woman who owned the Town House Motel on Peterborough Street in Christchurch, where we had stayed, thought that *he* was the member of the trio who was foreign-born. He enjoyed the fact that the team seemed symbolically to represent the tradition of the American melting pot. And despite his general dislike of McMurdo as being a dirty Antarctic "city," he liked precisely its melting-pot quality: the foreign surnames and the increasing presence of blacks and women. He thought the American Antarctic program nicely reflected the diversity of American society, and tended to reflect that society in a timely and current way.

All of which caused me to reflect on my own odd situation. My name too neither looked nor sounded "American" (it's pronounced Nyder, not Needer), I was foreign-born (Odessa, Russia) and although I had never been Jewish in any real sense despite my having had a Bar Mitzvah, with all the Hebrew lessons it entailed, I was sufficiently of Jewish origin (both my parents were Jewish), to have been killed by the Germans during the Holocaust had I been available, and I had close relatives who had been slain by them. My paternal grandparents, elderly people in Bessarabia, who had refused to flee the town of Akkerman because they were unable to believe the stories of German atrocities, had been locked in a synagogue together with other Jews and been burned to death.

While I did not represent my country officially in the way the inspection team did, I was in the Antarctic as my country's guest and, as far as I knew, I was the only literary writer and humanist working in the Antarctic, a peculiar role in that it seemed strikingly unrepresentative for a naturalized American Jew, if that was how I wished to regard myself (something I rarely did, and then only with much hesitation and difficulty). Very soon, although I had no inkling of this yet, I would become a guest of the British Antarctic Survey, with official approval of the National Science Foundation headquarters in Washington and of the British Antarctic Survey headquarters in Cambridge, England, and then I would in a more real sense—although still unofficially—"represent" my country; or at any rate my thinking and behavior would be modulated by the realization I might be regarded, however mildly, as its representative.

As for Akalovsky, I had first noticed him on the flight from Point Mugu, California, to Christchurch. He was, by comparison with the others on the plane, elegantly dressed and seemed to have certain meticulous habits, such as the way he lit his pipe, using a well-designed and expensive cigarette lighter. He was of foreign birth and spoke English, of which he had an excellent command, with an accent. As I mentioned earlier, he worked for the State Department in Washington.

John Combemale, the leader of the inspection team, was a Navy lieutenant commander. He wore Navy greens most of the time that I saw him at McMurdo and on the ship. He was on assignment to ACDA (Arms Control and Disarmament Agency), an independent federal agency responsible for inspections of foreign stations in Antarctica under Article VII of the Antarctic Treaty. United States Antarctic inspection teams always included representatives of ACDA, the State Department and the Department of Defense. And so here was an interesting paradox: A military man was representing a civilian agency, and a civilian (Mahncke) was representing the military as a member of the Technical Director's Staff of the Naval Surface Weapons Center of the Department of Defense. Nevertheless I thought it strange and perhaps undiplomatic for the United States to send to a demilitarized continent an inspection team the leader of which belonged to a military department of government.

There was an additional paradox in that the United States was going to a good deal of expense and trouble to carry out what was essentially a pro forma mission. Nobody really expected to discover flagrant breaches of the Treaty. (Of the possibility of subtle breaches I shall have something to say later.) However, there was method in this. The United States wished to keep Article VII alive and well so it might serve as an important precedent for other international treaties, or, more particularly, a lever with which hopefully to budge the Soviet Union in general on the matter of mutual inspection. The Soviet Union, on the other hand, had never conducted an inspection under the provisions of the article, possibly because it did not wish to commit itself to such a precedent even though it, the Soviet Union, was one of the Treaty's original signatories.

Article VII reads as follows:

1. In order to promote the objectives and insure the observance of the provisions of the Treaty, each Contracting party whose representatives are entitled to participate in the meetings referred to in Article IX of the Treaty shall have the right to designate observers to carry out any inspection provided for by the present Article. Observers shall be nationals of the Contracting Parties which designate them. The names of observers shall be communicated to every other Contracting Party having the right to designate observers, and like notice shall be given of the termination of their appointment.

2. Each observer designated in accordance with the provisions of paragraph 1 of this Article shall have complete freedom of access at any time to any or all areas of Antarctica.

3. All areas of Antarctica, including all stations, installations and equipment within those areas, and all ships and aircraft at points of discharging or embarking cargoes or personnel in Antarctica, shall be open at all times to inspection by any observers designated in accordance with paragraph 1 of this article.

4. Aerial observation may be carried out at any time over any or all areas of Antarctica by any of the Contracting Parties having the right to designate observers.

5. Each Contracting Party shall, at the time when the present Treaty enters into force for it, inform the other Contracting Parties, and thereafter shall give them notice in advance, of

(a) all expeditions to and within Antarctica, on the part of its ships or nationals, and all expeditions to Antarctica organized in or proceeding from its territory;

(b) all stations in Antarctica occupied by its nationals; and

(c) any military personnel or equipment intended to be introduced by it into Antarctica subject to the conditions prescribed in paragraph 2 of Article I of the present Treaty.

I had the sense the team members were restless and unhappy about being placed for such an extended time in the role of pro forma representatives. True, they were getting a prolonged and paid vacation from their work in Washington, but the trouble was that the vacation had become boring and claustrophobic and was developing problems for them individually in their home offices. For myself, I often felt I was on an extraordinary cruise, but in my case, because of my profession, I could never be sure what was vacation and what wasn't.

Overcast sky, grayish day, nothing much to do—and then I saw a fantastic double berg close to the ship. Sometimes I would spot a berg at a great distance and watch it grow as we neared it. Ice in any form helped give us a sense of our forward motion and I believe this was one of the reasons we were fascinated by it. Unless you stood on the fantail and watched our wake, or in the prow and saw our spray, it was hard to sense forward motion, you felt becalmed, and a desperate, trapped little feeling would try to find a voice inside you: "Help! There's too much space! We'll spend an eternity traversing it!" The ocean seemed endless and the flying birds seemed trapped in our gravitational sphere.

The taller berg was to the left of its mate as we swung abreast of them. The heavy swells slammed against them, throwing clouds of spray half as high as the shorter berg. The columnar berg suggested the fat, squat base of the mushroom cloud that follows the explosion of a nuclear device. It was fascinating to observe these floating giants unique to the Southern Ocean. A southern fulmar glided above us and three or four seemed to flirt with the ice masses.

1 FEBRUARY. Noon position: 66°40'S, 74°50'W.

Spectral effects of weathered bergs in fog. I yearned for the crystal sunlight we had left behind at Ross Island. Suddenly life was brightened by the appearance of a solitary snow petrel whose gleaming white body shone against the sea's deep tones. Shy and fluttering though it was, I had a good look at it as it flew close to the swells. It made several passes at us. With its departure the world grew dull again. I observed distant bergs enshrouded by mist.

At 2:45 A.M. I made a phone patch to the States with Bob Burton's help. It was interesting to see how much my relations with him had changed. He had signed me in when I had boarded the ship. He had been very correct and proper then, doing his official duty, and had been a bit embarrassed because, unlike the other civilians, I had been assigned a rack not in Temporary Officers Quarters but in Chief Petty Officers quarters. Then there had been the episode of my falling into his rack when he was asleep, and that had caused a cooling off between us for a while. But during the patches he could reassess me accordingly. And perhaps he had heard some of my pilot friends speak well of me.

For my part he was no longer the large, overweight, rather cumbersome man I had first met. Instead, he was a man who gave his time and skill very generously to make phone patches possible, and he was no machine: for example, he remembered the names of people I had called; for another, he was not simply passive about making patches for me but, as in the present case, at times urged me to make them and told me when the best times were. We had grown friendly despite the difference in our social status aboard ship.

2 FEBRUARY, WEDNESDAY. From the ship's log, midnight to 4 A.M.: "Radar landfall with Adelaide Island at a range of ninety-nine nautical miles."

As we neared Palmer the sea grew strangely calm and the ship was steady under your legs. It felt like sailing on a smooth lake. I was very happy to be at last nearing my primary goal, the Antarctic Peninsula, which many times I had feared I would never reach and which too often had seemed illusive. And so I was about to end a fantastic voyage on this moody, cold ocean that encircled a roughly circumpolar continent and whose health in large measure determined that of the world ocean. An ocean of relatively few species but containing vast numbers of those species. An ocean producing tremendous quantities of invaluable nutrients that eventually made their way to other seas. An ocean whose difference in temperature and salinity were immediately noticeable when you entered it by crossing the Antarctic Convergence. The fiercest, most remote, strangest, most unpredictable, most fascinating and, not least, most beautiful vast body of salt water on earth.

During our entire voyage we had never come upon a sea like this: rippled glass the color of light slate, with a bland sky several shades lighter. And riding on this was a weathered beautiful berg softly reflected in the water. Part of it was low-lying and flat, another part thrust up a squat tower. The mood was so gentle, almost tender, as to be unreal. Even the wide arc of our milky wake failed to disturb it. The whole effect was strangely sweet, as if this part of the ocean was fresh water.

And then the horizon filled with a glowing opal light, and several bergs of varied sizes, shapes and colors sailed on it, and the sea grew even calmer. Some of the horizon bergs were chalk-white, others were turquoise and amethyst. Nearer to us was a large weathered berg with a companion which resembled a sailing ship. Another berg had sweeping sides that sloped down to the water, but parts of it were hard-edged, angular cliffs. To the right and farther from us was a low berg suggesting a skyscrapered city made of cake frosting. Candy blues and whipped-cream whites. We were gliding on a lollipop sea that stretched upward to form part of the gentle sky. What a conclusion to an unearthly voyage.

The water was strewn with brash. The sea was now littered with ice bits that seemed to be remnants of an ice explosion. Our bow swept them effortlessly aside. They grew increasingly numerous but we paid little attention to them. We reached ice pancakes, some with a solitary seal, and spotted whole fields of pack. Sky and water were of almost the same thin shade of blue. A vague band of light above the horizon was reflected in the ocean. We created gorgeous satiny swells that made me think of slatey taffeta. And then we were surrounded by ice and had to push heavy chunks out of our way. We overturned some that revealed yellowish undersides and the degree to which this pack was rotten. Our voyage, which had begun with pack, was ending with it.

Some of the scenes felt dreamy, Venetian. Parts of the sky resembled the warmth of dusty rose. Maritime dreams peopled by ghostly white and bluish ice shapes. The white continent was an orchestration of ice. We moved through brash fields that gave way to stretches of clear, noble water. A blue light infused the horizon, blending with the blues of small bergs and setting off the larger, chalky bergs. Antarctic petrels joined us, dipping a wing against water. We passed a weathered berg containing a single large grotto. A rising wind shivered the sea, interlacing it with crosscurrent ripples.

Then we rapidly approached two spectacular bergs. Sea soundings showed a couple of thousand feet, but as we passed between the bergs we got a sounding of only a hundred feet, so clearly they were joined, or rather were parts of one berg. One of them was a large tabular berg whose top showed annual striations. Its sides looked like an earth cliff except for the pale blue color. The lapping of the water had sculpted the bottom of it very smooth. The berg loomed massive above us as we passed close to it. Its mate had a snow-mantled saucer with a turret on either edge. The turrets suggested the texture of a bone cross-section. The mate had the airiness of certain modern sculptures. I had not expected to discover art on the Southern Ocean. The twins were beautiful, pulsating blues and greens of electric intensity against a sky perfect as a setting for them, for it verged on black pearl.

A couple of hours later we sighted an immense tabular berg containing several caverns scooped out by waves. I hurried to the bridge, where I joined the captain, who informed me the berg was 140 feet high and the largest grotto was 87 feet high. The colors were the usual intense cobalts, light blues and rich greens. The berg, which had at least eight large caverns on the side exposed to us, was too tall for me to examine its upper surface from the bridge wing on which I stood. There were many men in the prow, perhaps twenty, and more were heading there. Looking at their light clothes, you momentarily had the illusion you were in temperate waters. They were mostly young men, and all were fresh from the ship's warmth. Soon there

were some fifty in the prow, Mahncke among them, conspicuous in his red parka.

The berg, a huge ice chunk, would have looked impressive
even without the grottoes, but the latter made it visually extremely exciting. The moody sky suggested twilight. The largest
grotto, high-vaulted, had brash streaming from it, which ought
to have alerted the captain to the fact that ceiling and wall pieces
were currently falling in it. He headed the ship directly toward
it. The grotto's ceiling gave the impression of being formed of
plaster of paris that, while still creamy soft, had been slashed by
a palette knife. The white brash on the black grotto sea resembled coins.

The captain decided to head into the largest grotto. Men in
the prow whistled loudly and in unison in the hope of causing
ice to fall from the cave's walls or ceiling. The PA announced
that the following blast would not signify an emergency. Then
the ship's horn gave a long, loud signal. Still no effect in causing
an avalanche. More whistles, and then shouts in unison. Meanwhile the bow was heading into the grotto.

And then a large chunk of the inmost wall collapsed, setting
up a powerful swell, and men in the prow raced headlong away
from it. The captain ordered the ship to back off but before he
did the men on the upper or safe decks, seeing the possibility of
ice action on the prow men, called for more, more of the ship's
horn, causing general laughter. The captain told me it was good
for the crew's morale for them to be called out on deck to see
such spectacular sights at close range. A little later he said a
small party would go over to Palmer tonight with some gear and
that Warburton's, Murphy's and my rooms were ready for us
there and we could move to Palmer tonight if we wished, or we
could stay aboard until tomorrow morning. When Murphy later
learned about this he decided, almost grimly as it seemed to me,
to move ashore tonight. Warburton and I decided to remain on
the ship.

This was a day of several extraordinary moments—it was as
climactic, for the voyage's final day, as if it was clearly staged—
and one of them came when I suddenly realized that the main
engines had stopped for the first time since I had come aboard
at McMurdo. It was strangely disorienting not to hear and feel
them, and the silence and lack of heavy vibration felt eerie. It

had been a most roundabout way to get to Palmer—California, New Zealand, Ross Island, a large track of the Southern Ocean from the New Zealand sector to the South American one—but what an unforgettable cruise it had been. Moving for the most part eastward along a high latitudinal circle for a bit more than twelve days and nights, we had come roughly between a quarter and a third of the way, or some 3600 statute miles, around the frozen, circumpolar continent.

The Northern Ocean is for the most part isolated in its basin, surrounded as it is by Eurasia, Greenland and North America. The Southern Ocean, circumpolar, isolating Antarctica from the globe's other major landmasses, is the chief conduit of the world's great seas. The furious circumpolar westerlies, which have no significant landmass to obstruct and moderate them, create an eastward and profound oceanic current. In addition, waters chilled by the continent flow northward and, being heavier, sink when they meet the warmer, southward-flowing waters of the lower latitudes. The meeting, forming a circumpolar belt, is known as the Antarctic Convergence. At the Convergence there is a dramatic difference in temperature, salinity and color between the two waters.

The Southern Ocean is generally considered to begin at 55°S, the approximate location of the fluctuating Convergence, but it extends beneath the great, floating, anomalous ice shelves, which are usually regarded as parts of the continent itself. Though a large portion of the Southern Ocean freezes over each winter, causing the continent to double in size and thereby pulse or fluctuate, about 1.5 million square miles remain still frozen at summer's end.

As might be expected, the Southern Ocean is extreme. It is very cold, low in salinity, dense, and contains much dissolved oxygen. It is also extraordinarily rich in both phytoplankton and zooplankton. But the number of species is relatively small. It contains perhaps the simplest, shortest and most effective food chain on earth. In sharp contrast, Antarctic continental life is extraordinarily sparse, with only two flowering plants, both on the Peninsula, and no indigenous land vertebrates. There are algae, mosses, lichens and a few minute springtails and mites.

Shortly after sunset I went ashore briefly. From my journal: "Guy Guthridge [the station USARP representative] greeted me, almost immediately told me that I'd probably go on the British ship, *Bransfield*, to Rothera Point on Adelaide Island, where BAS [pronounced like the fish—British Antarctic Survey] was building a new base, with an airstrip for Twin Otters. I'd be gone about a week. I was very pleased to hear this, told him so. Tremendously relieved I won't hang around Palmer, with little to do. Will leave on the *Bransfield* February 7 or February 8, come back on the British ship *John Biscoe*, or at least part way. The *Hero* will take me the rest of the way.

"Learned that mail situation at Palmer is very poor but that patches are easy to get. Lots of booze around, and warrant officers [from the ship] enjoyed it. The enlisted men [also from the ship] played ping-pong or pool in the recreation building uphill from the main building. Guy showed me my room—208. I'll have it to myself. Very efficient, attractive, private, comfortable. Liked the station at first sight. Neat, civilized, almost luxurious in some ways. Good music, books, maps, etc. There have been 11 men here this season, then 16, and there will be 21 when Joe Warburton, Bob Murphy and I and two of Warburton's colleagues arrive here."

I thought increasingly about the Peninsula and wondered how much of it I would encounter. *Sailing Directions for Antarctica* has the following description of it.

Antarctic Peninsula (Palmer Peninsula) (Graham Land) extends [almost 800 miles] southwestward and southward from near 63°14′S, 56°40′W to about 73°S. The northern extremity of the peninsula is the most northerly point of the Antarctic continent. The southern shore of George VI Sound (Robert English Coast) marks the southern limit of the peninsula where it widens to form Ellsworth Land. The peninsula is a snow-covered plateau, about 3,500 feet high in the northern part, which gradually increases in elevation to about 12,000 feet in the southern portion. The plateau is broken occasionally by snow-covered peaks rising above the heights of the peninsula. The western cliffs of the plateau are dissected by numerous glaciers and icefalls which descend to the coastal limits. Numerous bays and indentations form the western shore line which, for the greater part, is covered by piedmont ice with many islands, islets, and rocks lying seaward of the ice cliffs. The eastern coasts are broken by valley glaciers which fill long fiords, the seaward approaches being inaccessible to vessels owing to an extensive shelf ice formation which skirts the greater portion of the east coast . . . .

Between Cape Dubouzet and Cape Roquemaurel, about 50 miles southwestward, the land is comparatively low and covered with a continuous ice sheet with occasional rock outcrops. Offshore, for a distance of 10 miles, there are many rocky islets and submerged reefs. These waters have not been thoroughly surveyed and the mariner is warned to exercise caution when approaching this coast. The most prominent elevations are Mount Hope (Mount Bransfield), 2,480 feet high, Mount Jacquinot, 1,556 feet high, and Mount D'Urville, 3,553 feet high.

The Antarctic Pilot, a British publication, notes that the current name for the Peninsula was agreed upon by Australia, Great Britain, New Zealand and the United States in 1963. Prior to this time the Peninsula was referred to by the British as Graham Land (after James R. G. Graham, First Lord of the Admiralty at the time John Biscoe explored part of the western coast of the Peninsula in 1831) and by the United States as Palmer Peninsula in honor of Nathaniel Palmer. Argentina calls the Peninsula Tierra San Martin and Chile calls it Tierra O'Higgins after patriots who helped their respective countries free themselves from Spanish rule.

Postscript. Two years later I learned that the U.S. inspection team had visited the following stations: Scott (New Zealand) on January 12, Druzhnaya (U.S.S.R.) on January 19, Bellingshausen (U.S.S.R.) on February 4, Presidente Frei (Chile) on February 4 and Vicecomodoro Marambio (Argentina) on February 5.

The United States Arms Control and Disarmament Agency of Washington issued a report.

During the period January 3 until February 10, 1977, a team of designated observers from the United States of America conducted an inspection of certain Antarctic stations under the provisions of Article VII of the Antarctic Treaty . . . .

In accordance with Article VII of the Antarctic Treaty, all designations of U.S. observers were communicated to the other Treaty Parties.

In no case was any evidence of violation of the provisions of the Antarctic Treaty observed. . . .

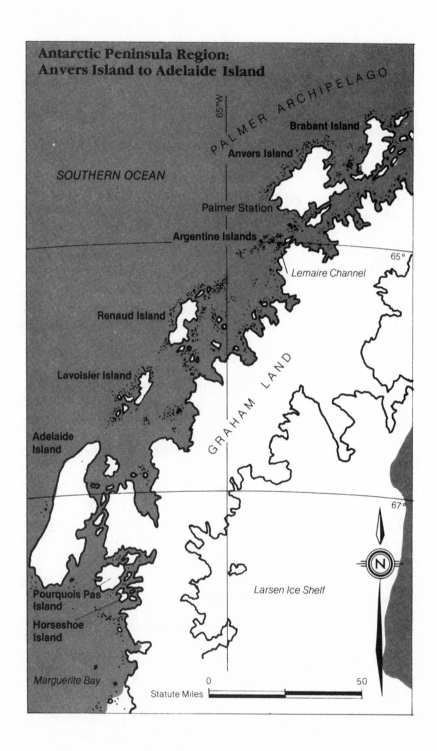

Antarctic Peninsula Region:
Anvers Island to Adelaide Island

PALMER ARCHIPELAGO

65°W

Brabant Island

Anvers Island

SOUTHERN OCEAN

Palmer Station

Argentine Islands

65°

Lemaire Channel

Renaud Island

GRAHAM LAND

Lavoisier Island

Adelaide
Island

67°

Pourquois Pas
Island

Larsen Ice Shelf

Horseshoe
Island

N

Marguerite Bay

0   50

Statute Miles

9 ❀ Palmer Station, Anvers Island

3 FEBRUARY, THURSDAY. "I finished packing, went on deck for early views: the Marr Ice Piedmont, blue-eyed shags (a kind of cormorant; only the ring around the eye is blue) flying low over ice and water, southern black-backed gulls (also known as Dominican gulls), Antarctic terns, brown skuas. Warburton attracting many birds with bread so he could photograph them. A crewman quietly fishing with rod and reel."

For some reason that faceless crewman remains steadfastly in my memory. He must have been a very dedicated fisherman. He was alone on the deck except for Warburton and me. There was something attractive about his body language, patience and silence.

Palmer, built on a rocky head stretching out brief and black under the Marr Ice Piedmont, which I shall also refer to as a glacier, was moody in the early morning close to dawn. The *Hero's* two masts showed against the overcast sky. Skuas flew boldly near the icebreaker.

The Marr Ice Piedmont, which covers the western half of Anvers Island, was named for James W. S. Marr, British marine biologist and first commander of the FIDS (Falkland Island Dependency Survey), 1943–45. He was also a member of Ernest Shackleton's expedition of 1921–22, during which Shackleton died of a heart attack. Shackleton is buried on South Georgia. Anvers Island, the largest island of the Palmer Archipelago, was named in 1898 after the province of Anvers, Belgium by the Belgian Antarctic Expedition under De Gerlache. Anvers Island is thirty-eight nautical miles long from northeast to southwest and twenty-four nautical miles wide. Its highest summit is Mt. Francais, 9258 feet high.

Quick, eager first views of the station in the early morning light revealed two large buildings on the spit emerging from under the huge bluish icecap. The main building, closer to the jetty at the spit's end, was of three stories and graced in front by a flagstaff. The lesser one was of two stories. Two large, squat, white fuel tanks showed on the farther side of them. The tanks fed not only the station's generators but the *Hero's* as well when the latter was moored at the jetty.

I had waited a long time for this moment of imminently joining the station and had often wondered if it would ever come. In Christchurch I had been in suspense about reaching the *Burton Island* before its departure from McMurdo. At McMurdo I had sometimes despaired as the time available to me on the Peninsula had been eaten away by the unavoidable delays caused by the unusual sea-ice conditions. On the icebreaker I had been uneasy because the voyage was taking longer than its originally scheduled nine or ten days. Each day was tremendously precious for me in its possibilities. Now at last I was here, full of curiosity about what the station and its environs were like, and wondering how much time I would spend in this region, and above all what I would be able to do with the time left to me before the season's terminal point: the *Hero's* departure on March 10 for Tierra del Fuego, that Land of Fire so-named by Magellan because of the night fires made constantly by the Indians.

I had exchanged the continental dryness of the Ross Island sector for the relatively high humidity of the Peninsula region; McMurdo's low temperatures for the higher ones of Palmer Station; Ross Island's endless counterclockwise daylight at this time of year for Palmer's two or three hours of gracious, blessed night; McMurdo Sound's rippled sea ice and the Ross Ice Shelf's windswept, windscarred, sastrugi-surfaced freshwater ice for the placid waters of Arthur Harbor, once the scene of

British activity; and McMurdo's staging-area bustle and mining-camp and wartime-dump looks for the handful of young men (scientists, logistic supporters and one or two administrators) of a very small, neat and relatively luxurious station. I had exchanged the proximity to the geographic and geomagnetic poles for the proximity to the Drake passage and Cape Horn; the proximity to the Dry Valleys and the beautiful Royal Society Range for the proximity to the Peninsula mainland and its equally beautiful mountain ranges; the proximity to the polar history of Scott, Shackleton, Amundsen and Byrd for the proximity to that of Palmer, Bransfield, John Biscoe, James Weddell, Thaddeus Bellingshausen. But there was one thing I had not exchanged: the sense of vast ice masses all around me.

"Last breakfast. No goodbyes. Into the landing craft with Warburton, the two bird watchers and the three members of the observation team. The team stayed for lunch. I moved into my room on the second floor, started unpacking, walked around the station, observed a helo take off from the *Burton Island* and land at Palmer, then return to the ship."

The *Hero* left the jetty and took up a position in the harbor. It was a tight, small, two-masted wooden motor sailer which had been designed to complement the station both scientifically and logistically. It carried sails for three reasons: as an added mode of propulsion, for greater stability in very rough weather, and for silent operation during certain oceanographic work. From the icebreaker's landing craft the *Burton Island* looked massive, squat, relatively short, its hull brilliant red, its wideranging superstructure, including the broad bridge and bridge wings, very white. Despite its special bow meant for riding up on ice it suggested it was strong enough to withstand the recoil shock of three-inch guns, and indeed it had once carried such weapons. On the forward part of the hull one could read in white: 283, a Coast Guard insignia and COAST GUARD. By comparison the *Hero* looked frail, innocent, anachronistic and romantic, suggesting shoal waters and inland waterways. But from the station and in profile the icebreaker looked quite long: a red horizontal line on the gray water, the massive icecap sloping to the rocky water's edge beyond it under a brooding sky, with a scattering of low, dark, rocky islets on its left. The red hull was a very warm color in the harbor's cool polar blues and grays.

I was grateful to Guthridge for letting me have a room of my own after the shared room at McMurdo and the no room at all on the icebreaker. I took it as an excellent sign of his good will toward me and my project and I responded accordingly. It made a great difference to me to be able to have my own place to work, spread out, secure data, think and rest: things that had not been made available to me on the *Burton Island* but which had been offered me in generous measure by the skipper of the *Staten Island*, the *Burton Island's* sister ship, during my second Antarctic expedition.

The room felt spacious to me from the moment I opened the door and looked in, yet in reality it was quite modest. I felt the hard bed. No more climbing up to my icebreaker rack in the dark. But that was not central. The important thing was my ability now to gather all my things together in one small place, and it was as if this convocation also had its counterpart inside myself somewhere or everywhere: in my mind, my hands, my emotions. I had been given back to myself in a certain way.

The room was approximately across the corridor from Guthridge's. Immediately on the right as you entered it were two bunks, upper and lower. I occupied the lower one. Beyond the simple bed was a small desk, at the left of which was the room's sole window. To the left of the door as you entered were two closets running the length of the room. The one closest to the window had a chest of drawers that I did not find time to use. I had so much with me—the five cartons, the two seabags and my own personal luggage and gear—that it was quite a feat to jam everything more or less out of my way so I could find some areas of freedom. But I used the room only for sleep and for writing at the desk. Under the lower bunk were two drawers that I found very handy for certain items, such as exposed film. I tried to keep the window open at all times in order to hold the temperature down as much as possible for the benefit of this film.

Shane Williams handed me some mail which had been sent to Tierra del Fuego and brought here by the *Hero*. How exotic the address seemed even though I had just left the globe's most exotic ocean. One of the strange and unforeseen functions of such mail was to assure you you still existed as a psychic entity, or rather that your inner self, like some delicate baroque instrument, was still in tune despite the hazards of sea travel.

"Last evening Guthridge said I should talk with Ian Dalziel, a geologist who was arriving on the *Hero* and departing on the *Burton Island*. So I got hold of him. He had been with David Elliot in the South Orkneys. He works at Lamont–Doherty Geological Observatory of Columbia University in Palisades, New York. I asked him about international relations on the Peninsula. He informed me, among other matters, that Chile has a law that obliges all publishers of maps of Chile to include Chilean Antarctic claims. An intelligent man, concerned about the growing nationalism in Antarctica by Chile and Argentina."

Dalziel's comments on Latin American nationalism in the Peninsula region were the opening notes of a motif that would grow during my first visit to Palmer and which was to color my stay in the region. I shall discuss it in some detail later. He did not suggest that there was any United Kingdom nationalism on the Peninsula (I use the word Peninsula to include the offshore islands, whether single or in groups such as the South Shetlands), and his British accent made me wonder if he had a patriotic bias. As the reader will recall, the United Kingdom as well as Chile and Argentina claimed the Peninsula sector. What was to surprise me in the coming days and weeks was the emergence or perhaps rather growth of my own patriotic bias. The more I heard of a thriving nationalism on the Peninsula the more I came to believe that the United States presence on the Peninsula was insufficient both scientifically and geopolitically. Global though my thinking was about the Antarctic, or at least I liked to believe it was, it seemed to me that a greater U.S. presence would strengthen the U.S. position with regard to sovereignty claims: like Russia, the United States neither made such claims nor recognized the claims by other nations. I liked the fact that the United States was the only nation with a base at the Pole itself, where it blithely sat astride the triangular apexes of all the claimed pie slices. But the United States, like the Soviet Union, also reserved the right to make sovereignty claims, and the explorations of its citizens in these waters were as old and respectable as anybody's.

4 FEBRUARY. "Janus Island was my first experience of the harbor's rocky islands. Dolerite. Very few erratics. Very boring gray shardlike rocks showing little if any action of the winds. The rocks often move beneath you as you walk on them.

"Came upon a tidewater pool containing a young elephant

seal, a crabeater seal on nearby snow and a fur seal who roared like a lion at us but was timid when I tried to approach it, moved away from me over rocks toward water. The female elephant seal had large bloody sores around its head and there were fresh bloodspots on nearby rocks and a bloody color in one edge of the pool. Its huge dark eyes observing us. The pale gray crabeater lay on its side, resting, occasionally scratching itself with a clawed flipper, paying little attention to us. Orange lichen and tufts of a greenish grass. Matt Sturm upturned some lichen to show me a tiny orange mite. I believe it's the largest indigenous animal in Antarctica. Luxuriant green and brown mosses. I looked for feathers, and though we saw skuas and were attacked by them with the usual dives and screams, I saw very few feathers of any kind."

The place was a gray-sharded wasteland. It was as if Nature had said, "Now I will show to what extent I can amass and exaggerate gray shards on a single island." The glut of gray rocks, of sameness of shape and color, of angularity, the vast surfeit of it all, began to irritate me. We had had a fine beginning—three seals, each of a different species, and one bloody, one yawning and one roaring—but the monotony of this rockscape was severe, and I thought the island's chief gift to me was to make me think of my own glut, own surfeit, own dull grayness, own monotony, own sameness of shape and color, own vast interior of angularity. Then I remembered that I didn't need to have my vision bound by such an ungifted place, and when I gazed outward from it I saw glassy, pale-blue water, islets, and sweetly white and blue and sloping small bergs sailing under a brightening maritime sky, and my spirits lifted and my view of myself improved.

When the skuas didn't attack us their scouts seemed to be following and observing us closely wherever we went, as if we were mere trespassers, which indeed from their point of view we were. They were more effective occupiers of this bleak island than we, and I gladly recognized their superior territorial claims.

The elephant seal suggested a large reptile as she lay in the pool, her body only partly submerged. She had what looked like bloody carbuncles on her head. Her mouth was open as if in pain but she was soundless. She had a wiry black mustache (no whiskers) and three black brow hairs for each eye. At one point she rested her chin on a tabular rock that sloped into the dark water. I was fascinated by her serpentine look and huge round eyes. Lifting her massive gray head with goitrous-looking eyes out of the water to study me, she suggested for a moment a bloodied hippopotamus. The poor thing was in trouble and showed it. I wondered what it was like to be such a creature and not have doctors and nurses and hospitals. There was nothing fair about fate. Here this seal slunk in the tidewater pool, very poor in health's estate, and the crabeater yawned and scratched its head and probably wondered the crabeater equivalent of what time it was and what was stewing up for dinner, and the young fur seal roared his head off to prove his toughness.

The crabeater lay decorously supine on a patch of snow beside the tidepool, idly scratching its head, the darker gray of head, tail and flippers exactly matching that of the dolerite. Its gray belly looked as if it had been spattered by white paint. The fur seal, young and strong, was on rocks. It kept bellowing a warning. I knew it could attack and give a bad bite but I headed toward it to test its courage, remembering all the fur seals that had been clubbed to death in the terrible greed-slaughter of the early decades of the last century. Retreating in stages, roaring at me, it gave the impression of being a quadruped.

Cullen and Sturm went at their task seriously: to put in a couple of brightly painted red drums of survival equipment. I didn't help, nor was I expected to. I was doing what I needed to do: looking around, getting impressions. Gray growths with spots of yellow the size of a dime. Views of ice-clad mainland mountains and of many islands in Arthur Harbor. The overcast sky set off the blues and chalky whites of floes and bergs and the brooding grays of rock islands. Sky and sea retreated together into a backdrop only faintly marked by objects on the horizon. The sea was a faint blue silken sheet against which flying birds were revealed with their flashes of white and their gracefully arched upbeating wings.

"After lunch I went with Guy Guthridge, Dick Wolak and Bob Murphy to Torgersen Island. It's directly across the water from the station, closer to the station than Janus is. Same kind of rocks but here you have many Adélies. I was curious about their brown color until we landed and drew close and I could see that many of the birds were large juveniles about to molt. They stood about, a mangy looking lot, and tried to imitate their parents' sounds but not very successfully. They let us approach closely, showing no fear. The adults showed no fear either. Skuas scouted overhead or stood close to a group of young penguins. Strong, fishy penguin smells. Saw penguins swimming and breaching in the harbor on our way out. I know Adélies but this was my first view of Adélie chicks so large."

Torgersen was the closest island to the station. Roughly circular, some 400 yards across and about 55 feet high, it was named for Torstein Torgersen, who, as first mate of the *Norsel*, was the first to enter Arthur Harbor in one of the ship's boats in February 1955. You left Hero Inlet in the Zodiac and went directly across water and brash to it. It was irksome to have to wear the yellow floatcoat over my parka. I felt at times I was a clothes rack whose chief purpose was to bear things. I always carried at least one camera and my shoulder bag. Like Janus, Torgersen was heavily sharded, but the presence of Adélies lessened its feeling of hostility. Some of the rocks had weathered into sharp pinnacles, and it was startling to come upon towering masses of orange rock, dolerite covered with lichen, beyond which we could see a mainland mountain range. In the harbor were other islands, or rather islets, small and low-lying. The water was very placid. Two adult penguins, distant from each other, were in the vicinity of the orange rocks, as if they had been attracted by the color. Given the fact they were very gregarious birds, their solitariness was as eyecatching as the lichen.

The rookery birds stood around in large groups as if in convention. The juveniles looked furry rather than feathery and seemed to be vegetating and having trouble staying awake. They were very plump and gave the impression of being ready to burst out of their "fur." Skuas flew near the rookery constantly, alert for a sudden tasty meal. Occasionally we came to flat spots full of little bits of gray caked mud and on one of these we saw whole or partial remains of killed chicks: a flipper, a spinal column, a foot, a feathered skull—all desiccated. Once we observed the vivid red remains of a freshly killed bird.

In some places the guano had browned or rosed the rock-earth. The warm colors contrasted sharply with the blue-grays of a rotting ice piedmont slope visible from the island. The glacier snout near Palmer was equally visible. In a little valley of sharded rocks we saw a thick carpet of green-brown moss, which forcefully reminded me that I was no longer in the Ross Island sector.

Adélies were no novelty to me, I had lived with them on Cape Royds on Ross Island, but I had never seen almost full-grown juveniles. These looked tattered and were funny in their apparent confusion between childhood and adulthood. They were almost large enough to be on their own, yet they were still dependent on their parents for food. A chick using a rock as a pillow. Many were flapping their rudimentary wings. The usual loud quacking. The youngsters grew silent and contemplative on our approach. Not so the adults, obviously used to human presence and still going into ecstatic displays with all the accompanying quacks and guttural mutterings. The rookery was quite extensive. Some of the birds were on a hill. Many were on a couple of rocky beaches. Odd to see a group of five big chicks sitting on a bunch of rocks about as high as my shoulders and occasionally quacking.

"Looked around for Adélie feathers but saw none, realized that Adélie feathers are tiny pin feathers. Again found very few skua feathers. What happens to them and to skua bodies? Skuas and Adélies have lived here for generations, yet there's almost no sign of bodies or parts of bodies such as skulls, feet. Saw a very funny sight: two large juveniles begging a parent to disgorge, give food. One ran after the gaunt-looking parent a long way until the latter finally stopped, faced it. The chick made motions with its beak which seemed at a distance to suggest it was tickling the parent's throat to aid in vomiting. The parent also made gestures: efforts to disgorge, which finally succeeded. Then the chase began again, continued through a couple of sub-rookeries, the parent heading lower and lower toward the sea. One of our group predicted the parent meant to escape by plunging in. We laughed at the persistence of the chase and at the disparity between the adult's leanness and the chick's fatness. As someone remarked, the chick hadn't gotten that fat through shyness. Overhead hovered the menacing forms of scouting skuas looking for a kill. I was moved by the simple, endless drama of it: life in the chick's efforts to thrive, the parents' duty to feed the offspring, death stalking and sometimes overtaking the young.

"A group of somnolent feather-downy chicks huddling to-

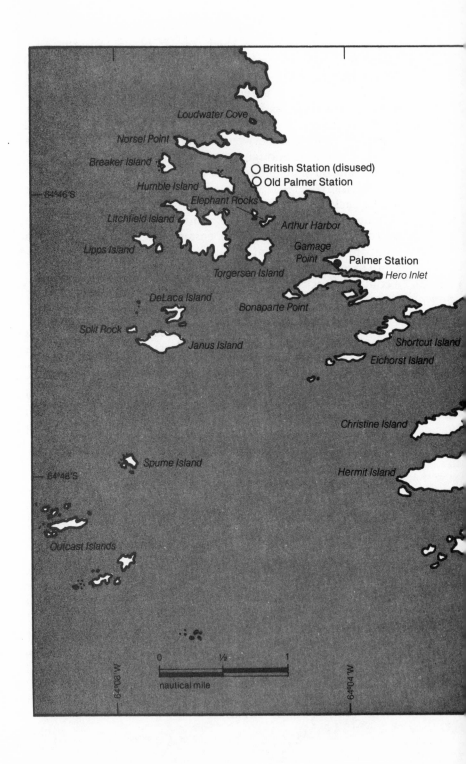

Loudwater Cove

Norsel Point

Breaker Island

Humble Island

64°46'S

Elephant Rocks

Litchfield Island

○ British Station (disused)
○ Old Palmer Station

Lipps Island

Arthur Harbor

Gamage
Point

Palmer Station

Hero Inlet

Torgersen Island

DeLaca Island

Bonaparte Point

Split Rock

Janus Island

Shortcut Island

Eichorst Island

Christine Island

Spume Island

64°48'S

Hermit Island

Outcast Islands

64°08'W

0   ½   1

nautical mile

64°04'W

Palmer Station and Vicinity

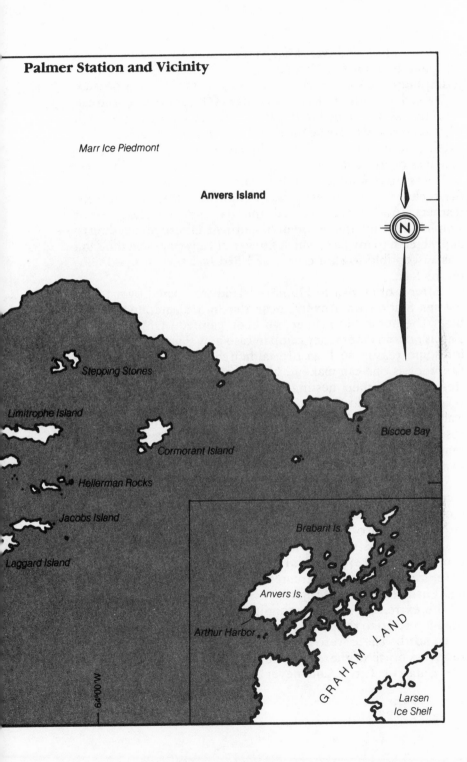

Marr Ice Piedmont

Anvers Island

N

Stepping Stones

Limitrophe Island

Cormorant Island

Biscoe Bay

Hellerman Rocks

Jacobs Island

Laggard Island

64°00'W

Brabant Is.

Anvers Is.

Arthur Harbor

GRAHAM LAND

Larsen
Ice Shelf

gether on a rise, and two skuas waiting close by, hoping to grab one, and no adult standing guard. An adult growling and muttering angrily at Guthridge and making a pass at his legs because he walked too close to it and it perhaps felt cut off from retreat. It bridled as we seemed to outflank it, tested its flippers to see if they were ready to strike us, cast sidewise nervous glances. [An Adélie can bruise you with its flipper.] We laughed at the humanness of its behavior.

"I was disappointed by the terrain, the endless sameness of the rocks, the lack of erratics, of colorful rocks, of ventifacts, feathers. And I was pleased the day was overcast, for it simplified for me the problem of getting sunburned, needing to apply cream to my face, which I never did anyway even though I was susceptible to skin cancer and had had several operations on my face.

"After a brief visit to Humble Island we boated over to old Palmer Station on Anvers, near the long-abandoned British base. The hut at old Palmer had been painted orange recently. This is now an emergency camp in case new Palmer is wiped out for some reason such as fire, although the new station is as fireproof as one can make it. Many attacking skuas because we trespassed on their nesting grounds. I found a long bamboo pole near the old station, with which I protected us as we walked to a rise to have a view of a pond or lake. Flocks of skuas rose in alarm. Their agonized, pleading, 'female' cries. I was reminded of Skua Lake near Scott's Terra Nova Hut on Cape Evans, Ross Island. Skuas are strong, beautiful fliers.

"Looking out at the scenes of the harbor, I found it hard to accept them as authentically Antarctic: smooth-surfaced water, mountains, the curving wake of a Zodiac, the *Hero* quietly at the jetty. I thought of resorts in Colorado, Switzerland."

I felt that this was not "my" Antarctica, the severely hostile continent, and I experienced a certain embarrassment in being here, for the beauty of Antarctica was for the moment pretty, and I had come to the Antarctic, as I always had come, because of the extremeness of its conditions. I had been invited on occasion to go to the Arctic, but after Antarctica I had no desire to go north. There were more than a million indigenous human residents north of the Arctic Circle. There were none south of the Antarctic Circle and never had been. There were polar bears and foxes and other animals north of the Arctic Circle. Aside from a few bird species, the only animals south of the Antarctic Circle were in the sea, and the birds had to live off the sea or die. It was precisely the continent's extremes that drew me to it, and the fact that it was not only pre-human but probably pre-mammalian as well fascinated me. There were scores of reasons why I could not share my attention with the Arctic. Which pained me a little when people still asked me how it was "up there" instead of "down there" and asked about the polar bears and, in rarer instances, about the Eskimos.

I told myself to be patient, that this too was the Antarctic and that I was broadening my knowledge of the place. And I added what I already knew: that I was disoriented, I had come too far too fast, which was part of being "modern," I had still not digested the experiences of Upper Wright Valley, the Dais, the hard cold and the smells of sprayed DFA of Victoria Valley, the killer whales, the fin and the vast stretches of the Southern Ocean, and the various people in those places, and now here I was, trying to comprehend the resort prettiness that Arthur Harbor now suggested. I told myself to be careful about mental slippages, to remember, despite what it might momentarily seem, that this was the Antarctic, with its own laws so different from those of the temperate regions, and to keep in mind that any use of low-latitude thinking as a crutch of comfort was dangerous in that it caused you to let down your guard, or was a signal that you had already begun to let it down. The Antarctic was a place whose strange laws you forgot at your peril. And yet, precisely because it was so foreign, your mind tended to slip a gear now and then, for it needed the solace of low-latitude images. I remembered the fierce daydreams and night dreams of gorging on food the Shackleton and Scott polar parties had suffered from as they were starving, dreams that were extreme examples of low-latitude crutches. There were many kinds of deprivations one could experience in the Antarctic.

"Guthridge had told me that several days ago four Chileans had come about fifteen nautical miles to Palmer to ask for help in repairing a piece of equipment and had been lent a similar piece while theirs would be repaired at Palmer. Going over to Torgersen, we saw their dory approaching Palmer. On our return to Palmer we met them as they emerged from the station and prepared to sail home. Small dark men in blue parkas and windpants. Their outboard engine made in the States. Round wool sailor caps. Talking Spanish with a couple of station members, Shane Williams among them. INACH painted on the bow, standing for Instituto Nacional Antartica Chileno. They had come from Yelcho Station. We squeezed hands warmly. I was suddenly moved: the sense of the Antarctic brotherhood. And I was reminded that I was indeed south of South America now, had come from New Zealand, left McMurdo. They sailed off. I thought it odd that they should use blue clothes that didn't contrast with blue water, and a gray dory that blended well with the gray of island rocks. We thought it incautious of them to travel 15 miles in an open dory.

"Forgot to say that as we boated from old Palmer to new Palmer we encountered fresh ice from a glacier breakage and decided to haul a piece of 'black' ice (it looks black while in the water and it's very dense and hard) to the station for drinks. Selecting a candidate, I reached out barehanded and got it out of the water. Later, when I icepicked and tasted it, it had no taste I could detect, or about as much as distilled water has. The ice was possibly several centuries old. Such ice pops and crackles in a drink as it depressurizes. It doesn't melt readily.

"Talked with X [who later, when we were back in the States, asked not to be named in my book in the following connection for fear of professional reprisals by the Argentines, who could make continued scientific research in the Peninsula sector difficult for him by refusing him entry into their country] and brought the subject around to nationalism on the Peninsula. He told me something I hadn't known: that the Argentines will not let USARPS depart Ushuaia for Antarctica without a special paper called a *ficha*, containing fingerprints, photo and the declaration that the USARP scientists are crewmen on the *Hero*. X is a very intelligent man whom I have known for years and whom I have every reason to trust.

"He suspects the following reasoning: The Peninsula is claimed by Argentina; it is unlawful for foreign passengers to move from one domestic port (Ushuaia) to another (Palmer Station) in a foreign vessel (the *Hero*). But 'crewmen' carrying the *ficha* may do it. X was angry because the U.S. lets itself be 'pushed around,' that 'it recognizes Argentine sovereignty claims in a de facto way'—claims supposedly placed in abeyance for the life of the Antarctic Treaty, to which Argentina is an original signatory. He believes 'the U.S. should take a forceful stand, stand up to them, in the interests of the Treaty and Antarctica,' that its 'acquiescent behavior weakens the Treaty.' I told him I think the U.S. has an insufficient presence in the Peninsula sector. He agrees, thinks we should manage to use Hercs [C-130's] on the Peninsula, that we should make ourselves independent of Ushuaia, that it was a mistake for us to move from Punta Arenas in Chile to Ushuaia in Argentina, that the Chileans would be delighted to cooperate with us again. He thinks it's unlikely that anything of sufficient economic value will be found on the Peninsula to strain the Treaty but believes the Treaty will be and is being strained out of nationalistic motives."

Well, I told myself, this was precisely why I had come to the Peninsula area. You learned very interesting things in the field. Antarctica was not a subject that could be well understood merely from reading papers and books.

A few words about Palmer Station and its history. The United States did not have a base in the Peninsula region during the International Geophysical Year (1957–58), when there was a great outburst of basic scientific research in the Antarctic. Leaving possible geopolitical motives aside, United States interest in the Peninsula after the IGY stemmed from its desire to include biology and related sciences, which had not been part of its IGY program. The British in 1955 had erected an eight-man hut on Norsel Point to facilitate their geological and biological studies in the area. The hut had been deactivated in 1958. Early in 1964, with the approval of the British, U.S. personnel occupied the hut while constructing a temporary base nearby: "old" Palmer Station, commissioned in February 1965.

Construction of the new and permanent base about 1½ miles north of Norsel Point was begun early in 1967 and completed in March of the following year. The main building, a three-story steel-frame structure, contained some 10,000 square feet of space. It included a biology laboratory, a storage area for laboratory equipment, an electronic workshop, a machine shop, storage space for the *Hero's* spare parts and supplies, living facilities for twenty-four men, a dining room, a kitchen, a small recreation room, oil-heating and electrical utilities and a power plant. The multipurpose secondary building, erected in the austral summer of 1968–69, provided additional storage space, a large recreation room, a garage, a dormitory for transient personnel, the station's amateur radio equipment and two 150-kilowatt generators. The two fuel tanks each had a 125,000-gallon capacity.

The station was named for Nathaniel B. Palmer of Stonington, Connecticut, the twenty-year-old captain of the sloop *Hero*, who, while hunting the southern fur seal in his 47-foot vessel, discovered Deception Island and who possibly was the first person to sight the Antarctic mainland, the latter in the form of a Peninsula mountain range. Palmer's sloop, of 44 tons, was built in Groton, Connecticut, in 1800. His exploratory cruise occurred in November 1820. During another exploratory cruise in the *Hero* in January 1821 Palmer unexpectedly encountered Bellingshausen in the strait between Deception and Livingston Islands and had a meeting with Bellingshausen aboard the latter's flagship *Vostok*. Bellingshausen was impressed by Palmer's youth and the smallness of his vessel. Bellingshausen was not the only important explorer Palmer met. He had previously met Bransfield and Weddell. Much later Palmer became famous as a pioneer clipper ship master and designer.

The National Science Foundation named its 125-foot Antarctic research ship in honor of Palmer's sloop. Palmer's name was also officially identified with Palmer Land (the southern part of the Antarctic Peninsula), as well as with the Palmer Archipelago, a group of islands off the Peninsula's northwestern shore.

5 FEBRUARY. During the afternoon someone out in a Zodiac reported spotting a vessel near Arthur Harbor but out of view of the station. Lenie, the *Hero's* captain, tried to contact it by radio but it didn't respond. There were rumors it was a whaler, which roused mixed feelings, for no one at the station approved of whaling in the Antarctic. There was also talk it was a Russian whaler and probably too embarrassed by its activities to answer our calls. Lenie climbed to the *Hero's* crow's nest to have a look with binoculars, decided it was indeed a whaler and went with a crewman in a Zodiac to check on it.

I admired him for doing that: his curiosity, energy, fearlessness despite his age (he was gray-bearded), his determination to know. I can still see him ascending slowly but steadily in his flowing, capacious khaki windpants, heavy plaid wool shirt, pile-lined cap with upturned brim and earflaps, gaily striped, heavy, calf-high boots.

When a fair amount of time passed with no word from him, the station tried to reach him by radio. No response. It tried to reach the whaler in the hope of discovering what had happened to him. Silence. Growing suspense could be felt around the station. Why wasn't he in touch by radio? There were jokes about his having been captured by the Russian whaler.

Finally he was overdue enough to justify sending a Zodiac to check on him, so Matt Sturm and someone else went out. Then he radioed from the whaler to say he was on board and chatting. He returned with a Polaroid picture of himself with three or four Russians and a harpoon gun on deck. He reported he had invited the whaler to visit the station but the captain had declined because a diver was cutting away something from their hull and because he didn't want to risk moving into the harbor with his "inadequate" charts. We were disappointed the whaler couldn't visit us. Now that we knew they had been cordial to Lenie our mixed feelings about their whaling activities had changed, at least temporarily, to friendly ones.

"After dinner several of us went over to Bonaparte Point by the little trolley. Guy Guthridge, Cliff Patrick, Dick Wolak, Gary Cullen. It was tricky getting seated on the simple arrangement and pushing off, and on the farther side you had to haul yourself in by pulling on the nylon rope. You weren't belted in. A fall into the water would have been serious because of the water's temperature, about 33° F. There were no life-saving devices around, such as a life preserver or even a rope."

Rock cliff from which you took off, rock cliff on which you landed, the single cable from which you were suspended; the icy Hero Inlet below, ice cliffs to the left, rocks and ice all around you. I was not especially eager to take the trolley ride. It seemed like a rather foolhardy and unnecessary thing to do, which is to say it was not part of my program, and normally I thought that anything not part of it should best be relatively safe. There was a considerable difference in my mind between taking risks for my project as against taking them through idleness, boredom or foolishness. I had been very lucky in the Antarctic, but partly because I believed luck needed all the help I could give it. Sometimes I was lucky without my own help. For example, aside from the fact I had survived the Erebus episode, it was extraordinarily lucky it had occurred near the tail end of my second Antarctic stay. If it had happened earlier it might have seriously damaged my work, for my frostbitten and partially injured hands were unfit for camping out for a while. Later, after my return from the voyage with the British Antarctic Survey, Jerry Huffman, Guthridge's replacement, would tell me bluntly he had no intention of using the trolley, which looked to him dangerous, and he was much younger than I. Even as I waited for my turn I saw Wolak tumble off the narrow board seat and proceed across the inlet upside down, but he was young and agile and no doubt enjoyed this divertissement. However, if he fell into the water it would be no joke. Still, there was nothing to do but put all negative thoughts out of mind and go across, which I did. I even managed to stay right side up.

"Subtle greens and blues showed on the glacier snout, and layers of lavender on the top. Guthridge and Wolak joined Patrick and me, and at one point, while I was reloading my camera, Guthridge said, 'Look what's here. The *Bransfield*. It's a darn big ship.' Knowing I was destined to live on it, I took my time looking up at it. I didn't want to risk spoiling the moment by being hasty. There it was: red, large, moving carefully toward the base, positioning itself for anchoring. Later we heard the clang of anchor chain and saw the chain spinning out of the ship like a delicate spider web."

The *Bransfield* looked very attractive: bright red hull and white superstructure. It faced the glacier. The sunlight fell gently upon its stern, highlighting reds and whites. The bow and bridge were in shadow. As I was to learn, its overall length was 325 feet, its beam about 52 feet, its gross tonnage 4816, its service speed 13.5 knots. It resembled the *Burton Island* with its red hull, white superstructure and stern helo deck.

I had a maritime sense about my present life: Everything seemed watery. It was odd to think I would soon take up residence on that foreign ship. Large boulders in the left foreground, with two shadowed skuas on one, watching me. Softly blue harbor faintly rippled. Large sloping glacier mass beyond the ship, parts in sunlight, others shadow-coated with gray-lavender cloudbanks above them. Pale blue sky with touches of cirrus. The ship etched sharply in the fine air and light. It had positioned itself where the *Burton Island* had been. No signs of life aboard, it looked abandoned. And then the ship's funnel let out a burst of dark smoke that opened into a brown cloud before drifting toward the sunlight.

A snout embayment cried out its sunlit whiteness. Palmer Station and the *Hero* at jettyside seemed to be napping. Panes of glass at the base reflected the light with a golden hue, spattering the water with yellow dust. The *Hero* looked like an interesting mongrel compared with the *Bransfield*. The glacier cliffs showed bluish corruption as of weathered copper against the gleaming ivory.

"Again Cliff Patrick was solicitous about my safety as I seated myself on the narrow board of the trolley. Returning, you didn't have to pull yourself in. It was a downward voyage and you spun freely until you could stand. The trolley pulleys clattered. Guy had returned first and I had seen him running toward the station. It was 9:50 and we were late. As I headed across rocks toward Palmer I heard him shout my name from a Zodiac. I went to a little rocky beach and boarded it. With him were Shane Williams and Wolak.

"We boarded the *Bransfield* by means of a rope ladder and had a good talk in the captain's cabin. The effect of boarding the ship and entering the rather posh cabin was quite dramatic. Consider: Just a little while ago I was clambering over the shardlike rocks of Bonaparte Point, attacked by skuas, then I went by Zodiac almost at water level over to the *Bransfield's* great metal hull, then I climbed the rope ladder to one of the *Bransfield's* decks, and now suddenly, while still wearing my American field clothes, I entered what felt like the drawing room of an expensive London hotel suite. Fine wood panelling, luxurious chairs and sofas, excellent rugs and other appurtenances of the good life, with four English gentlemen dressed in starched white shirts and ties under well-tailored jackets. These were Stuart Lawrence, the ship's young master, William Sloman, administrator, third in command at the British Antarctic Survey, Charles Swithinbank, an authority on glaciology and chief scientist of BAS in the field this season, and Don Hawkes, geologist and professor at a Birmingham university."

6 FEBRUARY, SUNDAY. "I went to Warburton's satellite communication gear again 5 to 6 and this time his side was okay—he had found a shorted diode—but he couldn't rouse Reno. 'VHF Reno, VHF Reno, this is VHF Palmer Station calling,' said in his Aussie accent. VHF stands for very high frequency. He transmitted that he would stand by tomorrow at the usual time. After dinner I was still very tired. So was everybody else at the base. Wolak helped me get a patch through to Joan, who said all is well. I explained that I'll probably join the British Antarctic Survey for a while, that there will be no patches while I'm with them because patches are illegal in the U.K., and no mail, that I hope to return to Palmer February 25 or 26, that I tried to reach her yesterday at home and at the Y. I gathered that matters are at a crisis point in the States regarding fuel and the cold weather. Wolak left the ham room while I talked and keyed the mike. The patch was run through Big John in California, to whom many Antarctic people are indebted. I explained to Joan my hope of returning to Palmer by hitching a ride on some vessel. She said I sounded tired. I guess I was feeling exhausted and somewhat disoriented. I was about to make another big move, yet I had spent only three nights at Palmer. It was only a short while since my last patch with her but for me it felt like months, and I think this perplexed her."

7 FEBRUARY. "To Shortcut Island in the morning by Zodiac. The usual climbing around on difficult rocky footing."

I never got much of a sense of Anvers Island. You had a worm's view from the station and harbor. You didn't relate much to the island as a whole. Mostly you dealt with the rocky head or spit on which the station was built, with several harbor islands and with the glacier or icecap behind the station.

We were attacked by skuas whose nesting grounds we had to cross. I was used to skua attacks from having camped out on Ross Island. They meant to hit you if they could. They would come at you at about your throat or chest level, diving very fast and working as a group, outflanking you or trying to get you from the rear. They had powerful claws, which luckily they rarely used for some reason. Usually they tried to hit you with the leading edge of a wing. The skua was a fairly large, heavy

164   BEYOND CAPE HORN

and fearless bird. I had been hit several times at Cape Evans. Once I had received a blow across the left temple that had almost knocked me out. I was on a beach then and had realized it would not be a good idea to get hit like that while standing on a cliff edge. The only time I had really been frightened was when a bird had come at me with its claws extended and I had imagined myself being blinded while far from medical help. We waved them off now and ducked and tried to pay no attention to them.

Again the hard, gray dolerite: cracked, fragmented, shattered. Giant petrels: parent and chick on a high rocky area. They were a lighter gray than most of the rocks. The giant petrel is also (and probably better) known as the southern giant fulmar but at Palmer and at Shortcut Island I heard it referred to only as GP or giant petrel. Adults have a wingspan of seven to eight feet. When they're annoyed or attacked they vomit a noxious stomach oil at their assailants. A very prominent nasal tube.

"Big pearly chicks growling and making threatening beak gestures. A chick's pale salmon beak. The adults growl heavily if you approach too suddenly. Brian Glass checking chicks, empty nests, eggs, empty-nest sitters. He was careful, gentle, slow in approaching, was therefore able to relax the birds, examine an egg, grab a petrel by the bill. Guthridge and I stood apart from him while he worked and made notes. A giant petrel sometimes had difficulty getting airborne. Not a pretty bird. A pretty one is the snow petrel, a nervous one Wilson's storm petrel, a cocky one the skua. Glass is a student ornithologist from the University of Miami."

Behind two birds was the massive curving ice snout beyond an inlet. An adult bird stood up and spread its wings as Brian Glass approached it. The chick, seated in the nest, observed Glass closely. "Ugly" is a word to be used carefully inasmuch as it's anthropomorphic, but one can say with caution that the giant petrel is ugly with its huge bill and large nasal tube. It's a wonderful glider. Glass squatted close to the birds, moving slowly. He wore a red indoor parka of a rather soft material, a wool cap, black trousers, leather work gloves and carried a blue rucksack. A parent bird opened its beak threateningly at him. He grabbed the bill. The bird looked unsettled, ruffled as it stood aside, revealing a single white egg. Glass made notes on a clipboard. A closeup of a nest showed some brown earth, moss, a depression amid empty limpet shells, and four or five large feathers: all set in the lap of the rocks. The giant petrel eats limpets and disgorges the shells. This was a home.

A moody, overcast sky with suggestions of cloud shapes and bluing-water hue. Mild gray of the rock foreground against water, distant bright bergs, sullenly beautiful sky. Fluidity of liquid, and hard edges of the angular, teeming rocks. Black-backed gulls, mosses, lichens. Guthridge wearing soiled red indoor parka with hood up, gray trousers, black moccasin boots, yellow leather work gloves, and carrying a large green net. Dark green dull background of a nest, and an adult bird warning him by growling, thrusting its neck forward and opening its bill. Flat stretches of brown-green moss. The chicks were light gray and furry, downy. Adults had dark bodies, mottled heads and necks. I wondered how long their kind had nested here, as I had wondered how long the Adélies had lived on Torgersen.

I was at last having enough exercise after having been deprived of it on the *Burton Island*, yet I could still feel the ship in my bones. It was fine to climb about, to feel raw rock underfoot, and it was exciting finally to come to grips with the Antarctic Peninsula, even if it might be only an illusion that I was coming to grips with it and even if I was doing so only on minor offshore islands of a single minor harbor. Yet I now discovered I had developed a powerful taste for the Southern Ocean, its mists and brash, its wild swells and birds, its wandering icebergs, its emptiness of human traffic, its at times exquisite beauty, which seemed to me to parallel the exquisite fragility of many of the continent's ecosystems. Life-rich sea, life-barren land: My love of Antarctica had grown, I now understood, to embrace the Antarctic waters washing the desolate continent and sending health to the world ocean.

Toward the end of the excursion, wanting to experience the place alone, I separated from Guthridge and Glass. We were still high above the beach and among a great sprawl of outcropping rock. They climbed up a rocky bank and disappeared while I stood viewing my surroundings. I heard the screams of skuas attacking them. I felt a little strange because I had left my companions. I trusted they didn't misunderstand. I needed to

BEYOND CAPE HORN

stop doing things and simply to stare, even if it was only at rocks, inlet, ice piedmont, two giant fulmars soaring high, and to listen to other sounds than our own voices and footsteps: stirring of wind, adjustment of snout ice, rustle of brash. And I felt it was essential to my well-being that I hear, at odd moments for which I was grateful, just silence. I needed by staring, by opening myself up, making myself vulnerable in some way, to lessen the psychological distance between me and my surroundings, even between me and something as prosaic and plentiful as the dolerite rocks.

It suddenly occurred to me that there was always some noise at the station. Even at night you heard the generators going in the power plant. And for twelve days and thirteen nights on the icebreaker there had been the endless noise of engines. I now realized I was fatigued by the pollution of silence and that, strangely, I was suffering from silence deprivation while on the world's most silent continent (most silent, that is, when the winds don't blow). I remembered the silence of Taylor Valley, the silence of Land's End on Cape Evans, the silence of other Antarctic places, and it seemed now possible to me that at times it was the Antarctic silence as well as the beauty, grandeur and solitude, the great Antarctic silence which could resemble that of an anechoic chamber, that had moved me to tears.

I remained in the area until my two companions appeared on the bank above me and climbed down. We proceeded in silence downward to the beach. Glass was a cool, blond, young man, absorbed in his work and very taciturn. He wore a beard and mustache. I noticed that he was cool not only in the field but at the station, not only to me but to others as well. He never spoke to me unless I addressed him first. Whenever I did he was always responsive and respectful. He struck me as a very competent person. He was going to winter over here. Guthridge was beardless, of medium height, wore glasses, was handsome and thirty-five. He tended to be a bit formal with me for the most part but he was very cordial nevertheless. Actually, it was he who most of all in the Division of Polar Programs of the National Science Foundation was responsible for my project and its success, and he gave me many times more than ample indication of his genuine goodwill toward me and toward what I was about.

"Sloman, Swithinbank and Lawrence came over to Palmer in the afternoon for drinks. Some of the Fids had stayed for lunch. Sloman told Guy he had turned down a request from a Royal Marine to travel on the *John Biscoe* in the style I had suggested [sleeping on deck or in a lounge in order to get passage back to Palmer] and that therefore he had to say no to me too, especially inasmuch as I was a writer and would tell about it. (Laughter by all.) Guy and I decided I'd board the *Bransfield* anyway.

"At about 2:30 P.M. Captain Lenie suddenly sent word around the station that the *Hero* would depart at three o'clock. Originally it was due to leave 'no later than six,' but 'with passengers most welcome at the last minute.' Laughter about his predictable unpredictability. Guthridge furiously and amusedly packing, hurrying to the ship. Many of us at dockside to say goodby. The *Hero* slid away at 3:20, let go three blasts of its horn, quickly rounded Bonaparte Point and disappeared from view."

As I stood on the jetty and watched the *Hero* slip away I had many mixed feelings. Above all I romanticized the ship, which had a much more intimate relationship with Antarctic waters than the icebreaker. Perhaps I would not have fully appreciated the *Hero* had I lacked the icebreaker experience. The *Burton Island* was large for me, restrictive, and my relations with the ocean were lessened accordingly. Also, it was a military vessel, with military formalities. The *Hero* (even its name was romantic, let alone its association with Nathaniel Palmer's 47-foot sloop) seemed like an outcast, a half-breed, almost a pirate ship by comparison. And its versatility in being able to navigate shoal waters as well as deep ones also excited my imagination. Not to forget that it was devoted to basic science and its logistic support, and I had nothing but admiration for such a cause and mission. In this latter sense it was perhaps poorly named, for Palmer's *Hero* had been a sealer, and his discoveries had been motivated by commercial profit. Paradoxically, there was a certain exoticism about its going off to Tierra del Fuego. Drake Passage, Beagle Channel, Strait of Magellan: what rich associations and daydreams these names conjured up. And yet it was more exotic to be on Anvers Island, was it not? Certainly it was more difficult.

In any event, as I stood there I wondered how the crossing of the Drake Passage would go for Guthridge and Elliot and how my own crossing would go and what mail if any the ship would bring back for me, and I felt very grateful to Guthridge, who had been of important, spontaneous and intelligent help to me, and I regretted certain moments of abrasion between us which I recalled from Scottsdale, Arizona, and I thought of him carrying part of my Antarctic journal now, which made me feel strangely bonded with him, and this moment felt heady in its complexity, a pleasant disorientation for a change, for all was going well, I had reached Palmer, my human relations were good here and I was about to go off myself but in the opposite direction: *south*, a word with exciting connotations for me.

"I went to Warburton's gear from 5 to 6 for his daily communication with Reno. This time there was no trouble."

From the station walkways you had intimate views of the glacial cliffs, snout and brash field on your left, the brash heaving with a current or wind or with a swell caused by a recent calving, and you enjoyed the brisk air with its taste of snow, and the feeling of cold penetrating deep into your skin, for you crossed from one building to the next wearing only indoor clothes. You realized then how intimately you could live in two worlds so close together, and this made you feel special: the indoor world of the station, with its music, magazines, whisky, hot food and its communications with civilization, and the outdoor world of the rocky, now watery but mostly icy Antarctic, which you never quite took for granted. This was when the *Hero* was away. When the ship was at the jetty you could live in three worlds, for the vessel had its own self-contained one, although while moored it ran an electrical umbilical cord to the base's power plant.

You were always on the alert for something unusual on land, harbor or ice: an unexpected Weddell seal sunning itself on the bouldery beach, a leopard seal swimming in the harbor, an unusual-looking rock, a heretofore overlooked tuft of moss, an odd growler or bergy-bit, a flight of blue-eyed shags, a sudden immense growling in the snout and then a calving there in a vertical collapse of ice suggestive of an old and massive building falling straight down as if from too much living but actually brought down by wreckers' skillfully placed dynamite. Often I told myself that some time I would leave the walkway and climb down to the beach to have a look there, but the reality was that I never had or made the time; while at Palmer I was usually in a hurry to do this or that, the place was hardly more than a way station for me.

The walkways led to the other building, with its garage, recreation room, ham "shack" (a room in the building), some living quarters, a large refrigerator, large storage areas for hardware gear as well as preserved foodstuffs, and, among other things, Warburton's satellite communications equipment in the rear or landward side of the building and close to the snout. His gear was just inside a side entrance there. His directional antenna was set up just outside, where you felt wonderfully close to the snout, although in actuality you weren't that much closer than when you were in the main building. The illusion of proximity was caused by the lack of man-made structures between you and the glacier. The laundry machines were in a corner of the garage on the ground floor.

The chief experience for me of moving about the station was one of paradox: the spaciousness and luxury of it all despite the base's smallness. There seemed to be a superfluity of everything, from paper towels to machines to food to fresh water to various supplies like leather work gloves to space to neatness. There was no doubt under whose flag this station had been built and was being run. Whenever I contrasted the station's spaciousness with the handful of men who would run it during the winter-over, I felt my mind boggling a bit. If McMurdo was the great "town" of Antarctica, by far the continent's largest station, then Palmer was the continent's luxurious showplace by contrast with the other small stations I had visited or was to visit. My own preference was for two or three less expensive American stations in the Peninsula sector rather than a single really comfortable one.

I was invited to dine on the *Bransfield* but I opted for dinner at Palmer. Shane Williams told me Palmer would have radio traffic with the *Bransfield* each evening at eight, in case I wanted to send messages. After dinner I entered a *Bransfield* launch and was taken to the ship, Shane Williams and Joe Warburton (station manager and chief scientist) coming along for drinks.

10 ✿ First Days with the British Antarctic Survey

WHEN I TURNED IN, the *Bransfield* was still placidly at anchor in Arthur Harbor. When I awoke, the ship's main engines were throbbing and she was in sea motion. She had steamed out of Arthur Harbor at 6 A.M.

The ship was named for Edward Bransfield, Sailing Master of the Royal Navy and one of the Antarctic's earliest explorers. Intent on claiming new land for England, he sailed in the ship *Williams* (with William Smith, discoverer of the South Shetland Islands, as master and pilot) and reached the islands in January 1820. Exploring them in January and February, he made a rough chart, then sailed southward and probably saw Trinity Islands, after which he proceeded northeastward parallel to the mainland coast and probably saw the Peninsula's northwest coast, which he named Trinity Land. As a consequence of this probable sighting it has been claimed he was the first to see the Antarctic mainland, but a similar claim has been argued respectively for Palmer and Bellingshausen.

Bransfield is the first mariner known to have sailed through the strait named for him which separates the South Shetlands from the Peninsula proper. The strait is some two hundred miles long and about sixty miles wide in a roughly northeast-southwest direction. Bransfield sailed to Elephant and Clarence

171

Islands, part of whose coastline he charted, then went south-eastward until he was stopped by pack ice at 64°50'S, 52°30'W in what later came to be known as the Weddell Sea. He claimed the newly discovered lands for King George IV.

I had begun a new major Antarctic sea voyage, not on the Southern Ocean now but in Peninsula waters, not moving east-ward or northeastward but in a southerly direction, not a closed voyage between points A and B (McMurdo and Palmer) but an open one both in time and place. I had no clear idea when this new voyage would terminate for me, nor did I have a firm notion as to how I would make my way back to Palmer in time to board the *Hero* for her last trip this season out of the Antarctic and back to civilization via Tierra del Fuego. All I knew was that I was extremely happy to be where I was, and that if cir-cumstances prevented me from hitching a ride back to Palmer (by what vessel or its nationality I vaguely hoped to find a ride I didn't know) I could always stay on the *Bransfield* until, in due and leisurely course, after various stops in the Antarctic and sub-Antarctic, it went to Stanley in the Falkland Islands before proceeding to Southhampton in England, and I could fly home from Stanley.

My position was anomalous and ambiguous. Although I was berthed on the Fid deck and dined (a fancy word for the Fid mess room) with the Fids, I had access to the spacious and luxurious wardroom, the seat of the ship's political power. I was much, much older than the Fids, who were mostly in their early and middle twenties, but I liked being with them and being treated as one of them and I enjoyed their informality of grooming, dress, language and behavior. They seemed at times to be free spirits just fresh from a jungle (odd thought inasmuch as we were in the barren Antarctic): young, muscular, long-haired, in many cases mustached and bearded, wearing the strangest conglomeration of what often appeared to be tattered clothes, and clothes that were usually much too large for who-ever was wearing them, often evidencing signs of personal ec-centricity mixed with high intelligence, a combination that charmed me.

I resolved that if I was to be served by them, as was inevitable when it came to meals, I would serve them in turn, and I sought out Tim Stewart, the King Fid, and volunteered to do my share of gash duties. Tim was tall, lean, bearded, serious, a bit forbid-

172   BEYOND CAPE HORN

ding except when he gently smiled or softly replied to you (he wore his title lightly), and liked to walk barefoot almost everywhere on the ship, even at times briefly on the weather decks. It must have seemed strange to him that I, a sixty-two-year-old, was offering to swab the Fid deck, to serve meals and to wash dishes, but his face betrayed no surprise whatever. All he said was, "Your gash duties will be posted on the board," meaning the notice board in the Fiddery, and he walked briskly and barefootedly away toward wherever he had been heading.

I had an English breakfast, with a heavy load of broad bacon that looked and tasted more like ham. Afterwards I spent much time on deck. The sea was mostly smooth and the ship rolled very little. We entered the Bismarck Strait south of Anvers Island, a dangerous passage containing many islands, and made our way slowly eastward toward the mainland. Mountains, passages, bays. The southern end of Wiencke Island. The Danco Coast. This was my first close look at the Peninsula mainland and I was moved by the solitude, the relative lack of signs of man's coming here, and the variety of beauty everywhere. Mountains looked like hills when there was no sense of scale, as there almost always wasn't. And so this was another way in which distance could be deceptive in the Antarctic: vertical as well as horizontal: vertical because of the absence of scale, horizontal because of the extreme dryness (in the nonmaritime parts of the continent) and purity of the air.

A world before man and which man hasn't yet spoiled. For thousands and millions of years it existed and went on existing without him and without any other primates and, so far as we know, without any other indigenous mammals aside from those, like seals, that tangentially, peripherally, visited it from the sea. Strange that the presence of birds seemed to "humanize" the place. Seals didn't do it. Dominican gulls between our ship and glaciers made the latter seem less hostile, more understandable, possibly even more decorative, even though one was staring at huge icefalls and mazes of crevasses. For the birds this was a place where one could make a living. An ice garden, one thought when our wake rippled the water and the ripples emphasized the land. Fifteen gulls scavenging in our wake. Scenes of strong yet serene beauty. Sunlight filtering through the web of flying wings and tail.

Black rock jutting massively out of blue-white mountains. It was lovely to observe icefalls, icespills, crevasse cataracts, a scattering of ice boulders (time-frozen avalanches), all from the safety of your ship perch. This was my first experience of dealing with the Antarctic intimately on a nonicebreaker ship. Clouds enfolding mountain waists. Exposed black ribs, some grayed by distance. The air so good to breathe. How to describe the joy?

Estacion Cientifica Almirante Brown, an Argentine station consisting of several buildings and communication towers, perched on a rocky landspit that tumbled down to Paradise Harbor. Behind and above it were crevassed glaciers and razor-backed mountains or hills. The base, dwarfed by its surroundings, looked fragile among rocky heads, glaciers, sea. We stood off it at around 9:30. It seemed half-real.

Our party went ashore by Gemini, the BAS equivalent of Palmer's Zodiac. Dominican gulls hovered around us, scavenging, alighting on floes—strong black-and-white bodies about the size of a skua. Emerald floe underparts: glowing color. Turquoise and emeralds in the water. A weathered creamy floe carrying a large black rock. A three-quarter moon resembling a cloud bit. Clouds looking like smoke. The Gemini raced back to the ship, throwing bow spray.

We moved southwestward to Wiencke Island, anchored in Dorian Bay, which indents a small peninsula with penguin rookeries along the shores, and sent a party in a red outboard-powered dinghy to inspect a BAS refuge hut at Damoy Point, the peninsula's extremity. As we headed towards the rocky, low-lying shore I saw two huts, one salmon-colored, the other the hue of cooked bacon. A huge cap like a glacier arched massively beyond the huts and swooped like a great white sand dune almost to the beach itself.

Gray rocks, gray water. Dolerite outcrops, some in the shape of boulders, many of the latter frost-split, cracked, fallen, partly snow-covered. A solitary Adélie greeted us at seaside, stared, quacked. The *Bransfield* waited off the coast, its red hull very visible, its superstructure looking unusually high. We boated as far ashore as we could, then made our way on foot from rock to slippery rock. The icecap, looming, suggested a moist gray sky.

We entered the cozy, prefab, wooden salmon hut. I presumed it was painted salmon-colored for greater visibility.

Windows were checked to make sure they were intact against wind and snowdrift. The coal supply for the stove was examined. And survival foods and gear were carefully inspected. I was reminded of refuge huts I had occupied on Capes Royds and Evans on Ross Island, but this hut was larger. It was important to BAS because Damoy Point was a transfer station early in the austral summer season before ships could move farther south than here. A ship could land personnel at the Point who could be flown to more southern bases by Twin Otter. Thus BAS was able to achieve a longer field season. Obviously one could not depend, in Antarctic weather and with the marginal harbor features of Dorian Bay, on an umbilical connection between ship and shore or between land and air, and it was essential that men could survive ashore if they were stranded. A number of marooned men could have lasted for months in the hut.

The "Argies" (pronounced *are-gheez*), as the BAS people referred to the Argentines, had left cheeses, candies and other goods, mostly tinned, in return for stores they had consumed during a normal visit. My companions were pleased with what had been left. Fascinated by the Argentine goods in their wrappers printed in Spanish, I experienced a quirk or a peculiar slippage of my mind in that I found myself doubting I was actually "under" South America, under Argentina, south of Cape Horn and the Drake Passage, that I had really traversed a significant part of the Southern Ocean and was no longer south of New Zealand. The goods, but especially the wrappers and the automatic belief of my British companions in their authenticity, brought home to me in an immediate way that Argentina was indeed involved in the Antarctic (as Chile was, and I recalled the Chileans from Yelcho Station who had dropped in by dory on Palmer), that some of its citizens were part of the Antarctic brotherhood and therefore by definition close to me, and that despite the conflicting territorial claims of Argentina and the United Kingdom, I was seeing and hearing visual proof that at least in the field, away from the power centers, the national capitals, international cooperation was still viable— even vividly so. There are various reasons for this, among them the internationalizing influence of basic science and the need for all to survive in the extraordinarily hostile environment. I was moved to hear my BAS friends speak warmly of the Argies, and this evening I would learn how Argies had risked their lives to search for the remains of British young men killed on an Antarctic mountain.

This was a new kind of mental slippage for me but it reminded me of another sort that I had described in *Edge of the World:* the difficulty of making a thorough working transition between the temperate regions and the Antarctic one. I remembered for example how I imagined seeing cobwebs in the rafters and corners of Shackleton's hut on Cape Royds—until I caught myself in surprise and reminded myself that there were no spiders in Antarctica, just as there were no flies, cockroaches, mosquitoes, ants, black gnats. I was somewhat accustomed to moving between radically different longitudinal regions at a low latitude and by air but it was clearly taking me some time to adjust to the fact that I had been transported a long distance longitudinally by ship and at a very high latitude, where the longitudinal meridians converge.

In short, I was still getting used to being in the Peninsula area and to digesting certain facts emotionally and imaginatively which I knew very well intellectually: that the region differed from the rest of the continent not only because of its maritime climate and its proximity to South America but also because it was *the* international sector of Antarctica. Another difficulty for me probably stemmed from the fact I had never been to South America and as a consequence I found it hard to grasp that I was close to it, and that as soon as mid-March, which paradoxically seemed both very distant and very close, I would be visiting Tierra del Fuego and Buenos Aires.

We went outside. Scuddy clouds, dappling light. And then a strange oval hole in the clouds, revealing a mountaintop. The metallic brilliance of sunlit rough waters: bands of platinum and a showering of silver coins. White mountains bristling with fierce light. Small bergs of dense, striated blue ice. The water indigo. The *Bransfield* had swung round. Its bow now pointed at us.

Ron Smith and a companion had gone wandering up the great white back of the icecap but remained visible as two tiny figures. Ron Smith, thin, trim, tall, wore hiking knickers, heavy woolen khaki socks, heavy boots, an anorak and a rucksack. The knickers and knee-length socks would have seemed odd at any American Antarctic station. Our party being ready to return to the ship, a couple of men tried to call Ron Smith and his buddy back but the wind frustrated them.

Charles Swithinbank, using his little portable radio, asked the ship to signal them with a blast of its horn. The blast was so feeble it only served to amuse us.

"Can't you do a bit better than that?" Swithinbank asked the ship.

More feeble blasts, now answered by guffaws.

The two men finally noticed our waving and came down.

We had arrived at near high tide. When we returned to the beach we discovered that the dinghy was fast on large rocks. We began struggling to free it.

A voice from the ship asked us by radio, "Would you like us to throw you a line and pull you off?"

It was a joke. The ship was much too far from us for a line. We realized we were being observed with binoculars from the bridge.

"No, thank you, we've just freed ourselves," Swithinbank said urbanely in his precise, somewhat musical voice.

And indeed we had.

We returned to Almirante Brown to pick up our Doppler party and to take on board a young Argentine scientist who would be visiting the BAS Argentine Islands Station. The sea was ruffled but without whitecaps. Glowering smoky clouds over a semiveiled mountain, a surly sea, muted glacial cliffs, ribbed dark rocks: That was one view. Another showed bits of marshmallow on the water: thirty-five sitting Dominican gulls. And a glowing light in the far distance. And ten gulls roosting on a floe, all facing the same direction: tight little soldiers standing at attention.

Now we headed southward for our night anchorage off the Argentine Islands. Bismarck Strait again (named for the German statesman, Prince Otto Bismarck, in 1874 by a German expedition under the German whaler Captain Eduard Dallman). Butler Passage. Lemaire Channel. Penola Strait. Names very new to me. The ship had much urgent work to do in the south: the dismantling of old Adelaide Island Station and the construction of the new base at Rothera Point.

Ron Smith as well as Charles Swithinbank had urged me not to miss the spectacular passage of the Lemaire Channel, named by De Gerlache for a Belgian explorer of the Congo, and Ron Smith came now to the Fiddery to alert me to the fact that the passage was about to begin. The Channel is about nine statute miles long in a northeast-southwest direction, about half a mile wide at the narrows, and deep, with strong northward currents.

I went to the helicopter deck (marked by a large H; but the ship had no helicopters), where I could see without obstruction to starboard, port and aft. I was blind in our forward direction (southerly) because of the ship's high superstructure. As a consequence fresh scenes leaped at me sidewise. However, there were many interesting scenes behind and to the west of us which I preferred not to miss, as I would have had to do had I taken up a forward position. And I liked the feeling of privacy the flight deck afforded me despite the fact that the deck was probably the most exposed place on the ship. The raw weather acted as a curtain, kept men indoors, and the crew on the enclosed bridge, the bridge proper, who would have been able to observe me had I been forward, had no views aft except from the exposed bridge wings. It was very cold and windy. I dispensed with gloves in order to handle my rangefinder Leica more efficiently. When my hands grew too numb for use I pocketed them in my red USARP parka, the only one on the ship, until they warmed up. Two of my many pockets were small and lined with synthetic fur.

Dark rocky mountains rising fiordlike. Great glaciers. Icebergs. Awesome ghostly light. Mists. Some sunlight in the far southwestern distance. We sailed rapidly. Scenes quickly rose, slipped by, quickly faded. At times we were very close to land. This provided a thrill, gave one a sense of intimacy with—what? Forlorn icescapes, seascapes? The fact that it was late afternoon or early evening, nearing the conclusion of a long first day with BAS, that the light shone from a low angle, that I was alone on the relatively large open spread of helicopter deck while everyone else was doing something else, some watching the movie, many socializing (they were no doubt familiar with the Channel), that it was raw cold and a bit gloomy—all this added to the experience.

Two huge black snowcapped rock towers, with just part of

the caps catching the light. On either side at their base, glaciers spilling into cliffs. Cloudbanks, in places windshredded. The ruffled Channel, dark, asleep, containing white icebits. In the great distance behind us were creamy mountains, violet clouds, touches of blue sky and, spread along the whole horizon, brilliant white dashes: icecliffs. The sea in the north, which we had so recently left, was already asleep, the mountains were nodding, the clouds were busy in their work of spreading moisture, and the blue sky, streaked by faint and partially transparent clouds, was pensive. The light in the north kept changing. Occasionally it would open up dramatically, and suddenly what looked like light-bristling white islands wearing conical caps would rise out of the inky, troubled waters. Nothing seemed to disturb the serenity of the several silhouetted silent Dominican gulls soaring close to us and which, for all I knew, had picked us up at Almirante Brown.

At one point the entire northern scene was indigo except for a narrow golden band just above the horizon, silhouetting mountains that looked like miniatures. The world glowered and the twin black towers lost all light but light filtered through in other places, and a razorbacked black mountain showed a hard white plate at its crest. Twilight-blue glaciers fell toward the Channel. Cottony, smoky clouds wreathed part of it or sailed northward just above it. Immediately to the south, adjacent to the Channel, a mountain rose like a naked black fang that seemed to touch faint, rippled, semilucent banks of cirrus pasted on a span of rich, mouthwatering blue.

How strange it felt to leave the raw helo deck and the very raw natural scenes, hands and face half-frozen, and so soon afterwards to enter the warm large wardroom with the artificial fireplace flames flickering electrically, with the solid good armchairs and sofa, the glass-cased books, the heavy drapes, the thick rugs, a room that suggested fine old London hotels, and to see the ship's officers handsome in their blues, and the civilians in starched white shirts, neat ties and jackets, Bill Sloman in a fine Harris tweed with a handkerchief discreetly showing out of the breast pocket, and all hands sipping fine brandies and conversing in well-modulated, ironic, quipping, dry tones. I not only was but also felt a stranger in this place, with my rough outdoor clothes, including unpolished hiking boots—tieless, jacketless, with my long hair and American accent, my body tingling and my cheeks aflush in the sudden warmth. I was received most cordially: softly, gently by Swithinbank, wittily by Sloman.

There was talk of the three young Fids, based at Argentine Islands Station, who had been killed while climbing Mt. Peary during a holiday last September. After being cooped up in the tiny rock- and ice-bound base during the long winter night, they had crossed the sea ice leading to the mainland (the Peninsula's west coast), reached the summit, radioed the station from there and had not been heard from again.

Mt. Peary is a very conspicuous massif almost 6250 feet high. It has a flat, snow-covered plateau summit with perpendicular cliffs on all sides. The southwestern face is a vast chaotic glacier marked by icefalls and crevasses. An Argentine helicopter, searching for the bodies, had found from the air only a tent and elsewhere a pair of skis stuck in the snow somewhere below the summit. A British land search party from the station was ordered to turn back when it reported it was encountering fast-souring weather. And so everyone was now freshly aware of the Antarctic's predictable hostility to life.

I heard speculation as to the cause of the young men's death. Had they fallen into a crevasse? Off a cliff? Been caught by an avalanche? Died in a storm and been snowed over? The speculation seemed to me subdued, cautious, evasive, embarrassed. Why had the young lives been thrown away? How could such a thing have happened and on such a relatively short mountain and on a mere holiday jaunt? Who was at fault, if anyone? The station commander who had approved the climb? The young men? BAS itself?

I tried to discover exactly what had happened, not as a journalist in order to report the appalling incident accurately but as someone who himself was dealing with the Antarctic and had dealt with it close to tragedy and who wanted to arm himself as well as possible against this exotic, mysterious place that could snuff out lives without a clue. But no one person seemed to know much. I tried to piece together whatever bits of information I could come across, now in the wardroom, later in the Fiddery.

Sloman informed me that a small party would be set ashore

tomorrow morning at Rasmussen Point on the mainland, from which the men had begun their fatal climb, and there in the open wilderness a memorial service would be held, good weather or bad. Big Al, the architect and builder with the huge frame and booming cockneyed voice and the lovely eye wrinkles and smile, had constructed a large memorial cross of English oak, which had been consecrated in a church in England with the parents of the lost men present, and it would be fixed into a rock cairn to which a brass plaque would be added.

Big Al listened silently as Sloman gave me this information.

I had learned in the wardroom that although the current spring/summer austral season was far from ended it had already been a terrible one for the Argentines, whose Antarctic operations were limited to the Peninsula area. Seventeen of their men had been killed and one had lost both legs. Eleven had died in a Neptune aircraft that had slammed into a mountain on Livingston Island, one of the South Shetland group. Six others had been lost in two subsequent helicopter accidents. All three crashes had been caused by the uncertainties of Antarctic weather, as had the crash of a BAS-owned Twin Otter in which miraculously no one had been seriously hurt.

The man who had lost his legs had had the misfortune to be standing in the wrong neighborhood of an anchor chain which had lashed out and hit him just above the knees.

I left my bunk and stared out of the porthole. Brash, pack ice and bergs were moving in and out of a mist-laden bay as if on ghostly errands, occasionally stunning me with electric cobalts, turquoises, watery jades. A troop of blue-eyed shags glided on the smooth water, dove and surfaced in unison.

I was up early, ready to attend the memorial service. We were lying off Argentine Islands Station. One could see nothing of the base, for the weather was scuddy, with fog and large snowflakes. I went to my cabin and stood by in case Sloman or Swithinbank wanted to get in touch with me regarding going ashore. Ron Smith came in and said we wouldn't be landing until around eleven. The tragedy and the thick weather had combined to create a complex mood of uneasiness mixed with lethargy. I oiled my boots with Sno-seal that I had brought from Palmer and I worked on my journal.

After awhile, feeling restless, I went up to the wardroom, where I chatted with Swithinbank. Sloman, joining us briefly, said people were feeling lumpy (meaning emotional), for many had known the three young men who had been killed. I returned to my cabin and resumed work on my journal. There were blasts from the ship's horn because a launch coming from the station to the ship got lost in the fog-snow and needed the horn for guidance. Lunch, normally served at noon, was delayed until one. A messenger from the captain came to the gashroom or scradge palace (mess hall) and said very few Fids would go ashore. A complaint from the Fids changed this.

Later Ron Smith, entering our cabin and stretching out on his bunk, informed me the service had gone smoothly but that it had made people very tired, for it had stirred deep emotions. The ship now, at 4:30, departed the Argentine Islands via French Passage, bound southwestward for the southernmost point of Adelaide Island, some 230 statute miles away, via Grandidier Channel, Crystal Sound, Matha Strait, Hanusse Bay, the Gullet and Laubeuf Fiord.

In the Fiddery after dinner Tim Stewart, the King Fid (elected by the Fids), informed me I would be a gashman tomorrow, duty I would share with Andy Smith, and I saw that my duty was duly listed on the Fiddery bulletin board. Andy, a roundfaced, large, somewhat overweight, very affable and intelligent young Ph.D., outlined for me what we would have to do together. Beginning at 7 A. M., we would clean the Fiddery, sweep and mop the Fid deck passageways, hand out breakfast in the gashroom, wash dishes, hand out lunch, wash utensils, dishes and pots, hand out dinner, wash pots, dishes and utensils, sweep and mop the gashroom and mop up the bogs (head).

I was up by alarm clock at 6:30 and proceeded with my gash duties. The psychological distance between the Fids and me decreased immediately despite the fact that I was having difficulty understanding their dialects and they were having all kinds of trouble making out my Yankee-talk. It was important to have a functional role in the Antarctic. To be too much the observer was to be too much the outsider. I had given this problem of participation a good deal of thought back in the States and had decided for literary as well as social reasons to try to be a functioning part of whatever groups I encountered in the Antarctic.

When Swithinbank invited me to visit Adelaide Island Station and to observe some of the offloading that was to be done today I hurried to prepare myself. We left the ship from the main deck by a rope ladder that swung above a ten-ton metal scow lashed to a powered launch. Launch and scow had been winched separately down to the swelling sea.

The least pleasant moment came when I stepped backward off the main deck into what felt like naked space and felt around for a ladder slat until my boot found it, and then began lowering myself over the side, temporarily gripping an upper slat or the deck's gunnel. Another undelightful moment was in leaving a heavy metal craft to ascend the ladder. If the swell was high and my craft was wildly rolling or pitching or both, and rising and falling dramatically, I had to mount the gunnel and grab the ladder at the craft's crest and swing myself up rapidly, otherwise the craft might slam against my legs instead of against the ship's hull. At such times the maindeck men wisely gave me a short length of ladder in order to spare me the temptation of trying to ascend it at a bad moment. But the ladder was also in motion, swinging from side to side and away from the ship and toward it, and at such times it seemed to be tantalizing me. I thought I had it, I touched it, and away it went. Meanwhile men were waiting to follow me and I was aware of anxious faces above me peering over the main deck's gunnel.

People around me on the main deck seemed to hold their breath whenever I prepared to go over the side, no doubt because of my age, and occasionally someone would urge me to be careful, as if for some peculiarity of character I needed to be reminded of my mortality, and this troubled as well as flattered me. I knew I was slower than most but I didn't need the suggestion that I might imminently injure myself, which only increased the risk that I might. I usually carried a fair amount of gear, including a rucksack and cameras, and on returning to the vessel from a trip ashore was often loaded down with collected rocks. Eventually I heard that someone had indeed fallen off a ladder (I believe on the *Bransfield* and that it was a relatively young person), bounced off a gunnel below, fallen into ice-crowded water and not been seen again. I don't remember when this happened. After hearing this I stopped minding my friends' overt solicitude for me. I realized it would have been most embarrassing for them to lose their American guest and to have to radio the National Science Foundation in Washington, "Sorry but your man got himself killed," and I determined to do all I could to spare them such a message.

Adelaide Island, discovered in 1832 by a British expedition commanded by John Biscoe and named by him for Queen Adelaide of England, and first surveyed by a French expedition under Charcot in the early part of the present century, is eighty statute (seventy-three nautical) miles long in a northeast-southwest direction and averages more than twenty statute miles in width. It lies eastward of the Loubet Coast and contains a mountain range that runs the length of the island. On the western shore is the vast Fuchs Ice Piedmont, named for Sir Vivian Fuchs, Antarctic scientist, explorer and former director of the British Antarctic Survey, whom I had met in Cambridge, England, in the spring of 1975. Adelaide Base was on one of the southernmost capes of the island and exposed to the broad sweep of Marguerite Bay in the south and to the Southern Ocean in the west.

Both Swithinbank and Sloman had told me this morning that they regarded it as great good fortune that no lives had been lost and no serious injuries sustained in the years the base had been operated, and that the selection of the base's site had been a mistake. The first hut at Adelaide had been constructed in 1961. They felt they had probably just about used up their luck and didn't want to challenge the fates any longer. Another reason for giving up the station was that deterioration of the icecap above it due to local warming of the climate and man-caused pollution made it increasingly difficult to land Twin Otters on the ice runway and to travel over snow between the runway and the base proper. At present a skeleton staff manned the base, which would be closed down permanently at the end of the austral summer season.

The idea of moving to a new station had come two years ago and an extensive search had been made before Rothera Point, on the island's eastern side and overlooking Laubeuf Fiord, had been decided on. The irony was that Rothera had originally been the site selected, but sea ice conditions had made it impossible to work with it at that time. I had heard it grumbled a number of times that Rothera had been named for an "obscure"

184   BEYOND CAPE HORN

BAS surveyor and that the station should be renamed for someone more prominent. I had wondered how Rothera himself would have responded to that.

Adelaide Base felt, like Palmer, marginal, clinging as it did to a small rocky cape or head, a huge icecape looming above it. The station did not look like its true self now, for the process of abandoning it was well under way. It was strange to feel heavy snow underfoot. I hadn't experienced walking on snow this season except for the day when I photographed the killer whales in McMurdo Sound. An uphill walk from the jetty to the station proper. Very dark sky—lavender—behind red hutlike buildings set on rock. A raw day with wind. People heavily dressed, many in red suits. A white lifeboat on shore some distance from water. The ship's white superstructure prominent, its red hull subdued. A weathered berg poking its jagged white head above a mass of snowstained dark headland rocks. Vehicle tracks in the snow roadway. The Union Jack flying from a pole anchored in the crest of a small rock hill. An old weathered hut with vivid blue piping. Lots of stuff lying about outside, waiting to be hauled away: piles of snow-covered wooden crates; black fuel drums; heavy black cables. A tracked vehicle was winch-loading the scow.

There were unpleasant things for me about the place: packed slick snow on which it was hard to stay upright without fresh cleats or crampons; ice-covered steep wooden stairs you could break your neck on; a feeling of rawness and desolation and of imminent transition to something worse: to abandonment, to being a frozen tiny ghost town in the vast middle of a frozen nowhere. I wasn't unhappy to leave: brief look, brief departure.

I boarded Big Red, the metal scow now very heavy with retrogaded crates. I sat on a crate in the after end, facing aft, Sloman and Swithinbank standing there facing forward. It was safer not to stand and they had insisted I occupy one of the very few places where one could sit. Soon after we left the jetty the sea grew rough and gave us sheets of intensely cold spray. I took heavy whacks of spray across my back. I was surprised by their strength. Swithinbank and Sloman were rapidly drenched. The wind now was loud. Leaning forward, I discovered the ability of my USARP pile cap to hold seawater. Water ran down off the brim in a stream. I joked with Swithinbank about this.

His Russian-made leather cap had no such talent. Luckily I had waterproofed my boots, so my feet were still dry, but my double gloves (woolen liner and leather shell) were soaked, my parka glistened with water, and my open throat and upper chest and my legs in their cotton corduroys over thermal longjohns were sopping. Glancing around, I saw that everyone was thoroughly wet and I remembered, perhaps for the first time, that this was Antarctic water, part of the world's coldest ocean, which we were becoming intimate with and which seemed to rise up higher than our gunnel as if to embrace us the better. Barrie Bromby, the chief officer (first mate), joked about the sea here living up to its reputation.

The launch maneuvered us alongside the *Bransfield* and we began to rock violently. The high swell slammed us against the ship's hull. The launch tried to keep control of the situation but was rapidly losing it. The scow lurched violently in a roll and the crates moved suddenly about. The wind was blowing now at forty-five knots.

The scow began to ship water. Whenever it pitched it looked as if we might go under, and the men in the launch began preparing to cut loose in order not to go down with us. A rope ladder hung ridiculously high above us on the *Bransfield*. The launch did its best to press us against the ship or to draw us away when nearness to the hull was too dangerous but it was now our captive. No one said anything. Cargo began to be winched out of the scow on pallets, looming above us, the wind heaving it. People were working urgently, rapidly, and not with the greatest of care. It was awesome to see the cargo lurching upward above you and to feel utterly helpless. There was no place to hide except in the death-cold sea.

Sitting there, I thought, "So now I'm doing it again, fooling around with Antarctica. I'm going to get myself killed one of these days, maybe now." And I wondered briefly what I thought I was doing there at my age, in that broad naked stretch of flesh-freezing sea, slamming against the *Bransfield*'s towering red metal hull, remote even from Ushuaia in Tierra del Fuego, the world's southernmost town.

The crates in the scow were moving violently about, and if one was not injured by one of them one might be hurt by something dropping off a rising pallet, or by the huge, swinging iron hook that was lowered to us for its pallet load. A Fid, missed closely by the hook, scrambled into a niche of the metal prow and seemed to do it as rapidly and instinctively as an animal might or as a ballet dancer who had practiced the part many times. I thought, "Nice to be young."

Barrie Bromby finally shouted to the main deck that we must be taken out quickly in a rope net, that this was the only way. There were shouts to the deck for a rope net to be lowered to us. They seemed imperfectly understood in the noise of the waves, the wind, the creaking of crates, the slamming of the launch against the scow and of the scow against the ship.

I spotted Brian Moore, a radio man, on the deck and cried, "Brian! A rope net!"

He glanced at me, signalled that he understood and disappeared. Seconds later a net was thrown down to us.

"Go ahead, Charles!" Swithinbank cried.

I scrambled on hands and knees like a wet dog across a world of heaving wet crates to the place where the net was being untangled by Barrie Bromby. Several others, including Bill Sloman and Ron Smith, got inside the net with me. We grabbed hold of the net and each other.

"Don't worry, Charles, we've never lost a journalist," Bromby said.

The hook descended, attached itself to us and up we went. It was the kind of physical intimacy human bodies strange to each other rarely experience. And then we stood solid on the main deck, which felt remarkably still.

It was raining hard now, something I hadn't noticed. I ran up a little flight of stairs to a place partially protected against the weather and from which I would have a better viewing angle in taking shots of the second and last human load to be ropenetted aboard. The swell was deep, the sea dark lead. I remember how strange it was to see human bodies treated (and treat themselves) like so many packages of meat, tossed into a bundle, hauled up like fish. Standing inside, in the middle of the rising net, was Swithinbank still wearing his old Russian leather cap gotten while living at a Russian station. There were others inside the net with him but most, all young, clung to the outside, using the rope mesh for handholds and footholds. Two were bareheaded and head-drenched. Barrie Bromby, wearing his tangerine waterproof suit and his black cap, clung to the net casually with his usual graceful style. Three men below—two in the launch, one in the scow—craned to watch.

Launch and scow were still lashed together fore and aft. A blue-suited, blue-hooded young man stood in the cockpit, which contained a red-and-white life preserver marked BRANSFIELD/STANLEY FI (Falkland Islands). The swell caused the launch to roll heavily toward the scow. The launch aft man, green-suited and wearing an orange hood and red gloves, threw out an arm at the scow to brace himself and fell onto a little housing. Spray shot high between scow and launch, drenching him. The cockpit man clung to a post. The dark water was threaded with bubbles. The launch righted itself, the scow heaved upward.

Over the gunnel the net came, twisting round and round. A green-suited, powerful, heavy-bearded, long-haired man, wearing a blue woolen cap and with a large sheath knife strapped to his waist, signaled to the crane operator on a higher deck. The net was set down on a litter of nets.

Unloading the rest of the crates, people were urgent and a bit careless, and a crate fell from its crowded pallet into the scow. But by now, luckily, the few men still below were in the launch. The scow when empty was hoisted up and then the launch was brought on deck. Some of the young men in the launch had been badly flung about and there was concern for their safety. But no one had been injured and no one had gone into the Antarctic sea. A sea rescue at this time might have been very awkward, and the sole BAS doctor in these waters, a young man himself, was currently at Rothera Point.

I went to my cabin, hung parka, cap and gloves in the drying room, dried and cleaned my camera carefully, made photographic notes. My feet were still dry, my trousers and shirt were evaporating nicely on me. It was less trouble to leave them alone than to change clothes. Ron Smith came in to invite me to have tea in the wardroom.

11 ❋ Glimpses of My Life on the "Bransfield"

11 FEBRUARY. It snowed heavily. I spent a good deal of time chatting with Sloman and Swithinbank. The latter and I had a long talk about the need for humanists in the Antarctic to bridge the gap between basic science and the general public. He said the public knew very little about Antarctic programs and problems, yet could control their destiny by affecting appropriations. He expressed pleasure that I, a humanist and a literary writer, was working in the Antarctic and hoped I would continue to work in Antarctica a long time to come. He had finished *Edge of the World*, which I believed he respected, for our friendship seemed to have deepened since he had read it. Sloman was now reading the book.

After dinner I went to the wardroom. Quiet drinking there, mostly port last evening, now chiefly brandy. You paid for your drinks, keeping score in a ledger. There was much mutual treating. Sloman asked me if I found their wardroom "stuffy" and if I thought them to be "stereotypical Englishmen."

"Not at all," I replied, "but then I should warn you that I'm prejudiced. I'm an Anglophile."

At times literary subjects were raised. Sloman admired Saul Bellow's *Herzog*. I felt very comfortable on the ship, both physically and psychologically. People turned in around midnight, after which Swithinbank and I were alone, standing at a window and looking out at ghostly gray bergs drifting by extremely close to the ship. He thought them benign.

He reminisced about his Antarctic experiences in a soft, slow voice. He had great range and depth of Antarctic experiences, an excellent memory and a quietly expressed but passionate love of the continent. I felt honored by his reminiscing to me at length. He spoke mostly about very human matters, of hairy times, for example of sledging on the Beardmore Glacier in the Transantarctic Mountains, the glacier traversed by both Shackleton and Scott, and of close calls in aircraft. Not all the experiences he described were his own personally. And he talked about life at a Russian station where he had wintered over. I felt a great fondness and respect for him.

12 FEBRUARY, SATURDAY, LINCOLN'S BIRTHDAY. From the ship's log: "Vessel departed Adelaide at 0600 [6 A.M.], arrived off Rothera 0830. Discharge of the vehicles and the setting up of moorings took place until an unsuccessful attempt was made to moor at 2000 [8 P.M.] and the vessel proceeded to anchorage off Jenny Island, arriving 2330 [11:30 P.M.]."

I had joined BAS the evening of the 7th with the idea of observing the construction of Rothera Point Station. I had been on the *Bransfield* only four days but they seemed a good deal longer, for much had happened in them. Now, this morning, I was finally having a look at Rothera but only from a distance and from the ship. The ice-covered weather decks were dangerous for the slick-soled, worn-down boots I favored. Twenty-nine degrees Fahrenheit and fifteen to twenty-knot winds, so it didn't take long to get thoroughly chilled if you were lightly dressed. A recent three-inch snowfall obscured much of the base that was normally snowfree.

The approaches to Rothera were very fine. Snowcapped mountains both on islands and on the mainland, some with jagged crests. Distant mountains in a blue wash. Dark water troubled by wind. Slashes of platinum among distant islands. Far piedmont glaciers asprawl. Some of the landmasses suggested black breasts veined with white. A small, pale-blue (yet vivid) floe, ribbed vertically, weathered: a tiny object in the foreground, the vastness of things beyond. Nature was so marvelously inventive here and its chief theme was ice.

We drew closer to the new station. Tiny figures and vehicles. Minute bits of color. An antenna tower on the head's highest point. Light, falling through gray clouds, silvered the textured sea, and beyond the silver was the antimony of a piedmont glacier. Snowmantled mountains, brash, glacial head, snout, razorbacks, piedmonts, cumulus: sprawled lavishly. The station was relatively quiet visually with its simple snowcover.

Swithinbank found me in the Fiddery, where I was chatting with Brian Moore, the Fid radio operator, to tell me I was free to go ashore at any time and to check if I had read the base commander's posted telex warnings about crevasses and other restricted areas. Moore had been telling me at length about his jobs at sea. He was a colorful man whom I liked very much.

I envied Scott, Amundsen and Shackleton, who had had much more time to deal with their experiences and who had kept excellent logs and journals (I excluded their sledging journals, written under extraordinary circumstances, and of course I did not have in mind Scott's awe-inspiring last notations, made while he was dying), and above all I envied the young Charles Darwin, who had spent almost five years (four years and nine months) on the *Beagle*, during which he kept logs, notebooks, journals and diaries and gathered much data in the form of plants, birds, rocks and other examples of his broad interests as a naturalist, as a consequence of which, granted always his great genius and not forgetting the financial independence which permitted him to work with a minimum of at least financial distraction (his health was not good), his account *The Voyage of the Beagle* is incredibly rich. I had grown to feel close to Scott and Shackleton, in whose huts on Ross Island I had been privileged to live through the courtesy of the government of New Zealand, huts of which I had been temporary custodian, and now I felt a new intimacy with Darwin because soon I would be navigating the Beagle Channel, named for the *Beagle*, as in a similar way I was beginning to feel close to Francis Drake, whose Passage I was due to cross in the *Hero*, and to Ferdinand Magellan, whose Strait I would overfly on my way from Tierra del Fuego to Buenos Aires. It goes without saying that I was also beginning to have new feelings about Nathaniel Palmer, Edward Bransfield, John Biscoe, Thaddeus Bellingshausen, and that I had by now become closely aware of the

Palmer Archipelago, the Bransfield Strait, the Biscoe Islands, as I had earlier been cognizant of the Bellingshausen Sea and the Weddell Sea.

In the Antarctic it was always painful for me to be torn between the chance to engage in fresh events—"events" were what one had come here hoping for—and the duty to record old ones, even if they were only three days, two, a day old. But I knew too well from painful experiences that however fresh they might at first be they would, without a journal to crystallize, shape and record them, be seachanged into episodes whose newness would deteriorate, and perhaps more rapidly than one expected, into ever less authentic and dependable memories. And after all, authenticity, I liked to believe, was what I was most about. Often I envied those aboard ship who were simply "living life," as if keeping a journal with a larger goal in mind or with a smaller one or with no goal other than the journal itself was not also "living life," and I envied those with a life of action who didn't have to answer daily and at times hourly to a cranky conscience that often cried stridently, "Self-betrayer! The journal, the journal!"

And so I stayed on board and worked, mostly in the Quiet Room, occasionally taking a break by going out to see what was happening. Much offloading of ship's cargo by scow and launches. The hold hatches had been removed, so you could look deep into the ship. People coming and going. Many new faces at dinner yesterday and at lunch today. I amused myself by going to the ship's store, called canteen on the *Bransfield*, where I bought razor blades, soap, shaving cream and three *Bransfield* T-shirts. The canteen was out of heavy sweaters and *Bransfield* plaques. Calum Cumine, the canteen's operator and the ship's purser, promised to sell me one of his own plaques. He said he had two in his cabin.

On my way to the canteen, which was on the second deck, or a deck below the main deck or two decks below the Fid deck, I heard a parakeet in a cabin on the main deck. The crew was quartered on this deck. I knocked on the door. A young steward, pleased by my curiosity and interest, invited me in and introduced me to the bird, which quickly landed on my shoulder, gently pecked my ear lobe and said "Pretty boy Joe" in a way that sounded precisely as if it had been uttered by the throat of its owner. The steward had brought the bird from the U.K. It had plenty of seed food, toys, a little mirror and was in fat shape. It flew happily around the cabin when the door was closed. There was another parakeet down the corridor and the two were sometimes brought together so they could play and exchange gossip. There were no insects visible on the ship. I thought of them when I observed this citizen of the low latitudes. Apparently they all died out by the time the vessel reached the Antarctic.

I spoke with Peter Fitzgerald ("My name is Peter but people call me Tweaky"), who was leaving the Antarctic after serving two years there with BAS. He had been stationed both at South Georgia and at Argentine Islands as an ionosphericist and was coming out to do Doppler work. He had boarded the ship during our layover at Argentine Islands. He would help set up an antenna at Rothera Point. Although in his early twenties, he gave me the impression of being about thirty. I wondered why. What had aged him? He was a handsome man with clear, sharp blue eyes but gave the impression of being extremely absentminded. At first, because of this screen, I wondered if he was intelligent and educated. I soon realized he was both, and not only intelligent but highly so. Whether his absentmindedness was affected I'm not sure, but I tend to doubt it. I was not unaware of the fact that eccentricity has a respected tradition in England. He almost always looked abstracted, even when he was in the midst of a conversation, but occasionally he would come into sudden focus, surprising you. Now and then, very unexpectedly, he would break into attractive, wholesome, infectious laughter that was only tangentially related, or so you felt, to what you and he were talking about. It was as if he had heard a funny, inner voice. If what he was after, either consciously or unconsciously, was to keep you in suspense and surprise, he certainly succeeded, although in the long run, after you got used to him, both surprise and suspense subsided.

He was rather short, with an immense shock of light-brown thick hair. He wore a huge beard and had a scraggly mustache that covered much of his mouth, so that trying to read his lips in the hope of better understanding him was at times a frustrating experience. However, I did not have as much difficulty in understanding his English as I had in absorbing that of many of the

Fids. By contrast, I had little if any trouble making out the wardroom speech. Peter wore baggy light-brown woolen trousers of standard BAS issue, in which he appeared to waddle, and very scuffed standard-issue BAS boots. His wool shirt and trousers were very frayed. He was wiry and had good, strong, blond-haired hands. He smoked a pipe with a tiny bowl, into which he tamped tobacco with the greatest of care with the tip of his pinky. He said he wanted to give up smoking altogether but wasn't prepared to go that far just yet and so he was doing it in stages. He added that he had expensive tastes in tobacco which he really couldn't afford.

I was attracted to him, sought out his company and enjoyed my meetings with him without exception. And apparently he was attracted to me. We both brightened whenever we met each other, and we seemed to have a good deal to say. He seemed more available to me than the other Fids in some special, pleasurable way. I liked the way his mind worked and I admired his honesty and directness in expressing his opinions. I thought that if I had to share a bad survival situation in the Antarctic he was the kind of person I would prefer to do it with, for despite his eccentricity there appeared to be something very sturdy and trustworthy about him.

I liked treating him to mugs of beer, which he drank slowly, methodically but with relish. He insisted on giving me one of his mesh vests (undershirts issued by BAS) because he had heard me admiring such shirts, which I had seen when I had lived with the New Zealanders at Scott Base and which I had meant to buy in Christchurch but never did. The ship's canteen didn't sell them.

Many of the Fids who had put in two years of isolated duty gave me the impression of being eccentric but Peter Fitzgerald was so odd he had the reputation of being somewhat mad both in the Fiddery and the wardroom. In the latter there was a kind of benevolent acceptance and understanding of him. I heard he was an excellent worker. I wondered how he would manage to deal with day-to-day life back in economically pinched England after two years of remote and celibate duty.

As we have noted from the ship's log quoted at the beginning of this day's entry, the vessel tried unsuccessfully to moor at 8 P.M. in what was unofficially called South Bay off Rothera

Point, and then proceeded to an anchorage off Jenny Island, where it arrived at 11:30. The chief disadvantage of Rothera Point as a BAS station was its lack of an anchorage for the *Bransfield*. HMS *Endurance* was scheduled to come here later this month to do soundings of the harbor, but no one expected it to find anything but that the harbor was very deep, too deep for the length of anchor chain the *Bransfield* carried. The *John Biscoe*, a smaller BAS ship, could push its bow gently against the rocky beach and stay in place. It was short enough to back out. But the *Bransfield* couldn't do that. It had a single screw, which meant that it swung to port on backing out. If it had had twin screws, like the windclass icebreakers such as the *Burton Island*, it wouldn't have swung out of control that way and possibly could have used this harbor. The other side of the Point, which was unofficially called North Bay, was rather shallow and had a further disadvantage in that bergs and pack tended to congregate there. And so we would commute between Rothera Point and Jenny Island some thirteen statute miles southwest of the base. The *Bransfield* had a good anchorage off Jenny, a rocky island about two miles in diameter and around 1600 feet high, which had been named by the French explorer Charcot for the wife of the second officer of his expedition of 1908–10, Sub-Lieutenant Maurice Bongrain of the French Navy.

13 FEBRUARY, SUNDAY. Ship's log: "Weather too bad to work at Rothera, so vessel remained at Jenny Island anchorage."

From my journal: "Ugly weather, twenty- to twenty-five knot wind blowing both wet and dry snow. We're enshrouded by mists and seaspray. Seaspray against a berg. Jenny Island, off which we're anchored, just barely visible beyond the choppy water.

"The heavy, overcast weather of the Peninsula is a good thing. In the Ross Island sector, especially on the plateau, you encounter the awe-inspiring side of Antarctica that abstracts things, so simplified do they become. Things are at their core. By contrast the Peninsula overwhelms you with scenes and you would become inured, blasé, if the weather didn't let you recover from them. One feels more intimate with the abstractions."

The overcast weather also had a personal value for me. Ever since I had started going to the Antarctic in 1969 I had been subject to facial skin cancer and had had to undergo several minor operations, which had left my face somewhat scarred. Certainly the great amount of ultraviolet radiation there during the austral summer when the sun never set played a part in triggering my cancer. I remember the severe burns I would get while camping out and how my facial skin would come off in shreds. At times I had the feeling the sun was pursuing me and that there was no escape. Often I wished it would go away or just shut down and sometimes I daydreamed about the joys of night. The extremely dry and clean air let much radiation through that would have been screened out in the temperate regions, and in the Antarctic (I'm speaking mainly of the Ross Island sector but I include trips to the great interior plateau) the sun bounced off everything, and "everything" was likely to be ice and snow, and there was usually little if any shelter if you lived in the field and were moving about. No trees. Few shadows.

My first sight of Giles Kershaw occurred when he entered the gashroom one day. He sometimes had a meal there. I took immediate notice of him because he was wearing mukluks of Japanese make of the kind that USARP was issuing this season. They had obviously had a great deal of use and it was equally apparent that he enjoyed being different in wearing them here. Nobody else in BAS wore mukluks, nor did they have any, so far as I knew. As for myself, I had some in my seabags but I didn't find that the Peninsula weather was likely to require them, presuming I ever went far inland once I went ashore. Kershaw, however, flew into the interior and at high altitudes, where they would be invaluable in a survival situation. He had been to McMurdo, to Siple and to the Pole, all of them American bases, and had done some flying this season with RISP (Ross Ice Shelf Project). I learned about this in a conversation with him.

He was a bit taller than middle height, was strikingly handsome, very lean and in excellent physical condition. He had curly, tousled, dark brown hair and a very easy manner that exuded self-confidence but in a surprisingly pleasant way. In someone else it might have generated resentment. Probably the reason it didn't was that one instinctively knew he had the goods to back it up. It was obvious at once that he was "special," that he knew it and was justified in thinking it. He flew in a sort of cowboy fashion, which is to say most casually. I heard a story, probably true, that he had buzzed McMurdo at an altitude of fifty feet earlier this season in his Twin Otter because on approaching Williams Field for a landing he hadn't been able to rouse them quickly enough on his radio. I also heard that the U.S. Navy people at McMurdo had made quite a flap about the incident.

When he flew his Twin Otter in Antarctica he always had his lights on and blinking. This was an oddity inasmuch as it was extremely unlikely that there was another airborne aircraft within hundreds of miles. At the season's end Kershaw and his navigator would fly the Twin Otter northward across the Drake Passage, the length of South America, across the Gulf of Mexico and the United States to Toronto, Canada, where it would be overhauled by the company that had made it.

As I explained in an earlier chapter, BAS had lost one of its two Twin Otters in a crash earlier this season. Kershaw and his navigator were flying the remaining Otter. Swithinbank told me that BAS knew it was incorrect to fly just one aircraft, for in case of an accident to this craft there was no backup plane available for a rescue. But BAS was so hard up for time and money they felt it was essential to fly the one Otter. Swithinbank informed me that if the Otter got into trouble BAS would not ask any other nation to come to its aid. He firmly believed that if BAS were to ask for help in such circumstances it would undermine the good will upon which international mutual aid existed in the Antarctic, for the helping nation would understand that BAS had behaved improperly in depending on only one aircraft and would be reluctant to help again. Kershaw had been told that if his plane went down no attempt would be made to call in outside help. I had my private doubts about this. I felt certain that if a life was at stake BAS would call upon the Americans or the Argentines for help. The situation had been explained to Kershaw, who had been given the option of flying the solitary aircraft or of leaving BAS at this time without prejudice. He had been told that in case of an accident he might have to winter over. He had agreed to continue flying even though he had a young pregnant wife back in England. I heard that he was flying more conservatively than usual, however.

In this connection, I was told a true story about a BAS pilot who had crashed some years ago and had had to winter over after having just spent a winter-over season. Someone at BAS in England had to phone his wife and inform her that her husband's return home would be delayed. After some conferences a woman employee of BAS was delegated to make the call.

"Well, how delayed will he be?" the wife asked.

"A year," was the reply.

The marriage survived.

My journal. "During dinner Peter Fitzgerald, whom I usually call Peter, not Tweaky, raised the point, as he did before, that there's a 'serious rift' between the Fid deck and the wardroom and that the 'supervisory people' (that is, Sloman and Swithinbank) are not doing their 'proper job at its best' when they don't come down to the Fids and get 'the buzz' from them about what's happening here and in the field, now and in the recent past. Peter says they are losing touch. Giles Kershaw debated this view, or at least suggested that the Fids ought to speak up, that probably Sloman and others aren't aware of the rift. Some emotions were aroused. Most of the Fids present seemed to side with Peter. Peter said he would mention his views to Sloman."

While I was with BAS I sensed class structures and distinctions I hadn't ever noticed with USARP. The Fids not only ate and dressed differently from the members of the wardroom, they also, it seemed to me, thought very differently. They were not at the bottom of the heap; there was the crew below them in status, and they were not at the base of financially hard-pressed British society, for they had been educated and had jobs. But by comparison with field employees of USARP their work and time were ill paid, which they knew. They considered the Americans to be lavishly treated and paid. However, the general economic plight at home made many if not most of them feel lucky to have a financial haven, limited though it might be. Unless you had strong connections it was hard to get started at home. It was also very difficult to get into BAS, for the competition was high, many young men applied to go to the Antarctic. In Great Britain the memory of Scott and Shackleton and other great Antarctic explorers was still strong and their deeds were well known. Scott's *Discovery* was moored in the Thames in London, and the famous last entry ("For God's sake look after our people") of his sledging journal was on display in the manuscript room on the ground floor of the British Museum, a relatively brief walk from the *Discovery*, where you could also see several early versions of the Magna Carta, pages of Beethoven and Mozart, and who knew what else.

And so you wanted to join BAS in the hope of professional advancement, either within the BAS structure or outside of it, say in the universities, and for the romance of it, because you were young and strong and had a romantic streak and a desire to travel which you could not afford to indulge with your own means, and because it was a damn sight better than the risk of being unemployed or, almost as bad but not quite, better than the dangers of a petrifying and eventually soul-killing job. I sensed both in wardroom and Fiddery a large gulf between the two as well as a sharp mutual awareness of it of a kind I would have been surprised to discover in USARP and which, I thought, reflected British society as a whole, just as USARP mirrored American society.

In the exchange between Giles Kershaw and Peter Fitzgerald I had the feeling the latter was being unusually courageous in stating his views so openly and that by doing so he was acting involuntarily as a spokesman for less bold Fids who wanted to have similar opinions aired. When he stated, after a pause the length of which seemed to me significant and which was a result, I couldn't help thinking, of Kershaw's goading, that he would go to the wardroom and plainly offer his views to Sloman and Swithinbank, I had the sense he was about to do something dangerous, perhaps risk his career because he might be judged a reckless upstart and troublemaker whose eccentricity had now gone too far, and I thought my apprehension was mirrored by the Fids, but what is much more likely is that I picked it up from them.

To say that Kershaw's position was unusual is a deep understatement. He was so needed by BAS, particularly now that the organization was down to only one Twin Otter, that he could do more or less as he pleased, and there was a freewheeling air about him—a pleasing one, for he was much too genuine and refined for even the suggestion of a swagger—that suggested as much. What supported his style, beyond the fact he had charisma and was an excellent pilot, was that old keystone: money. I had heard it often remarked how hard it was for BAS to fill certain jobs in the Antarctic these days for want of the ability to pay the required high salaries, that is, high relatively speaking, relative to BAS's increasingly restricted budget. As a consequence certain persons, especially ship masters, doctors and pilots, could almost call their own shots, and this was a situation that you could sense troubled and pained administrators and leaders like Sloman and Swithinbank regardless of what their personal feelings and opinions in the matter might be.

Once upon a time, in an era seemingly as remote as fairy tales, a ship master was content to spend a full austral spring/ summer season in the Antarctic, or at any rate was willing to put up with such a condition. Nowadays the *Bransfield* was mastered by two captains during a season simply because that was the best that BAS could bargain for. Stuart Lawrence would sail as far as Stanley in the Falklands, turn the vessel over to his counterpart and fly home to England. It had dawned on ship masters that Antarctic work was tricky, dangerous and exhausting, that the financial rewards were incommensurate and that they were wanted elsewhere at much better pay and infinitely better hours. As for doctors, who but a quite young person with a flair for romance would willingly place himself in a dead end, which Antarctic work essentially was, medically speaking. The Antarctic men were mostly young and fit, the air was bracing, there was plenty of exercise, bugs tended to be dormant, and so there wasn't much that needed to be done and rarely anything unusual, of the sort that could broaden a young doctor's experience and make him more valuable back home. Much better to begin establishing your private practice as soon as possible or lease yourself out to better-paying work and less hazardous, and without the severe prices of professional, social and domestic remoteness.

About aircraft pilots: They were the most independent of all. The Middle East oil nations with their burden of petrodollars and shortage of experienced pilots were a powerful and increasingly irresistible lure. Any individual Fid needed BAS more than BAS needed him, and this held also for any small group of

Fids, but BAS needed Kershaw infinitely more than vice versa, which all concerned well knew.

And so Kershaw was a sort of man from Mars as he sat there in the gashroom arguing with Fitzgerald and insinuating that the latter was not bold enough to make his opinions known to the wardroom. Kershaw, of whom it was rumored on the Fid deck that this was his last season with BAS and that he had already accepted an extremely lucrative job in Saudi Arabia, had little if anything to lose. He moved freely between Fiddery and wardroom, between ship and shore and between land and air, and the wardroom was glad to have his presence no matter how he was dressed. I never saw him dressed there other than very casually, usually in his huge, Japanese-made, USARP, much-battered, formerly white and now dark gray mukluks that had been given him, I believe, in the McMurdo region. I am by no means suggesting that he was anything but immaculate in his social behavior in the wardroom. He was an extremely attactive person in every way.

But Fitzgerald was correct when, in the exchange with him in the gashroom, he pointed out to him that his, Kershaw's, role in BAS was very special and that by its nature he, Kershaw, did not see things as they appeared to the Fids, nor was it so easy to beard the BAS lions as he implied. To Kershaw, it seemed to me, Fitzgerald was a malcontent griping behind his employers' backs rather than to their faces, and was an oddball to boot. There was little if anything that appeared to be substantively eccentric about Kershaw. His oddnesses were purely of style.

"Later we all went to the Fiddery, where I bought Peter a beer. Listening to the Fid chatter, I was very sleepy at times and had trouble staying awake. But then I cried with laughter when Peter told of Argentine Islands Station declining to let the *Lindblad Explorer* bury a tourist passenger at their base. As Peter told it, the old man, of about eighty, was asleep near the shore, waiting to be taken to the ship, and either fell into the water and had a heart attack from the shock, or had the attack and fell into the water. The station declined to accept his body because he hadn't actually died at the base, so he was buried on a small nearby island. The way Peter told it and the images he aroused made the story seem very funny to me even though I realized it was also tragic. I had trouble stopping laughing."

14 FEBRUARY, MONDAY. From the ship's log: "Departed Jenny Island anchorage at 0700, arrived Rothera 0900."

Rothera Point was named after John Michael Rothera, born in 1934, who while a member of FIDS (Falkland Islands Dependency Survey, the predecessor of BAS), was based at Horseshoe Island in 1957 and at Detaille Island in 1958. A surveyor, he completed the triangulation of Arrowsmith Peninsula and adjoining areas in those years. As a landing point, Rothera gave access to the interior of Adelaide Island.

"Fids on the tween deck shoveling out the scow's interior prior to the scow's being winched over the side. At breakfast I spoke with Giles Kershaw about the BAS Twin Otter and about the National Science Foundation possibly buying a couple of Twin Otters for the Ross Ice Shelf Project. Kershaw thinks they would save NSF a lot of money.

"I went ashore at Rothera Point for the first time at about 1:30 with Swithinbank and Sloman. Again the Jacob's ladder down to the scow. The scow lashed to a launch. Pack and brash had entered the harbor since we left it and this caused problems of movement for the launch and scow between ship and shore. I was told the shore is usually snowfree this time of year and all the rocks are visible, but now there was a snowcover of about 18", with drift in places of up to several feet, and this hindered the work of resupply. Floating jetty of empty fuel drums, and a vehicle with a strong winch on the beach."

As I understood it, the chief job at this time was to unload the elements of the main hut, bring them ashore and put up the exterior structure before the summer ended around the *Bransfield's* departure for home waters in mid-March, the equivalent of mid-September in the northern hemisphere. Work would continue on the hut's interior during the coming fall and winter, when the base would be cut off from civilization except for radio communications.

"I made my way up to the temporary main hut, which serves as a galley, dining room and various other things. It was a good climb over heavily rutted snow from the jetty to the hut. Warm and humid inside and there were some pinups I had trouble keeping my gaze from. Met many young and sturdy and bearded Fids new to me. I didn't stay long in the hut. Went out to have a look at the station."

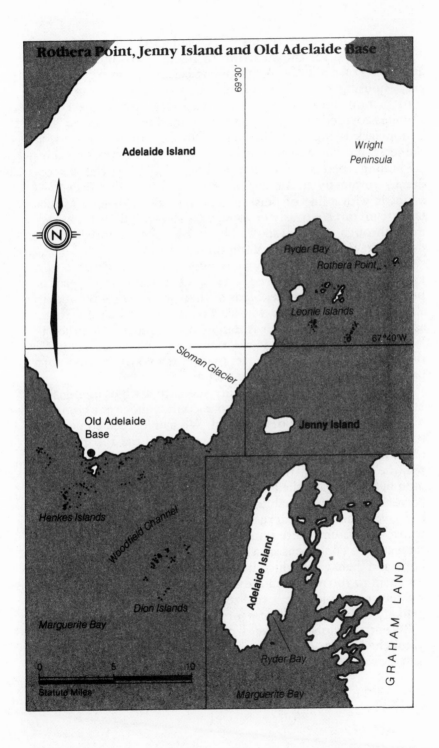

Rothera Point, Jenny Island and Old Adelaide Base

Adelaide Island

Wright
Peninsula

69°30′

N

Ryder Bay

Rothera Point

Leonie Islands

67°40′W

Sloman Glacier

Old Adelaide
Base

Jenny Island

Henkes Islands

Woodfield Channel

Dion Islands

Marguerite Bay

0   5   10

Statute Miles

Adelaide Island

Ryder Bay

Marguerite Bay

G R A H A M   L A N D

Foundation wooden beams of a large hut on concrete blocks, naked, waiting for the structure to begin. Two finished small green huts on a hillside. A row of conical tents, one red, the rest gray, housing men. Five warmly dressed men digging out a construction area. Antennas, a concrete mixer, gear and supplies covered with tarps, sounds of machinery working. The Union Jack flying on a hill. Men offloading the metal scow at the jetty. An orange-suited driver operating a red tracked vehicle pulling a blue cart with automobile wheels. The heavy snow deeply rutted by traffic and hard to walk on. The *Bransfield* majestic with a line of brash behind her, and Adelaide Mountains rising precipitously beyond that, showing their dark rock mass through ice and snow. South Bay slate colored. Black dashes of Weddell seals among the brash.

The close, immediate sight of men, many of whom I now knew and liked and admired, carving up a chunk of wilderness, profoundly disturbed me. Signs of their work and of the inevitable pollution were everywhere. And was I not a part of them, as I was a part of the larger Antarctic brotherhood, even though I could rationalize that I was only their guest, and didn't I therefore share, despite the fact that I was an observer and not a participant, in what they were doing?

True, of course, this was a tiny speck in a white immensity, but the time was long lost when one could believe any common on earth to be infinite or immortal. We had learned some scary lessons about the limits of our biosphere and the apparent lack of limits of our greed wherever a common was concerned, the sea, the air and now this continent that, like every other common before it, gave the absolute impression of being limitlessly powerful and impregnable, as the forests of medieval Europe had given, and the wilderness of the Americas, but a continent whose ecosystems were remarkably fragile precisely because of the extreme conditions in which marginal life managed to exist here, and damage to which it would take great stretches of time for them to recover from if ever. It was not that one was fighting the inevitable, but I realized that the Antarctic was most unlikely to be spared what every common had endured.

"Went off alone westward over rocky stretches and across untouched snow to the huskies chained within sight of the camp, aware of the snow road, marked by fuel drums, leading steeply upward onto the glacier on my left. There are some 45 dogs, two of them pregnant. Those two are in pens. Sank up to my calf in places. The tremendous cries the dogs made as I drew near. Their jumping, howling, wailing, cavorting, and their efforts to extend the reach of their chains. They seemed to be considerably larger than the dogs at Scott Base. Powerful creatures. I hugged a few but there were too many for individual attention, and they were rough, causing me to worry about my camera. Went up to the pens. Curiously, the two dogs there, who had been moaning as if from lack of sufficient attention, now stared silently at me."

Now, despite my solid attachment for certain people on the ship, I felt wonderfully released from human ties even if only momentarily, and perhaps in some senses I was inwardly howling and wailing and moaning and cavorting. Some of the dogs, aside from the pregnant ones, stared at me very intently, as if trying to make some contact much more powerful than a visual one. It was almost embarrassing.

I stared back or talked plainly to them, for there was no human to overhear me. I told them how fine they were, how glad I was to see them, how much I admired their handsome heads and coats. Surely we had a dialogue, for these half-wild animals listened intently, and I responded with surges of wildness and renewal in me, sexagenarian though I was. But I was puzzled by the silent staring of the pregnant bitches. What were they trying to tell me? Something about the state of pregnancy? Or of their isolation from the other dogs? Their embarrassment because, having moaned for attention, they were now receiving it more closely and intently than they had expected? Strangely, they caused me to behave as they did, with a certain inner distance. Even though I was a male I too could feel pregnant, and in this connection I remembered an intelligent woman, who did not intend to have more children, saying, "The important thing is always to feel pregnant with *some*thing."

"Went down to the jetty, shot some scenes there, walked along the very narrow rocky beach leftward. Sounds of beach waters. Gray clarity of the sea. Rocks underwater. And the stern of the *Bransfield* peering from beyond a snowbound point. It was good to be alone, to have escaped from the incessant vibration and small roar of the ship's generators and to hear the lapping of waves. The water looked very inviting, didn't suggest intense cold. Thoughts of taking a brief swim. Frost-shattered gray scree everywhere, and gray boulders of all sizes, and very few erratics, and little rock color. Glacier snouts, mountains, raw gray razorbacked peaks."

The extreme gray clarity of the water as I viewed it on returning to the jetty—small rocks, sand, soft ripples, a pure glasslike quality. I had the extraordinary urge to remove my clothes and jump in briefly, my body seemingly aching to be immersed in this soothingly cold liquid as if I had a fever of mysterious origin, an urge I hadn't had even at New Brighton Beach near Christchurch on that summer day that felt now so long ago. I wondered what would happen if I gave in to my imagining. But then I thought of the water's extraordinary temperature and of my considerable chronological age and how embarrassing it would be if I had a heart attack and became a burden to my hosts, and how much our behavior is based on fear of being an embarrassment, and how many good people, Ernest Hemingway among them, have killed themselves rather than endure this fear.

The icecap at Rothera flowed to the sea edge at South Bay just south of the new station and showed cliffed embayments, impressive in size and hard-edge shapes, where huge chunks had calved off. A tracked red vehicle with a yellow crane was offloading large crates from Big Red at jettyside and lowering them into a blue cart. The Fids working here were dressed drably.

"Went up to the main hut again and had coffee and very good but very hard shortbread and spoke with people, some of whom I knew. Everyone very polite and respectful to me. Brian Moore said he hadn't been able yet to rouse Palmer to pass them my signals of wanting word of my going north. One Fid declared to me, I forget in what context, that President Andrew Jackson had been successfully impeached, and when I disagreed he remained firm. So, smiling, I asked, 'Would you care to put some money up on that?' which silenced him."

It was getting on now, the last scow before dinner was soon to leave, so I hurried down to the jetty, where it was being unloaded, and observed the bay. About eighty blue-eyed shags were swimming in dense formation in two troops of equal number, all facing east and close to a brash field beyond, diving in unison, magically disappearing, staying under a long while, then suddenly popping up far from where they had gone under, and now facing in the opposite direction. It felt precisely as if they were playing a joke on you, a very funny optical illusion.

It was strange, or at any rate I thought I couldn't hope to explain the sensation, how the felt presence of a nearby glacial snout comforted you, perhaps because of all the mysterious recesses which were denied you and which you knew you would have neither the opportunity nor the bad judgment to explore, for huge pieces frequently fell there. Or was this a sexually deprived male's response to the idea of recesses?

"The scow couldn't successfully be pushed by the launch alongside: too much pack. So a line was attached and we were pulled though the pack. At the ship's side the white rope ladder had been shortened considerably. It hung high. This was an intelligent move, for it forced the scow passengers to reach high and to mount the ladder at the scow's crest, thereby diminishing the chance of someone taking to the ladder in a trough and being smashed by the scow coming up to its crest. But it took strength and agility and care to pull off the maneuver, which I wouldn't recommend as an exercise in personal safety. The scow was heaving and the gap between it and the ship often changed and at times grew too wide for crossing. You had to stand on the gunnel to reach the ladder at all, and to reach the gunnel you had to climb onto slippery wet cables piled in a heap and onto boards that structured the scow's side. The gunnel too was slippery, as were the soles of your boots. Even leaving the ladder and getting onto the deck was tricky: few handholds and poor footing. But with care and deliberate motion all went without incident. My hands got extremely cold from touching metal, and the ladder's rope felt as cold and hard as steel.

"After talking with Palmer I went to the wardroom, this time dressed up: whipcord trousers (Abercrombie & Fitch), white shirt open at the collar (Brooks Brothers), Harris tweed jacket. On seeing me enter, Bill Sloman pursed his lips in a silent whistle and arched his left eyebrow in that characteristic way of his, doing both in such an exaggerated manner that everyone noticed it, picked up his cue and took to joshing me about looking so elegant."

Glimpses of My Life on the "Bransfield" 207

Sloman was very handsome and distinguished looking, of upper-middle height, with a full head of silver-gray hair, an attractive and carefully trimmed mustache and intelligent, witty dark eyes unobscured by glasses. His teeth were white and strong. He was somewhat overweight and underexercised but he made up for this with an agility of mind. He dressed conservatively with a touch of elegance in the British style. He had a highly developed sense of play and loved to josh and tease people in a wry, understated but pinpricking, witty and very dry manner. He would deliberately arch his left eyebrow when making a special comment or challenging someone, and you realized he had developed this effect to an art, as you sensed also his self-irony when he did it, for his humor was broad enough to include his own foibles as targets. At times he could verge on being wicked, as if he enjoyed seeing his victims squirm, but he was noticeably more gentle with those less able to defend themselves.

As the third ranking BAS administrator, he regularly but not annually did a tour of duty in the Antarctic, flying from England to the Falklands and from Stanley home to Cambridge. The *Bransfield* wardroom was clearly his domain in terms of style, and he definitely set its tone. I was fond of him and always looked forward to my wardroom visits partially because of his lively presence. Also, he together with Swithinbank set the tone of my stay on the ship by their great and overt courtesy to me, amounting, I liked to believe, to real affection. He often focused the wardroom's attention upon me not only on my entrance but during my stays. I invariably received from him the feeling that I was appreciated even though I might not be entirely understood.

Toward Swithinbank I also felt very fond, but with him there was an added dimension. He was an Antarctic veteran, had wintered over several times, spent time with the Russians, lived with the Americans in Antarctica, taught in a Midwestern university in the States, was married to an American and had an accent that suggested traces of Americanisms. He was quiet and unassuming but because I knew him for an old Antarctic hand I never underestimated his inner strength. He had an excellent mind, was an authority on glaciology and possessed broad views of Antarctica and its problems. He was one of three scientists

208   BEYOND CAPE HORN

who ranked with Sloman in the BAS structure. He was in charge of Earth Sciences. The others administered Atmospheric Sciences and Life Sciences. When he expressed himself on a subject it was always with an admirable intellectual and emotional balance. His manner was bland and his views temperate but at times I sensed, I don't quite know how, that he was a stern disciplinarian regarding the Fids. He was not as quick and witty as Sloman but was capable of holding his own in a verbal duel. He dressed more simply and less expensively than Sloman but almost always wore a white shirt, tie and jacket in the the wardroom during the evening. He was Bill Sloman's buddy and at times his foil, as for example when Bill openly speculated on the etymology of the name Swithinbank and decided it meant "swine-bank." Charles quietly agreed. Charles was above all, as far as I knew him, a temperate man intellectually in the highest sense of the word. In his early fifties, he was youthful looking for his age. His thinning, graying hair was cropped very short. His features suggested the balanced life I felt he led emotionally.

Hugh M. O'Gorman ("Hughie" in the wardroom), the ship's radio officer, middle-aged, fixed in his sedentary habits, loved his work so much or was so compulsive about it he rarely left the ship even when his presence was not required on it. The radio room seemed twilit, complex, almost mysterious to me with its various consoles which he handled masterfully. He was always carefully dressed in shirt, tie and dark trousers and was very formal and properly cordial with me. He struck me as being a special kind of sea hermit. As far as I knew he was the sole inhabitant of a cabin on the bridge deck. He sometimes came to the wardroom, but even there seemed a man apart, as if his mind was always on the air. And indeed he had special duties and responsibilities. Usually his presence was required in the radio room during certain evening hours such as between eight and nine, the "goon show" time, as it was called at Palmer Station.

I frequently had occasion to hear him speak on the ship's radio and was able to note the surprising, marked difference between his normal speech and the clipped, almost machinelike speech he automatically assumed when he was on the air and which to some fine degree entered into his ordinary conversation. I supposed these professional mannerisms were necessary and perhaps inevitable if one was to make oneself understood across the chasms of static, fading and other problems of shortwave radio communications. The moment he got on the air he would concentrate ferociously and begin to twitch in very tiny ways, twitches that were in rhythm with his speech, as though they magically would help his interlocutor to read him more clearly, or as if he were a puppet being affected by the finest of strings and the gentlest of motions.

"Brrrr-*ans*field, Brrrr-*ans*field, Brrrr-*ans*field calling!"

How often I heard him say that.

I can hardly imagine a more cultivated sea captain than Stuart Lawrence. Surprisingly small and slight in figure, he had abstemious eating habits, say tea and toast on the bridge or a light soup such as consomme while we were making our way through dense fog among many looming bergs. He had a fine dry wit, which was obvious not only in his domain, the bridge, but in the wardroom, which he always visited very quietly but nicely dressed. He was not a regular wardroom visitor in the evenings, for there were times when his presence was needed on the bridge. When he did appear, much notice was taken of him not only because he was the ship's master and our lives were in his hands but because of his quick intelligence and humor. He was in his mid-thirties, I believe, and had married recently. He handled himself extremely well: He was cool and wry, with a graceful, quiet authority, and he gave every sign of enjoying his work except for those times when the ship was threatened in uncharted waters or by huge bergs sailing hard upon it. It is perhaps worth remarking here that a metal ship is more vulnerable in Antarctica than a wooden one because it is more brittle and because its metal skin is relatively very thin, suggesting that of a balloon. Lawrence was always extremely cordial to me. I quickly became very fond of him.

A word about Ron Lewis Smith, my cabinmate. He headed the terrestrial section of Life Sciences in BAS, had risen from the Fid ranks, had a doctorate and was married. We enjoyed sharing our cabin. I can see him now: tall, slender, with a rather small face and intelligent eyes set close together. In the field he wore heavy wool knickers partially covered by gray ribbed woolen stockings, and a rucksack for carrying botanical specimens. He often wandered off alone. I recall him as a solitary figure seen at a distance. He was in his early or mid-thirties. He was very quiet and very respectful toward his superiors when he was in the wardroom with them.

Good views of the ship from the conning tower. The prow filled with heavy crane machinery. Cranes on the tween deck too. The tween deck crowded with fuel drums. No persons in sight below. The helo deck red, with a large circle half of which was white, the other half light-coffee. The middle of the circle black. On it a light-coffee large H. Two white funnels with black tops like top hats, the two encased in a single yellow one most of the way up. Lifeboats in their davits. The launch making a sweeping pass at us, leaving a round wake.

The gashroom was at the aft end of the Fid deck. You queued up at a counter railed off from the rest of the room and waited for your food to be dished out onto a tray. There were lots of overcooked meat and overcooked vegetables, including lots of spuds, and lots of excellent, solid bread and wonderful jams and marmalade, and lots of yorkshire pudding, and often there would be a good but solid and simple dessert. Coffee, tea, milk and boxes of cereal would be available on a sideboard. Coffee was of the instant variety. Tea came brewed in a large pot. The milk was powdered, as were the eggs for the most part. The butter was of the kind that didn't require refrigeration.

The gashmen were on the other side of the counter in a room called the pantry, which contained a large refrigerator, a dumbwaiter, overhead cabinets, two large stainless steel sinks or basins, and the extensive serving area, into which newly arrived pots full of hot food would be placed and which was heated by electrically controlled hot water. The food arrived in stages by dumbwaiter from the ship's galley below. It was usually eaten on two long, rather narrow tables, but on occasion, when there was a crowd come from shore, a third was used, and there was a fourth which I never saw in use. Seats were not reserved. Everything was unadorned and styleless. On completing your meal you dumped the scraps, including any liquid, into the gash bucket near the pantry and placed your plates on a small pantry window ledge.

The Fids were roughly and at times oddly dressed. Often they would come to the gashroom directly from the outdoors, either from the weather decks or from work ashore. The gashroom was entirely functional and you did not tend to linger there, for it was a drafty, cold place.

Many of the Fids were a blur in my mind, but a few stood out vividly. One was Mike, with shoulder-length, gorgeous, light-brown hair, whom I first saw with his back to me as he was reading one of the Fiddery's bulletin boards.

I thought, "Good God, a woman! How wonderful!"

And then he turned around and glanced blandly at me with his bearded face. And I thought, "What the hell! These Fids are crazy."

Mike was shy and gentle and not obviously muscular and I wondered if he was capable of doing hard physical work. He very much was, as I later had the chance to see.

Without implying anything whatever about his sex life, let me say parenthetically that occasionally people in the States have asked me what I know about sexual activity in the Antarctic. My reply has truthfully been: nothing.

In connection with the Fids and Mike, I remember thinking, "Well, I admire their tolerance."

There was one Fid whose face and presence haunted me, a strange Irishman, older than most of the Fids, who was a terrible misfit in the gashroom and who never appeared in the Fiddery. For a while, not knowing his story, I couldn't understand what was happening. He was silent, dour and always alone, even during meals. He looked unhappy in the extreme. I never once saw him laugh or smile, and I wondered if his vocal cords were atrophying, for I rarely saw him talk with anyone, or anyone talk to him. I soon got the idea he was being severely ostracized but for what I didn't know.

He seemed to regard me as one of the Fids, or perhaps in his gray absentminded grief he wasn't even clearly sure who and what I was. I finally asked a couple of Fids about him and got a strangely mixed response: contempt because he had let them down, and admiration of his raw guts in doing what he believed had had to be done, regardless of the social consequences.

It turned out he had been enthusiastic about joining BAS for Antarctic duty, for among other reasons he had heavy financial responsibilities at home and this was a two-year job in which there was little opportunity to spend money. But by the time the ship had reached South Georgia on its way southward he had changed his mind and decided to resign, which meant that there was one less hand to help care for the station he was going to, and consequently more work for the other station members. From that moment he was ostracized by his fellow Fids and strictly isolated himself. I never learned what it was that had caused him to resign. He was of medium complexion and looked badly in need of some sun. There was little to distinguish his features but I remember them well. He worked willingly and hard when necessary and had his share of gash duty. I could easily imagine that his homecoming (by ship) would be blighted and that the would-be hero who had sailed for Antarctica might be returning in a condition akin to disgrace. I sometimes wondered how under the circumstances he managed to develop an appetite and find some solace in sleep.

Something strange happened to me in relation to him after I failed to make contact with him. I discovered I was beginning to share the general feeling against him as being an unwelcome member of "our" team even though I was a guest, a stranger, and I had to remind myself that this was not my business and that I should try not to resent his silence and remoteness toward me. He was a man in great distress and needed sympathy wherever he could get it. My odd behavior reminded me of that of certain animals toward an injured one or one in disfavor, and I recalled examples of huskies suddenly attacking and killing a particular husky out of mass hatred that was only minutes and possibly only seconds old.

Barrie Bromby, the first officer, on the bridge wing, looking very natty, wearing a carefully trimmed dark beard and mustache, a black cap worn rakishly, a USARP medallion attached to the forehead, a white, high-necked, heavily ribbed turtleneck, a black jacket with gold shoulder braid and gold buttons. He had handsome, weathered features, good lines in cheeks and around the eyes, an excellent smile, small ears. He was the sort of man who gave the impression of being likely to be cool in a hard emergency situation. He was often kidded by his superiors such as Sloman in the wardroom, partly because he was younger, I think, and partly because he handled the joshing very gracefully.

"A sunset came up at about 10 P.M., grew in splendor and I went to the starboard bridge wing. Alexander Island's peaks clearly visible in the southwest even though they're about 110 statute miles away."

The intervening water gently rippled. Long bands of cerise clouds lit from below. Yellow flames or copper-gold of a cloud line just above the horizon. Silhouetted peaks and islands glued to the horizon, that meeting place where the slate of water met the gold and orange and lime and blue of the sky. A silent, burning world. Eyes that had had a full diet of blues for weeks feasting on reds, cherries, cerises. The world darkened, grew more magical, hushed. About a hundred feet from us a group of some half-dozen white skuas caught the failing light, glowing on the muted, rouged, textured water. Cherries turning to dark violet. A skua flying blurred across my field of vision. The rouge turned to beaten copper with a reddish hue. More cherry in the sky, more ruddy copper in the water. In the south and southwest there was nothing at the moment to suggest an Antarctic scene: no blues, no ice, no snowcovered mountains: just open water, a horizon of black peaks, a flaming sky. The clouds were slowly being extinguished, the top of the sky was turning inky, the water was growing pale slate.

12 ❀ The Palmer Mystery and Argentine Islands

16 FEBRUARY. Bill Sloman came by and said the launch would go ashore in about five minutes. Did I want to see the airstrip? "Yes indeed!"

So off we went. Sloman disappeared to see about work on antennas on the hill. Swithinbank and I waited for the Sno-cat to come get us. The *Bransfield's* brilliant red hull stood out keenly against a blue sky absolutely devoid of clouds. In the foreground was the brilliant white of heavy snow. The bay was a mirror.

Some of the Fids were working on the main hut stripped to the waist, others were in mesh vests, still others were warmly dressed. All wore heavy sunglasses. Tim Stewart, the King Fid, stripped to the waist, a cloth band round his forehead, was a tall athletic figure in brown pants, brown boots and khaki wool gloves. His woolen shirt was tied around his waist. He had long brown hair and a huge dark beard and mustache. He was working on the main hut's flooring.

Swithinbank, Don Hawkes and I took the U.S.-built Sno-cat up to the strip, Charles insisting I have the front seat beside the driver. It was a four-seater and still quite new. We climbed the steep snow ramp at about four miles an hour. The cat got one mile to the imperial gallon (1.2 U.S. gallons). Later, when we

215

were on horizontal terrain, we did twelve miles an hour, churning snow and flinging it high in the air. It was three miles from the base to the strip.

On our left as we lumbered upward with great growling of engine and tracks, polluting the silence as well as the icecap, were jagged black razorbacks casting blue shadows on the virginal white. Long, sensuous lines, caused by tumbling and rolling rocks (from the sharded, frost-shattered peaks) that picked up snow as they ran, fell onto the tilted snow plain from the base of these razorbacks. At the bottom of each trail was a white ball. I wonder now why the dotted lines with the ball at the end of each fascinated me and whether there was anything more involved than visual novelty.

Abstract beauty has a haunting power. I find it difficult to explain in any other way why a certain image I still carry with me from the visit to the airstrip, and carry involuntarily and gratefully, keeps recurring in my memory, causing me to cherish it for the pleasure of a very high degree it gives me, like that of studying a great drawing. The scene I have in mind is very simple, yet at the same time prodigious, if such an adjective can be applied to nature.

Let me clarify with an example what I mean. I happened to be in London in the spring of 1975, when there was a great exhibition of Michelangelo's drawings at the British Museum. One of the things that excited me about it was that it drew all kinds of people. The rooms were massed with them, and they all came to be transported and were. It was a wonderful demonstration of popular response to the powers of an immense genius. You looked at the drawings and you saw no preparatory marks and no erasures. Nor was there anything precious about them, anything suggesting the artist's struggles for perfection. They were simply there in all their incredibleness. It seemed quite clear to me that you had to assume at least two special, prodigious powers to account for them in their great numbers. He was able to see very clearly on a screen in his mind, but beyond that, he was able also to project the seen image onto the paper and thereby give the impression of simply outlining and shading what was already obviously there.

I am looking westward from the airstrip across an absolutely untouched expanse of sparkling snow with a pinkish hue, an untouched monochromatic mass, with a hint of dancing because of the sparkles. Beyond it rises a sand dune all very simple and all in blue shadow because the sand is snow lying on a mountain arching as gently as any lovely dune. And so here are these two elements: pinkish, dancing snow plain and beautifully blue-shadowed dune. One could hardly ask for anything more, and yet there is a third and equally marvelous item: the crisply blue Antarctic sky. Three horizontal layers: sky, dune, plain; nonobjective, magical. What a gift the visit gave me. How could I have imagined that this particular scene would take hold in my memory more strongly than any other that day?

It is possible that the ambiguity of the middle element, snow/sand, sand/snow, and its mercurial fluctuations in one's memory create a dimension not easily grasped, perhaps unsuspected, but exerting its power nevertheless. An interesting possibility is that the Antarctic snow, because of the continent's very low humidity and temperature, is often the consistency of sand. This is something that would be more likely to hold in the non-Peninsula regions. However, I was new to the Peninsula and had brought with me non-Peninsula memories. Besides which, the snow I had already encountered at Rothera as well as on the airstrip was surprisingly dry. Does the mind unconsciously attempt to bridge the gap between a sand dune and a snow one or, to be more accurate, a snow/ice one, for beneath the relatively thin snow layer was the glacier or icecap. If so, why should this be pleasurable? Because of the added play of mind? Or because of uncertainty, an uncertainty, incidentally, which would be congruent with all the other uncertainties a low-latitude mind finds in the very high latitudes?

The Twin Otter (it had two turboprop engines), painted red, with black on top, stood off to the right of the strip, the port ski being worked on by a couple of mechanics. It gleamed as if enamelled, BRITISH ANTARCTIC SURVEY on its sides. It had three wheels and used skis. The fiord as background. Jagged black peaks ribbed vertically. The airstrip very pure. Swithinbank in pale tan windpants stuck into high boots, wearing a long khaki anorak, bareheaded, tanned, sunglassed, hands in muff-like pockets. Don Hawkes in red anorak, black pants.

Giles Kershaw rode up from the base alone on a snowmobile, helped load the plane with fuel drums and took off with his navigator, heading over the mainland. Swithinbank explained that the reason I wasn't invited to fly was that there was no backup craft for a SAR (search and rescue; rhymes with "far").

Swithinbank and I returned to the ship at around 6 P.M. South Bay was dead calm now. The ship was secured by two ropes, fore and aft. The aft one, lying in the water between the stern and some rocks, acted as a dam against ice coming close to shore. The water farthest from the shore was oily in smoothness. It changed to textured ripples on the shore side of the rope. We embarked, as usual, by a rope ladder.

After dinner I was reading in the Fiddery when John Dudeney came up to me and said Bill Sloman invited me to share an anniversary cake in the wardroom. Today was his thirty-first wedding anniversary. I accepted, changed clothes and for the first time wore a tie with my white shirt and jacket.

The cake (raisin with rich sweet topping) was good. Under Sloman's urging I accepted two servings of Drambuie to celebrate the occasion. He had injured his lower back at the base this afternoon lifting something heavy. Occasionally he had a severe spasm of pain, which was revealed when he would suddenly raise his eyebrows in a sophisticated way and purse his mouth as if saying a prolonged "whew." He had returned to the ship before Swithinbank, Hawkes and I had started for the strip.

"How did you manage to climb up the ladder?" I asked.

Lifting his left eyebrow, he replied, "With great tenacious courage," which brought forth a burst of fond laughter.

18 FEBRUARY. It's a bit curious to me now how terse my journal was on the subject of failing to reach Palmer. Palmer was my direct connection with home. Palmer *was* my home, in a sense. At times, in a reverie, I would recall my room there: bed, closets, the way the light came in over my left shoulder when I sat at the desk, the stuff I had stashed away in the drawers under the bed, such as exposed color film because that was the room's coolest place, the toilet on my floor, the shower, the ham radio room, the pool table, the frequent movies, the familiar faces like Warburton's, the pleasant feeling in the lounge. Palmer was the place I had a key to, hanging on my silver key ring wherever I went now in the Antarctic, the place I had carefully locked up on my departure from it for greater security of film and journals

and of such strange personal possessions as giant petrel and skua feathers, the place whose window I had left open just so, to keep the room cool yet hopefully dust free. Palmer was my home in the middle of nowhere, a limbo, and now I was in another limbo and longing for the Palmer one.

I would grow quite nostalgic in the strangest way, for Palmer wasn't my home at all, yet in another sense that was hardly surprising, for the base represented the sole spot in the entire Peninsula region which could be regarded as American. Palmer was where I could rest, where I did not have the responsibilities of being a working guest, where I was not "on show." Also, it was a place where I didn't have to strain to understand what people were saying and where they understood me with equal perfection. I'm sure I romanticized the place at a distance because it wasn't readily accessible to me, because I wasn't yet certain as to how I would return to it and my things there. I felt that because of those things it contained parts of me.

As I undressed to turn in, I wondered why Palmer had been off the air, for I had received the definite impression while at the base that they were invariably on the air during goon-show time and that I would have the opportunity to be in close touch with them if I wished to use it. About one thing I was very clear: Hugh O'Gorman, the *Bransfield* radio officer, had tried his very best to reach them. I had witnessed his efforts myself.

19 FEBRUARY. I was on the starboard weather deck and so close to an icemass I felt I was on it, and I could easily have jumped onto it. The sky now was black pearl and all of one hue, like a silk screen, not spotted or patched, with a couple of small castle bergs very white on the horizon, turrets gleaming. And there was this great arm of scalloped blue ice stretching toward the ship, agleam with highlights, and deeper blue in the trough. But at moments I sensed it was stretching with seeming rapidity *away* from me out to the horizon, with its gnarls and hillocks, one of them gleaming razor-sharp white. And beside the berg a mass of chalky white brash and jagged bergy-bits encompassed a slit of black sea. The scalloped sections looked as if they had been formed by careful, artful blows of a great round hammer. It was thrilling to be so close to a large piece of dense ice, centuries old.

The mass loomed higher and I observed scalloped or beaten

sapphire mountains, with true mountains, dark lead in hue, and a dark-lead sky, setting them off. The world was in riot, nature had exploded, there was even a superb, deep-blue patch breaking through in the sky, yet all that had happened was that a wind or current had blown brash into our harbor. The blue ice field south of us was particularly heavy and thick. Beyond it were large spilling glaciers, one of which was named for Sloman, but I was not sure we could see his from where we were. The scenes were wonderfully photogenic, with interesting compositions and play of light everywhere. Some large and beaten intense-blue bergs clogged channels to the south of us. You could see how blue they were because of the pure white of mountain snowmantles. The fact that they had been at sea a long time was evident from the degree to which they had weathered. Each had cliffs, turrets, a sloping shoreline, mountains, valleys. One of them had a frizzy substance that reminded me of the tight formal curls of ancient Assyrian beards.

"On the bridge during the run to Jenny Island via a new route. The sonar pen showed rock pinnacles or ground rising suddenly under us to about a depth of 35 meters when moments earlier it had been 200 meters. Stuart Lawrence noticeably upset by the change in the sonar reading.

"Once more failed to reach Palmer during the 'goon show' 8 to 9 P.M. Bill Sloman invited me to join BAS for a trip to Antarctica 'at any time,' said I'd be 'most welcome.' I was pleased. I want to reach Palmer to see what plans there are for me and if the *Hero* will pick me up at Argentine Islands and if there's any radio traffic for me."

It certainly was strange, most passing strange, that Palmer should be off the air a second evening in a row and without notice of any kind. What were they up to?

21 FEBRUARY. Launch and scow were winched over the side close to some ice bits. I descended into the scow and we moved away from the ship through brash. Glistening small ice masses, and the great crevassed glacier back beyond (I wanted to use the word "dorsal" at times). The ship looked massive above us. The light was now coming bristlingly from the direction of the glacier, whose cliffs were in blue shadow. I went ashore and took pictures of the station. Swithinbank was with me part of the time. We climbed onto a rocky hillock and viewed the scene

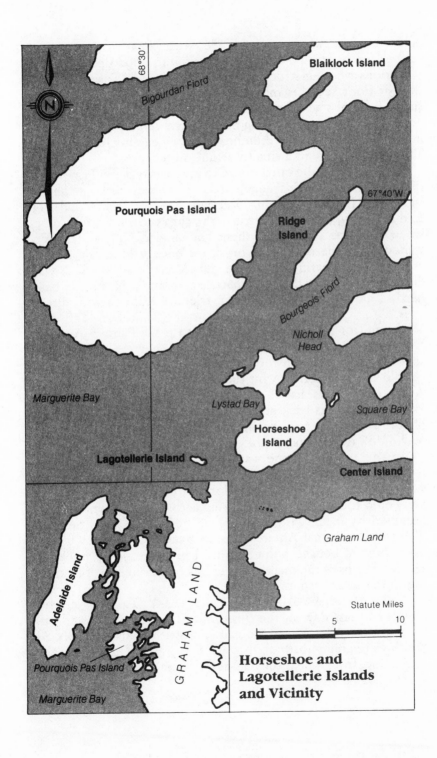

Horseshoe and Lagotellerie Islands and Vicinity

below us. The wind was cold. He wore khaki trousers, large rubberized boots and a brown anorak with hood up.

Various wooden structures all over the place. Large wooden wall or floor sections piled on the ground. Vehicle tracks on snow. Piles of stacked wooden crates on a flooring constructed on a bouldered, outcropping hill. Conical tents. Vehicles flaming in the brilliant light. Antenna towers gleaming like needles. The camp suggested a small wartime supply area.

I walked along the north shore to investigate a seal I saw lying there near the water's edge, making my way through heavy snowdrift. It was a sleeping Weddell. The red launch and Big Red the scow, coming to retrieve the ship's party, were held up when the rope connecting them got tangled underwater. We waited while the three men on board untangled it. Big Al the architect was wearing an orange anorak the hood of which was down. He had very thin hair that blew about on his mostly bald head, a graying beard and warm, friendly features with direct eyes.

"Again (for the fourth time) failed to reach Palmer. And the Doppler at Palmer is out too, John Dudeney reported. Much speculation in the wardroom about the 'Palmer mystery.' And people are wondering why the *Hero* hasn't been on the air. Argentine Islands hasn't heard from Palmer either. Tweaky Fitzgerald, who is back aboard the *Bransfield*, thinks Palmer is off the air in order to install new radio equipment. But if so, why didn't they signal us they were going off?

"In the evening in the wardroom Charles Swithinbank was reminiscing to me about wintering-over on an ice shelf, being two or three miles from camp, alone with the stars that you felt you could touch, the aurora playing across the sky, and feeling humbled by it all. 'Nicely humbled,' he added. Then he said, 'I've always felt that Antarctica is not against people . . . if they know how to behave politely in it.' I like the use of 'politely.' He again: 'I have the marvelous feeling of belonging, of belonging to the solar system.'"

22 FEBRUARY, WASHINGTON'S BIRTHDAY. This was my fifteenth and last day on the *Bransfield*. Tomorrow I would sail north on the *John Biscoe*. Sloman and Swithinbank and Big Al Smith were going north on the *John Biscoe* also. They would sail to Stanley, from which they would fly home. I would part with

222   BEYOND CAPE HORN

them at Argentine Islands. Ship's log: *"John Biscoe* alongside at 0630. Cargo stores, water and fuel transferred [from the *John Biscoe* to the *Bransfield*] until 1800."

"Charles Swithinbank, Ron Smith, Don Hawkes, the latter's graduate student Mike Crabtree, Hughie Monckton (extra second officer), Ian Clark (third officer) and a couple of other guys and I went to Horseshoe Island in two Geminis. The BAS people have a way of zipping along in these regardless of waves, and the consequence is a great deal of uncomfortable bouncing and much spray. We wear inflatable life jackets."

Horseshoe Island is high, conspicuous, crescent-shape and about eight statute miles long and six and a half miles wide. It lies in the entrance of Bourgeois Fiord. The British established a base there in 1955, which was evacuated in 1960. The old station now remained as a refuge. Lystad Bay is about three and a half miles wide.

We landed on a rocky coast of Horseshoe Island. Massive outcrops of tan rock like partially freed boulders. However, much of the coastline was ice-covered or ice-cliffed. Swithinbank carried one of several radios we had taken along to stay in touch with the *Bransfield*. Looking back at the two ships lashed together and facing the island, I could see that the *John Biscoe* was about half as large as the *Bransfield*. The bay close to the island was clear but about half a mile out were a number of sizable bergy-bits. Hawkes wore a woolen cap, red anorak, black trousers and a large green rucksack. A heavy smoker, he was smoking a cigarette soon after we went ashore. Swithinbank wore his snug-fitting Russian leather cap with the earflaps down (which reminded me of an aviator's cap of the 1920 vintage), a khaki anorak and off-white windpants. Also, he wore a blue sweater over a freshly laundered white shirt.

Toward the southern part of the island were large black talus slopes or fans that had accumulated at the base of Penitent Peak and Mt. Breaker and which entirely occupied the beach there. Apparently they resulted from frosts which had flaked the mountain crusts. They resembled great coal heaps.

It was exhilarating to walk freely, first on land, then on sparkling, crunching snow. I was alone for most of the hike. On my left was a snowcovered freshwater pond. The glare of the snow fields was severe. I could see Charles far away and then I lost sight of him as he went behind a hill but I could follow him easily by his tracks almost as far as the former small station that was now a refuge hut.

Adélies in the hut's vicinity studied us silently. They came from Bourgeois Fiord. The long hut was of unpainted wood. The shuttered seven windows and one door on the fiord side were painted red. The veins of pale-green copper sulphate on the nearby hill seemed to be encrusted on granite. Under a magnifying glass the copper sulphate appeared to be a film of shiny green globules.

We went off to Lagotellerie Island, which last evening had looked naked, with a chocolate, solid color. One was curious as to why it wasn't snow-covered like the other islands. I hoped I wouldn't find frost-shattered rock but something more intact and possibly even ventifacted. I was greatly disappointed. Shattered, shattered, flaky, angular rocks everywhere. Some Adélies and Weddells on the beaches, the seals smelling very fishy. Hardly a ventifact to be seen. Most of the people who came ashore started climbing to investigate the geology of a col or saddle high up, browner in color than its surroundings and seeming by its shape to suggest the position of a former alpine glacier. I was more interested in some tidal pools. Climbed about on rocks and took pictures of Adélies and seals until the rendezvous time. The weather was now overcast. Lagotellerie Island, off Horseshoe in Lystad Bay, is much smaller than Horseshoe.

Lagotellerie is a mile long, about half a mile wide and has steep sides of metamorphic and igneous rock, the highest of which is about 1000 feet in elevation. It lies some two miles west of the southwestern shore of Horseshoe Island. By now the day was cloudy, with patches of sunlight breaking through. Because of the impressions I received of the island from shipboard during sunset of the previous day, I had great expectations of exploring this chocolate place. But the chocolate was an illusion, for the island turned out to be a granite gray. Calum Cumine, the ship's catering officer and the person in charge of the canteen, was at my side a good deal of the time at first on Lagotellerie—we were alone together—and I suspected he had been detached to stay close to me to look after my safety because I was an older person, and this perturbed me. I shied away and, I think, caused him to drift off and give me much-needed solitude and space. But later, after we separated, I changed my mind, although he never wandered off out of range of any shouts I might make. I supposed he had come ashore for an interesting excursion and to get some exercise and I was sorry I had misunderstood his presence.

I looked across the body of water between Lagotellerie and Horseshoe islands at a lesser glacier, one still unnamed on my map. The clouded sky was dappled with light that silver-coined the water. Iced and naked peaks flanked the glacier. Between me and the glacier was a very strange, looming formation resembling a spouting whale. It was in shadow. Its dorsal, arched side was outlined with light. I could not be sure whether the form was rock or ice. The scene was eerie, primordial and extraordinarily suggestive and beautiful. But what made the visit to the island especially rewarding for me were the Adélies and Weddells.

I encountered seven Adélies on a snow bank near the rocky beach. They were standing as if in thought. Occasionally they preened themselves. We regarded each other in silence. This wild island was home to them. I could not see, smell or hear a rookery. They let me photograph them at fairly close range. Beyond the snow bank and contrasting with it were massive gray rocky outcrops and very large boulders, some eight or ten feet high. I photographed a couple to show how successive frosts and thaws had cracked, split, shattered, flaked and sharded them. The flat rock shards, which looked powder gray with streaks of dusty rose—they were all in soft, pastel hues—clinked metallically when struck together. In little rock runnels I saw thick black moss beds, no doubt fed by melting snow, attached to dolerite. The "trunks" of the moss were off-white.

Walking toward a beach inlet, I came upon some sprawled, sleeping Weddells—gray cigar shapes with plenty of snow space between them. They barely stirred as I walked among them. The beach was composed of huge outcrops and many gray boulders. It was here, on a large gray rock as high as my shoulders, that I photographed the solitary Adélie whose portrait appeared prominently in black-and-white on the op ed page of the *New York Times* some three months later. The bird quacked at me. Quacking back to galvanize its attention, I approached it slowly. We exchanged remarks as I drew close. I knew something about Adélies, having lived with the world's southernmost rookery on Cape Royds, Ross Island, during my second Antarctic trip. I believe it was my willingness to talk with the bird and to mimic its comments that kept it in place. The published photograph of this individual, by the way, showed a remarkably dignified bird, hardly someone you could accurately refer to as a member of a tribe of court jesters. One of the nice things about the picture, at least for me, is that the subject is higher than the photographer. Because of its position on the rocks, I was looking up at it, but just barely. Not only does this individual look dignified, it also looks solemn as it tries to appraise the unusual and probably unprecedented situation with one eye and a stern beak. A friend of mine, Richard Falk of Princeton, New Jersey, said to me about the published photograph, "It looks as if it was taken by another penguin."

I also came upon a sleeping Weddell lying on rocks of granite, throat resting against vertical blocks of the stone, dorsal side dark velvety gray, setting off the granite's stippled paler gray, a ridge running from the top of the head dorsally toward the tail, the flanks spotted white. The animal looked very contented and very oblivious of me. The scene was a lovely mixture of grays, a bit of ice and parts of the stone darkened by moisture. An island idyll.

"Back to the *Bransfield* to deliver some men, then over to the scree slope on Horseshoe Island to have a look at the geology (Hawkes and his graduate student; Ron Smith; Hughie Monckton; one other person and I). The slope had looked yellow-green last evening. Now it looked pale tan. I assumed the sunset had disguised true colors. The sea now was heavier, with more swell and therefore more spray for us.

'The huge long beach and incredible badland. Relief to find something so visually exciting after the disappointment of Lagotellerie, and to be able to enjoy gathering rocks again. My parka was so stuffed with them I could hardly stand erect, and there was an unpleasant pressure on my nape and shoulders from rocks, shoulder bag and two cameras.

"Informed I join the *John Biscoe* in the morning. It sails at 10:30 A.M., earlier than we had expected. Am delighted to be returning to Palmer. Would like a change from the BAS visit.

Hope to see a station belonging to Argentina or possibly Russia. In any event I want to touch 'home' base again, read the mail if any, make a phone patch or two, prepare to return to the States."

Once again I tried and failed to reach Palmer, and now there was some concern in the wardroom as well as new teasing of me.

"My dear Charles," Bill Sloman said, arching his eyebrow, "it's clear that Palmer has been taken over by the Argentines [pronounced Argen*tynes*] as part of their sovereign Antarctic territory. The British Antarctic Survey will be glad to take you to Stanley as a political refugee."

"Thank you but I do not in that case care to go to Stanley inasmuch as Stanley is an Argentine port."

This was an allusion to Argentina's claim to the Falklands.

It was a rather full wardroom evening. Among other interesting things that happened, the Rothera base commander who had given me such stern advice about phone patches being bad for morale and in general had impressed me with his belief in the stiff-upper-lip mode of life got drunk enough to turn suddenly very openly sentimental about his girlfriend back home and how badly he missed her and how hard it was not to be in close touch, and so on, and had to be helped to walk out of the room and, as I gathered, was gently, tenderly, aided on his way back to shore life. It should be noted that he behaved attractively as well as with embarrassment, knowing he was overextending himself, yet at the same time realizing he was among good friends, and that he made an appealing figure in his rough shore clothes, to such an extent that one could imagine him smelling of the bracing snowy headland air. He was aware he had drunk too much in the too sudden transition between the ruggedness of camp life and the wardroom luxuries, that he had misgauged the effect of the amount he had drunk and that he had been abetted in this error by the well-meaning pressure on him by all in the wardroom, myself excepted, to forget for a moment the station responsibilities and to give himself up to the camaraderie of the room, part of which was symbolized by the fine brand of ten-year-old Scotch he had consumed. I sensed among the permanent wardroom residents a kind of guilt toward anyone like him who had to be left behind in the Antarctic while carrying a specially heavy responsibility, and I thought I detected in him a certain embarrassment because he was in the presence of persons who wielded power back home.

I could not help but wonder at the strange things the Antarctic existence could do to one, particularly how it was able to bring about cleavages in one's emotional and even one's perceptual life.

Swithinbank informed me I had been assigned an aftermost cabin in the poop house of the *John Biscoe*, where the dispensary and hospital were.

"It's a notorious cabin," he said, "over the screw and full of rolling and heavy vibrations. It will be extremely rough and noisy even in good weather. Everybody gets sick there. May I offer you a couple of sleeping pills?"

"No thanks," I replied.

"Do you have seasickness pills?"

"I don't think I'll need them."

I awoke by alarm clock at 6:30 A.M., packed mostly in the dark of my cabin while Ron Smith slept, and finished packing before breakfast. A Fid named Bill helped me carry my gear from the *Bransfield* to the *John Biscoe* over a gangplank that swayed and heaved with the motion of the ships and below which you saw icy, brashy black water. There was a considerable swell now and the *John Biscoe* was bouncing, whereas the *Bransfield* seemed solid by comparison. Yesterday's poor weather was turning to bad. I discovered that I would share my cabin with a young Fid radio operator, Alf Cheshire, whom I had already met but only vaguely and who was heading for a winter-over at Argentine Islands. Business of crossing the smaller ship's narrow main deck, turning left to go further aft, entering a housing and then immediately afterwards the door of the poop cabin. The cabin struck me as being astonishingly small and crowded. A double bunk, closets, a sofa, desk, sink in a room barely large enough for one to walk into.

I filled the cabin with my gear: two orange seabags, five cartons, blue airline bag, green small suitcase, heavy parka and so on. Alf hadn't lugged his stuff in, yet there was little place to put mine. I was forced to occupy the little sofa, the space between it and the desk, and small odds and ends of other space. The shallow, small closet was useful only for hanging up an item of clothing or two. After debating what to do with my blue airline bag I laid it on the tiny desk. Just to the right of the desk was the tiny wash basin, which almost abutted on the doorsill. The door opened inward, and this made the cabin even smaller than it might otherwise have been. You felt you were treading on eggshells as you moved around in it.

I wondered why the lower bunk, which I appropriated on the grounds of priority (I was the first to enter the cabin and stow my gear there), had two mattresses, the upper of which was sheathed in heavy plastic and consequently was very slippery. That slipperiness was to be the cause of some comic as well as potentially dangerous episodes. The double mattress meant that my face almost touched the bottom of the upper bunk.

I looked around the cabin in the hope of finding some place to put the sheathed one but soon realized that was one of the sorriest hopes in recent Antarctic history. Who was I to question the hospitality and wisdom of my hosts, I who would have been happy to sleep on a wardroom sofa or in a gashroom chair just to be able to move northward a bit? Anything to move northward. This was certainly a curious and unexpected turnabout for one who constantly had the yen to move south, south, south to the Pole itself.

I went on deck to look up at the greater hulk of the *Bransfield* and to think and feel my farewells and to have the sense that once again I was a traveler among travelers, an outlander, on this haunting continent but a traveler who, regardless of how strange he might be, was living in a state of grace because he was here.

I have already noted the name John Biscoe. Unlike Bransfield, who was a Sailing Master of the Royal Navy, Biscoe was a sealing ship master employed by the unusual London mercantile house of Enderby Brothers. I say unusual because one of the partners was a founder of the Royal Geographical Society and because the firm encouraged its masters to discover new lands in the high southern latitudes as well as to hunt for seals. Other ship masters employed by it and whose names may be found on the map of Antarctica are John Balleny and Peter Kemp. In 1832 Biscoe, with the brig *Tula* and the cutter *Lively*, discovered Adelaide Island and the Biscoe Islands and landed on Anvers Island, which he believed to be a part of the mainland. He named this section of the coast Graham Land after the then First Lord of the Admiralty.

We cast off from the *Bransfield* at 10:55 A.M. by my watch. Those of us who had transferred from her—Sloman, Swithinbank, Alan Smith, Ron Smith, John Dudeney and I—were on the *John Biscoe's* main deck, waving. Stuart Lawrence was on his port bridge wing, smiling down at us. Both ships sounded their horns loudly for what seemed a long time. It was a bit weird to be saying goodby in the middle of nowhere. The horns moved you powerfully despite your inclination to resist sentiment. You were so close to them and they were so strong they vibrated all through you, rattling your teeth and bones as well as stirring up your gray matter. You might as well have tried to be indifferent to being doused with a bucket of Antarctic water. Besides which there was something electrifying in hearing them go off suddenly and listening to them echo off the icy mountain peaks. A shattering of the Antarctic silence. It must have stunned some penguins and seals.

I was very excited now to be going homeward and brimming with anticipation as to how Palmer would look after my absence and full of wonder about how I would be greeted and what sort of mail might be waiting and what plans for more Peninsula travel I could hope to find, and I was eager to see my room and to unload my new treasures in it (rocks, journals, exposed film, the *Bransfield* T-shirts and plaque, etc.), and not a small part of my daydreams was devoted to thinking how nice life would be on land, without the relentless heaving under one's feet or back, the relentless swaying and the unending roar and vibration of engines.

A number of people were missing at lunch, Sloman among them, and John Dudeney abruptly left the table without returning. I was surprised to find that my appetite was good. Swithinbank told me he had taken a seasickness pill and would take them regularly during the voyage. I debated whether to take one and decided against it although I had some with me, urged upon me by the purser of the *Burton Island* for use on the *Hero* in crossing the Drake Passage. As I understood it, it was part of my job not to shelter myself overmuch from the realities. I might as well find out just what seasickness was like and what it did to me and how much it put me out of action. After all, I told myself, Charles Darwin on the *Beagle* had never conquered seasickness and he had not had pills to help him. Also, I might as well discover what this notorious poop cabin was like without modern aids. I succeeded brilliantly.

The vibrations in the poop cabin were incredibly heavy. The loudest of a variety of odd sounds emanated from the basin, and I told myself not to be surprised if the basin soon disengaged itself from the wall. If I thought the ships' horns had shaken my teeth and bones, now I understood what a real shaking up was like. As for my brain, it was being stirred by a blender.

Deciding that it was in the best interest of my sanity to avoid the poop cabin if I could, I returned to the wardroom, where, alone, I napped until about four o'clock. However, the effects of the beating my mind and inner ear had received lingered much longer than I had expected. We were by now in the open sea and being buffeted by swells and wind, and the ship's relatively small size made itself felt throughout its length and depth but especially in the poop cabin, which rode like a roller coaster. Soon after awaking, I realized I wasn't well enough to risk staying in the wardroom any longer, so I made my way down a narrow corridor and up some stairs to the poop cabin, where Alf Cheshire was lying on his back in the upper bunk.

Turning over and studying me, he said, "You're not handling it too well, are you?"

"I'm afraid not."

It was almost impossible to remain standing in the cabin, and certainly it was hazardous to insist on doing so, consequently I lay down. And now I slid around on my double mattress, and the upper one, sheathed in its plastic casing and being therefore very slippery, kept threatening to fly off the bunk and deposit me onto the basin. One certainly felt better lying on one's back than standing up, but there was a limit to what one could take even lying down. When it came I left the bunk groggily and retched into the basin. Soon Alf Cheshire was jumping off his bunk and retching. He sounded surprised and angry.

"I've never been sick before in all me years at sea," he growled. "I'm going for a walk."

I offered him a seasickness pill. He said he had some and had already taken a couple. I debated whether to change my mind and take one, then turned the idea down. As he went out the door I thought, "Son, I doubt if a walk is what you need at this moment."

I was right, for he returned just in time to retch.

We spelled each other at the basin. I now felt somewhat tender toward that piece of equipment and prayed it wouldn't tear itself off the wall.

If the ship was heaving with the heavy sea running, as it was, the poop cabin was flying, but its flight was not a controlled one. In the poop cabin there was too great an input of rolls and pitches for our balance computers to process. I had taken heavy rolls on the *Burton Island* and I could probably take a good deal of pitching but now there were exotic and infinite combinations, and the vibration roars of the screw, especially when the screw was lifted out of the water, at which times it raced insanely, added to all the rest, was too much for my inner-ear to handle. By now, if I moved in the slightest I was immediately prone to be sicker, so the tendency was to lie extraordinarily still and to keep even a muscle, a tendon, a finger, from moving.

It was now early evening but neither Cheshire nor I made an effort to undress and slip between sheets. Undressing and sheets seemed to be totally beside the point, and in any event I doubt we had the strength and will to manage it. We were very sick now and making regular voyages to the basin. Meanwhile my slick mattress kept sliding every which way and I was surprised that both mattress and I were still in the bunk. I had blankets but didn't bother to use them although the cabin was cold and I had lost body heat through being ill. I lay flat on my back in my clothes and covered myself with my heavy parka.

I discovered that my blue airline bag had fallen onto the floor and that the contents had spilled in all directions. Neither Cheshire nor I had either the ability or the inclination to deal with them. When we used the basin we straddled them as best we could. The feeling in the poop cabin was nightmarish.

Once, when I had to use the basin, a lurch of the ship as I sat up threw me out of my bunk. I landed heavily on hands and knees on the floor among my airline-bag litter. I realized with a shock that I was not as aware as I should be and that I might easily have been seriously injured if I had allowed myself to be flung against the basin. I was not in sufficient control of myself. I was only partially conscious.

The chief steward came by to claim my upper mattress. He expected me to drag it off the bunk and remake my bed. Standing dazed, I informed him slowly that I didn't think I could fulfill his request without more vomiting. He called an assistant, who removed the mattress and carefully made up my bed, which I was never to use except to lie upon it fully clothed. The assistant asked if I wished him to clean up the mess on the floor. I said I would be obliged to him if he did that. He gathered the contents quickly, replaced them in the bag, zipped the bag and sensibly left it lying on the floor.

"Do you get seasick?" I asked.

"Not too often. Many people are very sick now, up forward as well as aft. The master is feeling poorly even though he took a pill."

Watching him work so efficiently and easily at a time when I felt half human, I found myself regarding him as a super-being. At the same time I felt almost like his child, although he was much younger than I. It was not a feeling I often had, and I doubt that I had ever had it before in the Antarctic. It was much more likely for me to feel like a father there, even toward a ship's master like Lawrence. I had had very strong fatherly feelings toward the three men with whom I had crashed on Mt. Erebus. And not only did I feel like a child now, but a child who had wet his bed or had done something similarly childlike. It was quite wonderful to see this stranger rescuing me by bringing order into my suddenly disordered existence.

After he left I glanced out the porthole at the great swells and judged we had a Force 7 sea*, which was later confirmed by the captain. I fell asleep again. I was awakened by the radio operator, who came to tell me he had Palmer Station on the air and did I wish to speak with them. Realizing with relief that the Palmer mystery had ended, I sent my greetings and regrets. Merciful sleep.

Some time after 8 P.M. the radio operator came again, said he had Palmer and that they wanted to speak with me. I followed

*See *Wind Forces* in Glossary.

him groggily down a flight of steep-pitched stairs, down a long corridor forward, up two flights of stairs. Chris Elliott, the ship's master, followed me to the radio room. I spoke with Shane Williams, who said the *Hero* would probably be at Argentine Islands on the 26th and bring me to Palmer on the 27th, a Sunday. He was making reservations by radio for flights out of Ushuaia in Tierra del Fuego and wanted to know my plans: how long I expected to stay in Ushuaia and Buenos Aires, whether I intended to spend any time in Rio and so on. Using his suggestions, I decided to depart Ushuaia on the 15th and spend a day or two in Buenos Aires. I said my Stateside destination was San Francisco. I asked him about the silence. He said they had been putting in new radio gear. Peter Fitzgerald had been correct.

I just about managed to talk with Palmer without retching although I was at times very uncertain if I'd be able to pull the thing off, and I cast uneasy glances around the radio room to see where I could vomit if necessary. No place seemed suitable.

I returned to the poop cabin alone, stopping off at the toilets near the Fiddery to throw up for the last time. I had so little to bring up that I tasted gall strongly. The taste remained for hours. I fell asleep instantly and slept through the night.

I got up at 10 A.M. and felt woozy but much better. Swithinbank dropped by the poop cabin to see if I had survived and to tell me I would go ashore around noon in the launch's second trip. I had no appetite. Alan Smith (Big Al) came in to say goodby. Even while we were at anchor off Argentine Islands Station the poop cabin heaved uncannily. My brains felt scrambled. It was heavy work carrying all my gear forward in stages onto the deck below the poop house. The gear made quite a pile near the Fiddery.

I waited inside the Fiddery, where Sloman came to say farewell and to repeat his offer to put me and my wife up in Cambridge whenever we might go there. Big Al came to the Fiddery to present me with a BAS tie, to say it was from "everyone" and to apologize because it wasn't boxed and wrapped. He added that I was the first American to receive it. I took that as a rhetorical flourish caused by the emotions of the moment. However, it didn't matter what I thought, I was very moved to get it nonetheless. Swithinbank came to the Fiddery to say goodby, as did Chris Elliott. Swithinbank and Big Al

234

seemed apologetic about my bout of seasickness. Other people, Ron Smith among them, came to say goodby.

I could make out very little of the station from the ship. The huts were inconspicuous from even a mild distance, being constructed on a low-lying rocky spit. I was eager to leave the ship.

The launch was winched up level with the deck, my gear was handed aboard, I climbed aboard, we were lowered, there were goodby waves and off we roared over choppy water, I sitting forward in the covered cockpit. I was ashore at 1:15. I said goodby to John Dudeney and Peter Fitzgerald near the little jetty. They were heading for the ship. Fitzgerald was wearing a black felt sombrero. The station had been his home for a long while.

One of the painful things for me about going to the Antarctic was constantly saying goodby to people who had become meaningful to me and whom I would very likely not see again. At times I felt this was carrying American nomadism to an extreme. True, I was a wanderer and had been born one in a sense and should by now have gotten thoroughly used to being one. I had been born in Odessa on the Black Sea, been raised on the western side of the Dniester estuary in a town then called Akkerman and now called Belgorod Dniestrovsk, and in my childhood I had been taken by my mother to Siberia to visit my father, who was stationed there a while during the First World War. I had come to the United States just under the age of six and been raised in Richmond, Virginia. And I had somehow or other continued to be a wanderer. I knew what it felt like to spread yourself thin, to say goodby to meaningful people here and there, this coast and that, and to feel you were leaving vital pieces of yourself.

My journal: "I met Ken Back, new base commander, waited in the wardroom lounge a couple of hours, still feeling woozy and rocky. Fifteen at the station, including me. Nine will winter over. Everything still 'rolling' from shipboard life. Very sore muscles in upper and lower back and in abdomen. Some sore throat. Feeling a bit under the weather. Am living in the 'surgery room,' with green down sleeping bag on a hospital bed. Room rather cold but otherwise comfortable and has the great advantage of privacy, a good chair, a desk and a desk light. To bed about 9."

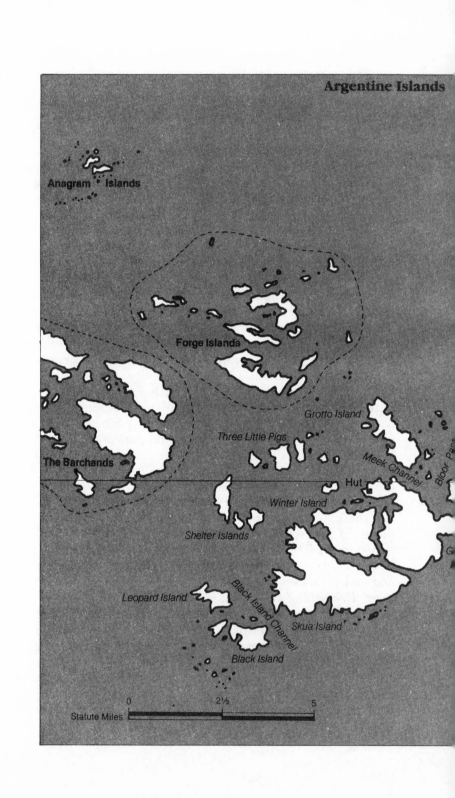

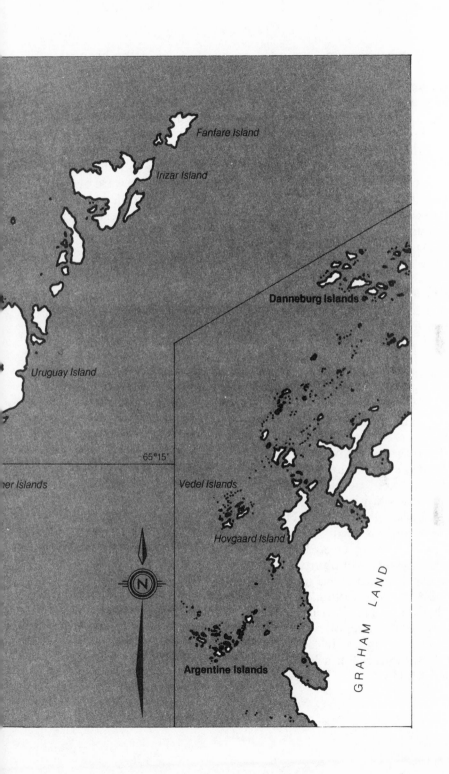

The surgery room reminded me very much of the hospital room I had been assigned to when I lived with the New Zealanders at Scott Base on Ross Island during my second Antarctic trip. That other room had been cold, too, and had had a hospital bed and a small desk and I had slept in a bag so snug it had been called a body bag.

Some well-meaning friends had on occasion warned me I was returning to Antarctica the third time to finish the job I had left uncompleted on the second: that is, my death. There were even friends who warned other friends against my so-called death wish and urged them not to drive in a car with me, for example, because I didn't care whether I lived or died, was in one piece or many. I liked to think I understood the need for people to make myths as well as trouble.

I got up early, used my chest expander, took aspirin for a sore back and went outdoors with binoculars. The weather was still overcast. I was surprised and depressed by the amount of man-made litter outside. There wasn't much for me to see or do. It felt like being on a tiny version of Lagotellerie Island.

I chatted with Ernesto Landera, the young visiting electronics technician from Almirante Brown. He had serious and somewhat sad eyes and a serious, old-too-early look about him in general. His dark straight hair was cut short. His English was sufficient. Although his government and that of the base were in disagreement about sovereignty of the Falkland Islands (Islas Malvinas to the Argentines) and although both claimed just about the same Antarctic territory (together with Chile), he was clearly made to feel welcome at the British station, for he moved about with an air of self-confidence and pleasure, as if he was among good friends. He would return to his own base when the *Bransfield* made its last call of the season in mid-March. When I tried to engage him in a discussion of the problems of overlapping sovereignty claims he looked clouded and unhappy and so I dropped the subject.

But he was willing, almost eager, to talk about tourism in Antarctica. He informed me that Argentina sometimes or perhaps even regularly sent some 5000 tourists a year to the Peninsula region. It can be imagined how difficulties arise at tiny stations when a horde of tourists descends, older people and children included. Not only is a great amount of litter

238

inevitable and much time lost from scientific work. There is also the problem of physical safety, for people tend to wander off, and some of the areas are dangerous, although they may not look it to an unpracticed eye.

I worked hard to catch up on my journal but found it difficult to write inasmuch as my desk seemed to be rolling. My footsteps were uncertain. I knew the base was stationary—it was, after all, a station—but I could not convince my muscles, ligaments and tendons of the fact. It was disquieting to try to converse with men who were solidly grounded whereas you yourself were still very much at sea. You feared you gave the impression of being absent-minded, for half of you was responding to signals unseen by your interlocutors. I wondered if this approximated in some way how schizophrenics experienced social relations. I sensed they couldn't give all of themselves to a conversation because there were other secret voices that demanded their attention. The sea—I thought of Chris Elliott's phrase "a heavy sea running"—was still demanding tribute of me. I felt its swells in my bones and heard its smoking whitecaps in my secret auditorium. I had been aboard ship every night since 22 January with the exception of four at Palmer and last night here. By a quick reckoning that came to thirty-five nights.

The BAS station* was on the peninsula that forms the north-western end of Galindez Island. It was first established on Winter Island in 1947 and had been moved to Galindez in 1953. Marina Point, containing the jetty, was the northwest-ernmost extremity of Galindez Island. The island was named by Charcot for Cdr. Ismael F. Galindez of the Argentine Navy, who was dispatched in the *Uruguay* to search for Charcot when the latter's expedition was feared lost in 1905. Charcot also named the island group Iles Argentine (Argentine Islands) in recognition of Argentine help to his expedition of 1903–5. The base was the oldest operational one in the Peninsula region. Research there was predominantly in what BAS called the Atmospheric Sciences.

Now that I am about to conclude my narrative of my voyages

---

*Argentine Islands was the name of the station when I lived there. It was subsequently changed to Faraday Station after Michael Faraday (1791–1867), the English physicist. The name Argentine Islands is still used to refer to the island group. The terms "station" and "base" are used interchangeably for BAS stations.

with the British Antarctic Survey, perhaps a few remarks about the differences between the BAS and USARP programs are in order. I had heard some American criticisms of the British Antarctic program. The chief points made were that BAS mechanically gathered field data without any guarantees they would be used back home by senior scientists, and that the latter were too often absent from the field. In other words, the data-gathering process had its own momentum and bureaucracy. The American claim was that the American program gathered data for specific projects and with an understanding of their needs and uses, and that senior scientists were almost always involved, often in the field.

The American program was relatively heterogeneous and decentralized and in these respects seemed to me to reflect American society. The British program was more homogeneous and centralized and in its way reflected British society. Much of the basic science in the American program was funded and administered by the National Science Foundation, an independent federal agency, but mainly through grants to universities and other nongovernmental institutions, and the scientists themselves were both government and nongovernment people, the latter being in the large preponderance and stemming from the universities. The logistic support was provided by the Defense Department through a naval task force containing units of the Coast Guard and leasing certain units of the Air Force. The university people were assigned to Antarctic work on the basis of special and relatively temporary projects. The BAS program, although it did include university people, was a good deal more governmental, which is to say that the majority of persons connected with it worked for the government, and this included scientists, administrators and logistic supporters.

Swithinbank told me he thought both programs were good ones, that the American one was lavish and costly and probably quite inefficient, as befitted the nation's affluence, and that the British one was less costly and more efficient but that its danger was in inbreeding.

BAS's broad spectrum of Antarctic research included ionospherics, meteorology, atmospheric geophysics, glacier geophysics, field geophysics, glacier physics, glacier chemistry, structural geology, mineralogy, petrology, geochemistry, paleontology, stratigraphy, taxonomy, microbiology, physiolo-

BEYOND CAPE HORN

gy, biochemistry, terrestrial biology, freshwater biology, marine biology, seals and birds, and human biology and medicine. It had a project in marine geophysics in cooperation with the Department of Geological Sciences, Birmingham University. It had no ongoing research in oceanography, which was a pity inasmuch as the British had done pioneer and great work in this field. Some British Antarctic research was done independently of BAS. For example, the Scott Polar Research Institute of Cambridge was doing glacier physics and glacier geophysics.

At the time of my visit BAS maintained five permanent bases in the Antarctic and sub-Antarctic, which were manned throughout the year. Three other bases were used in summer only.

The Fids were relatively young, had to be unmarried, and normally had a duty of two and a half years in the Antarctic, after which they spent up to two years analyzing and preparing the results of their research for publication. Many Usarps went to the Antarctic for a month in the austral spring/summer, some went for two or three or four, but those who wintered over were relatively rare. Extremely rare were the Usarps who wintered over two years in succession. In my opinion it would not be possible for USARP to get American young men to accept Antarctic conditions such as BAS did with its Fids. I believe the essential reason is that there are too many other opportunities in American society, with which USARP must compete. The Fids did have a telex allotment with home, but I no longer recall how many words were permitted and how frequently. I remember that the allotment struck me as meager and that it was my impression it served as a sorry kind of substitute for a phone patch. I never got a clear understanding as to why phone patches were illegal in the UK.

In the afternoon I observed Ken Back and another man butchering a young female crabeater seal to feed Rachel, the last remaining husky at the place. The seal had been shot with a rifle and a .22-long bullet. Ken Back wore a plaid yellow shirt, BAS brown trousers and high rubber boots. His sleeves were rolled. Barehanded, he wielded a large meat hook as well as a knife. The other man wore rubber boots and a white coat resembling a surgical gown. The seal, which lay on its back, was sliced down the middle, the mottled gray skin was peeled back and the pink blubber flensed off. The other man removed his white smock and rolled up the sleeves of his dark plaid shirt. He wore jeans. This took place on a little icy plateau above an arm of Stella Creek. The ice and snow were rotten, yellow and greenish in places. There was much sharded rock in the vicinity, reminding me of the sharded grays of Lagotellerie Island. The day was cloudy, the creek very still. Rocky low islets, inlets, large snow patches, moody sky.

A third man came out, wearing a skivvy shirt, brown pants and tennis shoes. Ken Back got chilled and donned a soiled orange anorak. He hacked through the seal's ribcage with a hatchet. The men exposed the dark-hued innards, tore them out, scattered lilac intestines and purple-brown organs for the gathering brown skuas and black-backed gulls but reserved the liver for themselves. The men, bent over, working hard, taking strong angular poses, reminded me of workers in Goya paintings. A skua pecking chunks out of the dark liver was chased away by the third man. The gulls with their white breasts brightened the scene. The ice looked increasingly gory. Meanwhile the seal gave the appearance of smiling contentedly. Her skin was pearly, her whiskered mouth almost tender. Even after she was cut up, some of her large muscles twitched. The men chopped off the bloody head and tossed it aside, then hacked at the carcass, bright red with fresh blood, and cut it up. After the carcass had been removed, the forty-odd birds feasted at the gory place with its meat and blood-soaked snow. Among them were speckled birds that were Dominican gull yearlings.

The skuas were more ambitious and aggressive than the gulls. They began to challenge each other for morsels. One skua, who was particularly aggressive, struck me as being sadly foolish, for he spent so much time fighting off other birds that he saved no time for eating. He was very macho but proving it seemed to be all he was getting out of the fray. I observed him with fascination, thinking of his human counterparts, myself included. He stood his ground against all comers and took to the air against them, but while he was airborne some of the meat he was defending was stolen from him, if one could assume he had ever possessed it.

The scene made me think of territorial sovereignty claims in the Antarctic and I wondered if the Third World or the United

Nations or some other congregation of birds would successfully peck away at Antarctica while the Antarctic Treaty signatories, club members as I thought of them, kept debating how to carve up the prize to which they had few if any claims of greater authenticity.

From near there I studied the main hut, or rather two long joined huts that gave the impression of being one. They were built on craggy gray rock close to the water. Their unpainted wood had weathered dark. I counted eighteen windows, the frames of fourteen painted white, the rest red. Several cylindrical metal chimneys stuck out of the slanted roof. The end doorway, which opened onto a small uncovered porch built on stilts, was blood red. From the porch you looked down onto a large snowpatch on which the husky Rachel was quartered, and you could also see the radiosonde balloon hangar hut.

I went now to have a look at Rachel from the porch. Sometimes, feeling lonely, I would go out there to observe her. A couple of times I called out to her. Squat-footed, stolid, she responded by looking up silently, intently, staring. Her face and body haunt me still. I see her sitting on her haunches, studying me, pearl-gray head, dark muzzle, short ears, both chain and running line beyond her, as I try to listen to the subtle resonance of my memory. I think I could write many groping, surmising pages without drawing close to the haunting place. The ghost of those moments of silent staring among some barely inhabited Antarctic rocks will probably never be laid to rest. But possibly the landscape—gray rocks, rotten ice, over-ripe glaciers, creek and channel arms and inlets as sinuous as octopus arms—found its psychic resonances in us both, and I wonder if that too was what her staring meant to convey.

Did she think a stranger like myself needed chaining? I recalled zoo animals who needed the bars for a feeling of protection against humans. Or was she speaking about being solitary, the last of her tribe, of having no dog to gambol and bark and cuddle with? It saddened me to see her cooped up in bondage on the wild snowpatch, a token dog living a token life. At no time during my stay did I see anyone approach her, much less fondle her, nor did I ever see her released from her chain. She had a running line but she rarely used it. Usually I saw her in one small area. She looked undersized, very different from the huskies at Rothera. She never invited me to come down and play with her, never suggested by a look or a wag or a grin or a lolling of tongue that I even visit her.

"Keep your distance and I'll keep mine," she seemed to be saying. "You're a very strange person and I'm not at all sure what your intentions are. Leave me in peace, and if you stop staring at me, that will free me to stop staring back."

Feeling rejected, I would turn away with an imagined shrug and try to reassure myself with the thought that I was a busy man.

I remembered my response to the two pregnant huskies at Rothera. Rachel had no means of getting pregnant here and now. Was she silently speaking about the sterility of her present female life? Why was she allowed to be so solitary? Why wasn't she invited into the station? I meant to ask someone that but somehow never got around to it, probably because of the criticism the questions implied. We two were marginal in this Antarctic place and felt it. We were luxuries. A crabeater had been killed for her, yet she did no work. A room and food had been set aside for me, the American supernumerary. I left her to her running line, chain and snow patch, and she left me to my handful of young men, the remote station and my restlessness.

During the remainder of the afternoon and at dinner I tried to obtain more details about the Mt. Peary tragedy but received only vague replies. I did not have authoritative details until I received a copy of the British Antarctic Survey *Annual Report, 1976–1977* in October 1978. The three men were Geoffrey Hargreaves (meteorologist, age twenty-one), Michael Walker (cook, age twenty), and Graham Whitfield (geophysicist, age twenty-four). They set out from the base on September 3. According to the *Annual Report*, their five-day trip had been planned with care and they had provided themselves thoroughly with equipment and food. Two parties had previously climbed the peak, and the general area of Mt. Peary was fairly well known. The men marched seven miles from the station to a mainland depot. They reached the summit on September 6, at which time they radioed their success. This was their last contact with the base. The mountainous area was known to cause difficulties in radio communication. Also, the men were due back at the station on the 8th. And so there was no cause for alarm at Argentine Islands until they failed to return on schedule.

The base commander alerted BAS headquarters and with two men set off to look for the lost party. The weather was bad, however, and deteriorating. An appeal was made to the Argentines for help with their Antarctic aircraft. The response was immediate but the weather prevented any ground or air search for three days. On September 11 an Argentine Otter, flying low over the Mt. Peary area, spotted two pairs of skis and what looked to be a ground sheet about 1000 feet below the summit. There was no sign of activity. Heavy snowfall and avalanching had descended onto the glaciers below. The ground party was unable to reach the crucial area. The Argentines flew to Adelaide Island Station and picked up three expert mountaineers with the intention of landing them near the summit, but bad weather made a further search impossible. The aircraft was diverted to the Argentine base, Vicecomodoro Marambio. The severe weather continued. By September 14 "it was reluctantly decided that conditions had exceeded human endurance and the missing men must therefore have perished." This was the first fatal accident in BAS for ten years.

Wanting to get outside, wanting to *do* something, I went with Ken Back to an outlying hut where the radiosonde gear was. We crossed and climbed craggy rocks to get there, dipped down, crossed snow, climbed again. I watched him inflate and release a balloon. He spoke of how expensive these things were, how BAS was having trouble affording them, how up they went and weren't recovered, and sometimes you got no signals at all and so lost them entirely, but usually you could track them awhile and get weather and other data: air temperatures, barometric pressures and so on. We observed the khaki balloon rising into the gray sky. Suspended beneath it was a square, wire-grid antenna, and hanging from the antenna was the instrumentation package. The balloon quickly disappeared from sight.

Back was of middle height, attractive looking, with especially fine features, and wore old, baggy clothes, usually with uncombed middle-length hair. He gave the impression of being shy and very capable. Like everyone else at the station, he was very cordial to me and eager to be of help.

Two of the Fids stood out. One was Mike Smith, a new Fid who tried to make a place for himself by the use of wit, flip remarks and such expressions as "My dear boy." Underneath it all was his unsureness about himself. He had a strange name for a dandy and knew it, and sometimes said as much. He was a wintering-over meteorologist/physicist. He had a small head on a tall, gangly body and long neck. Peter Wait the radio operator was tall, handsome, taciturn and waddled in huge, baggy, dirty, brown wool trousers and large wool shirt. He was rather remote but very obliging.

One made one's own breakfast but lunch and dinner were served. You took turns washing dishes. While having a late breakfast in the tiny mess room one morning I noticed that the box of Kellogg's corn flakes I was using advertised a contest. The closing date was 1961.

After dinner we went to the small lounge, where Beethoven's Ninth was playing on the stereo. The coal stove was hot. A young Adélie penguin, a wanderer from a distant rookery, was seen outside a window, clambering on the shards of frost-shattered rock. It was picked up gently and handed into the lounge.

"Don't bring him here, he'll shit all over the place," somebody complained.

But the bird was continent. Uncharacteristically, it did not bite or squawk. Observed at close range, it observed back silently, a bit nervously, its eyes rolling a little in fear. When someone carefully stroked its immaculate, white, glistening, pin-feathered breast, it backed up a bit on its bright pink feet, a humble visitor but gallant, brave.

And then it opened its dark beak and I saw a pink, narrow, fluted tongue thrust out, and the bird began to pant.

"It's overheating," I said.

It was ushered toward the open door and down the long crowded corridor. Waddling, it cast an eye backward to see if its rear was secure. It remained silent. The double doors of the hut were held open. It walked out into the sunlit night.

13 ✷ A Talk with Sir Vivian Fuchs

HAVING JUST COMPLETED the narrative of my visit with the British Antarctic Survey, I should like to present a taped interview I had with Sir Vivian Fuchs, former director of BAS and one of the very few persons to be knighted for Antarctic exploration. The conversation took place in Sir Vivian's home on Barton Road in Cambridge, England, on April 10, 1975.

From my journal: "Fuchs was working in his garden. He approached me in high rubber boots, a flannel shirt open at the collar, and heavy maroon sweater. He led me to a place in front of the house to show me his huge emperor penguin fashioned out of privet hedge, with a chick between the feet. I had a laugh. Fuchs was still amazingly fit at sixty-seven. He said he played squash regularly and had played yesterday. He looks hard, rugged, has most of his hair, beetling eyebrows, a seamed, lean, handsome face."

I had first met Sir Vivian at a USARP Antarctic orientation conference at Skyland, Virginia, in September 1970, prior to my second Antarctic trip. I remembered being struck then by his wonderful physical condition and by the vigorous and informal manner in which he tossed a frisbee, an informal manner that in the spring of 1975 puzzled me when I compared it with the formal tones I heard in letters and in one or two telephone calls I made to him from London.

"The interview went better than I had expected but, given the circumstances, it couldn't be a really complex, long one such as the one with Sir Charles Wright. Fuchs is not an expansive man. After we taped a whole cassette (ninety minutes) I asked if he wanted to pause. He seemed surprised that I still had a fair number of questions to ask.

"Rising, he said we'd have a drink. We had whisky and soda. Lady Fuchs came in and invited me to stay for lunch, which I did. But my heart wasn't in it, for Fuchs smilingly said he wouldn't allow me to spend the whole afternoon in talking, that we'd wind the interview up in a half-hour. With that kind of pressure it's impossible to do much that's creative. Still, the interview is better than I had hoped it would be. Fuchs very kindly insisted on driving me to my place on Tenison Street in his twelve-cylinder Jaguar, which he handles with great relish and aplomb."

The interview as it's now published, although based on the taped one, is in many respects different from it as a consequence of Sir Vivian's various and excellent changes by correspondence. I too made some changes. I am now very happy with the conversation, as I believe he is also.

He was born in February 1908, was married in 1933 and had one son, two daughters, one of whom is deceased. He was a graduate of St. John's College, Cambridge. He was well experienced in geological and administrative field work, having been geologist with the Cambridge East Greenland Expedition, 1929, the Cambridge Expedition to East African Lakes, 1930–31, the East African Archeological Expedition, 1931–32 and leader of the Lake Rudolf Rift Valley Expedition, 1933–34. During the war he served in West Africa, 1942–43, later in Europe, and was demobilized as a major. His chief recreation was squash and swimming.

He was the originator and commander of the Commonwealth Trans-Antarctic Expedition, 1955–58, which realized Shackleton's frustrated hope of making the first transcontinental traverse, a distance of almost two thousand miles, from the head of the Weddell Sea on the eastern side of the Antarctic Peninsula to Ross Island in McMurdo Sound south of the Ross Sea. He published a book about the expedition, *The Crossing of Antarctica,* to which Sir Edmund Hillary contributed some chapters. In it he outlined the general plan. The Weddell Sea party would use tracked vehicles supported by dogs and aircraft. After vehicles had served their purpose as traveling depots they would be abandoned. The Ross Sea or New Zealand party under Hillary would establish a route from Ross Island over the mountains, onto the continental plateau and on to the Pole and would lay fuel and food depots along the way. The expedition would explore the unknown area between the Weddell Sea and the Pole and would map the western side of the mountains surveyed by Scott and Shackleton from the east during their attempts on the Pole. During the continent's crossing, seismic soundings and a gravity traverse would be made to explore the depth of the icecap and the shape of the rock surface under it.

Whereas Fuchs started from the Weddell Sea, Hillary set up a station on Ross Island (Scott Base) and then proceeded to lay depots to just short of the Pole. Being head of the expedition, Fuchs expected to reach the Pole first, then meet Hillary there. Hillary, restless, and already knighted for his exploit in reaching the crest of Mt. Everest, broke the plan and marched to the Pole, thus becoming the first man to reach it overland since Scott in 1912. This, as I understood the matter, created a flap, since technically Hillary was Fuchs's subordinate on the expedition and inasmuch as the New Zealand part was definitely a subsidiary element of it.

The success of the expedition brought Fuchs many honors, chief of which was knighthood in 1958. He was director of the British Antarctic Survey from 1958 to 1973.

Neider: You were involved in expeditions to Greenland and Africa early in your career as an explorer, and one of the fascinating questions is: How did Antarctica come into your life?

Fuchs: Antarctica came in very much later on, because between Greenland and Africa came the war, and it was at the end of the war—of course, I had thought of going back to Africa but by that time the opportunities had changed. It wasn't all that suitable. And so I was casting around, and an old friend of mine, Launcelot Fleming (later Bishop of Norwich), who was a geologist himself, said to me, "They're looking for a geologist to go to the Antarctic. Are you interested?" As I had always had that in mind as a possibility, it fitted well and away I went.

When I applied to join as a geologist, one of the men who was organizing the thing said, "Will you take command of the whole expedition?" I was then older, I was in my thirties—in fact, late thirties, for I arrived in the Antarctic in time to have my fortieth birthday. But that was a long time after starting expedition work, for I went to Greenland in 1929 when I was twenty-one. There was therefore a long gap in time before going back to polar work. When I did reach the Antarctic I expected to stay one year but fell into a trap because we were isolated for two years—it wasn't possible to get in to relieve us. We were isolated completely. At some point in this period I remember saying, "Ah, yes, but you know we didn't do it like that back in Greenland in '29." And a queer look came over my companions' faces, for some of them were hardly born back at that time. Yes, I learned a lot then, of course—all the techniques. It was a wonderful experience. And it was then I thought of crossing Antarctica—back in '49. On one journey, in my second year down there, a geologist was with me—Ray Adie. When we were 400 miles out from base we wanted to know what was beyond where we were, but hadn't enough food and supplies to go on, we had to go back. So I said, "The only way to do this is to go across all the way." If you plan to do that you can go on forever, so to speak; so I sat down in the tent and thought, this will have to be more than just a little expedition, a Fid show, so we'll make it a British Commonwealth show. Bring in other countries. And that's how it all started—in the field in 1949. Of course, I didn't start the wheel turning—I couldn't—until 1954. You see, I left this country for the Antarctic at the end of '47, wintered '48, wintered '49, and came out in '50.

Neider: So it was while you were in Antarctica that you picked up the idea of Shackleton to cross the Antarctic.

Fuchs: Well, of course, it wasn't connected with Shackleton. We had our own reason why we wanted to go. Later it turned out that instead of continuing on the route we were then on, it would be easier and more practical to start from the head of the Weddell Sea, and that meant it had to be from where Shackleton intended to start.

Neider: I hadn't been prepared to encounter Africa in your career.

Fuchs: Ah, Africa was another story. When I came back from

Greenland I was a recently qualified geologist and had acquired a little expedition experience. There was an expedition going to East Africa and Central Africa which wanted a geologist; would I go? Splendid, I thought, so off I went on that. That was 1930. Then later I organized my own African expedition, the Lake Rudolf Rift Valley Expedition, in 1934. Then another African expedition, Lake Rukwa Expedition, in '38. So I did quite a lot of coverage: as far west as the Congo, north up to the Abyssinian border and south to Nyasaland. I did eight years of African work, five in the field.

Neider: You were on the Greenland icecap, I presume?

Fuchs: Well, not quite. The object was to climb Mt. Petermann, which was then the highest known mountain in Greenland. It *isn't* the highest mountain but it was thought to be at the time. It's just under 10,000 feet. Wordie—later Sir James Wordie—who was my tutor here [Cambridge]—he had been Shackleton's Chief of Scientific Staff on the 1914 expedition, when the *Endurance* was lost—was taking periodical expeditions to Greenland, and I ended up going with him on this one in '29. I suppose I was conditioned to these things not only because I liked open air life but because of my association with him.

Neider: That's a fascinating connection—a personal connection, that is, with Shackleton via Wordie.

Fuchs: At that time, here in Cambridge, there was also Priestley, who was with Scott *and* with Shackleton, and there was Debenham, who was with Scott. These three were a triumvirate of older people when I was an undergraduate, and I knew them all. Debenham was Professor of Geography. I knew him very well. Priestley fairly well, and later very well. The presence of these three in the University naturally provided encouragement towards exploratory work.

Neider: But I think the Greenland expedition—

Fuchs: It wasn't a major expedition but we succeeded in climbing Mt. Petermann, and in doing so learned the geology, and so on.

Neider: What sort of geological work were you doing on top of the mountain? Taking rock samples?

Fuchs: Yes, we were trying to map and geologize in an area between the coast and Petermann. You see, at that stage the region was only partly known, and certainly the geology wasn't known, for nothing had been done in the interior at all. So everything one encountered—practically everything—was new and we were the first people to traverse inland to Petermann.

Neider: So, in '49, then, you had other reasons than Shackleton's to cross the continent. Shackleton's main, perhaps sole, reason was that it was the last big thing to do on the continent.

Fuchs: This wasn't our reason, you see. We were trying—or I was trying, if you like—we wished to know what happened in the interior, geologically speaking. Would we find an extension of the heavily overthrust and folded sediments we had been studying in 1948–50? What was beyond? There were vast snow fields and doubtless mountains, but we didn't know what was there. Everybody who does these things has a sense of curiosity, the driving force is wanting to know something. It was that which was the reason for the expedition. Of course I believed and always have believed that you should never make an expedition without an object. At one time it was a question of: Is there a mountain range, are there people or are there not (apropos of African and such expeditions)—things like that. But by the time *I* was operating, the scene had changed from purely geographical exploration. People were going on expeditions to work in various scientific fields. Not only to find what was there, but what it was made of, what were the rocks, what were their ages, what were the fossils, how did it fit with the rest of the world—and in all the other subjects similarly. In our case, for instance, how deep was the ice.

Neider: Your prime interest was scientific, then.

Fuchs: Scientific interest was the purpose of the Trans-Antarctic Expedition but, of course, one had to play the adventure side—not only did one enjoy the adventure but you had to play it—because if you were going to get public support (it was necessary to raise money), it would be through the interest in the adventure side. They would enjoy that bit and contribute in various ways. In the end, in addition to public support, I think we had 490 firms supporting the expedition. We had also got support from four countries, and that was about a third of the total cost—a little less that a third.

Neider: You mean from the private firms?

Fuchs: No, from the governments.

Neider: Only a third?

Fuchs: Yes, it was ₤180,000. From this country, New Zealand, Australia and South Africa. The rest of the money had to be raised from all kinds of people—subscription, firms, institutions. The total cost was just under ₤750,000.

Neider: Were you very good at this kind of thing?

Fuchs: I didn't *think* I was. I can remember saying to Wordie, "You know, if somebody was to place me down there at the head of the Weddell Sea, with all the equipment, I'll get across. No doubt about that. I have no worries about that. What I worry about is how I'm going to raise the money. I've not the experience to get big money." I remember I tried to get a newspaper contract, and I saw the editor of a newspaper and I had an interview and he said, "How much do you want?" I said "You won't like it but I want ₤25,000." He said, "You're joking." I said, "Not a bit." I said, "₤25,000 or nothing." He said, "Oh if you were talking about two or three thousand I might consider it." I said, "Well, I'm very sorry." It was quite clear that you had to think big. On all the other expeditions I had done—on my African expedition I had six men for a whole year in Africa—the voyage out and back, food, vehicles, camels, donkeys, and all the rest—for ₤2,000. Now the whole scene was a different one. When you start thinking about ships and aeroplanes and many men and several bases and supplies for the year, and the backup supplies for the extra year that you may need, and so on, this constitutes an enormous amount. So I had to think quite differently. But I must say that everybody was extraordinarily good. The newspapers were friendly in their approach. They helped. Just naturally. It wasn't suggested to them that they should, but they did. Firms picked it up. British Petroleum was the big one. They gave a lead very early. They put up ₤50,000, and it cost them a lot more in the end. And then there were countless other firms. British Petroleum provided all the fuel for ships, aeroplanes and tractors, and all the lubricants—at both ends of the continent.

Neider: Once you've embarked on this kind of voyage—that is, the raising of money—there must be a lot of suspense, you wonder whether you're going to reach the other side, if the money will be forthcoming.

Fuchs: Of course, I had by this time not a doubt we were going. We had an executive committee, a science committee, a finance committee—it was highly organized. In fact, we were

A Talk with Sir Vivian Fuchs　　　253

never in the red, but we were always going to be in the red in the next month or two months. We never had the whole money all the way along. We were always needing more, and in the end we finished up with a surplus of what turned out to be £33,000.

Neider: And what happened with that?

Fuchs: That was turned into a trust, which now provides money for Antarctic work—if anyone in New Zealand, Australia, South Africa or the U.K. wants some equipment or an air passage or to publish something—but it is only for the Antarctic. They can apply to get a grant—for £100 or £500, that sort of amount.

Neider: Am I incorrect when I assume that the main scientific hope of the Trans-Antarctic Expedition was to measure the icecap?

Fuchs: When you say the main, it *was* in a way, because it was a study we could make from one side to the other. But in those days we didn't have radio echo sounding. It hadn't been invented. So we had to make spot soundings by firing explosive shots and getting seismic soundings of the ice depth. And, between those shots, which we made every thirty miles, we took gravity measurements. These can give you a reasonable idea of the depth of the ice between the seismic shots. So there was a gravity traverse, and a seismic shooting traverse, along the same line. There were also geological studies done at our end (the head of the Weddell Sea and the mountains beyond)—geology and survey. At the other end Hillary had parties out in the mountains, surveying and geologizing as well.

Neider: Once you had left your base on the Weddell Sea and encountered the icecap, aside from the seismic soundings there wasn't much to do.

Fuchs: No, there wasn't. There was meteorology, radiation, ice soundings—and the gravity, of course. We didn't know what was ahead in the way of mountains. We didn't know that we were going to find the Theron Mountains in our path, nor the Shackleton Range in our path, nor the Whichaway Nunataks. When we found them we worked on them before actually setting off on the crossing journey. We sent parties ahead the year before the main journey started. At the other end, of course, much more was known from the Scott and Shackleton and other expeditions. But still there were various mountains which had never been traveled in nor examined up to that time. So Hillary's group had also had a great deal to do.

Neider: Going back to what you told Wordie, you never really had any doubt about crossing the continent.

Fuchs: No. I'm a practical sort of chap, and through the years one gets to know one's capabilities, what you can and cannot *do.* Again, one must believe in what one wants to do, it's no good thinking that perhaps it is impossible. If you think that, you'll never start. You've *got* to believe in yourself, and to believe that the capability is there. When the problems arise, one deals with them. You cannot know what they're going to be—but you can anticipate *some.* What will hold you up? Will it be endless bad weather? You can allow for such things in your planning, to some extent. And you prepare for what you're going to do if you get caught. For example, we took with us light bridging members for getting Sno-cats out of crevasses. Of course, we dropped a lot of them into crevasses but we got them all out, and never actually lost a vehicle.

Neider: Seeing some of the photographs—that are in your book—of the Sno-cats down in the crevasses, it's extremely difficult to imagine how they were pulled out. You must have had very strong vehicles to pull them out.

Fuchs: In each case the arrangements were makeshift. You looked at the situation and then decided how it could be managed. You're thinking of one particular picture of a Sno-cat with its right side bridging a very deep crevasse, a very wide one, with one pontoon pressed up against the far side, the other two over the edge of the crevasse. Well, of course, if it had been pulled back, the whole thing would have dropped in at the front. So what we did was to attach two Weasels to the front end with a steel cable, then two Sno-cats behind to pull it out backwards. We then had to straighten the pontoon, which was hanging vertically. This had to be pulled to the correct angle to allow it to come up over the crevasse edge. So we had to have a fifth vehicle pulling that pontoon into position as the cat came back. Having the fallen Sno-cat suspended by cables at either end, the Weasels on the far side of the crevasse slowly gave way as the two 200-horsepower Sno-cats were pulling it backwards.

Neider: From the geological point of view is there any scientific advantage or excitement to wintering over?

Fuchs: From our point of view there always was the need to winter because we needed all the summer months to make the crossing. For other expeditions there is not now so much need to winter because of the increased long-range flying capability in many areas. For instance, the Argentines often fly planes to one of the islands off the tip of the Antarctic Peninsula. On the other hand the British Antarctic Survey does not have large enough planes to fly people into position and they have to be put down by ship early in the season. The small Twin Otters then pick them up where they're landed by the ship, and fly them south into the field. The biologists need to winter in order to know what happens in wintertime as well as in summer, so that they can study the life cycle of creatures or plants. The loss of light, the snow cover, the lack of radiation or the increase of radiation, all these things affect all living matter.

Neider: Getting back to the scientific results of the Trans-Antarctic Expedition, were you entirely satisfied with them?

Fuchs: Yes—except that we haven't quite finished publishing even now. We should have done, but we have one or two papers to go. It's only because people have jobs, and they're delayed, but we have practically finished.

Neider: But I suppose the results that were most interesting to the general public were the seismic shots?

Fuchs: Yes, perhaps they were for the general public, but I think it is true to say that they would today be regarded as rather weak. They are not as accurate as they could have been. There were various reasons for this, such as the depth at which we were able to fire the explosives and the nature of the snow, so some of the reflections were not too good, but we *did* get a general guide as to what the ice thickness across the continent was. *Now*, of course, you can fly in an aeroplane with radio echo sounding and you've got the whole thing in the form of a continuous trace.

Neider: Did you continue the seismic soundings from the Pole down to Ross Island?

Fuchs: We stopped at the top of the Skelton Glacier, which is on the edge of the continental ice sheet.

Neider: Were you knighted for your work as a whole or because you mounted the expedition and it was a success?

Fuchs: I'm sure it was for the expedition.

Neider: In that sense, then, I think you're one of the very rare people who have been knighted for Antarctic work. Sir Charles Wright wasn't. I believe you're the only one.

Fuchs: Shackleton was.

Neider: I mean in modern times. It was very strange, actually, because he was knighted while Scott was still alive, and given the somewhat difficult feeling between them, that must have been something for Scott to consider.

Fuchs: I'm not quite sure what happened there. Of course, I'm sure that Scott would have been knighted had he got back from the Pole.

Neider: Going back to your very great self-confidence in being able to cross the continent. Perhaps I ought to qualify that. There was this time when Hillary was worried and thought you ought at least to winter your gear at the Pole, and fly out and come back to the Pole. I thought that was a very bad suggestion on his part because—

Fuchs [laughing]: The public thought so too.

Neider: It was quite a flap. If you had done that I think it would have marred the expedition.

Fuchs: Well of course. It wasn't practical. The thing was, he wasn't in a position to judge. He had been to Antarctica on our side of it just to get the feel of it, to know what was going on. And then he had been there with the New Zealand party. He was a tremendously energetic chap, you see, a great goer and with a tremendous drive—"Let's *do*"— you know. But he hadn't very long experience of the Antarctic. We had assessed our equipment and we were geared to travel in temperatures down to minus 60° F if we had to. Such low temperatures were not to be expected even on the high plateau until very much later in the season—at the end of our journey the temperatures were dropping to just below minus 40. That is easy stuff. It's not anything to worry about at all. Below minus 60 it begins to get difficult to travel, but we were confident that if we had to we could work down to minus 60. And that wasn't going to happen on the continent until some time in late March or in April.

Neider: Apparently, from what you say, you didn't have great difficulty in starting the vehicles in the morning.

Fuchs: We prepared the vehicles to do it. The original engines were modified enormously. We changed the compression ratio, we installed preheating systems for the engines and for the batteries, there were hot-air blowers, and heaters in the coolant systems. It took half an hour to start the engines.

Neider: But there was no danger of oil seals cracking?

Fuchs: All the bearings were pre-packed with special greases. We changed all rubber—the insulation on wires, rubber seals on doors—all these things were changed to a silicone rubber, which was still flexible at minus 60. When we got those Sno-cats over from the States we tried them out in Norway and found hairline cracks in most of the welds on the tracks. That would have been nothing to worry about in this country at all, but for the Antarctic we had every weld cut out—thousands of them. All were replaced—all except two or three, the ring welds on the steering transmission systems. They were big, circular welds and were the only ones that broke; they broke on three of the four Sno-cats.

Neider: What we come to is that you feel that there was a genuine difference of opinion in Hillary's evaluating the circumstances. But what did he really think? That you'd have mechanical difficulties in making your way from the Pole before the end of the season? It isn't really pinned down.

Fuchs: The differences have never been pinned down by me.

Neider: We get these communications between the two of you and I'm puzzled. Is he worried about life and death, or is he worried about the fact that the machines are going to break down?

Fuchs: I think the implication was that he thought it a dangerous operation to go on another 1200 miles from the Pole. He was also concerned to get his party out so that they didn't have to winter again. He was anxious about that, I suppose. I am sure that he was also anxious that we shouldn't get into difficulties.

Neider: Was there or wasn't there a flap? I've heard rumors that there was some sort of feeling because Hillary went to the Pole first and wasn't supposed to, really.

Fuchs: It wasn't in the plan, but this was neither here nor there, I had no objection to this at all.

Neider: It didn't bother you.

Fuchs: Not a bit. I was crossing the continent. The thing was, Hillary sent me a message saying, had I a suggestion as to what he should do next? I sent a suggestion but by that time he had pressed on. Our communication was not very good. We had to communicate—I forget—either through McMurdo or through the Pole. Pole to McMurdo, McMurdo to Scott Base, and Scott Base to Hillary. So he had gone on before getting my reply. In any case, he wanted to go to the Pole, and I'd known that he wanted to at the time. This was taken up by the press, who said it was something which he did against my interest in some way. But then I wasn't thinking like that. Nor was my party. The only thing we didn't appreciate was the message suggesting we should stop, and that it was released to the press. That was what caused all the furor.

Neider: There were members of the press at the Pole when you arrived.

Fuchs: They got there the day before we did.

Neider: And who arranged for that?

Fuchs: Dufek.

Neider: He wanted the publicity, then?

Fuchs: Well, the press wanted the publicity. And anyway, it's American practice to put press men into position to get news.

Neider: It's also to the advantage of the press to have a conflict between two explorers.

Fuchs: Of course, my answer to Hillary, which was a very private message, had to be released too.

Neider: I think Hillary is a great man but it seems to me that it was a mistake on his part. New Zealand had not initiated the transcontinental expedition. They had come in, been very helpful, and certainly it was absolutely essential to set up a base at Ross Island. But really it had been an English initiative operation. And I think it would have been better all around—

Fuchs: But you see, Hillary's committee, the Ross Sea committee, which was the counterpart to the U.K. committee, they were upset by this business of the messages, because they didn't like it any more than we did. The point is that it was a private message to me, and my message back was a private one to him. It was said that the message was handed to the press by mistake but we don't know how it got out, really. But it got out, and that was the error that caused all the misunderstanding. I just got a message and I replied to it, saying that if you feel like that, you do your bit and I will continue to do mine. Since I was in command of the whole expedition I just continued.

A Talk with Sir Vivian Fuchs   259

Neider: It didn't cause you to hesitate in any way.

Fuchs: Not at all.

Neider: You had a triple career. You had a career as a scientist and one as an explorer and a third as an administrator. I'd like to have some sort of summary of your career as a geologist.

Fuchs: Well, you see, I never have counted myself as a very *good* geologist. I've been an enthusiastic geologist, very interested, very keen, good at field work. I found it more laborious to write up—most of my geological publications have been on Africa. Once I had started with the Antarctic I had specialists with me, and although I did do field geology, I found myself so tied up with organizing, administering and arranging for other people's work that I gradually dropped out. In later years it's been invaluable to have a scientific background and to understand—not only geology but the general picture of scientific needs—I was also trained as a biologist, I also had that background. I couldn't have done the job that I have done without the scientific training, and indeed practicing it for some years.

Neider: Do you expect to go back to Antarctica?

Fuchs: I suppose there's no real reason why I should, but if somebody offered me a trip to Antarctica I would certainly go. And it's quite possible that I might, as an elder statesman, visit some of the stations. It has always been my feeling that it is good to have people of the past, older people, making contact with younger. I believe the younger people feel that interest is being taken, they can get a bit of advice if they ask, and enthusiasm can be enhanced, or over-enthusiasm modified—you can contribute things. It's been my life for over twenty-five years, you know, and therefore it's always a welcome scene.

Neider: Have you been to various sectors? Of course you've been to the Weddell part and to Ross Island.

Fuchs: I haven't been around to the Australian sector. I've only dealt with the Peninsula and the McMurdo sides.

Neider: If you had to advise a younger man on mounting an expedition to Antarctica what would you counsel him to be particularly aware of in the selection of people?

Fuchs: It usually starts with meeting a man—a formal interview, or a casual drink in a pub, or something. You get a first impression of a chap. It is very important that the leader is going to get on with and can handle all those with him. It isn't that he's better than the others. It's just that he must be able to feel confidence in the men, that he can handle them, that they will work with him. By choosing people from that point of view, he is building automatically a kind of mutual understanding in the group. If he feels in tune with A and in tune with B, the chances are that A and B have something in common too. So as he goes on choosing more and more people, he is building a common factor amongst them all, because they all relate to him in some way. On the other hand, if you have an *official* organization which is choosing people who are going to be put together on an expedition, and then say So and So is to be the leader, that leader has not been able to exercise any kind of selection or adjustment. In such a case the responsibility devolves on the selecting group, and they must have experience of the scene for which they are selecting people. It's no good having a lot of people sitting on a board who've never seen the Antarctic. They must know the Antarctic and know what goes on and how people behave and how they react in various ways. Very quickly, at an interview, you get an impression of the over-confident fellow or the weak number. Some oddities begin to show up. And we have developed, in this country, our own particular way. After the first interview we decide whether we're going to offer the chap a job or not. If we do so he's put through a training course of some kind—in his subject but related to the Antarctic. Then he starts reading up and learning all that's gone before in the Antarctic, in his subject. So you gradually get to know him, and he begins to show how he works with others. Then we have a week when everybody, I mean literally everybody—doctors, scientists, carpenters, cooks—all of them come here to Cambridge. They have lectures and talks and discussions, so that everyone understands what the objects of the work are and the environment in which they will find themselves. Then we send them out by ship, which takes several weeks, and they get to know each other closely. Most of them will visit several bases before they're deposited at their destination. During this time they help in unloading and in doing various jobs ashore and on the ship. How do they work? Do they work willingly? Do they get difficult about this or that kind of thing? All the time the senior people keep an eye on them. Sometimes it has been necessary to bring a man out after he's actually arrived in the Antarctic. If he's not going to make the grade to winter, it is better to bring him back. One rotten apple upsets the rest of them. On rare occasions we have made a mistake and in practice we've found it best to say: "Any doubt: out." By the time we leave them to winter, with ships and aircraft gone, we've had them under our hands for five months. In that time we've learnt to know them all. So the selection is not as simple as it might seem. It's over a long period, in which a great many people have contact with a man—you've seen how he operates in his own field and in other people's fields, how he mixes, when he gets angry and why, how he controls himself. The basic thing is a healthy body and a stable mind. I think we have advantages in the slowness of our operation. In the American operation everything happens very quickly because of their capability, the capability of bigger aircraft, many aircraft, and numbers of ships. All that is efficient in being able to perform their task quickly. We haven't got that capability and have to do the field work more slowly. What the Americans might do in a year, might take us two or possibly three. Yet I believe the built-in slowness produces the best use of what we've got, and lengthy experience which leads to safe traveling. Because most of our people spend two years in the field they become proficient in their Antarctic techniques and the methods which aid their work.

Neider: Do you consider yourself primarily a scientist or an explorer?

Fuchs: I suppose that having said I have dropped from active, constructive, scientific work, then you must say I'm an explorer if you like. But I wouldn't have begun it if I wasn't scientifically inclined. I've seen my function, and have for many years, as making Antarctic scientific work possible. And to do so, to find capable chaps, young chaps, then make it possible for them to produce the results. In this I have been aided by knowing what is possible and what is not possible in practice.

Neider: There's the question of the possibility that Antarctica will soon be taken out of the hands of scientists, and *that* gets into the whole difficult matter of the pressure of a growing world population causing a greater need for energy resources, and there is talk of changing the Antarctic Treaty to make it possible to go in and exploit the continent.

Fuchs: The situation, as all of us who are in this game know, is that there have been considerable political disputes over ownership claims. When the IGY came along in 1958, scientists managed to get the nations to agree that the continent was to be open to scientific work during the IGY to anybody anywhere, regardless of claims. This gave the opportunity to make the Treaty. The only thing they missed out on—and for a reason—was what was to happen if anybody found anything valuable. It was too tricky a problem to solve at that time, so it was left out of the Treaty. It still had that gap. Well, of course now we have the need for energy, and it is probable that somewhere in that continent or in the continental shelves around it there *may be* resources, so the time is coming when the Treaty powers are going to have to make a decision as to how they are going to manage that. Meanwhile, in these last seventeen years, they have been producing rules and regulations regarding conservation of animals and plants. People who go there, whatever they do, have to face the existing regulations concerning what they may do; for instance, plants and animals may not be introduced, nor live or dead animals taken out without a license.

Neider: But technically, if you don't belong to the Treaty, or even if you do and don't care, you can send ships down there and do what you please. Who is to stop them?

Fuchs: Nobody could stop them, but I think you would find that the nations would unite to bring certain pressures to bear upon the offenders. And it would be very difficult for them. There would be no support, no communications, no assistance to anybody who operated in that way. The whole thing would be totally impractical for them. There could also be other sanctions.

Neider: You're not terribly worried about the situation, then.

Fuchs: I'm worried that if any of these nations that have signed the Treaty went out on a limb and started to do something against the Treaty, it might cause the whole Treaty to collapse.

Neider: Well, maybe the geopoliticians among the Treaty powers may decide that it's to their advantage to change the rules of the game—but changes have to be by unanimous consent.

Fuchs: I think that Nature is going to have the last word in this, she is going to make it extremely difficult to start extracting oil—because you've got to go through five, six, eight thousand feet of ice. There'll be problems. If there was a leak from a bore under the ice cap—no one knows what's going to happen. On the continental shelf the problem will be with sea ice and icebergs.

Neider: One of the unfortunate things is the secrecy with which such matters are treated by the Antarctic Treaty nations.

Fuchs: I do not believe there is secrecy; their deliberations are published. There are, of course, difficulties with unknowledgeable people raising too many hairs. For instance, the worst damage that is done to the cause of conservation is done by conservationists themselves. They overplay their hand by insisting on absolute bans and not using balanced judgment, thereby they make their ideas appear impractical, if not ridiculous. It is easier to achieve results by keeping to what is practical and sensible to do.

Neider: The United States effort in Antarctica, as well as that of the British, since the IGY has consisted almost exclusively of basic scientific research with logistic support. In the United States the logistic support is provided largely by the Navy. How do you feel about a program that would allow the humanities to come in? And how do you feel about the fact that women are playing an increasing role down there?

Fuchs: They're not really, their part is *very* small. As for the other thing, there is no justifiable reason that I can see to spend money on taking people down just for an experience at public expense. There are plenty of people who want to go, but then they'd be taking the place of somebody else who would be productive. Not all the time, but in most years we have taken one or two reporters, photographers, BBC people, on the ships, during the summer, and shown them around. But they must be limited, and must not be a nuisance to what is the main purpose. There is quite a problem in selecting from all the many who want to go. And then there's the question of women. Well, I wouldn't have any—for very sound reasons. It's not just sex as sex (which itself would cause problems in a small isolated community of men), but they can't physically play the part. You can't say to them, "Go and pick that up and carry it over there." A man has to do it. They can't pull their weight for sheer lack of strength, and everybody has to pull their weight. If you have a large body of people, then you can afford to introduce those who do not have to use their physical strength. Sooner or later somebody is going to say, "Now for God's sake, it's time she did something. Why am I always carrying the heavy load? Why am I always starting the engines?" So, the larger the operation is, the easier I can see it would be to have one or more women with it. There is no sense, in my view, for a woman to insist that she has a right to go—because she has only a right insofar as she is strong enough to stand up to what the man stands up to, and do exactly the same. There are very few women in the world who have that capability, the physical capability of a man. I just don't agree that sending them is a practical proposition, nor a useful one if the total number of people is small. When the community is large, say a hundred, this objection on the grounds of strength would disappear, but could remain in small traveling groups.

Neider: What has been the main thrust of British scientific work in Antarctica?

Fuchs: Like other nations, we have a very broad scientific program, ranging from marine biology to actual survey of terrain—glaciology, geomagnetism, seismology—all these things—human physiology, the physiology of animals, tides—all this. It's a very complex program, all running side by side at different stations. When you ask the question, "What is the main thrust?" you can't pick out a single subject.

Neider: I suppose really what one is doing is dealing with the sector that one is in, and handling that sector.

Fuchs: But you see, if you want to know something regionally you need to know about the whole region, so the important part about how the scientific community in Antarctica works—and the Treaty itself—is that everybody exchanges the information. So when you're working in a particular subject, a particular region—in our case the Peninsula—we can relate the studies to those from other areas. It makes the whole picture more complete and much more important. And I would interject here that what is really happening is that we are looking at an enormous portion of the earth's surface—the region that the Treaty controls: from 60°S to the Pole. That is something like a sixteenth of the whole globe. We tend to think, especially in the populated regions, that we know it all. But we don't. And if you want to understand globally any one science you've got to understand it in the Arctic and the Antarctic as well as in the rest of the world. As an example, take the case of life. As you move towards the Equator and dry desert regions you have extremes. Likewise, as you go towards the Poles, you have cold desert regions and extremes—of a different kind. But life—both botanical and zoological life—adjusts itself to these extremes, and in doing so it specializes. So we need to understand these adjustments and how they come about. Then there are the geophysical and other sciences. What I am saying is, that to have a complete picture you need to study each science over the whole globe.

Neider: Do you believe that there is such a thing as an Antarctic addiction? You know, Shackleton's need to keep going back, and your going back, and Sir Charles Wright's going back.

Fuchs: Yes, but you see, all you're really saying is it's a way of life. When you become knowledgeable in a thing, it's something that you probably do better than anything else. So, in order to get your own satisfaction out of life, you continue to perform and enjoy those things which you understand and which you're interested in. The principle of the thing is that everyone develops their own way of life, and it seems to me perfectly natural that, once having gained experience, they should continue in the same line. You take the artist or the actor—he wants to follow his bent, it's his role and he keeps to it.

Neider: But there is some other thing that Shackleton, Cherry-Garrard and other people have written about.

Fuchs: We must leave each man to decide for himself. Some people might say they go back for the isolation, some might say they go back for the companionship of that kind of person, some people may like to be self-sufficient and to do things for themselves. There's a host of reasons why people do these things, but for each person, perhaps, there's a different one. I don't think that there's a common factor.

Neider: I gather you've led a rather happy life.

Fuchs: Oh yes. I have no regrets, and I think this is one of the great things for anyone to be able to say. As they look back they shouldn't think, "Oh, if only I had done so and so." I have no feeling like that. I would do it all again if I could.

Neider: Has you wife ever felt as if she were widowed because you went off for such long periods?

Fuchs: She's been very understanding, very good. She's a

great traveler herself. She's been to many places in the world—canoeing in northern Canada, crossed the Sahara with me, visited Australia, New Zealand, Spitzbergen and other places.

Neider: Do you think there are dangers to the Antarctic ecology that the public should be made more vividly aware of?

Fuchs: I think that there were dangers to the Antarctic ecology but I think that they have been very largely covered by the measures that the Treaty nations have taken.

Neider: Were you happy with your life as an administrator?

Fuchs: Yes, because I was doing what I was interested in doing. I always regarded myself as a benevolent dictator.

Neider: Were there times, when you were the head of the British Antarctic Survey, when you would have preferred to be out in the field, doing research?

Fuchs: Oh yes! You see, my whole way of life was geared to field activity. What I really do best is running a project, doing the practical things of life and dealing with people, overcoming difficulties. You have to believe what you say, and you must believe in what you are doing; if you do not you will lose the battle. Never entertain a course that you can't see through to the end. You see, I'm not a betting man, because when I bet I do so in the knowledge that I happen to know the answer. You must be quite confident you can achieve what you set out to do.

14 ✿ The "Hero's" Cruise to the South Shetland Islands

27 FEBRUARY, SUNDAY. The *Hero* was sighted from the kitchen about 8 A.M. Then it disappeared to find a better anchorage, and because of the snow blowing heavily, at first there was some question as to whether a ship had really been seen. I was in the mess room adjoining the kitchen when the cook came in to tell me quietly my ship had come. For a fleeting moment, it seemed incomprehensible to me that he should inform me of such a momentous event in so mild and controlled a tone, and then I realized it was momentous only for me.

Your time sense could play strange tricks on you in the Antarctic, possibly because your emotions were occasionally out of focus, your needs were strong, your deprivations very real. The poop cabin experience on the *John Biscoe* was to have more lasting effects than I had counted on. As it turned out, it sensitized me to ship motion in a way that was fresh for me, as if it was possible for an extreme bout of seasickness to make an enduring impression on one's inner ear, just as the frostbite my hands had suffered on Mt. Erebus had sensitized them to cold permanently.

I have sometimes wondered whether a large part of what affected me during the transfer from the *Bransfield* to the *John Biscoe* and during the voyage to Argentine Islands was noise. I have already described the sudden noise of the ships' horns as they signalled farewell, and the great noise of the *John Biscoe's* screw, particularly as it went wild when it was lifted out of the water, and the noise of the basin, which seemed to be coming from the basin's efforts to rip itself from its moorings. There were many other sounds as well. Did all this noise, coming on me suddenly after the relative quiet of my stay with BAS, disorient me, and is there a profound connection between noise levels and the action of the inner-ear mechanism?

The *Hero* was a romantic vessel to me and I had been looking forward eagerly to spending some time on it, particularly after the larger ships I had sailed Antarctic waters in. As we know, she had been named after Nathaniel Palmer's 47-foot sloop, in which he had discovered Deception Island in 1820 and quite possibly had been the first, or if not that then certainly among the very first, to view the Antarctic mainland. The modern *Hero* was a laboratory-equipped, shallow-draft polar research trawler designed for inshore as well as offshore marine biological research. Ketch-rigged, she could carry some 1700 square feet of sail (mainsail, foresail, jib and mizzen). As I have already noted, the sails had three functions: to maintain ship control if the main propulsion system failed, to reduce roll and to permit silent operation during certain kinds of oceanographic research, such as bio-acoustic studies of marine animals.

Built in South Bristol, Maine, of native oak timbers, she became operational in 1968. Her masts were of Oregon fir and her keel and sides were sheathed with tropical greenheart from Guyana, South America. Sheathing along the hull's forward part was overlain by metal plating. She was very sturdily built, with unusual thickness and closer spacing of her framing. Her skeleton was an 18-by-18 inch keel and 6-by-6 inch framing spaced only eight inches apart. Her length was 125 feet, her breadth a trifle over 30 feet, her draft 16 feet (almost half that of the *Burton Island*), her gross tonnage 300, her horsepower 760, her cruising speed 10 knots and her range 6000 nautical miles. She could carry 30 tons of fresh water.

One of her unusual features was her backup systems. She had two engines, a double boiler, standby heating and circulating pumps, two generating power plants, two evaporators, and spare propeller and sails. She had two decks and a superstructure. The main deck was exposed amidships, with a hatch leading down to the general room, which was a combination lounge and messroom. Atop the bridge or pilot house was a conning bridge known as the ice bridge or ice house, to which you had access from the bridge via a vertical metal ladder and a scuttle.

I was on a steadily diminishing course in terms of ship size: I had moved from the *Burton Island* (5922 tons, 269 feet) to the *Bransfield* (4816 tons, 330 feet) to the *John Biscoe* (1584 tons, 220 feet), and was now about to embark on the *Hero* (300 tons, 125 feet). I was to have five sea voyages in the Antarctic this season: on the *Burton Island* (thirteen nights), on the *Bransfield* (sixteen nights), on the *John Biscoe* (one night), on the *Hero's* northern trip (five nights) and on the *Hero* from Palmer Station to Ushuaia in Tierra del Fuego (four nights).

It occurred to me only a good deal later that my present Antarctic visit was essentially a series of sea voyages. Once this thought took hold, I was open to numerous childhood sea memories: little voices that spoke to me in the form of elusive, fragrant images. I recalled oily mud baths along the Black Sea, and the squeaking of mud as it caked and cracked in the sun, and being forced by my father to bathe naked like the other beach children despite my complaints, and walking hand in hand with him around some estuary arm, and losing my French sailor cap while sailing because it blew off and sank—memories that had beautifully weathered more than half a century and the upwelling of which led me to feel, perhaps unjustifiably, I had some right to embrace the Antarctic sea voyages as part of my continuing past.

I went to the kitchen and then out on the porch to view the ship. It looked spectral in the falling snow blown by a thirty-knot wind. A ghostly small vessel with sailing masts, rigging, anchored in the Meek Channel. The mizzen sail up. Stars and Stripes flying from the head of the mizzenmast. A bright electric light aglow on the mainmast above and forward of the crow's nest. Low-lying ice-covered rocks showing dimly, vaguely beyond the craft. The foreground island rocks (Galindez Island) snowsalted. And a dangerous harbor rock barely showing its dark head in the channel between station and ship. Full of thoughts and images about the fact I would soon be on my way back to Palmer and mail and phone patches, my own room, own speech patterns, hot water aplenty, showers, movies and so on, I began packing.

I recall almost nothing about leaving the station for the *Hero*, nor of boarding the vessel. I suppose I was too preoccupied or excited, or was unable to digest all that was happening to me. After all, it wasn't so long since I had left the *Bransfield* and then the *John Biscoe*. To a certain extent I had to shut out the external world, I suppose, in order to hang on to my inner continuity. In addition, I suspect there was for me a "military" side to this sort of thing. You told yourself to do this or that, in a sense you gave yourself orders, just as you did when you ordered yourself to work at your journal, and you did it with or without sweat but you did it, at times quite mechanically. And this part of you actually pleased you although it also grieved you because it made you opaque to certain experiences and robbed your journal of details that might later be very useful. And you could only rarely tell in advance which items you would, in writing the book, find especially valuable.

So you had to trust to luck a great deal, as you had when taking photographs, and to depend on memory as well as on the certain knowledge a good deal would be lost. In short, you did the best you could, and when you did less you felt very guilty. There were also times when you weren't at all sure a book would result, when you wondered unhappily if it would all end in a terrible embarrassment and if you weren't one of the greatest frauds on two legs, an in-between creature, not scientist, not logistic supporter, not administrator, just a hopeful and very eager human being. And, having already published *Edge of the World*, a quite large book about the Antarctic, in the bad times you asked yourself if you had written yourself out on the subject. And if you had, how would you pay off the great psychological debts you were incurring? But thankfully there were still other times. After all, *Edge of the World* had gotten written, and it might well not have, for I had had that close call on Mt. Erebus.

But I do remember the flurry of goodbyes—never turn around for a second look—and Ken Back's particular and very appreciated warmth to me. I had lent him the copy of *Edge of the World* that traveled with me and which had been cacheted and signed now many times in the Antarctic, and he handed it to me together with a folded note, which I read on settling down on the *Hero* and which moved me. I reproduce it here out of fondness for him and the station, and in gratitude for their sheltering me at a time of some mourning for them.

BASE 'F'
ARGENTINE ISLANDS
c/o BRITISH ANTARCTIC SURVEY,
PORT STANLEY,
FALKLAND ISLANDS,
SOUTH ATLANTIC.
FEBRUARY 27TH. 1977

DEAR CHARLES,

IT HAS BEEN GREAT HAVING YOU TO STAY HERE, AND I WISH THE TIME FOR DEPARTURE COULD HAVE COME LESS SUDDENLY!

I HOPE THE LONG JOURNEY HOME GOES WELL, AND IF YOU CAN FIND TIME TO VISIT US AGAIN NEXT YEAR—SO MUCH THE BETTER.

WITH BEST WISHES,
YOURS SINCERELY,
KENNETH BACK,
BASE COMMANDER,
ARGENTINE ISLANDS

Aboard the *Hero* I was introduced to Vera Alexander, a fine-featured, soft-spoken woman to whom I was attracted at once and with whom I got along well. The other woman on board was Marjorie Young. I suspect I wasn't entirely surprised by the women's presence. I must have vaguely recalled hearing about the Barsdate project (that was how it was called inasmuch as he was its senior scientist) during the orientation week at Scottsdaie, Arizona, in September 1976 and on my visit to Palmer Station directly after leaving the *Burton Island*. This too may have played a significant role in my strangely opaque reaction. But perhaps part of the reason I was so little affected— who knows the full complexity of the human mind?—was that I had already been exposed in my imagination to a woman in the person of Mike the Fid, with his gorgeous long hair. In addition, I was close to the end of my Antarctic trip now and very soon would be seeing women aplenty in Tierra del Fuego and

Buenos Aires, and so the rarity of two *Hero* female companions was decreased a great deal.

Robert Barsdate had a fascinating way of speaking, or rather of not speaking. I had never in my life met anyone who paused so frequently and for so long. A sentence became an elongated paragraph full of space.

"Ah . . . I think . . . ah . . . it would . . . ah . . . maybe . . . be better . . . ah . . . if . . . ah . . . we did . . . ah . . . it . . . this way."

He was tall, blond-bearded, blue-eyed, rugged, intelligent and very quiet, usually silent. He had a wonderful, infectious smile. His body language sometimes gave me the sense he was as uncertain about himself as an adolescent might be. He carried himself rather timidly, although he had a good body and was still a relatively young man. He would shake his head gently sideways, as if trying to communicate something. He rarely laughed, but when he did you were pleasantly surprised by the brilliance of his teeth and by the fact he had a good sense of humor and a well-developed sense of play. And although in general his eyes avoided yours, he could defend an intellectual position capably, and then he had no hesitation in looking fully at you. Sometimes, when he was suddenly impelled to speak by a mechanism mysterious to me, he could be forceful, incisive and articulate. Although in the beginning I was put off because I spent so much time wondering about his pauses, I grew to like and admire him. He was up and about in all weather. I would see him lowering a bucket over the side to collect a water sample, wearing a blue wool hat and being often gloveless. He and his two colleagues worked in the small lab aft of the general room and in another lab still farther aft on the main deck.

Our route was northeastward through the Penola Strait and the Lemaire Channel, then north and northwest across the Bismarck Strait. At the western side the Strait opens onto the Southern Ocean.

Once we left the Lemaire Channel and were exposed to the western waters of the Bismarck Strait we encountered heavy swells and took to rolling accordingly. I did not get sick but I was not well either, and I ascribed this fact to the poop cabin experience, for the *Hero's* rolls were not extraordinary. True, as a small vessel she could manage an interesting combination of

The "Hero's" Cruise to the South Shetland Islands   273

rolls and pitches that the *Burton Island* achieved only rarely, but I still believed I was feeling the effects of the brief voyage on the *John Biscoe*. I photographed the heavy seas from the main deck while partially protected by a hatchway leading down to the engine room. Heavy, veined waves rose abreast of our starboard rail. The sea foamed, spat upon the ice-covered gunnel and the ice-covered tops of two lashed fuel drums. I got an intimate sense of the surging swells that occasionally exploded above the gunnel, drenched me and rushed out through the scuppers. There was a rare moment when sunlight, spilling out of the clouds, showered bits of gold satin all over the rough, dark Strait.

"Arrived at Palmer about 4 P.M. to warm greetings. The wanderer returned. Very tired. Drank Scotch to quiet a queasy tummy, enjoy dinner. Relief to talk, hear American after all the Fids' accents and dialects. Tried and failed to get phone patches. Played poker, won $7, to bed late."

Almost immediately on reaching Palmer I was informed by Jerry Huffman, the USARP rep who had replaced Guy Guthridge, that I would indeed be leaving on the *Hero* the day after tomorrow, March 1, for Deception and King George Islands. The ship would make the northern journey, which would last five days, for two reasons: so the Barsdate group could take water samples at certain stations along the way and so Huffman and I could visit the Russian and Chilean bases and especially the Polish one, Arctowski, which was now being constructed. I liked Huffman immediately and sensed we would get along well. He was easygoing, intelligent and had a good sense of humor. He had less of the bureaucrat in him than almost any other civil servant I had ever met.

The room I had so looked forward to seemed impersonal from the moment I entered it. It no longer felt mine. I examined the things I had left behind on my desk, in the drawer under my bed and in my closets. I shrugged inwardly, as if to say, "Strange, most strange." I was beginning to feel soul-tired now. My time on this remarkable continent was fast running out. I got into bed and lay there awhile, trying to believe the room was not in motion. My body gave evidence against me. It swore I was still rolling and that engine vibrations were penetrating both it and my mind. I would not be here long enough to regain my land legs. Very soon I would be on the Antarctic waters again, heading for the South Shetland Islands, whose very name was a kind of music for me, and learning the ways of the *Hero* intimately so that the ship and I would hopefully be congruent by the time we began to cross the infamous Drake Passage a fortnight from now. The Drake was widely considered to be the worst body of water in the world and it was never far from one's imagination.

I was running out of steam. I had found some mail waiting for me, brought from Ushuaia by the *Hero*, and it made me pensive about the States. My thoughts increasingly strayed to Tierra del Fuego and Buenos Aires. Part of me was no longer in the Antarctic. I had had enough, temporarily, of observing, experiencing and recording. My mind felt peppered by buckshot. I would find myself thinking, "What am I doing here? The job is finished."

Then I would remember Rachel sitting on the snowpatch below me, refusing my advances and staring forlornly at me as if I were a resident of a far planet who had come there specifically to mystify and disturb her; the butchering of the crabeater; the gulls and skuas that feasted on the remains; the *John Biscoe* that had brought me there; the *Bransfield* and the storm beach at Horseshoe Island; gash duty; Big Red the metal scow; Sloman, Swithinbank, Big Al and the BAS tie. Images, thoughts and emotions poured over me in their abundance and I was not sure what to do with them at the moment. I was almost embarrassed by the secrecy of my inner life.

I resumed my friendship with Joe Warburton and visited him and his gear in the outlying building. He had made much progress with the gear and was proud of the way things were going. Two colleagues, John Kleppe and Paul Lagé, had arrived from the States to assist him and would remain until the *Hero's* departure for Ushuaia. I joined him and Paul Lagé on the roof of the subsidiary building, where they were working on a small directional antenna. Hatless, he wore a USARP parka. He had a prominent brow and nose, straight muddy-brown hair worn rather short, was full-bearded, small-eared and of medium height. Lagé was younger, sensitive, wore his hair long and had buck teeth.

Warburton often wore a strangely serious semi-frown, as if he was concentrating on something important. On the *Burton Island* he had spent a good deal of time playing solitaire and had frowned like that then too. When I first met him at McMurdo he was very talkative and told me much about his scientific program. He was originally from Australia and had settled in the States. He was connected with the Desert Research Institute of the University of Nevada in Reno. He had quick, birdlike gestures and a great deal of professorial dignity even when, as at McMurdo and on the icebreaker, he wore very baggy black windpants.

I was fascinated by his gear at Palmer. The antenna was aimed at a U.S. satellite in a geostationary orbit about 22,500 miles above the Equator. He had a direct line-of-sight communication with the satellite, as did similar equipment in Reno, Nevada. For someone like myself, who was absolutely new to this kind of communication, it felt eerie to make a phone patch with it, as I did on my return from the northern voyage, because the reception was static-free. It sounded exactly like a very clear phone call and not in the least like the usual patch with its scratchy static or fading. Occasionally you were aware of a slight echo, which was your own voice. This was due to the fact that the round-trip distance of a signal from you to the satellite was 45,000 miles, which meant that it took the signal, traveling at 186,000 miles a second, almost a quarter of a second to cover the distance. Consequently there was a quarter-second lag or echo.

Looking from the roof across a couple of large white fuel tanks, I received a stunning view of rocky islands in the harbor, spotted with snow and stretching rightward like bony fingers. A mountain range sprawled on the mainland, its peaks icebound. Deep grays of water and islands, middle gray of sky, chalky white of the range, and the incredible, ringing, beryl-blue of a growler in the scene's center. I could see the main building with its three stories and cannon-gray metallic exterior, and the *Hero* at its jetty, Stars and Stripes on the high mizzenmast. The harbor water was calm.

A *Hero* crewmember I enjoyed from the beginning was John Lohr, the radio operator, who had literary skills and ambitions and who was eager to discover from me what the trade of literature was about. He had published some small articles about

Antarctica through the Pacific News Service and hoped to write a book based on them. He was in his late forties or early fifties. We would get to know each other quite well. I would meet his wife, who lived in Buenos Aires, in Ushuaia, and in 1978 both of them would visit me in Stanford, California. He had decided that this would be his last season on the *Hero*. He had been working on the ship for several years and had had, not so long ago, an experience that had convinced him his luck was running out and that he had better stop working in such perilous waters. He had fallen one night into the waters between the ship and some dock or jetty, had tried to climb out but had been unable to, had shouted for help as the cold water took increasing possession of him and had lost consciousness just after gripping a life preserver thrown to him by John Polkinghorn, the first mate, who very luckily had heard his cries. He had been pulled aboard and been given emergency treatment: a very hot shower, massages, whisky, and being put into a bunk with many blankets over him.

Another crewmember I noticed was Dan Reed, a large, dark-haired, sensitive, somber, shy young man who was an oiler. He struck me as being lonely and in need of friends but not knowing how to go about making them. He would stand around like a wallflower, watching you for example when you were playing poker, and then suddenly vanish. He could be articulate at rare times. Most of the time he appeared to have lost his voice. He and John Lohr liked to frequent the station but they ate on the ship. Reed was as awkward with his body as an adolescent, and often would stand hanging his head while listening and while obviously feeling left out of whatever it was he wanted to be a part of. I think he had some literary ambitions.

Then there was Conrad Paul, the ship's engineer, a gregarious older man whose enlarged red nose and volubility I ought to have suspected but didn't. He filled me with stories about how terribly the *Hero* rolled, how easy it was to be thrown out of your bunk and how he would handle everything for me by showing me how to prop up the side of my bunk in such a way as to guarantee to keep me inside it. He would usually sit around the forward, lounge area of the large station room that blended without demarcation into the dining room and then the kitchen, and would busy himself with magazines. I rarely saw him speak with anyone other than myself, and this too should have alerted me to something.

He actually fulfilled his promise, insisting, when I boarded the *Hero* next day, on creating a great Chinese wall in the outer side of my bunk by lavish use of blankets and other materials, and succeeding so well that I had trouble getting in and out of the bunk, which was a lower one. This may have been Paul's last official or unofficial act on the ship, for he promptly disappeared after it and I never saw him again, either during the cruise or in Ushuaia. When I inquired about him I learned he had a problem and would be discharged as soon as the ship reached Ushuaia. Meanwhile Dan Reed would take over many of Paul's functions. But I am getting ahead of my narrative.

It didn't take me long to realize that Paul's architectural ability with blankets and other soft materials was not being applied in any direction useful to me. As a matter of fact, it could do me harm, for although I felt as snug as in my mother's womb when I lay in my bunk, I had to fight and climb my way out with too great an expenditure of time and energy at a time when the ship was hardly rolling at all, and it occurred to me that during an emergency, if one were to occur, I would lose invaluable time in being pinned in my bunk. To cap it all, the bunk looked ludicrous, I felt ludicrous, and I was certain I would look ludicrous if I permitted anyone to see me in it. And so, not without reluctance, for human ingenuity, however partially deranged, had gone into the great construction, I tore it down.

Orange foredeck of the *Hero* as we departed Palmer. I was on the starboard bridge wing. The station on its dark rocky spit, with the great sweeping glacier beyond. A white berg with many vertical blue seams. Elegantly carved blue and greenish bergy-bits as we proceeded toward the Neumayer Channel. A blue-eyed shag flying past us close to the water: white-bellied, white-throated, the rest glossy black. The mainland guarded by majestic bergs. Poor weather, high wind in the Neumayer Channel, the land obscured by mists. We spotted a humpback whale.

The *Hero's* bridge wheel was fastened tight inasmuch as the ship was invariably on automatic pilot, at least when I was on it.

But you could see and hear the wheel axle moving heavily in staccato fashion and like a wild puppet clockwise or counterclockwise in response to the automatic pilot connected to the gyroscope in the general room a couple of decks below. You set your course and stood by to watch for unexpected events. You could control the movements of the ship manually by turning a dial to manual and operating a small hand-held black gadget on a long black cable. I would see Pieter Lenie, the captain, at times carry the gadget with him out onto one of the bridge wings for better visibility and use it from there, as when he drew alongside a jetty or another ship.

2 MARCH. "We anchored inside Deception Island, a flourishing place for Antarctic work until two volcanic eruptions (1967 and 1969) ended man's residence here. The old graveyard now under volcanic ash. Poor young Adélie limping too far from the safety of the beach, molting its young down, a sure victim for any skua."

Six of us went ashore, including Adolfo (Zornoza) and Carlin (Carlos Gohde), of whom I had already become very fond, and I confess that one of the reasons I was fond of them was that as Argentines they gave me the impression of being European. They were warm, outgoing, eager to be helpful and strained to overcome the considerable deficiency in their command of English. And they had a wonderful sense of humor. The others in the shore party were Jerry Huffman, John Lohr, a third crewman and I. Meanwhile the Barsdate group were taking water samples.

Deception Island, by far the best known of the South Shetlands and, with the possible exception of Ross Island, the most famous of all Antarctic islands, is a caldera, or drowned volcanic crater, surrounded by hills and mountains thirteen nautical miles south of Livingston Island. I haven't been able to discover why Deception was named that but I think I know why. When approached from the sea you don't realize it's a safe harbor: It looks like a mountainous island. Located at 62°56′S, 60°34′W, it is annular in shape (that is, shaped like a ring), some eight nautical miles in diameter, and encloses a large harbor (Port Foster) which is the sole port of entry in the South Shetlands and the entire Antarctic Peninsula. Access to the harbor is had by Neptune's Bellows, a narrow opening at the island's south-

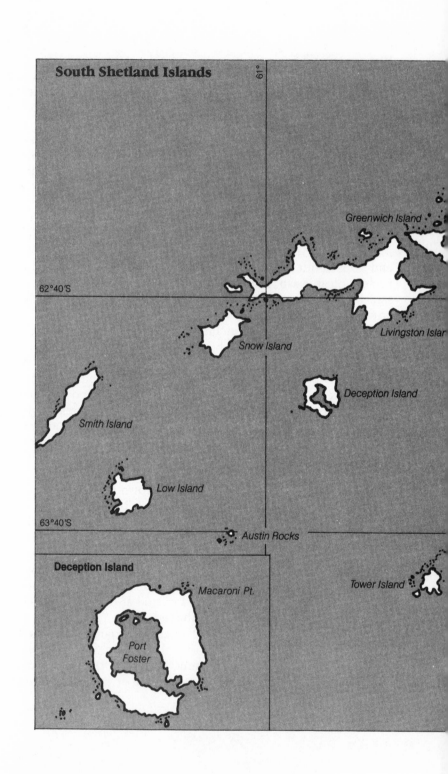

South Shetland Islands

61°

Greenwich Island

62°40'S

Livingston Islar

Snow Island

Deception Island

Smith Island

Low Island

63°40'S

Austin Rocks

Deception Island

Macaroni Pt.

Tower Island

Port Foster

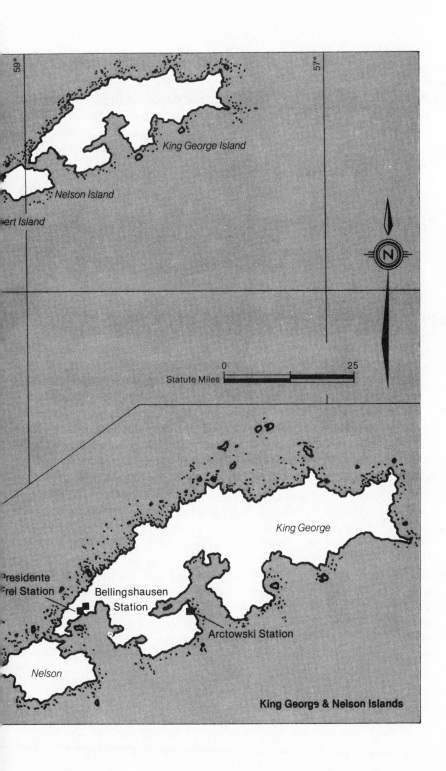

King George Island

Nelson Island

ert Island

0   Statute Miles   25

King George

Presidente
Frei Station

Bellingshausen
Station

Arctowski Station

Nelson

King George & Nelson Islands

eastern end, whose name was given by early American sealers because of strong gusts encountered there. The harbor itself is a landlocked basin about five nautical miles long northwest and southeast and about 3½ miles wide at the broadest point.

It was used by American sealers in the early part of the last century and by various whalers in the present century. According to *Sailing Directions for Antarctica*, the caldera "forms one of the most remarkable crater islands in the world." Along the beaches are numerous steaming fumaroles, much volcanic detritus and scoriae, dark basalt, pumice and various volcanic rocks such as brickstone. There are some hot sulphurous springs, and vessels near the shores of Whalers Bay have experienced blistering of paint because of high water temperatures. There is less snow and ice on the island than elsewhere in the South Shetlands, and no verdure.

In January 1930 an earthquake occurred at the island, without damage to any buildings. *Sailing Directions* says, "The whaling station is reported to have been destroyed in 1941 by a British cruiser to forestall the use of the station by German commerce raiders," and I saw holes in the blubber-rendering tanks that looked very much as if they might have been made by three-inch shells. The station was reported to be in ruins by 1957. In modern times Chile, Argentina and the United Kingdom had bases on it until it suffered the volcanic eruptions of 1967 and 1969. It was deserted at the time of our visit, but various small scenes evoked for me both the tenacity and smallness of man's efforts in the face of volcanic events.

We came upon a fur seal on the beach, large, growling, barking, very aggressive. I was reminded of the fur seal I had encountered on Janus Island in Arthur Harbor, who had also barked and threatened but whom I had faced down by walking boldly toward him. But possibly he was much younger than this Deception seal, or was unfamiliar with the terrain, or was a female, which is to say more docile, or had not encountered man before. The present seal was resting on his four flippers as if on dwarf legs and had a sleek, powerful tan body and sizable fangs. From the way he roared and made passes at us I suspected he was an adult bull. The third crewman, named Dick, a blond Texan, a man with a short temper and bad poker manners, was carrying a remnant of a broomstick, with which he pretended to fence with the animal. The seal grabbed the end of the stick with his teeth and began to break it off. The crewman let go and retreated. The seal then dropped the stick and glared at all of us, as if daring us to take him on. The light gleamed sharply on his eyeball. Although fur seals can be fast and dangerous, it was hard to take him seriously, for in the midst of challenging us he took time off to scratch himself with a three-clawed hind flipper in the way a dog does, and you saw his tiny ear, walrus mustache and doggie black nose.

The scene struck me as being very wonderful. Here was this cocky representative of a species that had come perilously close to being wiped out by man, especially by Englishmen and Americans, and he was challenging the lot of us, for no doubt he felt we had invaded his territory, as indeed in a sense we had. And because of the convention for the protection of seals in the Antarctic, which had been signed some years ago but had not yet been ratified by the Antarctic Treaty nations, but meanwhile nevertheless was on the whole being respected by them, he was left intact. In the sealing days such animals had been clubbed to death in the millions for their fur to satisfy the voracious Chinese market, and by sealers who were competitively secretive about discoveries of islands, populations, weather, routes. It was a tremendous slaughter that in the beginning was very profitable and that petered out only because its cost, with the rapidly diminishing supply, became exorbitant.

I thought of this fur seal as belonging to the new, liberated kind. The Third World was struggling to get on its feet politically and technologically and was already demanding a share of whatever riches the Antarctic common might provide. Women were in political and social revolt among the developed countries and had many men deeply confused and on the defensive. And here was the wonderfully cocky fur seal, reminding us that the beach was *his*, not ours.

John Lohr, Jerry Huffman and I explored the ruins of a BAS station. A large long hut with a sign at one door still reading BISCOE HOUSE. Doors ripped away, glass windows broken, part of the roof sagging over a large opening, stuff strewn about inside and out. Odd to walk about inside, staring at the remains of a kitchen, a radio room, sleeping quarters. Huffman hunting for man-made souvenirs. Lohr matter of fact, having been ashore here many times. Just westward of the hut was a long green fibreglass structure put together in sections. Ropes and pipes lying about outside. Much of the pumiceous shore was barren of snow and revealed the soft stuff one walked on, with its basic dark gray ground that here and there sported chunks of rust-colored or dirty yellow tuff.

The remains of a red Twin Otter outside a gray hangar: engine, wings and tail gone, doors gone, instruments missing, nothing left but a fuselage shell, a flaked-red hulk with a gaping side door, four little portholes in a row like black buttons, and the aborted, gaping cockpit looking out into nothing. To sit in it would be like sitting on a headless horse. The words ANTARCTIC SURVEY still visible in white on the side. The forward wheel struts still in place. The fierce red, even though flaked down to metal, hitting you in this place of cold colors. The hangar's exterior still largely intact. Cold, damp, disordered, abandoned inside. It was strange poking around in this ghostly place, thinking of work and play done here once upon a time and so remote from the rest of the world.

Structures that seemed to have collapsed abruptly. One side of a hut down, so that the building listed one-leggedly. A couple of cylindrical metal towers tilting thirty or forty degrees from the vertical. Two squat metal tanks. A conglomeration of piled metal wreckage.

John Lohr in front of a rotted old wooden hut with slanted metal roof, many of the latter's panels rusty but some looking surprisingly fresh. The boarding of one end of a structure gone quite to hell, whole large boards missing or hanging precariously, the interior looming black. A vast door missing, also some metal pieces at the very crest of the roof. Lohr with parka hood rising in a gnomish peak over black felt cap, gloved hands in orange parka pockets, green pants tucked into gaily striped waterproof boots. Dark beach, blue water and gray hillsides around and behind him

The sky now clear. The *Hero* at anchor (Lenie didn't come ashore) in the wine-dark sea beyond the brown beach strewn with long snow patches. Wine-colored snowcapped mountains beyond it. Bow pointing at us, masts rising straight, crow's nest high aloft, and something on the starboard deckside throwing back the afternoon light. Rotten whaleboat half-buried in the shore, bow pointing seaward. Gray rotting timbers and rusting metal prow, and loaded with volcanic stuff partly capped with snow. Half a dozen khaki metal fuel drums lying on their sides. Clear sky, naked hills.

Jerry Huffman seated on the whaleboat gunnel, wearing a fresh red indoor parka with the hood over his black cap with USARP embroidered in gold on the forehead, a white-belted, dirty, salmon life preserver over that, green pants, standard-issue hiking boots, brown leather gloves and dark glasses, and with a long black radio suspended round his neck. I remember the surprisingly quick agile way in which his legs moved when he walked or climbed. In no other way did he give me the impression of being athletic. More fuel drums scattered about, and the U-shaped col in the hills which I later climbed and from the crest of which I viewed the open ocean. A whaleboat with its stern rising in a slow crescendo of gray, weathered, curving, grained, nailed wooden planks and looking somehow noble.

There was a whalebone field nearby: tumbled gravestones intermingled with snow clumps on an aggressively black beach, and a stretch of harbor in a curve of the land, and a mottled cloudcover, and tilted cylindrical rusty tanks in the background, and barrel staves and hoops, all broken loose, and four figures walking away from me: red parkas, red hoods, green pants, and one with yellow rubber hip boots. Gray sloping planes of mountains beyond the purple sea. Mountains suggesting black-and-white film negatives. An etched world across the water—white scratches on a dark plate, the scratches indicating mountain ribs, earth lines flowing, rising, falling. The flung bay: a blue finger thrust into the black-and-white shore's guts. The *Hero* tinily at anchor.

3 MARCH. We had three pet krill in a large white barrel lashed to the *Hero's* starboard maindeck gunnel very close to the hatch amidships that led to the engine and general rooms and galley below, or to the bridge and ice house above. I would sometimes go outdoors to observe them idly swimming about: shrimplike crustaceans 1½ or 2 inches long, pink or red in color.

Occasionally I glimpsed Barsdate lowering his bucket over the side. He wore horn-rimmed glasses the side pieces of which were tucked under a black wool cap. He was rarely to be seen without his pipe. His blond beard was brown in places.

"We anchored in Potter Cove, King George Island, in preparation for the run tomorrow morning to Maxwell Bay and the Fildes Peninsula to visit Bellingshausen and Presidente Frei Stations."

King George Island is some forty-three nautical (about forty-seven statute) miles long and sixteen nautical miles wide at its broadest part. It is highly glaciated. Much of it is covered by an icecap. Potter Cove offered a protected anchorage at moderate depths, with good holding ground in stiff clay.

Next morning, as we sailed westward from our night's anchorage, we had Three Brothers Hill conspicuous on our port side. The hill is what is left of the neck of an old volcano. It's like Castle Rock on Ross Island, only it's three distinct towers, whereas Castle Rock is one. The day was subdued, with heavy cloud cover, the cove was mildly choppy, the shore was icecapped and snowstrewn, and the ice rose two-thirds of the way to the top of the hill, which is almost 700 feet high. The hill had been described as a "clenched fist" but I found this hard to accept. It was more like black stumps huddling together and showing themselves as a three-headed nunatak. One of the southernmost points of King George Island, it was a striking sight because of the contrast with the flat and low terrain in its vicinity. Several red refuge huts could be seen near the shore.

We entered Maxwell Bay and headed north, passing Marion Cove, until we were off Fildes Peninsula, which sloped down to an extended, flat-lying head mostly devoid of snow and ice. Large black volcanic rocks jutted out of the water near the shore. The peninsula is the westernmost part of King George Island and is fairly close to neighboring Nelson Island. Maxwell Bay sits between the two islands.

Drawing near Bellingshausen Station on the peninsula, one at first became aware of some dozen high antenna towers rising like long and slender pencils out of the snowy low ground, on the other side of which, not visible to us, was a sea which could be described in at least three ways: the confluence of the south Atlantic and the south Pacific, the southern part of the Drake Passage, or part of the circumpolar Southern Ocean. The inshore waters were dangerous for a vessel of even our draft, so we anchored on the far side of a huge rock or small rock island, where we were invisible from the station. The top of our rock was salted with snow. An antenna tower, beacon or marker crested it. It was very overcast at the time and the water was dark and rough.

"Up very early, excited to be visiting foreign stations today. I've been especially looking forward to seeing Bellingshausen, which before now seemed impossibly remote. The very name conjures up remoteness: the man who sighted the Peninsula so long ago. Went to the bridge, from which I watched our movements. We sailed from Potter Cove to Maxwell Bay, and Lenie, Huffman and I went ashore in a Zodiac. Later the Barsdate group joined us. The station looked empty as we walked from the rocky beach towards the buildings. Then a Russian figure appeared and we were shown to the station leader's office. The leader spoke some English. We were served coffee, tea, cake, and Pepsi Cola bottled in Russia. Polite conversation, exchange of patches, medallions, other souvenirs. I was given a Bellingshausen medallion and a Lenin pin. I was also given a blue-and-white station pennant, which gave the base's location (62°12'S, 58°54'W), a picture of Thaddeus Bellingshausen's vessel and a date (28/1/1820), as well as other information, the latter in Cyrillic letters.

"A brief tour of the building. Met some hikers from the new Polish station, Arctowski, who had come over by traversing inland and were about to return."

Slavic faces of the three Arctowski men. Large backpacks. Two of the men wore red down parkas that were very bulky as compared to the USARP parkas. The third wore a yellow waterproof jacket. Two wore woolen sailor caps, one tangerine, the other coffee, the third wore a lavender cap that suggested a beret. All three wore heavy tan boots with white lacing, and long woolen stockings into which trouser legs were tucked. One wore blue socks , the second white, the third fiery red.

Someone, using my Leica, took a couple of frames showing me and Lenie standing beside them. Lenie was short and rather handsome. His gray beard had much white in it although his mustache and the hair just under his nether lip showed brown. His nose was strongly aquiline, his face tended to smile with sarcastic, ironic and condescending overtones. He wore a plaid blue shirt and loose dark trousers, gaily striped calf-high boots, and a khaki-green cap the brim and furlined back and earflaps of which were turned up. He also wore a new orange USARP parka without hood, and with a U.S. flag as a shoulder patch. On the upturned brim of his cap were two medallions, a USARP one and a Bellingshausen one.

Bellingshausen: many buildings, constructed off the ground to avoid snowdrift and for thermal protection against the permafrost. Many high antenna towers guy-wired down. Almost everywhere you looked around the station you saw the complex rigging of taut wires. The huts were mostly prefab metal, and the vertical panels were pastel: pale lilac, pale green, pale blue. Much snow and ice on outlying slopes, but the close station surroundings were drab, cindery, rocky, dark. Three flags flying: Soviet, Polish and U.S. in descending order. Lots of heavy gear around, such as huge amphibious artillery wagons converted to civilian use. Covered yellow cockpit or drive cabin of one, a tracked vehicle with six wheels per side. Many wooden crates stacked outdoors. A heavy barge on the gray beach. A launch beached on rollers. Outlying huts.

"We were shown some hats for sale: squirrel for men ($35), golden fox for women ($60), and some lacquered, painted boxes that looked expensive."

I surmised that this hospital mart had been set up primarily to cater to and profit from tourist ships like the American *Lindblad Explorer*, and it seemed to me likely that this was the first such tourist shop in the Antarctic.

"I had heard there were interesting geodes in the outlying areas. Remembering my luck at McMurdo when I had investigated the ground near the Lodge and the Earth Sciences Center, I explored the vicinity of one of the entrances to the meteorological building and found numerous odd-looking rocks that had been gathered elsewhere and thrown away. Vera Alexander and Marjorie Young having coffee with a Russian scientist in the met building. He insisted on giving me a can of instant coffee, and two packs of cigarettes with a penguin and a map of Antarctica on them. As we were about to leave, Americans and Russians took pictures of each other.

"We walked across fields to Frei (pronounced Fray by the Chileans). (Many people in the Peninsula region pronounced it Chil-*lay*-uns. I believe the practice comes from the Chilean word Chi-*lay*-nos. Some, like Joe Warbuton, said peninshoola, I don't know why. Many said Wed*dell* instead of *Wed*dell.) Very sufficient place and quite comfortable. I was told there are good relations between it and its Russian neighbor. Vera Alexander was given a large piece of lichen that she studied intently."

Long, red, single-story buildings of the Chilean station, set on cindery terrain west of Bellingshausen. The Chilean flag flying alone. Three men walking outdoors, one in gray military uniform, the other two in long, salmon-colored parka-like coats. A modest station by comparison with its neighbor, it was the communications and meteorological center of the Chilean Antarctic program, and it also had a weather forecasting service.

"We were invited to lunch, which was somewhat formal, with white tablecloth, pleasant silverware, red and white Chilean wine. The meal consisted of a huge rich bowl of splendid seafood."

I was given a pennant: FUERZA AEREA DE CHILE [Chilean Air Force]—DOTACION 1977—BASE ANTARTICA PDTE. FREI. It contained a map of Antarctica showing Chile's claimed slice of the pie, from 53°W to 90°W and running south to the Pole. It also had a list of station personnel—twenty-one including the leader, A. Perez.

"Frei an airforce station, with some civilians employed by the military. Relatively short, dark men. The leader stiff, with a strange macho smile and manner, wary, straight hair parted exactly in the middle."

We slid along the northwestern side of the bay in the deepening twilight, amazed to see the great number of fuel drums stretching out along a strand of Point Thomas and indicating the potential power of the newcomer station, Arctowski, and of Poland's strong intentions here. We murmured remarks to each other on the bridge. We knew we would visit the station in the morning and this was our introduction to it. Someone studied the fuel drums with a pair of binoculars and reported on their extent.

Why was Poland making so bold an effort here and so belatedly? The answer, true or false, was quickly forthcoming among us: to harvest krill. Few on the bridge believed Poland's main thrust here was basic science. Poland was already busily harvesting krill on a unilateral basis, as were several other nations.

The "Hero's" Cruise to the South Shetland Islands   289

As we rounded Point Thomas on our port side and headed westward into Ezcurra Inlet toward Dufayel Island, we saw the Polish stern-trawler *Dalmor* anchored near the island. Lenie by radio requested and received permission to lash alongside the *Dalmor's* starboard. It was night now and, working with his magic black box on the port bridge wing, he inched us along by the stong lights of both ships. Soon we were secured and a long rope ladder was hung from the *Dalmor's* maindeck gunnel onto our foredeck. Our own maindeck was so much lower than the *Dalmor's* and we were separated from the larger ship by so many bumpers in the way of old tires and hawsers that the ladder did not hang vertically but at quite an angle. It was more like a sagging bridge than a ladder. It was admirable how skillfully Lenie brought the *Hero* alongside the *Dalmor* by a series of maneuvers, and all with adjustments of dials on the little black box in his hands.

Faces peering down upon us from the *Dalmor's* maindeck gunnel. Our seamen on our foredeck. I remembered the *John Biscoe* lashed alongside the *Bransfield*. That had been a harbinger of much discomfort for me. But this now would lead to nothing unpleasant, I told myself. I could not help but feel that what I was observing was a clever stage setting and a stage rehearsal. Antarctica around us in the night. Black icy waters below us. The shores of Ezcurra Inlet and Admiralty Bay somewhere near us. The island's great icecap out there somewhere. The heavy-swelled waters of the Bransfield Strait not far away. The Drake Passage within miles of us. But life in this inhuman place was now very human, focussed by the spotlights of both ships, and Poles and Argentines and Americans were about to socialize.

"Many of the Poles visited our ship, and there were an accordionist, a guitarist and many people eager to dance. Our general room became a dance hall. The taller men, forgetting themselves in the excitement, slammed their heads against the metal rafters and bolts. When our guests could not persuade our two ladies to dance, they danced with our men or with each other. This continued a long time."

A small man with a huge accordion sat on the bench on the starboard side of the room and squeezed and bellowed out music with an east-European flavor. I admired the generosity of his effort. Although he was not paid for his labor he put a great deal of muscle into it. He seemed oblivious of everything in the room except his instrument, which he gazed at lovingly with bent head. In dress there was nothing to distinguish him from any of the other visitors. The accordion music reverberated through the general room and down the passageways forward and aft. In volume of sound the guitar was hopelessly outclassed by the accordion, but the guitarist, a large bulk of a man in black work clothes and caked muddy boots, seemed as imperious and as proud a music-maker as Andres Segovia.

Vera Alexander and Marjorie Young did dance a bit, I seem to recall, but there were many suitors with a lot of energy, the presence of women came as a great surprise to the Poles, the day had been long and crowded, and soon the two women begged off. For a while they sat at the dining table, observing the wild goings-on, but the suitors' pressure was too much, and they retired to their cabin across the room from mine. This was a disappointment to the men but not for long. Quickly men's bodies joined in contredanses, jigs and God knows what else. When the Poles danced with the Americans or Argentines it was a Babel of tongues. Polish would speak to American with what appeared to be absolute confidence of being understood, and Spanish would speak to Polish in the same way. Of all the *Hero's* crew Carlin seemed to be the wildest at enjoying this event. His gold earring, secure in its lobe, flashed in the ceiling lights. There was not a Pole on the *Dalmor* who would have dared to wear a ring like that. Carlin was the most charming pirate of them all. His vitality and great human warmth endeared him to me. Adolfo was not far behind him in his dancing antics, his flowing black pirate's mustache waving as he pirouetted.

"When the dancing at last stopped and the room looked empty though somewhat frazzled, I turned in in my cabin just off the dining table. But visitors kept coming all night—until 6 A.M."

5 MARCH. "A huge amphibian tracked vehicle came around to our starboard to take us ashore to the new station. Lenie insisted I wear a life preserver, muttering that these craft had been known to go down. He, Huffman, Barsdate, the two women and I were the Americans that went ashore."

The "Hero's" Cruise to the South Shetland Islands 291

Lenie now had four or five medallions on his upturned brim. He wore a long green parka and a new, yellow, zippered float coat with CAPITAN lettered roughly by hand over the heart. Jerry Huffman had on green pants and two parkas, one indoor, the other outdoor. He had a crazy way of wearing the hood of the red inner one over a leather cap, which gave him a domed, forest-creature look. Vera Alexander, hatless, showed dark brown hair. Marjorie Young was much overdressed as usual. Barsdate had a pipe in his mouth even on the amphibian. Some thirty or forty people came ashore in the craft at one time. Many wore orange life preservers, dungaree-type work clothes, dirty knee-high rubber boots and sported black leather caps with the earflaps down. Foreign faces again, many bearded. The amphibian was painted a brilliant, fresh orange. It was probably Soviet-made. Like those at Bellingshausen, it had six wheels on each side. Two old car tires hung as shock absorbers on its starboard. JOREK was painted in black on its side. Also on its side was a white circular insignia reading POLISH ACADEMY OF SCIENCES ANTARCTIC STATION.

Approaching Point Thomas. Many large rocks looking like threatening squat towers rising out of the inshore waters. Stony beaches and dark landspits gray with whalebone. A low gravelly beach extending out from a cliff. Choppy blue water, cloudy day, windblown inshore brash, a whole whale spinal column, pale gray on the dark cindery beach, suggesting a crazily sculptured fence. Beyond it a great line of fuel drums lying double-tiered on their sides.

Arctowski Station was being built on a low-lying land finger stretching out from Point Thomas into Admiralty Bay. From it you could look across the bay at other parts of King George Island. The station was named for Henryk Arctowski, Polish geologist, oceanographer and meteorologist of the Belgian Antarctic Expedition, 1897-99, the expedition of which Roald Amundsen was first mate. As we know, because the *Belgica* was beset by ice, its crew became the first people to winter over on the continent.

"The amphibian is certainly efficient: rumbled out of the water and up a rocky beach and past long lines of whalebone debris right into the station."

The station was already a large complex. Most of its structures and vehicles were bright orange, like the lichen on rocks in the vicinity, but a large metal structure going up was pale blue. Sign on a central one-story building: POLSKA ACADEMIA NAUK STAKJA IM. H. ARCTOWSKIEGO. The building was prefab, wooden, painted orange with brown trim, and had a little unroofed fenced porch at the entrance. The long-haired photographer with his Hasselblad, dressed in black, with gray calf-high rubber boots. The station leader tall, hatless, wearing a huge red down parka and talking intensely. Barsdate, Alexander, Young, Huffman. People came out of the building to look at us. They cast long shadows as they blinked in the sharp light. Gray dry hills with rock outcrops behind the long building. Three flagmasts in a row in front of the building, Polish flag in the middle, Stars and Stripes on one side, the other empty.

Wandering along the beach, I came upon two giant petrel chicks. Chick's black eye on a white feathered circle, long downy gray body feathers, pale salmon beak. Whalebones bulldozed into neat bright piles.

Blue-panelled prefab long metal building going up. Yellow truck with a long yellow crane. Workmen adding siding slabs to the building. The cindery earth of the station wet, rutted by vehicles and meltwater. Some men cutting metal strips outdoors with an electric saw. The whole looking like a messy, bombed wartime dump with water-filled shell holes. A large wood-framed building rising, the frame almost complete. And the little red bunting hanging from one end of the roof for good luck.

The station leader, Dr. Stanislaw Rakusa-Suszczewski (Stan), was assistant professor in the Institute of Ecology of the Polish Academy of Sciences. He was dark-haired, clean shaven and with hair cut pleasantly short. In addition to his red down parka he wore plum pants and white boots with white lacing. The boots reminded me of American bunny boots. From him I learned that the station would conduct research in ichthyology, marine biology, geomorphology, hydrography, meteorology and medicine. He expressed perplexity and concern about the tourist ships that poured visitors ashore to roam freely in the rookery. The ships disrupted scientific work and posed a responsibility for the passengers' safety.

6 MARCH, SUNDAY. "Overcast, snowy. In transit from King George Island to Palmer Station."

The Neumayer Channel was choppy, the landscapes were

screened by mists. Our orange fo'c'sle and furled red sails were snowcovered, our shrouds and rigging icy. Somebody shovelled snow off the main deck. Occasionally we broke through lines of brash. A snowy sky showed behind a ragged, spectral berg. The weather stayed foul until we reached Arthur Harbor. At Palmer, I had to contend with a land that was rolling under me. The table seemed to be heaving as I sat at supper.

One of the pleasures of being in the Peninsula area was that one felt closer to historical figures who had previously seemed very remote. I had drawn closer to Scott and Shackleton by living in their historic Ross Island huts. Now one felt closer not only to Palmer, Bransfield, Biscoe, Weddell, Bellingshausen, but even and perhaps especially to Drake, Magellan, Darwin, Richard Henry Dana, Joshua Slocum. I had long ago admired Dana's *Two Years Before the Mast* and Darwin's *Voyage of the Beagle*. I remembered descriptions of rounding the Horn. I had heard of all the vessels destroyed off Staten Island just east of Cape Horn. The Beagle Channel, on the northern shore of which Ushuaia sits, was named for the ship Darwin had made famous. I had read how Magellan had discovered his Strait and how Francis Drake, wanting to be the first Englishman to circumnavigate the globe and in a sense the first navigator *really* to do it, for Magellan had lost his life on his voyage, had made an east–west passage through the Strait and had then been blown by storms until he was south of Tierra del Fuego. This was how it was discovered that Tierra del Fuego did not extend to the Pole, and how the Drake Passage was found.

Later, in the spring of 1978, I read an early account of Drake's discovery: "The World Encompassed, by Sir Francis Drake, Being his next voyage to that to *Nombre de Dios* formerly imprinted; Carefully collected out of the notes of Master Francis Fletcher *Preacher in this imployment, and divers others his followers in the same*: Offered now at last to publique view, both for the honour of the actor, but especially for the stirring up of heroick spirits to benefit their Countrie, and eternize their names by like noble attempts. London, Printed for Nicholas Bourne and are to be sold at his shop at the Royall Exchange. 1628."

Now when our Generall perceived that the nipping cold, under so cruell and frowning a Winter, had empaired the health of some of his men; hee meant to have made the more hast againe toward the line, and not to saile any farther towards the pole Antartick, lest being farther from the Sunne, and neerer the cold, we might happily be overtaken with some greater danger of sicknesse. But God giving men leave to purpose, reserveth to himselfe the disposition of all things: making their intents of none effect, or changing their meanings oft times cleane into the contrary, as may best serve for his owne glory and their profit.

For September 7 the second day after our entrance into the South sea (called by some *Mare pacificum*, but proving to us rather to be *Mare furiosum*) God by a contrary wind and intollerable tempest, seemed to set himselfe against us: forcing us not onely to alter our course and determination, but with great trouble, long time, many dangers, hard escapes, and finall separating of our fleet, to yeeld our selves unto his will. Yea such was the extremitie of the tempest, that it appeared to us as if he had pronounced a sentence, not to stay his hand, nor to withdraw his judgement till he had buried our bodies and ships also, in the bottomlesse depth of the raging sea.

In the time of this incredible storme the 15 of September, the Moone was ecclipsed in Aries, and darkened about three points, for the space of two glasses: which being ended, might seeme to give us some hope of alteration and change of weather to the better. Notwithstanding, as the ecclipticall conflict could adde nothing to our miserable estate, no more did the ending thereof ease us any thing at all; nor take away any part of our troubles from us: but out ecclipse continued still in its full force, so prevailing against us, that the space of full 52 dayes together, we were darkened more then the Moone by 20 parts, or more then we by any means could ever have preserved, or recovered light of our selves againe, if the Sonne of God which layed this but then upon our backs, had not mercifully borne it up with his owne shoulders, and upheld us in it by his owne power, beyond any possible strength or skill of man. Neither indeed did we at all escape, but with the feeling of great discomforts through the same.

For these violent and extraordinarie flawes (such as seldome have been seene) still continuing, or rather increasing, September 30 in the night, caused the sorrowfull separation of the *Marigold* from us, in which was Captaine *John Thomas*, with many other of our deare friends: who by no means that we could conceive could helpe themselves, but by spooming along before the sea. With whom albeit wee could never meet againe, yet (our Generall having aforehand given order, that if any of our fleet did loose company, the place of resort to meet againe should be in 30 deg. or thereabouts, upon the coast of Peru, toward the Equinoctiall) wee long time hoped (till experience shewed our hope was vaine) that there we should joyfully meet with them: especially for that they were well provided of victuals, and lackt no skilfull and sufficient men (besides their Captaine) to bring forwards the ship to the place appointed.

From the seventh of September (in which the storme began) till the seventh of October we could not by any means recover any land (having in the meane time been driven so farre South, as to the 57 deg. and somewhat better) on this day towards night, somewhat to the Northward of that cape of America (whereof mention is made before in the description of our departure from the straite into this sea) with a sorrie saile wee entered a harbour: where hoping to enjoy some freedome and ease, till the storme was ended, we received within few houres after our comming to anchor, so deadly a stroake and hard entertainement, that our Admirall left not onely an anchor behind her, through the violence and furie of the flawe; but in departing thence, also lost the company and sight of our Vice-admirall, the *Elizabeth*: partly through the negligence of those that had the charge of her, partly through a kind of desire that some in her had to be out of these troubles, and to be at home againe; which (as since is knowne) they thence forward by all meanes assayed and performed. For the next day October 8 recovering the mouth of the straits againe (which wee were now so neere unto) they returned backe the same way by which they came forward, and so coasting Brasill, they arrived in England June 2 the yeare following.

So that now our Admirall if she had retained her old name of Pellican, which she bare at our departure from our countrey, she might have beene now indeed said to be as a Pellican alone in the wildernesse. For albeit our Generall sought the rest of his fleet with great care, yet could we not have any sight or certaine newes of them by any meanes.

From this bay of parting of friends, we were forcibly driven backe againe into 55 deg. towards the pole Antarticke. In which height we ranne in among the Ilands before mentioned, lying to the Southward of America, through which we passed from one sea to the other, as hath beene declared. Where coming to anchor, wee found the waters there to have their indraught and free passage, and that through no small guts, or narrow channels, but indeed through as large frets or straights, as it hath at the supposed streights of Magellane through which we came.

Among these Ilands, making our abode with some quietnesse for a very little while, (viz. two dayes) and finding divers good and wholesome herbs together with fresh water; our men which before were weake, and much empaired in their health, began to receive good comfort: especially by the drinking of one herbe (not much unlike that

296   BEYOND CAPE HORN

herbe which wee commonly call Pennylease) which purging with great facilitie affoorded great helpe and refreshing to our wearied and sickly bodies. But the winds returning to their old wont, and the seas raging after their former manner, yea every thing as it were setting it selfe against our peace and desired rest, here was no stay permitted us, neither any safety to be looked for.

For such was the present danger by forcing and continuall flawes, that we were rather to looke for present death then hope for any delivery, if God almightie should not make the way for us. The winds were such as if the bowels of the earth had set all at libertie; or as if all the clouds under heaven had beene called together, to lay their force upon that one place: The seas, which by nature and of themselves are heavie, and of a weightie substance, were rowled up from the depths, even from the roots of the rockes, as if it had beene a scroll of parchment, which by the extremity of heate runneth together: and being aloft were carried in most strange manner and abundance, as feathers or drifts of snow, by the violence of the winds, to water the exceeding tops of high and loftie mountaines. Our anchors, as false friends in such a danger, gave over their holdfast, and as if it had beene with horror of the thing, did shrinke downe to hide themselves in this miserable storme; committing the distressed ship and helpelesse men to the uncertaine and rowling seas, which tossed them, like a ball in a racket. In this case, to let fall more anchors, would availe us nothing; For being driven from our first place of anchoring, so unmeasurable was the depth, that 500 fathome would fetch no ground: So that the violent storme without intermission; the impossibility to come to anchor; the want of opportunitie to spread any sayle; the most mad seas; the lee shores; the dangerous rocks; the contrary and most intollerable winds; the impossible passage out; the desperate tarrying there; and inevitable perils on every side did lay before us so small likelihood to escape present destruction, that if the special providence of God himselfe had not supported us, we could never have endured that wofull state: as being invironed with most terrible and most fearefull judgments round about. For truly, it was more likely that the mountaines should have beene rent in sunder, from the top to the bottome, and cast headlong into the sea, by these unnatural winds; then that we, by any helpe or cunning of man, should free the life of any one amongst us.

Notwithstanding the same God of mercy which delivered *Jonas* out of the Whales belly, and heareth all those that call upon him faithfully, in their distresse, looked downe from heaven, beheld our teares, and heard our humble petitions, joyned with holy vowes. Even God (whom not the winds and seas alone, but even the divels themselves and powers of hell obey) did so wonderfully free us, and make our way open before us, as it were by his holy Angels still guiding and conducting us, that more then the affright and amaze of this estate, we received no part of damage in all the things that belonged unto us.

But escaping from these straites and miseries, as it were through the needles ey (that God might have the greater glory in our delivery) by the great and effectuall care and travell of our Generall, the Lords instrument therein; we could now no longer forbeare, but must needes finde some place of refuge, aswell to provide water, wood, and other necessaries, as to comfort our men, thus worne and tired out, by so many and so long intellerable toyles: the like whereof, its to be supposed, no traveller hath felt, neither hath there ever beene, such a tempest (that any records make mention of) so violent, and of such continuance, since *Noahs* flood, for as hath beene sayd it lasted from September 7 to October 28, full 52 dayes.

Not many leagues therefore to the Southwarde of our former anchoring, we ranne in againe among these Ilands; where we had once more better likelihood to rest in peace: and so much the rather, for that wee found the people of the countrie, travelling for their living, from one Iland to another, in their canowes, both men, women, and young infants wrapt in skins, and hanging at their mothers backs; with whom we had traffique, for such things as they had, as chaines of certaine shells and such other trifles; here the Lord gave us three dayes to breath our selves, and to provide such things as we wanted, albeit the same was with continuall care, and troubles to avoid imminent dangers, which the troubled seas and blustering windes, did every houre threaten unto us.

But when we seemed to have stayed there too long, we were more rigorously assaulted by the not formerly ended, but now more violently renewed storme; and driven thence also with no small danger; leaving behind us the greater part of our cable with the anchor; being chased along by the winds, and buffeted incessantly in each quarter by the seas (which our Generall interpreted, as though God had sent them of purpose to the end which ensued) till at length wee fell with the uttermost part of land towards the South pole, and had certainely discovered how farre the same doth reach Southward, from the coast of America aforenamed.

The uttermost cape or hedland of all these Ilands, stands neere in 56 deg. without which there is no maine, nor Iland to be seene to the Southwards: but that the Atlanticke Ocean, and the South sea, meete in a most large and free scope.

It hath beene a dreame through many ages, that these Ilands have been a maine, and that it hath beene *terra incognita*; wherein many strange monsters lived. Indeed it might truly, before this time, be called *incognita*, for howsover the mappes and generall descriptions of

Cosmographers, either upon the deceiveable reports of other men, or the deceitful imaginations of themselves (supposing never herein to be corrected) have set it downe, yet it is true, that before this time, it was never discovered, or certainely knowne by any traveller, that wee have heard of.

And here as in a fit place, it shall not be amisse, to remove that error in opinion, which hath beene held by many, of the impossible returne, out of *Mar Del Zur*, into the West Ocean, by reason of the supposed Easterne current, and levant windes: which (say they) speedily carrie any thither, but suffer no returne. They are herein likewise altogether deceived: for neither did we meete with any such current, neither had we any such certaine windes, with any such speed to carry us through; but at all times, in our passage there, we found more opportunity to returne backe againe, into the West Ocean, then to goe forward into *Mar Del Zur*, by meanes either of current, or windes to hinder us, whereof we had experience more then we wished: being glad oftentimes, to alter our course, and to fall asterne againe, with francke winde (without any impediment of any such surmised current) father in one afternoone, then we could fetch up, or recover againe in a whole day, with a reasonable gale. And in that they alleage the narrownesse of the frete, and want of sea-roome, to be the cause of this violent current; they are herein no lesse deceived, then they were in the other without reason: for besides, that it cannot be sayd, that there is one onely passage, but rather innumerable; it is most certaine, that a sea-board all these Ilands, there is one large and maine sea, wherein if any will not be satisfied, nor believe the report of our experience and ey-sight, hee should be advised to suspend his judgement, till he have either tried it himselfe, by his owne travell, or shall understand, by other travellers, more particulars to confirme his minde herein.

Now as we were fallen to the uttermost part of these Ilands Octob. 28 our troubles did make an end, the storme ceased, and all our calamities (onely the absence of our friends excepted) were removed, as if God, all this while, by his secret providence, had lead us to make this discovery; which being made, according to his will he stayed his hand, as pleased his majestie therein, and refreshed us as his servants.

At these Southerly parts we found the night, in the latter end of October, to be but 2 hours long: the sunne being yet above 7 degrees distant from the Tropick: so that it seemeth, being in the Tropick, to leave very little, or no night at all in that place.

15 ❁ Conversation with Laurence McKinley Gould

ANTONIO PIGAFETTA'S narrative of the discovery of the Strait of Magellan was published in translation by the Hakluyt Society in 1874. Magellan was seeking a strait across the southern end of South America, which he discovered on October 21, 1519. He was killed in a fight with natives in what are now called the Philippines on April 27, 1521. The Strait separates Tierra del Fuego from the rest of South America. Pigafetta sailed with Magellan and returned to Europe with Elcano, the man who completed the circumnavigation of the globe after Magellan's death. Pigafetta's is the fullest account of the voyage.

After going and taking the course to the fifty-second degree of the said Antarctic sky, on the day of the Eleven Thousand Virgins [October 21], we found, by a miracle, a strait which we called the Cape of the Eleven Thousand Virgins, this strait is a hundred and ten leagues long, which are four hundred and forty miles, and almost as wide as less than half a league, and it issues in another sea, which is called the peaceful sea; it is surrounded by very great and high mountains covered with snow. In this place it was not possible to anchor with anchors, because no bottom was found, on which account they were forced to put the moorings of twenty-five or thirty fathoms length on shore. This strait was a round place surrounded by mountains, as I have said, and the greater number of the sailors thought that there was no place by which to go out thence to enter into the peaceful sea. . . .

300

The captain sent on before two of his ships, one named *St. Anthony* and the other the *Conception,* to seek for and discover the outlet of this strait, which was called the Cape de la Baya. And we, with the other two ships, that is to say, the flagship named *Trinitate,* and the other the *Victory,* remained waiting for them within the Bay, where in the night we had a great storm, which lasted till the next day at midday, and during which we were forced to weigh the anchors and let the ships go hither and thither about the bay. The other two ships met with such a head wind that they could not weather a cape which the bay made almost at its extremity; wishing to come to us, they were near being driven to beach the ships. But, on approaching the extremity of the bay, and whilst expecting to be lost, they saw a small mouth, which did not resemble a mouth but a corner, and (like people giving up hope), they threw themselves into it, so that by force they discovered the strait.

Seeing that it was not a corner, but a strait of land, they went further on and found a bay, then going still further they found another strait and another bay larger than the first two, at which, being very joyous, they suddenly returned backwards to tell it to the captain-general. Amongst us we thought that they had perished: first, because of the great storm; next, because two days had passed that we had not seen them. And being thus in doubt we saw the two ships under all sail, with ensigns spread, come towards us: these, when near us, suddenly discharged much artillery, at which we, very joyous, saluted them with artillery and shouts. Afterwards, all together, thanking God and the Virgin Mary, we went to seek further on. . . .

If we had not found this strait the captain-general had made up his mind to go as far as seventy-five degrees towards the antarctic pole; where at that height in the summer time there is no night, or very little: in a similar manner in the winter there is no day-light, or very little, and so that every one may believe this, when we were in this strait the night lasted only three hours, and this was in the month of October.

The land of this strait on the left hand side looked towards the Sirocco wind, which is the wind collateral to the Levant and South; we called this strait Pathagonico. In it we found at every half league a good port and place for anchoring, good waters, wood all of cedar, and fish like sardines, missiglioni, and a very sweet herb named appio [celery]. There is also some of the same kind which is bitter. This herb grows near the springs, and from not finding anything else we ate of it for several days. I think that there is not in the world a more beautiful country, or better strait than this one. . . .

The American, Richard Henry Dana, Jr., in his *Two Years*

Before the Mast, had vividly described his experience of rounding the Horn in 1834 on the brig *Pilgrim,* bound from Boston for California.

Wednesday, Nov. 5th. . . . During the first part of this day the wind was light, but after noon it came on fresh, and we furled the royals. We still kept the studding-sails out, and the captain said he should go round with them, if he could. Just before eight o'clock (then about sundown, in that latitude) the cry of "All hands ahoy!" was sounded down the fore scuttle and the after hatchway, and hurrying upon deck, we found a large black cloud rolling on toward us from the south-west, and blackening the whole heavens. "Here comes Cape Horn!" said the chief mate; and we had hardly time to haul down and clew up, before it was upon us. In a few moments, a heavier sea was raised than I had ever seen before, and as it was directly ahead, the little brig, which was no better than a bathing machine, plunged into it, and all the forward part of her was water; the sea pouring in through the bow-ports and hawse-hole and over the knightheads, threatening to wash everything overboard. In the lee scuppers it was up to a man's waist. We sprang aloft and double reefed the topsails, and furled all the other sails, and made all snug. But this would not do; the brig was laboring and straining against the head sea, and the gale was growing worse and worse. At the same time sleet and hail were driving with all fury against us. We clewed down, and hauled out the reef-tackles again, and close-reefed the fore-topsail, and furled the main, and hove her to on the starboard track. Here was an end to our fine prospects. We made up our minds to head winds and cold weather; sent down the royal yards, and unrove the gear; but all the rest of the top hamper remained aloft, even to the sky-sail masts and studding-sail booms.

Throughout the night it stormed violently—rain, hail, snow, and sleet beating upon the vessel—the wind continuing ahead, and the sea running high. At day-break (about three, A.M.) the deck was covered with snow. The captain sent up the steward with a glass of grog to each of the watch; and all the time that we were off the Cape, grog was given to the morning watch, and to all hands whenever we reefed topsails. The clouds cleared away at sunrise, and the wind becoming more fair, we again made sail and stood nearly up to our course.

Thursday, Nov. 6th. It continued more pleasant through the first part of the day, but at night we had the same scene over again. This time, we did not heave to, as on the night before, but endeavored to beat to windward under close-reefed topsails, balance-reefed trysail, and fore-topmast staysail. This night it was my turn to steer, or, as the sailors say, my *trick* at the helm, for two hours. Inexperienced as I was,

I made out to steer to the satisfaction of the officer, and neither S——— nor myself gave up our tricks, all the time that we were off the Cape. This was something to boast of, for it requires a good deal of skill and watchfulness to steer a vessel close hauled, in a gale of wind, against a heavy head sea. "Ease her when she pitches," is the word; and a little carelessness in letting her ship a heavy sea, might sweep the decks, or knock the masts out of her.

Friday, Nov. 7th. Towards morning the wind went down, and during the whole afternoon we lay tossing about in a dead calm, and in the midst of a thick fog. The calms here are unlike those in most parts of the world, for there is always a high sea running, and the periods of calm are so short, that it has no time to go down; and vessels, being under no command of sails or rudder, lie like logs upon the water. We were obliged to steady the booms and yards by guys and braces, and to lash everything well below. We now found our top hamper of some use, for though it is liable to be carried away or sprung by the sudden "bringing up" of a vessel when pitching in a chopping sea, yet it is a great help in steadying a vessel when rolling in a long swell; giving more slowness, ease, and regularity to the motion. . . .

Towards the evening of this day the fog cleared off, and we had every appearance of a cold blow; and soon after sundown it came on. Again it was a clew up and haul down, reef and furl, until we had got her down to close-reefed topsails, double-reefed trysail, and reefed forespenser. Snow, hail, and sleet were driving upon us most of the night, and the sea breaking over the bows and covering the forward part of the little vessel; but as she would lay her course the captain refused to heave her to.

Saturday, Nov. 8th. This day commenced with calm and thick fog, and ended with hail, snow, a violent wind, and close-reefed topsails.

Sunday, Nov. 9th. To-day the sun rose clear, and continued so until twelve o'clock, when the captain got an observation. This was very well for Cape Horn, and we thought it a little remarkable that, as we had not had one unpleasant Sunday during the whole voyage, the only tolerable day here should be a Sunday. We got time to clear up the steerage and forecastle, and set things to rights, and to overhaul our wet clothes a little. But this did not last very long. Between five and six—the sun was then nearly three hours high—the cry of "All star-bowlines ahoy!" summoned our watch on deck; and immediately all hands were called. A true specimen of Cape Horn was coming upon us. A great cloud of dark slate-color was driving on us from the south-west; and we did our best to take in sail (for the light sails had been set during the first part of the day) before we were in the midst of it. We had got the light sails furled, the courses hauled up, and the topsail reef-tackles hauled out, and were just mounting the fore-rigging, wen the storm struck us. In an instant the sea, which had been comparatively quiet, was running higher and higher; and it became almost as dark as night. The hail and sleet were harder than I had yet felt them; seeming almost to *pin us down* to the rigging. We were longer taking in sail than ever before; for the sails were stiff and wet, the ropes and rigging covered with snow and sleet, and we ourselves cold and nearly blinded with the violence of the storm. By the time we had got down upon deck again, the little brig was plunging madly into a tremendous head sea, which at every drive rushed in through the bow-ports and over the bows, and buried all the forward part of the vessel. At this instant the chief mate, who was standing on the top of the windlass, at the foot of the spenser mast, called out, "Lay out there and furl the jib!" This was no agreeable or safe duty, yet it must be done. An old Swede, (the best sailor on board,) who belonged on the forecastle, sprang out upon the bowsprit. Another one must go: I was near the mate, and sprang forward, threw the downhaul over the windlass, and jumped between the knight-heads out upon the bowsprit. The crew stood abaft the windlass and hauled the jib down while we got out upon the weather side of the jib-boom, our feet on the foot-ropes, holding on by the spar, the great jib flying off to leeward and *slatting* so as almost to throw us off of the boom. For some time we could do nothing but hold on, and the vessel, diving into two huge seas, one after the other, plunged us twice into the water up to our chins. We hardly knew whether we were on or off; when coming up, dripping from the water, we were raised high into the air. John (that was the sailor's name) thought the boom would go, every moment, and called out to the mate to keep the vessel off, and haul down the stay-sail; but the fury of the wind and the breaking of the seas against the bows defied every attempt to make ourselves heard, and we were obliged to do the best we could in our situation. Fortunately, no other seas so heavy struck her, and we succeeded in furling the jib "after a fashion;" and, coming in over the staysail net-tings, were not a little pleased to find that all was snug, and the watch gone below; for we were soaked through, and it was very cold. The weather continued nearly the same through the night.

Monday, Nov. 10th. During a part of this day we were hove to, but the rest of the time were driving on, under close-reefed sails, with a heavy sea, a strong gale, and frequent squalls of hail and snow.

Tuesday, Nov. 11th. The same.

Wednesday. The same.

Thursday. The same.

We had now got hardened to Cape weather, the vessel was under reduced sail, and everything secured on deck and below, so that we had little to do but to steer and to stand our watch. Our clothes were all wet through, and the only change was from wet to more wet. It was in vain to think of reading or working below, for we were too tired, the hatchways were closed down, and everything was wet and uncomfortable, black and dirty, heaving and pitching. We had only to come below when the watch was out, wring out our wet clothes, hang them up, and turn in and sleep as soundly as we could, until the watch was called again.

I was living with a certain amount of historical resonance, some of which was personal, for I could not forget that I had as a very young man heard Rear Admiral Byrd lecture in Richmond, Virginia, after his first Antarctic expedition (1928–30), had met him backstage, had become an admirer of his and had made futile attempts to go to the Antarctic. Nor could I forget that much later in my life I had had the great good luck to meet the man who had been science leader and second in command of that expedition, Laurence M. Gould.

Early in February 1978 I interviewed Gould in Tucson, Arizona, for the chapter to which these pages are an introduction. By now Gould was a kind of Antarctic superstar. He had directed the Antarctic program of the United States National Committee for the IGY, had been chairman of the polar research committee of the National Academy of Sciences, had been the United States representative on the special committee on Antarctic research of the International Council of Scientific Unions, and so on. The chapter is based on the Tucson conversations together with subsequent changes made during a correspondence between us.

Gould kindly met me at the airport and drove me to the Plaza International Hotel, where we immediately set to work. He was marvelously easy to get along with. He was still fit physically and was wonderfully congenial, enthusiastic and vital.

Neider: Do you think there's such a thing as an Antarctic addiction? Cherry-Garrard seemed to think so. There's no doubt that Scott would have gone back if he'd lived, and Shackleton kept going back. *You* have kept going back.

Gould: Well, I guess you could call it an addiction. I've been there six times and I'd still like to go back.

Neider: Why?

Gould: No one ever said it so well as Nansen, the greatest of all polar explorers, in a speech at St. Andrews University, I don't know how long ago, it doesn't matter. "The history of the human race is a continual struggle from darkness toward light. It is therefore of no use to discuss the use of knowledge. Man wants to know, and when he ceases to do so he is no longer man." It's the lure of the unknown. Probably every one of us, however, if we knew that we could never come back from Antarctica, would have quite a different feeling about it.

Neider: Are you suggesting that one has a feeling of immortality while there?

Gould: No. No, no. I've never been aware of any such feeling. I know a few people who think that, but I have never been on an expedition with one of them.

Neider: What about the religious or quasi-religious or neo-religious experiences that some people have there?

Gould: I'm not aware of ever having any myself, nor was I aware that any of us on the first Byrd Antarctic expedition had such experiences. At least I never heard anyone speak about them. And mind you, on that first expedition there were forty-two of us living in quarters designed for twenty-five. But Dick Byrd and I and other members of the community discussed several times whether we should have some kind of religious service. They wanted me to do something about it. Well, I decided along with the rest that it would be better to avoid it entirely. We had Catholics, we had Jews, we had several varieties, and I can't imagine a service that would have appealed to all of them. And I think it was one of the good reasons that we didn't have any serious trouble on the first Byrd expedition.

Neider: What about the beauty of the place? Does that play a role?

Gould: It does with me. It's beyond description. As it does with you. And the night is so beautiful. I had thought the long winter night would be so tedious. Ninety percent of the clear weather we had aurora displays. And when the moon was full you could read the headlines of a newspaper. It's so clean. Beautiful beyond description to me. Of course, that's one of the lures. I want to go back and look at it again.

Neider: You can't believe it's true. Do you have a sense of unreality after—?

Gould: Yes, in some sense you do. I want to be reassured that what I saw was really there. It's that magic. And I'm not talking foolishness, either. I'm a foolish man in some ways but I'm not about Antarctica.

Neider: How did you get started in Antarctic work?

Gould: Well, I had been in the Arctic on two expeditions. I was up in Greenland in 1926. In 1927 I was on Baffin Island and so had some polar experience, but no American geologist had yet set foot on Antarctica.

Neider: Why didn't you return to Antarctica with the second Byrd expedition?.

Gould: Just before I left for Antarctica I became engaged to Margaret Rice. I would have been glad to have spent another winter in Antarctica except for that. Furthermore, I didn't think I wanted to spend my life as an explorer. I wanted to be a scholar in my own field of geology. I wanted to return to the academic life. I did so. I came back and married Margaret Rice and returned to my geology.

Neider: So when did you go back to Antarctica?

Gould: When the IGY was being organized in 1955 I became a member of the United States National Committee for the International Geophysical Year and of its Executive Committee, and chairman of the subcommittee on Antarctica. When the IGY became operative I was appointed director of the United States IGY Antarctic program. I went to Antarctica in December 1956 and again for a longer period in 1957 to confer with Rear Admiral George Dufek, commanding officer of the Naval Task Force which provided all logistic support for our scientific program. One of our proposed stations was to be at the South Pole. This involved the unprecedented task of delivering all supplies by air drop. I soon was aware of a lack of enthusiasm amongst some of the pilots for this, and I conveyed my worries to Admiral Dufek. He looked at me and said, "Goddamn it, Larry, I'm in charge of the Navy operations and you're in charge of the scientific program. Don't tell me how to run the Navy and I won't tell you how to run the scientific program. We'll put your goddamn scientific stations wherever you want them." And the Navy did exactly that. There began a historic partnership between science and its supporters which still obtains.

Neider: What were some of the most memorable moments of your long sledging journey?

Gould: Oh, there's no doubt in my mind about that. Long before we had reached the Queen Maud Mountains we could see far ahead of us these great, high, beautifully snow-capped mountains topped with flat-lying rocks. They surely looked like sedimentary rocks to me. But as we reached the foot of the mountains and began climbing up the foot to reach the rocks I became nervous as to whether these *were* the rocks I really wanted to find or not. And I picked up a piece of sandstone and held it in my hand before I realized that this was surely a piece of the Beacon sandstone which Ferrar had identified over near McMurdo and had been identified elsewhere in Antarctica. We had a little radio. We communicated daily with Byrd back at Little America. And I can remember the radiogram I sent to him. I said, "No work of art before which I have stood in awe, no symphony I have ever heard gave me quite the thrill I had when I reached down and picked up a piece of this rock and realized that it was sandstone, that it was the very rock I had come all the way to Antarctica to find." And another thrill that we got as we sledged along was the realization that we were looking at mountains and glaciers that no one else had ever seen.

Neider: Why was it such a thrill to find the Beacon sandstone?

Gould: That's the same kind of formation of rocks of the same geological age that we find in India, Australia, South Africa and South America. And we found, as had been found before, that it contained Glossopteris, a fossil plant found in the above places. But the skeptics about continental drift wouldn't take that seriously. They said plant spores can be blown across the ocean. The fact that they had been found on all these continents didn't mean any more than that. It wasn't until the Lystrasaurus was discovered in '69 that the geological facts about the relationship were pinned down beyond any question.

Neider: Do you have any regrets about your Antarctic career?

Gould: My only regrets are that I did not do more. I look back upon it, especially the first Byrd expedition, and the things that I could have done and didn't. Several people, including Alfred Knopf, have tried to persuade me to write an autobiography. Every time I try to think of it, I think of the things I *didn't* do. If

I write an autobiography it's going to be a negative one. Things I didn't do that I should have done. Suddenly I think of a lad's definition of a "sin of omission." He said it was a sin one should have committed but didn't.

Neider: What didn't you do on the first Byrd expedition?

Gould: I could have done a lot better job in my geological studies in the Queen Maud Mountains. I was in too much of a hurry. I could have done more glaciology. Of course, I had a lot of things to do. I was executive officer and that involved a good deal of work.

Neider: I don't think you had much choice, as I remember. Byrd in his book *Little America* over and over praises you for your work in building the camp while he was on the ship. You were doing a lot more than just being a scientist.

Gould: I was, but I'm telling the truth, though. I wish I had done more science. I neglected science for these other things.

Neider: Well, I'm going to speak up on your behalf. This was the first attempt to camp on the Bay of Whales since Amundsen, and there was a great deal of exploration work necessary. Although the idea was to have a good combination of exploration and science, I think the problem in your particular case was that you were not only science leader but second-in-command of the expedition and I think that consequently your role as an organizer conflicted with your role as a scientist.

Gould: One can't deny that. You see, we really had a unique opportunity. We were the first American expedition ever to set foot in Antarctica. I was the first geologist of *any* nation to sledge inland to the geological features there. And when I think how much more I *could* have done, then I regret it. I want to draw attention to the fact that the first Byrd expedition was the transition between the "heroic age" of surface travel and the more sophisticated modern age. Most of the techniques of travel and communication which make the greatly extended scientific study of Antarctica possible today were pioneered on the First Byrd Antarctic Expedition (1928–30). Today aircraft are immensely more flexible and efficient, oversnow vehicles are infinitely more effective, and radios perform much better.

Neider: You say that's a transition but perhaps one could say that the last very long sledging journey on a scientific mission was in a sense the end of the heroic period.

Gould: It was, because nobody has ever sledged that extensively since, and of course we long ago stopped using dogs ourselves in Antarctica. The New Zealanders have a few dogs but that's more for the sake of the tourists and the visitors than it is for any field use.

Neider: What are some of your sharpest memories of Antarctica?

Gould: Oh, its sheer, utter, magnificent desolation. It is so desolate that it's impressive and inspiring. That may sound like a contradiction but it isn't, as you know yourself. And its beauty, its beauty. It's such a simple beauty. There isn't a great variety of colors but somehow it penetrates, and when I got off the plane and stood on the ice once again, a year ago now, I had what amounted to almost a physical thrill. I was back to my spiritual home.

Neider: I've never heard anyone refer to Antarctica as their spiritual home.

Gould: Let's call that poetic license, Charles. When I was back there for those few days in 1977 I felt better physically and spiritually than in a long time. That trip added ten years to my life, Charles. That's an exaggeration, of course, but it gives an idea of how much better I felt as a result of that journey.

Neider: If you had complete control of Antarctica what would you do geopolitically there?

Gould: That's a good question indeed. I think I would let my imagination run and explore the possibility of making the Antarctic Treaty permanent. We work so wonderfully well under it, and I shudder to think what may happen at the end of the Treaty.

Neider: You mean in '91.

Gould: I think we might do a lot more talking and planning now than we are doing about what's going to happen in '91.

Neider: How do you feel about the fact that the consultative meetings are almost always held in secret? Do you think that's necessary?

Gould: No. And under the present conditions I don't think they should be. We can't keep anything secret very long. You know, one of the reasons why our program in Antarctica from the IGY on down through has worked so beautifully is that there's no classified research. Everyone has free access to

310   BEYOND CAPE HORN

everyone else's bases. We have had a continuing exchange of scientists, and look how wonderfully it's worked. There have been no serious questions in the operation of our program nationally or internationally since we began in 1957.

Neider: So what you would want to focus on is to strengthen the Treaty. Now, one of the great weaknesses of the Treaty at the moment is that it doesn't deal with the problems of exploration and exploitation of mineral resources and fossil-fuel reserves.

Gould: But if we had tried to solve such economic problems as those we would have had no treaty.

Neider: Primarily because of the claimant nations?

Gould: Yes. I think the Treaty was possible only because we set aside all questions of claims for thirty years.

Neider: The Treaty is devoted to keeping the continent a peaceful place. The whole ideal of the Treaty is not to have physical force in the Antarctic—that is, south of 60° latitude—and the question that has come to my mind over and over is, "Is this too utopian an idea?" Let's say that a nonsignatory nation, a nonacceding nation, decides to go down there with a heavy ship and do whatever it wants to do. How are you going to stop it?

Gould: No way that I know of.

Neider: So we're walking a tightrope and we hope we don't fall off. We hope that somehow reason prevails.

Gould: We're in a mess if it doesn't.

Neider: How do you feel about Third World demands that they share in Antarctic resources if and when the latter are discovered and exploited?

Gould: I think it is a utopian dream in the context of the way these nations are thinking about it.

Neider: Their argument is that of the common heritage of mankind, that Antarctica—the Antarctic, which is larger than the continent itself, it includes the seas around it—is the common heritage of mankind, and it should not be taken away from them merely because they are slow in developing technologically. They're afraid that by the time they have the technological capabilities for harvesting whatever wealth there is there, most of it will be gone. I don't know how fruitful the argument is in practical terms, nor do I know in philosophical terms whether it stands up to a counter argument.

Conversation with Lawrence McKinley Gould   311

Gould: It is unrealistic to suppose that the more advanced nations are going to postpone any possible exploitation of resources until the Third World nations have caught up with them technologically. Actually, the more affluent nations have been operating on a sharing basis for some time. Ever since the initiation of the Marshall Plan after World War II the United States has been sharing to the extent of billions of dollars with Third World nations. Should the United States participate in exploitation of rich Antarctic resources, presumably Third World nations would be beneficiaries.

Neider: How do you feel about a nonsignatory and a nonacceding nation going down to Antarctica, if it has the capability, and doing its will in the Antarctic? Do you feel that the so-called "club," the Antarctic Treaty nations and the others who have acceded to the Treaty, have a prior moral right?

Gould: I think we do have on the basis of our achievements there and our record of wonderful cooperation. Maybe a united front of the Treaty nations, and there are a lot of powerful nations in it, could prevent it—not by active conflict but by protest.

Neider: I have a related question that comes to mind, and that is from reading the paper that you sent me by Brian Roberts, who was in the Foreign Office for quite a while. He believes that we are not so far away from the technological capabilities of drilling through ice masses, either over the continental shelves or through the ice shelves themselves, as some people think we are. He believes that the capabilities, say in the Arctic of the big multinational oil companies, makes successful drilling almost imminent. Do you have any information about that?

Gould: No, I don't, but I don't agree with him. I think the situation is quite different. Consider the Ross Ice Shelf and the area there. You'd be confronted with icebergs, and if one of those great tabular icebergs started floating towards your drilling machine there's nothing in God's world that would stop it. Add to that the hazard of the pack ice, which is in much greater motion than it is in the Arctic Ocean. In the Arctic Ocean it's so tightly tied in with land that the ice, that the pack ice, drifts around slowly and rarely gets out. In other words, there's a great deal more activity of the ice in Antarctica than there is in the Arctic. Furthermore, the fantastic weather. You don't have in the Arctic the Roaring Forties, the Howling Fifties and the Shrieking Sixties: the stormiest seas in the world. I don't think there is a parallel.

Neider: Are you worried about the current viability of the Treaty?

Gould: No, I don't see any other greater worry than those we've had. It gathers strength as it continues to operate. It's stronger now, I think, than it was when we built it.

Neider: If you could arrange it would you at this point try to broaden the Antarctic Treaty so that it includes the question of exploitation, whether it's in the seas or on the continent?

Gould: Oh, I would, yes.

Neider: You think it would strengthen the Treaty?

Gould: Well, if it isn't done that way, then I fear the exploitation will be a kind of random operation. Dog eat dog.

Neider: And do you think that it's possible to have exploitation in the Antarctic without a dog-eat-dog situation?

Gould: It's possible. It's a dim hope.

Neider: The problem here again is that the Antarctic Treaty is a moral force essentially. It doesn't have physical force as teeth.

Gould: None whatever.

Neider: So it's a moral issue, really. And perhaps for that reason it's extremely important to try to keep it alive.

Gould: Yes, I think it is. The alternative is unthinkable.

Neider: What are your views regarding territorial claims in Antarctica? We can go into that historically. For example, I think you were part of a group that went to Marie Byrd Land and felt that you were claiming that territory.

Gould: Sure, we did that on my sledge journey. When we went beyond the 180th meridian we had a little flag that we put up, and we took off our hats and I solemnly said a few words to the effect that we claimed this land for the United States in the name of Commander Byrd. We just did it. But it made news in New Zealand and our State Department opined that such claims were not valid, that the policy stated by Secretary of State Hughes in 1924 was still our policy—that claims to be valid had to be followed by effective occupation.

Neider: How do you feel about the matter now? Are you completely behind the United States position that we do not make any territorial claims?

Gould: I am entirely. But if the Treaty were to disappear tomorrow and there was no possibility of reinstating anything like it, I would recomend that we hurriedly lay down claim to the unclaimed slice. Of course, we have reserved the right to make claims and we have done extremely important work of exploration in other areas.

Neider: You've played practically every role there is to play in Antarctica. That is, as an explorer, as a scientist, as an administrator and even as a political scientist. Are you concerned about conservation in Antarctica?

Gould: Of course I am. This is the one part of planet earth that hasn't been despoiled. Neither by accident nor design have we yet introduced any new species of plant or animal into Antarctica. Yes, I'm completely dedicated to the idea that we should strengthen the agreed measures on conservation in every way we can. I think, by the way, the way we have operated internationally at that level has been very good indeed.

Neider: And do you believe that the Treaty nations are doing all that can be done in this respect? I mean, do you believe that conservationist groups have a right to feel fairly relaxed about what's being done in Antarctica?

Gould: I think so. Outside of whaling, of course. We couldn't do anything about that, and for obvious reasons.

Neider: How do you feel about the introduction of women into Antarctic life and work?

Gould: It was inevitable. With the kind of social atmosphere in which we live we couldn't have stopped them if we had wanted to. And actually some of them have performed superbly. It made it more complicated, of course, and more expensive. We kept them out as long as we could but I think it was inevitable.

Neider: Why did we keep them out? Was that a Navy matter?

Gould: Partly and partly the expense. You have to have duplicate facilities—toilets and all of that sort of thing, and the barracks. In those days the idea of having men and women in the same barracks would have been intolerable. Our whole social atmosphere has changed. My God, down here in the university—most colleges and universities have mixed dormitories. When I was a lad that would have meant excommunication or something worse. It's one of the things that we could have done without more easily but there was no way to do it.

Neider: What do you mean, one of the things we could have done without?

Gould: Well, ideally, I'd rather not have any women around in Antarctica.

Neider: Why is that?

Gould: They pose little personal problems that I can work in the field or the laboratory more easily without. That's all, and that isn't serious at all. Any man can put up with it.

Neider: How do you feel about possibly expanding our program to include more of the humanities?

Gould: I would like to involve every program with more humanities. That has been the thrust of my whole life. Just a bit of history. When I was inaugurated president of Carleton College in 1945 the subject of my talk was Science and the Other Humanities.

Neider: How do you account for the fact that you, who had a scientific education, are so full of humanistic thinking?

Gould: I don't know, but I think some of my humanistic thinking came from great science teachers, including a teacher of chemistry in high school, but perhaps more of it came from reading. My earliest heroes were Socrates and Lincoln and they still remain my heroes.

Neider: How do you feel about the fact that since the IGY, pure science has had a kind of monopoly in Antarctica, which is to say that the Treaty nations, almost all of them, enact legislation for basic scientific research and they put up the money for it, and then each of them deals with the problem of logistics in its own way. I mean, the British operation, for example, is very homogeneous. It's mostly governmental. *We* have civilians and academics doing the scientific work and then we have a task force of the Navy doing the logistics, and so on. But essentially, as I see it, science in Antarctica has a monopoly of the continent. Do you think that's an unfair statement?

Gould: I don't agree with it. You know very well when I learned about you and knew you wanted to go to Antarctica, I took it up in your behalf with the National Science Foundation. I said, "It's time we had some more objective view about the meaning of what we're doing. A few scientists may know its significance but we do need the humanistic approach. I think it's

Conversation with Lawrence McKinley Gould   315

a shame that we've neglected it so long." I'm glad you came along, my friend.

Neider: What worries you most about Antarctica?

Gould: The possibilities of finding mineral resources that are so rich and so necessary to mankind that they'll forget all about this magnificent, unspoiled part of the planet and do anything to exploit it. That's the biggest fear.

Neider: What is the chief scientific problem as you see it in Antarctica at this time?

Gould: Of all the things we're investigating there, I have the strong feeling that the effect which the great Antarctic ice sheet and the pack ice have on world climate may be the most important. In recent years the *National Geographic Magazine* has given increasing space to first-rate scientific articles about subjects of widespread interest. Some time ago it produced a fine article on plate tectonics which any intelligent person could understand. In the November 1976 issue there appeared an equally good piece on world weather and climate. The article appraised the role of Antarctica as follows: "Ice at the bottom of the globe may hold the power to change world climate. Is the Antarctic ice cap, which holds 90 percent of all fresh water on earth, rapidly melting away and raising sea level? Is that enormous ice cap itself the crucial control over climate?" With the scientific uncovering of Antarctica in the International Geophysical Year and the years since, climatologists have been confronted with data that demand a new appraisal of the role of Antarctica in world climate. There is no single factor on planet earth which affects short-range weather or climate as much as the variation in the pack ice—because of the great difference it makes in the albedo of the earth. When the sea is covered over in the midwinter of Antarctica, the continent is climatically twice as big as it is in the summer, when the pack ice is largely gone. Ice or snow can reflect as much as eighty percent to ninety percent of the solar energy which it receives, whereas the ocean may absorb that amount.

Neider: You were trained as a geologist and you were in Antarctica in the first Byrd expedition as scientific leader of the expedition, and as a geologist. You were also in Antarctica in 1969 when Lystrasaurus was found, and your name was mentioned on the front page of the *New York Times* when you stated

316   BEYOND CAPE HORN

that this was the most important fossil yet found in Antarctica and one of the great fossil finds of all time. That find certainly nailed down the theory of continental drift from the point of view of paleontology.

Gould: Yes, it certainly did.

Neider: That being the case, can a geologist go very far in extrapolating from the other landmasses and coming to the conclusion that Antarctica must possess valuable resources?

Gould: Well, that's quite simple. If you put Gondwanaland back together again, the geological provinces tie up perfectly. I mean, the rocks which carry great rich ore deposits in South Africa have their counterpart in Australia, and the rocks at least have their counterpart in Antarctica. Well, this is more than analogy. You can't escape the assumption that there are rich mineral resources in Antarctica. Every other continental landmass does have or has had important mineral resources, but I hope they never find any in Antarctica.

Neider: Let's go back for a minute to Little America. Apparently you and Byrd believed with Amundsen that there was no real danger of your camp calving off the ice shelf and going out to sea.

Gould: No.

Neider: You took that risk, right?

Gould: We took that risk. With all the information available it seemed to have been a good risk and so it worked out.

Neider: But eventually it did break off. So, Amundsen's claim that—he may not have been wrong, he said that if Shackleton had based himself on the Bay of Whales he would have been the first man to reach the South Pole. You remember that Shackleton took a look and it seemed to him it was too dangerous and then he backed off. Both men were right, then.

Gould: I think so. Even so, I think Shackleton made the greatest sledge journey of all. I mean, to have gotten within ninety-seven nautical miles of the Pole, as he did, and have the courage to turn back, knowing that if he carried on, his party could not make it back to Ross Island, was perhaps the most critical decision made by any polar explorer.

Neider: Are you worried about the fact that krill is being exploited on a rather unilateral basis at the moment and that probably the krill ecosystem is not sufficiently understood?

Gould: Yes, I am. We have some awfully good oceanographers who have worked on that. El Sayed of Texas, one of the foremost, thinks that sixty million metric tons of krill could be harvested per year without disturbing the ecology. But how can we limit the exploitation to sixty million metric tons? That's a hell of a lot. That's about as much as the total production of all the rest of the oceans put together right now.

Neider: What Antarctic books are you especially fond of?

Gould: Cherry-Garrard's *The Worst Journey in the World.* That is a classic in terms of the content and the style. I don't want to flatter you, but I've said publicly and to NSF, if I had only one book to hand to somebody to get a feeling of what Antarctica is like now, I would tell them to read your *Edge of the World.* I think I've read most of the books. Amundsen's is very dull. Scott's is one of the most interesting. Shackleton I loved, of course. Sir Douglas Mawson's *Home of the Blizzard* gives one of the very best accounts of the real character of Antarctica. A recently published book, *Mawson's Will,* by Lennard Bickel, describes the incredible manner in which Mawson survived after the tragic loss of his companions. For sheer tough going it is in the same class as Shackleton's *Endurance* episode, described in his book *South,* one of the truly great classics in polar exploration. Of Byrd's books I think *Little America* is the best. It is a fine account of the First Byrd Antarctic Expedition, in which he gives generous credit to his men. Richard Lewis's *A Continent for Science* is an excellent description of the coming of science into Antarctic exploration. I suppose I ought to include my own book, *Cold,* in the books I like.

Neider: I think it's a very good book. Byrd was not in a position to handle its subject inasmuch as he didn't make that very long sledging journey and he wasn't with you when the plane went down and when you were stranded because the wind blew it over and destroyed it. Also I liked very much the last chapter of *Little America,* which *you* wrote. Do you have any regrets about the administrative side of your Antarctic career? A lot of your time went into it.

Gould: Well, I have regrets about everything I've done. I could have done a better job with my science if I had not been second-in-command or executive officer for a group of forty-two men living in quarters designed for twenty-five. We did get through the winter night without any serious problems. After all, it is not the big problems that are of major concern. It's the little things like the way a man butters his bread or parts his hair or eats his soup that drives you up the wall.

Neider: I should say for the record that I have never encountered anybody else with the intensity and breadth of Antarctic interests and work that you have. Let us take our relationship, for example. You have accepted the work I'm doing. You have not begrudged the fact that I'm an outsider, that I am not a scientist. Also you have a global view of Antarctica despite the fact, or perhaps because of the fact, that you had a very prominent role to play in the United States program. And this is very impressive to me.

Gould: Flattery *does* get you someplace. But I reject completely one statement you made. You're no more of an outsider than I am from the standpoint of what should be our human concern for the welfare of this unique continent. There *are* no outsiders to those who love it.

Neider: Well, you see, that is exactly the point I'm making about your point of view. Strictly speaking, in terms of the United States program, essentially it's set up and financed for basic scientific research, and with logistic support in the form of various parts of the military, acting in a nonmilitary way in Antarctica. I'm very lucky that I've been able to go to Antarctica. I wouldn't have been able to without governmental support, as a guest of the government. But I'm particularly lucky to have encountered somebody like you, in a position of authority and great experience, who takes this view that Antarctica can use all the friends it can get from whatever source they come from. And I think that's what—

Gould: We *need* the kind of view that a humanist like you can give to it. Too many scientists aren't very good at interpreting their science. Too many of them see it through a very narrow aperture, so to speak. We need, the whole field of science needs, generalists, people who can see the broad pattern. We've gone hog wild with specialization, and it's dimmed the luster of science in the mind of the public and in our own minds.

Neider: Is there anything you'd like to talk about that I haven't yet touched on?

Gould: Before the IGY had really started, the scientific community of which I was a part realized that in a year or eighteen months we could only scratch the surface of Antarctic science. And so we recommended to ICSU, the acronym for International Council of Scientific Unions, that some kind of continuing organization should be created to keep the program going after the IGY was over. And since I was the official representative of the National Academy of Sciences, I was the United States delegate to the conference in The Hague in February 1958 to help design the organization which would carry on our scientific programs after the IGY officially ended on December 31, 1958. Delegates from the twelve nations operating IGY programs in the Antarctic wrote the founding document or constitution of the Scientific Committee on Antarctic Research (SCAR), under which the twelve IGY nations still carry on the highly successful scientific cooperation of the IGY. As the official representative of the National Academy of Sciences I was a charter member of SCAR. In 1963 I was elected president of SCAR. I served in that capacity for seven years. I continued as a member of SCAR until I retired in 1972. I was then elected an honorary life member. Likewise the Academy's Committee on Polar Research, of which I had been chairman since its organization in 1958, kept me on as an ex-officio member. The committee's name has been changed to the Polar Research Board. While the National Science Foundation funded the IGY, the scientific programs were operated by the National Academy of Sciences. The Academy is not designed to be an operating agency, and at the end of the IGY both the funding and the operation of our scientific programs (SCAR) were taken over by the National Science Foundation. Like other federal agencies, the Foundation turns to the Academy for advice, and the Academy's Polar Research Board provides long-range plans and programs for the Foundation's Division of Polar Programs.

As for ICSU, it is a nongovernmental organization of the scientific committee of most of the countries in the world under which major international scientific programs are developed. Even as ICSU was studying in the fall of 1957 ways in which IGY Antarctic programs could be continued after December 31, 1958—and this led to the creation of SCAR in February 1958—the United States Department of State was making a comprehensive review of our Antarctic policy on the assumption that some kind of political instrument or organization was needed to protect our Antarctic program after the end of the IGY. Thus the movement that led to the Antarctic Treaty originated in our State Department, and all of the meetings leading to its ratification were held in Washington. United States participation was master-minded by Paul C. Daniels and Herman Phfleger of our State Department. After the exchange of much information amongst the twelve SCAR nations, our State Department sent notes to the other eleven members on May 2, 1958, inviting them to gather in Washington for preliminary talks. These talks began in June 1958 and prepared the way for the final conference convened in Washington on October 15, 1959. So successful had been the preliminary talks that within six weeks agreement was reached and the Treaty signed on December 1, 1959. The Treaty then had to be ratified by each of the participating nations. It went into effect on June 23, 1961. I think the Treaty is a document of great importance in pointing the way toward a more orderly world. It is the first treaty in man's history designed to protect a scientific program.

SCAR is a purely scientific nongovernmental organization. It has no authority to make decisions or take action in political matters. Thus the Antarctic Treaty fills a real need. For nearly twenty years the scientific and political organizations have cooperated with great benefit to man's last great unspoiled area of his planet earth. Perhaps the most outstanding example of the cooperation is the agreed measures of conservation, which are truly effective in protecting the life of the land and the sea about it. There is no single segment in the pattern of our world society where cooperation is easier than at the scientific level. The IGY was so successful that there have been many programs like it. The International Hydrological Decade and GARP (Global Atmospheric Research Program) are spinoffs of the IGY, which has been aptly called the greatest peacetime activity in man's history. The two outstanding programs of the IGY turned out to be the space science–satellite program and the uncovering of Antarctica.

Neider: I think I've already asked you what are some of the poetic moments of the sledging journey. And I believe you answered the knowledge that you were seeing geographical places for the first time in mankind's history.

Gould: That's right. And the sandstone, of course, the Beacon sandstone. Well, I think I was born at the right time, Charles. I was a mature man before World War I when the world was at peace and when economists demonstrated that there couldn't be a world war because it would bankrupt the whole world. They were right. In some ways we've been going downhill ever since. I was born at the right time. I'm not sorry I'm nearly 82 years old. I'm so glad that I was able to participate in the last Antarctic expedition which depended solely on the dogs for oversnow transportation. You can't tell other people about dogs and what rapport you develop with them, unless you have driven them month after month for a long time. Often when we would get into a dangerous crevassed area, where the crevasses were covered over with snow, we would tie long ropes on the rear of the sledges and let the dogs go across, and if they got across we thought probably *we* could. Never a word of command. They could sense better than we could whether they should lead us through this maze. They were magnificent. And I still remember also how often, when we had stopped for the day and the dogs had been fed and were settling down for the night, one dog would stick his nose in the air and start to howl. Not bark, but howl. Presently he might be joined by another one. Soon the whole pack would be howling in unison and, after they'd traveled for three months together, in the same pitch. And then just as cleanly as a symphony orchestra conductor brings his orchestra to a close, these dogs would all stop howling together. That's one of my lovely memories too. By the way, while I'm talking about dogs, these sledge dogs were wonderful dogs. The idea that sledge dogs are inherently mean is complete nonsense. They are mean if you treat them meanly, if you don't feed them. But they love to be petted. They're great friends.

Neider: I remember well that Byrd's first expedition, like Amundsen's, took a lot of dogs along. They did not make the mistake of Scott and Shackleton in insufficiency of dogs.

Gould: If Shackleton had used dogs, of course he would have been at the Pole before anyone else. Scott wouldn't have gotten anywhere near the Pole on his first expedition. His preparations were inadequate. But Shackleton would have done it. Of the three competitive leaders for the South Pole I think Shackleton was the greatest. Amundsen was a rigid disciplinarian, as was

322   BEYOND CAPE HORN

Scott, who carried naval discipline to the extreme of drawing a line across their one-room cabin, which enlisted men were forbidden to cross. On the contrary, though Byrd was a naval officer there was no naval discipline on his first Antarctic expedition. His was a truly democratic group. Byrd saw more of Antarctica for the first time than any other man ever did and was the dominant figure in Antarctic exploration for three decades.

Neider: Do you believe that his Antarctic work damaged his health?

Gould: I don't think the first expedition did. But I suspect a very tough thing to which he subjected himself on his second expedition, going out a couple of hundred miles and getting snowed under and inhaling a good deal of carbon monoxide, may have adversely affected his health. I wasn't close to him after the first expedition, or at least not until the IGY. He was not the man I had known. He was not well.

Neider: What about alcohol on the first Byrd expedition?

Gould: We may have been too careful. We took only a few bottles of gin or whisky or whatever it was, and there was no beer. We made no provision for issuing alcoholic liquors to the members of the expedition. But we had two great big hogsheads of grain alcohol which we needed for drying our aerial films. We had to develop them in Little America and we needed the alcohol to dry the film quickly before it froze. Well, somebody who had no business to do so got into one of these barrels of alcohol and found that, mixed with the jellied kind of orange juice which the Eli Lilly Company had made for us and which was the first antiscorbutic orange juice in the world, it made a potable drink, but it was so terrific that it soon had the name of Blowtorch attached to it. Dick Byrd and I talked at some length about this and we decided that maybe it would be a good idea to have an occasional party, so every few weeks we'd get a tub and we'd put a lot of this grain alcohol in it. We'd pour out a lot of fruit juice and all kinds of things to dilute it and then let every man drink all he wanted to. Some of them got tight. I had to stay sober because I had to make sure that nobody got outside and froze to death. But it was quite amusing. Taffy Davies, our Welsh physicist, came up to me one time and he always started like this. "Dahm and blast it, Larry," he said, "this is wonderful.

When I get like this I can say insulting things to my friends and be forgiven that I wouldn't dare say if I were sober," and it was true. We had one man, the most wonderful, lovable man, who was one of the most gentle souls, on the expedition, but when he got drunk he became very pugnacious, and one time the supply officer and he both were drunk at one of these parties and the supply officer became very sentimental and he walked up to Mac, the aerial photographer, and he put his arm around him and said, "Mac," he said, "you're wonderful. Everybody loves you." And Mac backed up and socked him in the jaw, and he said, "I'm tired of being loved. I want to be a son of a bitch." And I remember this same man the morning after, when he had a most fantastic hangover, say to me, "Oh, my God, Larry, I've got to die or get well. I can't stay *this* way."

Neider: Is there any light that you could throw on the first expedition that wasn't discussed either in *Cold* or in *Little America?* Some lighter aspect of life that perhaps at the time you and Byrd didn't think was worth publishing?

Gould: Our primary recreational activities were games. Bridge became very popular and widely played. And checkers and acey-deucey and things of that sort. We couldn't have any competitive games because we didn't have anywhere to play them. It suddenly comes to me that the most important single asset in terms of recreation was our library. When we were getting ready in New York to go, Dick Byrd asked me to assemble a library. Well, the expedition was great publicity in those days. So, most of the books were given to us. We had the famous Harvard five-foot shelf of books, we had the Encylopedia Britannica, we had an awfully good selection of first-rate novels, and it was very interesting to me to watch the reading habits of my companions. Indeed, after I came back I wrote a little paper on "What do explorers read" for the *American Scholar.* The most widely read book in Little America was *Green Mansions.* You know the book, of course. A beautiful romantic novel of the tropics. Not too widely read were the books of other explorers. We were locked in the ice and the snow and we wanted to escape, so a lot of the reading was what I would call escape literature. Detective stories were very popular, and one man, a wonderful Irishman without much education, had his life almost made over by the discovery of O.

Henry. He'd never read anything of O. Henry. But the funniest episode of reading was Parker, a pilot. With a long winter night ahead of us and little to do, Parker came and talked with me one day, and he said, "Larry, you know what I'm going to do during this long winter night?" And I said, "No," and he said, "Well, I'm going to read the Encylopedia Britannica through." I said, "That's a wonderful idea. You'll be a pretty well educated man when you finish." I was there in the library when he finished. He threw the book down and he said, "That damn book is of no use to a pilot." He'd gotten down as far as ammonium tetrachloride. I myself think I'd like to spend another winter in Antarctica just to read. Never in all my life have I enjoyed the luxury of reading as I did during the winter night. I had much to do getting ready for the coming summer of 1929–30 and the geological sledge journey into the Queen Maud Mountains and being executive officer of the camp. But there was still much time to read. I read Walt Whitman's *Leaves of Grass* in its entirety, which I had never done before. I came to the conclusion that "When last the lilacs in the dooryard bloomed" is the greatest American poem. Because I loved Lincoln, I suppose. I read a lot of detective stories and many novels and all of Shakespeare's plays. One of the most rewarding books was Robert Burton's *The Anatomy of Melancholy.*

Neider: Did you have electric lights?

Gould: No, we didn't. We used Coleman lanterns. And of course we didn't have any running water. We didn't have any showers. We didn't have any indoor toilets, and our outdoor toilet was not a flush toilet. When I was at McMurdo a year ago, Charles, I slept between the sheets, I had shower baths, I had a flush toilet. My God, the romance is gone. But I do not bemoan this. There's no credit for doing anything the hardest way. A scientist or anyone else will work better if he is in a comfortable environment to work. I applaud all of these things that make life easier for the people who go there. They'll do better work. Nevertheless, I'm awful glad that I was born in a day when I could be second-in-command of the First Byrd Antarctic Expedition and do everything the hardest way.

Neider: How did your current teaching career come about?

Gould: It began when I was a lad only a little less than eighteen years old and had no money to go to the University of Michigan but found out that there was a great shortage of teachers in Florida. A family from the town where I lived had moved to Florida, so I wrote down there and found out that if I passed the teachers' examination I could get a job in the school of Boca Raton. I went down to Florida. I had never had any exposure to education as such. I bought two books on elementary education. I boned up on them and I took the teachers' examination and I passed with higher grades than anybody else in Florida except a man with a Master of Arts from Columbia Teachers College. That just shows you the status of education in Florida in 1914. I stayed two years. I went back to Michigan in 1916. I got all three of my degrees there and I thought I was going to become an oil geologist and make a lot of money. And I had a tentative offer of a job with an oil company in Mexico when Professor Hobbs, the chairman of the Department of Geology at the University of Michigan, organized a small expedition to go to Greenland, on which he took me along in the summer of 1926. The following summer I was geologist and geographer on the Putnam Baffin Island Expedition. And that was the extent of my polar exploration when Isaiah Bowman, director of the American Geographical Society, persuaded Dick Byrd that I would be a good man to take along as geologist and senior scientist on his first Antarctic expedition. I went to the University of Michigan thinking I was going to study law. The first money I ever earned was picking strawberries, and I invested it in a life of Abraham Lincoln, and from that day to this he is my hero without parallel in all history as a source of inspiration to me. If you get down to my office, even now you'll find a great lithograph of Lincoln on the wall, which I brought with me from Carleton College, where I had it hanging above the door through which people came in to see me during the seventeen years I was president of the college. My visitor would sit down opposite me at my desk and if I found the conversation too annoying, and lest I show my irritation, I would look up at Lincoln and my poise would return. So, I was going to study law. And I was going to be an Abraham Lincoln and I was going to be a politician. And at the University of Michigan I had no money, so I had to work, and Hobbs, head of the geology department, had given me a room in his home for taking care of the furnace, mowing the lawn and doing all that sort of thing. And he was so nice to me, I took a course in geology. And I decided that it seemed to be a lot more interesting than law. Well, I've had a much more interesting life in geology and where it has led me than I would have had as a lawyer.

Neider: I would like to go back a bit. You said something earlier that sounded a bit paradoxical. You said on the one hand that you felt that you were born at the right time and then you proceeded to talk about the devastating effects of World War I and how things have been running downhill.

Gould: Well, the years just before World War I were a happy, balanced world, at peace. And when I look at the future, with all of the ominous signs, I'm not sorry I'm as old as I am, Charles. If I had to depart this world tomorrow I would have no complaint. It has been good to me.

Neider: When you say ominous signs I assume you're talking, for one thing, about overpopulation.

Gould: That's the first one, isn't it? I don't see how this world can ever get organized to support itself unless some curtailment on population comes about. There is no major problem facing mankind which is not complicated by too many people.

Neider: Do you have any advice for me?

Gould: Get back to Antarctica again as soon as you can. You've got a lot yet to do. I'm pinning a lot of hopes on you. With what you're doing and with what you're writing you will enlighten a lot of people. You will help to promote the idea that conservation is terribly important in Antarctica and that we must do everything we can to preserve this last, vast part of our planet from being despoiled.

Postscript. As second in command of Byrd's first Antarctic expedition, Gould helped usher the air age into Antarctica. Ironically, he was in Antarctica near the end of November 1979 when the modern world caught up with the continent in the form of the fourth greatest single-aircraft crash in history: the loss of a New Zealand Airways DC-10 with all 257 persons on board. The aircraft smashed into a lower slope of Mt. Erebus. A further irony is that Gould was on the continent to celebrate the fiftieth anniversary of Byrd's historic flight over the Pole.

During the ceremony at McMurdo, Gould was presented with a gold medal as part of the National Science Foundation's Distinguished Public Service Award.

16 ❧ The Drake Passage and Tierra del Fuego

7 MARCH. "Up early. Many chores: repacking, preparing to leave Antarctica. Phone-patched a couple of my editors in New York. Climbed the glacier behind Palmer in the afternoon."

I climbed the glacier out of a sense of duty, because my conscience reminded me that Guy Guthridge had twice suggested I do it. In prospect it felt like a chore, so I kept putting it off. For some reason I imagined him climbing up there primarily for the exercise because he was too confined to the station and its environs. I didn't need the exercise. My sea wanderings had exercised me enough. What I needed now was land rest and for the land to stop rolling under me. My sea voyages were not yet over. The worst was still to come. Also, in some strange way I had become used to being on Antarctic waters, or among Antarctic sea ice, to such an extent that the land seemed to bore me, appeared to be merely a place for repacking, for preparing for another sea journey. Antarctic sea vessels had got into my blood. My land experiences on this Antarctic visit now felt remote. Only my intellect could convince me I had visited Victoria Valley on my third and not my second trip. Lyle McGinnis and Don Osby felt to me like persons I had met on another planet.

The light was brilliant, the kind we didn't often get at Palmer.

328

In some ways my love of Antarctica was closely related to my love of intense sunlight and what the latter did to one's moods and perceptions. As I climbed I could see how the icecap jutted out on the small capes, how it crumbled and crevassed at the embayment, where chunks calved off and drifted westward toward the Southern Ocean.

I approached the glacier over rocks and snow. The way was marked by frozen, gleaming footsteps and by red fuel drums. I knew better than to stray far from the broad path, for the area was heavily crevassed. I walked on snowcover, not ice—the ice was deep beneath the snow layers—but the snow was crustfrozen and slippery. I could break through it with a sharp heel kick. I had no ice ax or crampons with me.

It was fine to come in contact with a large Antarctic ice sheet after the weeks of viewing such ice from a safe distance. The glare was terrific and I soon became uncomfortably warm. I was tempted to leave my parka, cap and gloves behind me on the trail but when I reflected that a cold wind might catch me offguard and give me a nasty chill, I carried them.

Solitude could be a hard thing to come by in the Antarctic, as I well knew, if only because it was generally considered to be dangerous. No need to be polite now, to consider other people and their feelings about themselves and you. No need to have social emotions or any emotions unrelated to the joy of experiencing this solitude and beauty. You could give yourself up completely to your surroundings. You were released not only from groups but in a profound sense from yourself as well. The perceptual and receptive sides of you were now supreme, and whatever emotions you had were subordinated to these and supportive of them. You were rolling along in a perceptual/emotional circle that was perfect.

You cut yourself off from the rest of the world, undistracted by memories of family, lovers, children, friends. It was experiences like this that Antarctica could give you in fullest measure and which made the Antarctic discomforts and hazards worthwhile.

It reminded me of the time I crashed on Mt. Erebus, and yet there was a significant difference. You had been obliged to tie an umbilical cord to Palmer by signing out on a bulletin board your destination, time of departure and estimated time of return. And so you could not simply give way and linger endlessly in case that was what you wanted to do, not if you didn't want to become a burden to the station. You *could* commit suicide, though, easily and without anyone knowing for certain you had done it. All you had to do was head for the crevasse field and fall in. The temperature in a deep crevasse, presuming the fall itself didn't kill you, would quickly finish you off with hypothermia. You would leave no footprints, for the snowcrust today was too hard to make them. Your body might or might not be found but if it were, who could be sure you had done the thing deliberately? Perhaps you had merely overextended yourself in having a close look.

Such thoughts, instead of chilling you, had the opposite effect. They were comforting in that they were real. There was something good and part of the Antarctic experience in feeling the closeness of death and in accepting with grace your end. If you had come howling from your mother's womb into this world, you meant to balance your personal budget by dying softly: no kicking, no wailing.

The spit of dark rocky land on which the base sat faced west. The icecap sloped massively. The silence was intimate (no birds, no station or harbor sounds, no wind). The absence of birds reminded me that no one had yet explained the presence of an occasional solitary skua in the neighborhood of the Pole itself, hundreds of frozen miles from the sea and sustenance.

The base sat serenely on its rocky spit: antenna masts, main buildings, a couple of well-stocked set-apart refuge huts in case a disaster overtook the chief buildings, two squat white cylindrical fuel tanks, the masts of the *Hero*, and, showing as dark as dolerite at the station's tip, the Hero Inlet.

I was slowly ascending, growing hotter, The icecap stretched out before me in a vast dome, a miniature of the great Antarctic plateau. The embayment cliffs were in stark blue shadow but the embayment water glistened brilliantly. As I kept glancing at the crevasses above it I was looking almost directly at the sun, which was approximately in the northwest. The ice was broadly textured by old winds: pitted, scarred, gray-shadowed.

I began to make out the Neumayer Channel that runs east of Anvers Island, between Anvers and Doumer and Wiencke Islands, and I could see the Bismarck Strait in the west. Bonaparte Point stretched out before the icecap like a dirty, gray, gnarled finger. The ribbon of sea darkness had broadened. Looking west, one did not see mountain ranges but one was content, for the soft, sweet sea with its low naked islands and broad span of upper sky rested you. If you wanted visual excitement you looked leftward and found it in range on range of ice-clad or rock-ribbed mountains.

Occasionally the glacier boomed like thunder as ice adjusted itself. Aside from my footsteps and breathing and the rustle of my clothes this was the only sound I heard. The crevasses suggested crumbling blue cheese. A mountain peak began to show itself inland.

The surface I now walked on was scalloped by waves whose crests gleamed ivory and whose troughs were gently shadowed innumerable finer waves. A lacelike pattern seemed to have been formed by benign winds. The white crests of two inland mountains had risen into view. More mountains showed themselves, and boot tracks and red fuel drums met in perspective in their direction. The sun was now almost directly above the crevasse field, so there was tremendous glare in that direction but not enough to obscure ice field textures. I was now on a line with many of the parallel crevasse slashes. I looked across Arthur Harbor, Loudwater Cove, Wylie Bay and at Cape Monaco northwestward of me. The piedmont surface was now more hardcrusted than before and gleamed like plates of roughly etched and scoured metal. The inland scenes felt increasingly desolate and suggestive of what it would be like to have a stubborn strong wind sweep across here. Inland from me smoky clouds seemed to rest on the icecap itself and to wreathe the base of several blue-shadowed mountains. I could see Biscoe Bay now and Mt. Rennie, Mt. Moberly, Shrewry Peak, The Minnaret, Mt. William and Mt. Hindson. A gay feather cloud in the west arched brightly northward.

The ice surface close to me resembled a section of a terrestrial relief globe. Mountain ranges, valleys, plains: the color of blue-gray sand. Ice and snow crystals glittered. I was occasionally breaking through snowcrust as I advanced. Old frozen boot tracks revealed the tread of gleaming soles. The light was so sharp and low now that even faint depressions contained deep, stark, lunar shadows.

I returned to the base at 5:30. As the sun was about to disappear, the clouds were bloody, the horizon black. The glacier aged rapidly in color, taking on hues of old and weathered copper and in places shining like polished brass. The sun vanished. The reddish gold clouds cast an apricot glow on the rippled water. Islands and bergs melted into each other in a single black plane. Above Litchfield Island the sky was lime.

"Lost $3.50 at poker. Moonlight, insomnia."

I was sure I had lost at poker to pay some kind of dues for my great pleasure on the glacier. The moonlight excited me, made me feel half-crazy. That was what I told myself, but I sensed that what was making me feel so strange was the imminence of my departure from Antarctica mixed with the fear I would never see the continent again.

8 MARCH. "Time for departure rapidly approaches. Some apprehension about crossing the Drake. Had *ficha* photos taken for entry into Argentina. In the afternoon, seeing some bergs in Arthur Harbor, took a Zodiac out to photograph them. Matt Sturm and Cliff Patrick with me, Matt steering. I wanted to get very close to the bergs and shoot in ways not possible with telephoto lens: looking straight up from water level."

One berg was quite large. When we drew close to it we felt lost in its mass. Two ice turrets connected by a col or saddle, reminding me of the col I had climbed on Deception Island. Blue ribbons alternating with white. The sky beyond the col a dead gray. In places the berg suggested veined blue marble. The veins were about 40 degrees from the horizontal. Humanoid shapes: a disembodied staring eye with iris, a bruised, closed eye with bony brow, a profiled nose. Part of the berg extended underwater, where it paled and blued the cloth-gray harbor and emerged in a strange, fragile, flower shape that contained a pear-drop of open air.

The sky was now a brooding gray with only hints of warmth. The gray color, steadily deepening—we were getting nasty weather—set off beautifully one muscular corner of the berg, which, after a long, gentle cape, arched rightward and upward to end in a bullet shape: all this in a variety of blues that had deepened with the closing of the light. The form was full of skyward motion, but also of great interest were its textures of elephant skin. The water was dark, colorless.

Rounding a corner, we spotted a leopard seal and turned to approach it. The reptilian head with its mouthslit seemed to be resting its chin on the water. The submerged body, close to the corner, showed as a dark wavy mass in blue water that appeared to phosphoresce. I was familiar with Weddell and crabeater seals. They would lie cigarlike on the ice, basking, half-asleep, sometimes scratching their face with a flipper claw, occasionally yawning and revealing surprisingly large teeth. If you waked one with your voice it would look at you with soft, dark, sleepy eyes, making you think of a cow's temperament. They were gentle even if a pup was lying near.

There was nothing bovine about the looks and behavior of this leopard seal, this oceanic predator who had only the killer whale to fear. He was on station, waiting for prey: blue-eyed shags, Adélie penguins, perhaps a young seal. His dark, cavernous eyes and nostrils gave the impression of total concentration. A creature with a tremendous capacity for visual focus was observing us. His gaze was hypnotic.

Photographing him, I was rapt, saw him only in my viewfinder, had no sense of the distance closing between us, kept urging we get closer until Matt Sturm said in his deep voice, "That's close enough," which caused me to realize how close we were and to laugh.

With my butt on the pontoon inches above the water, I felt vulnerable. The deathly cold water was dangerous enough. If you fell in, you were in an immediate and very serious survival condition. With him close by, capable with a lunge of pulling me out of the rubber boat or with a bite of deflating the pontoons, the situation, fascinating though it was, was becoming untenable. After observing us a moment full-face he dove toward us with litheness and huge dark power. We raced the engine and sped away.

Seeing the embayment cliffs at fairly close range and from water level, you got a different sense of them from the one you got in viewing them from the deck of the *Burton Island*. There was clearly a recess in the jutting land here, and the ice apron or sheet as it approached the sea began to collapse for lack of local support. The collapse resulted in crevasses and finally in calving. I wondered what happened to the parts of the sheet that ended on landspits. Did they ablate? Degrade through weathering? From where I was observing it the sheet didn't calve off but rather stopped at the land's edge and, through weathering, sloped gradually to the shore. The ice here seemed older, looked vaguely dirty and yellowed, raggedy, patchy. A couple of skuas flew strongly near the cliffside.

I spied what I instantly called the Sphinx berg gazing majestically northward, its features and breast outlined dramatically by the sky's deepening gray. I was taking liberties in calling it the Sphinx berg, for the face also suggested a baboon. Meanwhile we were constantly bobbing on the water, occasionally shipping spray, twisting and tacking, and I felt precarious, sitting as I was on the narrow, low pontoon and trying to catch hold of something with my boots for a feeling of security although there was nothing to grip. Both my hands were involved in camera work.

The berg was massive and suggested soap sculpture. At closer range the face was sharply clear. The eye was deeply recessed, the brow bold, the nose long and rather doglike, the mouth a bit petulant in its feline slit, the ear massive. In all my experiences with bergs I had seen none so suggestive of having been deliberately and carefully sculpted. The closer we drew to the ice mass the more the white bled from it and the more the berg looked a luminous, jewel blue. The features held firm, but now the Sphinx seemed to be a great outflung broken wing reminding me of the Winged Victory of Samothrace. The ice at very close range showed remarkable textures: vertical scalloped ribs from water level up to the face itself, ice slopes, and a series of parallel creases that made me think of a carefully combed beard. The mouth was now seen to be open, the jaw slack, the nose and cheek pursed, the eye staring in horror.

"Marvelous moods of oily water, weather closing in. Barely perceptible ice and landforms."

Spotting several blue-eyed shags sitting on the water just where the ice cliffs tended to calve most thunderously and often, we changed course to approach them, curious to see how close we could come before they flew off. Eight question marks huddled together, all facing north, or leftward. Long black bills, black heads, white throats. Alarmed, the flock turned to face south, then propelled themselves through the water away from us, heading for the cliffs. They spread out in a line, now ran on the water and suddenly lifted off with a rapid beating of large black wings, wingtips opening while arching upward. They quickly left us far behind, turned north and disappeared.

"After circling and shooting a couple of bergs we went into thick brash toward the glacier snout, had to push our way through. The dense, hard, blue glacial brash, formed under great pressure, glistening, pockmarked by weathering, popped as, melting, it depressurized. John Lohr, the *Hero's* radio operator, radioed me from shore to bring blue ice for cocktails (the kind that pops and crackles). Cliff Patrick tried and failed to board a huge piece, then he and Matt Sturm succeeded in landing a moderate one, all glistening, cold, pockmarked. Possibly it dated from Shakespeare's time or Chaucer's."

A thick fog came in from the sea, obscuring islands, ice cliffs, icebits. Sleet and hail as we headed for Hero Inlet.

We placed the chunk of blue ice on a wooden bench of the porch outside the station lounge and there occasionally someone icepicked at it. I tried the pick myself and, not surprisingly, found the ice very hard and brittle. When struck by the pick it flaked in sharded ways unlike those of normal ice, and a detritus of fine particles resulted. Occasionally I put a piece in my mouth for the fun of it. It had no taste I could discern. I melted some in a glass. The water had no taste either. The chunk melted very slowly next day, not only because the sun wasn't strong but because the ice was so dense. It was great fun to consume ice that was centuries old, and doing so infused you with a very special feeling of luxury.

Warburton, in a fine moment of one-upmanship, declared he had once served cocktails at a Reno party in which the ice was thousands of years old, having come from a core brought up by the drill rig at Byrd Station. That drill project had reached rock. Inasmuch as the ice showed annual layers, you could study pollution and weather going back many thousands of years. I had either read somewhere or heard it said that the core showed very clearly, because of layers of particulate matter, when the Industrial Revolution had begun. The contamination spread round the world by industrial pollution and by other forms such as pesticides like DDT and by the after-effects of atomic explosions like strontium 90 could be detected in the farthest reaches of Antarctica as well as in its shoreline residents.

Everywhere in the station you could sense the excitement of the *Hero's* imminent departure for the last time this austral season. Pat Moriarty, the cook, was getting help in hauling foodstuffs from remote storage areas to ones near the galley. Others like him who would winter over were getting set for the sudden departure and loneliness. A social cleavage had developed between those who would stay and those who would leave. Last-minute letters were written by those who would stay, and there was the usual exchange of addresses. People seemed more absentminded. The winter-over crowd was bracing itself against darkness and coldness, frozen seas, frozen harbor. The others were already beginning to thaw out, and in addition to looking forward to seeing Tierra del Fuego, women, children, night, stars, green hills, gardens, were getting themselves inwardly ready for the intemperate and moist heat of Buenos Aires, where it was reputed to be in the nineties. But no one, not even Lenie, looked forward to the crossing of the Drake Passage.

9 MARCH. "Up early. Short on sleep for two nights. Moved the last of my gear to the ship. Left Palmer 2:50 P.M. Eight people on the dock. Seven will winter over."

The jetty was covered with snow. I could make out an emergency motor launch on the dock, partially under a tarp. The dockside spotlights, mounted on a mast with ladder rungs and with a loudspeaker atop, were on, looking yellow by daylight. The gap between us and the jetty rapidly widened.

10 MARCH. "Several people ill and keeping to their bunks—Warburton, Shane Williams, Dave Neilson, Paul Lagé, Vera Alexander among them. Our route: Gerlache Strait to the west of Low and Smith islands to the open sea. Great swells once we reached open water. The ship rolls, pitches, yaws, creaks loudly. Taking Bonine every twelve hours. Brains feel as if they're splashing around in the cranium. Not possible to work in any sustained way. The only time one is comfortable is when one sleeps, and even then I'm sometimes awakened by the ship's heavy rolls, for my bunk is athwartships and a good roll makes me lie on my head or feet.

"Hazardous to move about the ship, and difficult. No great storms, but the ship is so small in the huge swells that it gets a considerable battering. The wind is against us, so Lenie can't put up the main sails for greater stability: They'd be shredded, he says."

I remember how I would spend a good deal of time sitting half asleep on the starboard bench in the small, crowded general room, which was partially filled by a large gyroscope. And I recall that at times it was difficult to keep my place on the bench, for the ship's heavy movements threatened to unseat me. And how long it would take me to gather my will sufficiently to enable me to stand up, walk to the linen cabinet nearby, remove one or more of my cameras, check them, and climb to the bridge to see what was happening if anything, what the sea was like, what was visible.

Beautiful "cavern" berg in the morning. This blue berg rose up on our starboard and turned out to be huge, slanted and tabular. A faint light broke through the restless sky and scattered silver coins on the sea. We encountered a heavy swell in which we pitched, our bow slapping the water hard and causing it to spray heavily onto the foredeck. Our maindeck was heavily awash, and when we rolled, the sea was often high above the gunnel.

I hoped for a great storm so I could experience the Drake at its heart and I made the mistake of mentioning this half-jokingly to some of my companions. I was thought to be crazy and a jinx, especially by Matt Sturm, who had put in a hitch in the Coast Guard. The wooden vessel creaked loudly, the engines labored.

11 MARCH. From the *Hero's* log. "0700—ran slow ahead most of the night in dense fog with scattered bergs. No visibility. Vessel pitching heavily."

From my journal: "Still sleeping a great deal. Skipped meals. Uncomfortable but never sick (that is, never vomiting). Can function when I need to. I suspect that a high degree of motivation is very important in keeping off bouts of seasickness. I have the ability to fall asleep anywhere and to sleep a long time. Not many passengers visible. Didn't shave. Ship's bow in swells: bow awash, pitching."

At times we pitched and rolled simultaneously, or stood on our stern, with the bow lifted so high it obscured a large part of the horizon. Down it would come crashing, sending white water flying. The sea was leaden, the sky gray. Our red sails were furled. The port maindeck was taking spouts of white water through the scuppers, and the green gunnel contrasted with the white and with the purple sea.

"Am very irritated with the ship's movements, as if they are made to spite me personally."

I needed to reassure myself that I was going to the bridge and *seeing* the Drake. It seemed easier to take the battering it gave you when you could see what was happening, for example in the precise relationship between swells and ship. You could brace your footing accordingly. Things didn't surprise you as much. It was like the difference between driving a car and being a passenger. On the other hand, when things got very rough and you saw the mainmast's and bow's extraordinary motions in the great mountainous swells, your queasiness increased and you considered yourself infinitely better off in your bunk, dead to the sea world. But once having got to the bridge, after all the effort of will and battle with things to get there, you stayed as long as you could, turning your eyes away from the sea if necessary when the latter looked most awful. Getting to the bridge was a sizable investment that you weren't about to relinquish easily, even if continuing to stay on the bridge nauseated you.

Compounding everything was the fact you felt trapped. There was no way in which you could leave the situation. And although you realized it was unreasonable to have such a thought, the feeling that represented the thought nevertheless persisted. "I'm trapped," it said, "and I'm furious about it. I don't *like* to be hemmed in like this." The ambiguity of it came from the equal understanding that the ship you felt trapped in was also preserving you. When you saw the vessel falling down a mountainous swell as if it were a roller coaster and felt yourself falling with it, most notably in the pit of your gut, you were thankful to be trapped. The ambiguity as well as the physical strain added to your weariness. Yet at the same time, as if to prove the complexity of the human psyche, you enjoyed the swells and the smallness of the ship and still hoped for a storm that would leave a lifelong impression on you. I supposed this was man's hubris in the face of Nature. It was hard to believe that Nathaniel Palmer and sealers like him had crossed the Drake in a 47-foot sloop.

The main feeling I had on the bridge was a sense of the ship's smallness in the huge swells. The vessel would fall down one

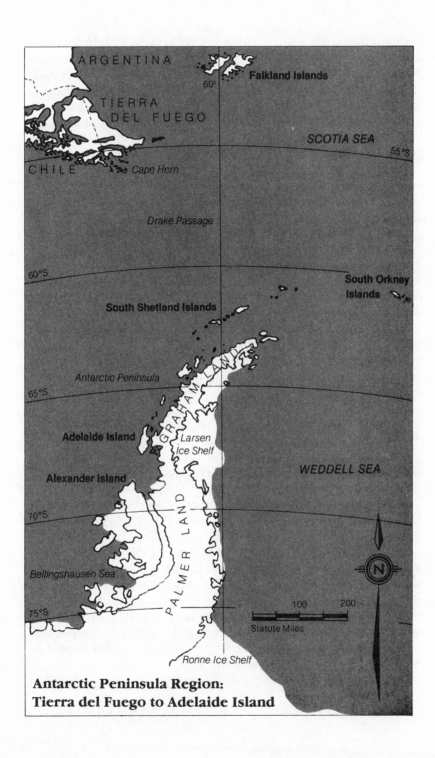

**Antarctic Peninsula Region:
Tierra del Fuego to Adelaide Island**

ocean hill and be hurled sideways by another while still descending. You saw the rolls vividly from the bridge because you could note them by the swaying of the mainmast. Lenie seemed apprehensive, as though bracing himself for a fierce storm. Early this season the ship had had a bad experience, it had torn open part of its hull while trying to move a small berg and had had to go to South America for repairs. Possibly this colored his present crossing. The crew would sometimes tell about bad crossings: how long they took, the frightful storms, the wild rolling and pitching, the torn sails, the fear. But for all the relative mildness of the present crossing, there were some special things to see and hear: spectral bergs in ashen, blood-drained fog, and always the ship's heavy, labored creaking.

Still, there wasn't much to see. The Drake was lead-gray now. The only colorful things as you looked forward from the bridge were the orange fo'c'sle and the furled red mainsail and jib. It did fascinate you to see how far the mainmast could tilt from the vertical. The mast served as a good inclinometer. When the vessel took to pitching heavily, the fo'c'sle rose high and the unpainted mast seemed about to fall on you. When the bow fell it usually didn't hit square. Often it touched portside first and white water would madly fly away from the ship.

After awhile you grew used to even the wilder gyrations. Nobody ever exclaimed about anything. You were crossing the Drake Passage, that was all. The best moments were when the white water flew back onto the foredeck. The air all around the vessel then turned misty, and the bridge windshield dripped. Some of our rolls were at least thirty degrees. I have no way of judging to what degree we pitched.

The hours slipping by, and almost everyone ill. Huddled bodies in bunks, faces turned to the wall. A challenge to leave your bunk and reach the head without falling, being slammed against something. The toilet bowl heaving. You had to brace yourself to manage the act of micturition and you needed patience while the urinary sphincter relaxed. Your breath came in short rhythms. You closed your eyes often in order the better to endure the discomfort, but at times it was dangerous to do so. Things fighting you: a heavy metal door, a steep-pitched metal stairway, your bunk, the floor. Luggage and other gear in my cabin were all piled up by the ship's gyrations.

The ship's motion made you despise your consciousness, to

be disgusted with it, which was partly why you slept. You didn't despise the Drake or the vessel. The Drake was Nature. The ship preserved you. *You* were at fault, and when you handled ship and ocean well, your regard for yourself made a quantum leap forward.

The sudden absence of people when we hit the open sea on our way northward. Warburton, Kleppe, Lagé, Shane Williams, Dave Neilson, Vera Alexander all absent. And the re-emergence of people the morning we sailed in the Beagle Channel to Ushuaia. But Barsdate was a good sailor, as was Ed Born, long-legged, silent, often on the conning bridge.

The experience of crossing the Drake in a small vessel was neither of saltwater nor ship as much as it was of being brainwashed, brainsloshed. Thinking and writing about the crossing ten months later, I felt somewhat seasick, awoke one night sweating, my bedroom heaving.

12 MARCH. "Calmer waters. Lots of time on the bridge now. Foresail and mainsail up. The air sharper. Sky clearing. The Drake has turned blue, the swells have declined. An albatross. Hilly land on the horizon."

It was fine when the sails were hoisted, for then you had the illusion of being on a sailing vessel, and the time between you and the sealing days and the later days of *Moby Dick* seemed to shrink. An albatross took to wheeling around us. When the sun turned the horizon to platinum there were lovely contrasts between red sails, platinum band and glowering, purple sky. The sun broke loose and spilled over the ship, casting foredeck shadows and making your heart dance.

We saw land, lying low and bluish on the horizon, and knew it was another continent, South America. Civilization. Home.

"Sighted Staten Island on our right, parts of Tierra del Fuego dead ahead. We sailed at night by radar, with very poor visibility, rain. Entered the Beagle Channel, decided to anchor for the night, meet the pilot very early tomorrow. To bed at midnight but couldn't fall asleep, people were chatting at the mess table outside my cabin. Dressed and joined them. Vera Alexander visible for the first time since leaving Palmer. Young and Barsdate there too. Chatted till 4 A.M.

13 MARCH. "Up at 9 A.M. to photograph our arrival in Ushuaia in rain. The green hills of the Ushuaia environs. The sudden ocean smells."

The Drake Passage and Tierra del Fuego

Dry mountains beyond a line of low hills. Some green showing. The green hills were my first since Christchurch. Overcast sky, the air misty with rain, the Channel calm. A brooding maritime morning in Tierra del Fuego. Mountains with snow patches coming into view. Ushuaia in the distance above our fo'c'sle: a whitish sprawl of houses at the foot of hills and snowpocked mountains blue with mist. The town looming.

It was flat but larger and less primitive than I had expected. White buildings with red roofs, some of the buildings multistoried. Paved streets running down to the shore. Wild hillsides. A small warship in the harbor, ships at the dock, Wilson's storm petrels flitting low over the water. We moved leftward of the dock and began to sidle in. A large freighter at dockside with WESTBURY/LIVERPOOL on its stern.

"Was surprised to be handed a packet of mail. I knew there would be some but I was caught off guard when John Lohr handed me mine as I was packing something in my cabin. Yesterday I typed up my *ficha* paper, gave it and my passport to Lenie. We can't go ashore until we get our *ficha* and passport back from the prefect of police. It's illegal to be on the street without identification. Yesterday I had an argument with Lenie about the meaning of the need for us to declare ourselves crew members of the *Hero*. He asserts this has nothing to do with Argentine Antarctic claims, results only from the fact the *Hero* is not classed as a passenger carrier in the States. But if that is so, why do the Argentines stamp an entry mark only on our *ficha* papers and not on our passports?

"Left my two orange seabags on the *Hero* for return to USARP in the dock warehouse. We tied up in front of the *Westbury*. The *Hero* looked like a rowboat beside her."

Ushuaia, the world's southernmost town, was styled the capital of the Territory of Tierra del Fuego, Antarctica and the South Atlantic Islands. It is a Yahgan (Indian) word meaning "a bay penetrating to the westward." At the time of our visit it had about 5400 inhabitants. The Hotel Albátros, at the corner of Maipú Avenue and Lasserre Street, was built by the government in 1966. Overlooking Ushuaia Bay, it was the public center of town. It contained a bar, restaurant and conference room. We lived in the new annex, which was on the corner of Maipú and 25th of May Street. The main street of town, a block behind the hotel, was San Martín Avenue: paved, wet, cars parked on one side only. A half-faded sign: "30 KM VELOCIDAD MAXIMA." The end of the street cloud-wreathed. HOTEL CAPRI. Muddy wet side streets leading upward. Houses with picket fences, greens shrubs. A small beached boat: ICHTHUS on the bow. Directly across the street from my room in the Hotel Albátros: a little shop with barred-iron front, red sign with white letters: IMPORTACION MARCO POLO REGALOS. From the town itself you got the impression of smallness and relative poverty.

John Lohr and I walked the rocky shore opposite the town. Many seashells. Unpopulated green hills across the Channel. A thick, sodden, greenish growth along the shore. Smoky clouds forming a curtain behind the town, but the town itself looked sharp. John Lohr: brown street shoes, blue, stylishly cut pants, unzipped blue lightweight parka, blue turtleneck, black beaver hat at a rakish angle. A good, warm smile.

"Yesterday I told Lenie I wanted to stay on the ship rather than in the hotel. He denied the request with the explanation that he wants the ship cleared for cleaning, etc. Today I learned that Shane Williams, Dave Neilson, Matt Sturm and Ed Born are living on board. In the mezzanine lobby of the Albátros extension this afternoon I criticized him openly before Barsdate, Warburton, Alexander, Young, Lagé and Kleppe. Lagé defended him but unfortunately not well, for he was drunk on too much Scotch and insufficient food and finally tottered off to our shared room, where he fell asleep dressed on his bed."

It was fine to be alone again. The last time I had really been alone outdoors was on the Palmer glacier. I enjoyed walking strange towns, and Ushuaia was certainly an odd one. I went down along the harbor and into shops to get the feel of things. The place felt marginal, an outpost, and there were many signs of the military around. It was not unusual to see soldiers carrying burp guns. There was increasing tension between Argentina and Chile because of three disputed islands in the Beagle Channel. As for Americans in the country, your dollars were excellent but there was official resentment and anger because President Carter had cut off foreign aid on the ground that Argentina was violating its citizens' civil liberties. One had heard many stories of people disappearing permanently for political reasons. I had been warned by Lenie not to get caught on the streets without my passport and *ficha*.

In Antarctica you didn't have to worry about humans as a threat. The greatest threats were your own negligence, ignorance and stupidity: these and the sudden changes in weather. You had a great sense of serenity because you were free from human threat, the kind of threat you felt in the great cities. In New York there were mindless crimes. In Buenos Aires there were political crimes. Both were equally inhuman and terrible. In Antarctica your guard was down. You hiked in the middle of nowhere and there was nothing on earth that could harm you except weather and your own foolishness. No animals, microbes, viruses, insects, plants or whatever to attack you. Above all no humans. In Ushuaia I began to sense my guard coming back.

"Chores, mostly packing and organizing, till about 1:30 A.M. in my room while Lagé slept. I find Ushuaia very interesting, even attractive, although many of the side streets show unpleasant degrees of poverty. Poor sleep: much auto, scooter and truck noise, sounds I haven't heard for a while."

14 MARCH. "Up at 9 and breakfasted continental style at the hotel. Returned my seabags to USARP via Natalie Goodall in the dock warehouse."

Scenes from the dock: a mass of cup-shaped fishing nets in a boat. A rusted large boat like a tug, still at dockside. Moody day with some sun. Glassy harbor. The *Hero* looking very small. A parked bus on a side street off Maipú, the harborside avenue, with the legend above its windshield: TERRITORIO NACIONAL DE LA TIERRA DEL FUEGO ANTARTIDA E ISLAS DEL ATLANTICO SUD.

"Walked the main street to the beginning of the naval station. A horribly mangy dog barely able to stand, his penis and scrotum black and shrunken. Rafael, the town 'character,' pathetic in clothes that hang on him, sweeping the gutter aimlessly with a last-gasp broom, full hair uncombed, red-rimmed eyes, features strange and half-wild."

I lunched at the Albátros with the Warburton group, then took a tour of the nearby national park. I stood outside while we waited for the car to come for us. A military truck coming up the hill to the main stret was emitting a cloud of blue smoke, which lingered after the vehicle disappeared. The cloud was so large and dense that for a while it obscured the street.

"As we drove out of Ushuaia in the direction past the airport we were stopped by a roadblock of about eight army men with burp guns slung across their shoulders and chests. They wanted to see identification. We showed passports, the young driver showed an ID card. Trigger fingers at the ready. I noticed a young man sitting on a knoll partly obscured by bushes, aiming a machine gun at the road we would traverse.

"We drove into the mostly unpopulated countryside: mountains, streams, Irish-green fields. It was strange to see so much green and to smell odors of fields, herbs, flowers."

It was, however, a land denuded of trees. Tree stumps prominent. Ashen tree skeletons. In the 1840s Darwin wrote of Tierra del Fuego's magnificent forests. Many mists, low clouds, wetlands. Boggy green turf, yellow wildflowers, green hummocks, many rabbit holes, fast-flowing narrow stream. A black lagoon, with rotting tree stumps drowned in smoky water. My companions in city clothes.

15 MARCH. I got up at 5:30. There was no way of having breakfast or even a cup of coffee. The elderly desk clerk politely inquired where I was going. When I said San Francisco his eyes opened wide, as if I had said I was heading for the moon. He asked if I liked Ushuaia. I said I did. That seemed to please and reassure him. The town was still dark as we waited outside. I thought of the *Hero* down at the dock and of John Lohr asleep in the Hotel Mustapic.

Two cabs took us to the airport, where we waited for our local agent, a large stout older man, to appear with a small entourage and take care of overweight charges. He was a big fish in this pond. Many people were waiting in the airport lounge.

"Took off at 8:20 in a Fairchild 27. Two propellers. Forty passengers. Barren landscape between Ushuaia and Rio Grande, flat after we crossed razorbacked mountains like those in the Peninsula islands. Lay over in Rio Grande airport lounge from 9 to 11:45. Young men, looking moronic, with burp guns. Left Rio Grande in a Boeing 737, stopped briefly in Rio Gallegos (about a half-hour), arrived in Bahia Blanca at 2:40. Temperature: 90°F. Took off at 3, arrived Buenos Aires 3:55. A feeling of unreality as we banked over the city. The many white skyscrapers looked at first like tombstones."

The crowding and uproar at the Buenos Aires airport were unbelievable to one like myself who, seemingly, had never visited a major airport. And the heat, and the sweating, and the sticking of clothes to one's body, and the noise—they were all very funny, in a way. One hadn't just crossed the Drake Passage in a small vessel for nothing. It was all part of decompressing after Antarctica.

We had an agent, though, who had come to rescue us: a middle-aged woman, very efficient. Before we knew it we were out on the street, and for one reason or another Hugh Dakers, the *Hero's* cook, and I were less encumbered than the others and so we were ushered into a waiting car and off we went into the city, for we were all going to stay at the same hotel, the Hotel Tucumán Palace (not exactly a palace) on Tucumán Street in downtown Buenos Aires. It was a place often used by Usarps going to and from the Peninsula.

The city was noisy, trafficky and smoggy and we got stalled at the height of the rush-hour traffic by a freight train blocking a major artery alongside the harbor. The sea breezes made the heat not at all oppressive.

I got room 309. It was beat-up and had no view but I did not care. I had no bathtub or shower stall, just a shower head that ran into a drain in the bathroom floor, but that was fine with me too. I was looking forward to seeing the city, not the hotel room.

I slipped away for a walk. I went down Tucumán Street to Florida Avenue, which was a shopping mall, took a right on Florida and strolled and window-shopped until I reached a park. I was impressed by the elegant goods, which promptly gave me a financial inferiority complex. A daily *New York Times* cost 1000 pesos ($3.30), a Sunday one more than 3000 ($10). I was glad to see the large newsstands selling Borges's complete works.

Walking back to the hotel, I took pleasure in thinking I would have a night and a day in this city: that is, I would fly out at 9 A.M. the day after tomorrow. It came as quite a shock, therefore, when, in the lobby, John Kleppe, who knew some Spanish and had been a kind of volunteer father for us in dealing with the locals, notified me that the agent had brought my air ticket (which he handed to me) and that I was scheduled to fly out from a distant airport at 8:30 tomorrow morning.

I awoke at 5. A khaki shirt I had washed the night before was thoroughly dry. I had been instructed to be ready in the lobby between 6 and 6:30 for the car that would take me to the airport. On my way down to the lobby I stopped off to knock on Barsdate's door on the floor below mine. He had asked me to do it. Hearing his murmured "Thanks," I proceeded downstairs.

A beat-up black American-made car, a Dart, came precisely at 6. An elderly man with an alarmingly loose cough insisted on helping me with my luggage. He knew practically no English and I no Spanish. The car was parked across the street. I was in much better shape than he was, and I tried to spare him the physical effort but he insisted on doing most of the carrying and on lifting the luggage into the car trunk.

Buenos Aires was very much in night at this hour. We drove through the downtown section. I saw women huddling in doorways, waiting for buses. I saw lights go on in apartment houses and tried to imagine the individual lives, so different from mine, that were coming awake. Occasionally I saw trucks and buses on the move, and men's bodies lifting things darkly. We drove a long time on spacious streets that reminded me vaguely of Paris and Madrid and then we rolled along on residential ones. The old man was silent. I wondered how much time he had left in this world, and how much I had left.

We departed the city and drove on highways and past surburban highrise complexes. We were overtaken by dawn in the broad countryside. It seemed like a very long drive indeed. We were stopped twice at sudden roadblocks by armed young soldiers for passport control. Burp guns, vacant faces. I was reminded of the burp guns in Ushuaia, Rio Grande, Rio Gallegos, Bahia Blanca, and of the young man just outside of Ushuaia, sitting on the half-hidden knoll with the machine gun between his legs, trained on the road. And I recalled the *ficha*, which I carried in my rucksack along with my passport as an American. I felt unwelcome in this country and I had serious doubts about this country's intentions in the Antarctic. But I was also aware I was being self-righteous and that I was scapegoating, and I remembered it wasn't Argentina that had started Antarctic sovereignty claims, it was the United Kingdom as long ago as 1908.

My Stateside life was about to resume. My third Antarctic trip was ending as it had begun: in solitude. I had disengaged myself (or been disengaged) in stages: from McMurdo, the *Burton Island*, the *Bransfield*, the *John Biscoe*, from Argentine Islands, the *Hero*, from Palmer, the *Hero* again, from people and friends. But I had just begun. The trip, in my mind, was nothing without a book to describe and justify it. In terms of challenge, the trip was only the visible part of the berg.

We arrived at the airport. The old man, coughing, insisted on carrying the lion's share of my baggage. His honor was at stake. He had been paid to help me. I checked in at the Avianca counter. My solitude had followed me from the drive to the counter itself. I was relieved to see my baggage go. The old man stood quietly by, ready to serve if I needed him. He coughed into a large handkerchief. I had a feeling he was losing part of his lungs. I imagined him driving alone back to the city and to wherever it was he lived or worked.

Then we sat on a bench in a dirty, deserted section of the airport. He stayed at my side. We couldn't converse, and I was glad about this in a way. We waited for emigration and customs control. No one seemed to be in charge. Occasionally uniformed figures wandered vaguely about.

It was well the old man stayed with me, for there was a moment when an official who spoke no English said I couldn't leave the country because I hadn't officially entered it. At least this was what I gathered he was saying as he angrily pointed to my open passport. The old man spoke carefully. He knew he was dealing with bureaucratic power and that the official, who already looked offended for some reason, could easily delay my departure by hours.

The old man pointed to my *ficha* and to the special exit paper that the agent had prepared for me. The official stamped the *ficha* and handed it to me together with my passport. He kept the exit paper. He didn't trouble to wave me on.

The old man indicated that I was to go to the waiting plane. I tried to give him an American bill. He declined it with a smile, making it clear with a gesture that it wasn't necessary.

Saluting him, I turned away and headed for the plane.

The Antarctic Treaty

The Governments of Argentina, Australia, Belgium, Chile, the French Republic, Japan, New Zealand, Norway, the Union of South Africa, the Union of Soviet Socialist Republics, the United Kingdom of Great Britain and Northern Ireland, and the United States of America.

Recognizing that it is in the interest of all mankind that Antarctica shall continue forever to be used exclusively for peaceful purposes and shall not become the scene or object of international discord;

Acknowledging the substantial contributions to scientific knowledge resulting from international cooperation in scientific investigation in Antarctica;

Convinced that the establishment of a firm foundation for the continuation and development of such cooperation on the basis of freedom of scientific investigation in Antarctica as applied during the International Geophysical Year accords with the interests of science and the progress of all mankind;

Convinced also that a treaty ensuring the use of Antarctica for peaceful purposes only and the continuance of international harmony in Antarctica will further the purposes and principles embodied in the Charter of the United Nations;

Have agreed as follows:

ARTICLE I

1. Antarctica shall be used for peaceful purposes only. There shall be prohibited, *inter alia,* any measures of a military nature, such as the establishment of military bases and fortifications, the carrying out of military maneuvers, as well as the testing of any type of weapons.

2. The present Treaty shall not prevent the use of military person-

349

nel or equipment for scientific research or for any other peaceful purposes.

ARTICLE II

Freedom of scientific investigation in Antarctica and cooperation toward that end, as applied during the International Geophysical Year, shall continue, subject to the provisions of the present Treaty.

ARTICLE III

1. In order to promote international cooperation in scientific investigation in Antarctica, as provided for in Article II of the present Treaty, the Contracting Parties agree that, to the greatest extent feasible and practicable:

(a) information regarding plans for scientific programs in Antarctica shall be exchanged to permit maximum economy and efficiency of operations;

(b) scientific personnel shall be exchanged in Antarctica between expeditions and stations;

(c) scientific observations and results from Antarctica shall be exchanged and made freely available.

2. In implementing this Article, every encouragement shall be given to the establishment of cooperative working relations with those Specialized Agencies of the United Nations and other international organizations having a scientific or technical interest in Antarctica.

ARTICLE IV

1. Nothing contained in the present Treaty shall be interpreted as:

(a) a renunciation by any Contracting Party of previously asserted rights of or claims to territorial sovereignty in Antarctica;

(b) a renunciation or diminution by any Contracting Party of any basis of claim to territorial sovereignty in Antarctica which it may have whether as a result of its activities or those of its nationals in Antarctica, or otherwise;

(c) prejudicing the position of any Contracting Party as regards its recognition or non-recognition of any other State's right of or claim or basis of claim to territorial sovereignty in Antarctica.

2. No acts or activities taking place while the present Treaty is in force shall constitute a basis for asserting, supporting or denying a claim to territorial sovereignty in Antarctica or create any rights of sovereignty in Antarctica. No new claim, or enlargement of an exist-

ing claim, to territorial sovereignty in Antarctica shall be asserted while the present Treaty is in force.

ARTICLE V

1. Any nuclear explosions in Antarctica and the disposal there of radioactive waste material shall be prohibited.

2. In the event of the conclusion of international agreements concerning the use of nuclear energy, including nuclear explosions and the disposal of radioactive waste material, to which all of the Contracting Parties whose representatives are entitled to participate in the meetings provided for under Article IX are parties, the rules established under such agreements shall apply in Antarctica.

ARTICLE VI

The provisions of the present Treaty shall apply to the area south of 60° South Latitude, including all ice shelves, but nothing in the present Treaty shall prejudice or in any way affect the rights, or the exercise of the rights, of any State under international law with regard to the high seas within that area.

ARTICLE VII

1. In order to promote the objectives and ensure the observance of the provisions of the present Treaty, each Contracting Party whose representatives are entitled to participate in the meetings referred to in Article IX of the Treaty shall have the right to designate observers to carry out any inspection provided for by the present Article. Observers shall be nationals of the Contracting Parties which designate them. The names of observers shall be communicated to every other Contracting Party having the right to designate observers, and like notice shall be given of the termination of their appointment.

2. Each observer designated in accordance with the provisions of paragraph 1 of this Article shall have complete freedom of access at any time to any or all areas of Antarctica.

3. All areas of Antarctica, including all stations, installations and equipment within those areas, and all ships and aircraft at points of discharging or embarking cargoes or personnel in Antarctica, shall be open at all times to inspection by any observers designated in accordance with paragraph 1 of this Article.

4. Aerial observation may be carried out at any time over any or all areas of Antarctica by any of the Contracting Parties having the right to designate observers.

5. Each Contracting Party shall, at the time when the present Treaty enters into force for it, inform the other Contracting Parties, and thereafter shall give them notice in advance, of

(a) all expeditions to and within Antarctica, on the part of its ships or nationals, and all expeditions to Antarctica organized in or proceeding from its territory;

(b) all stations in Antarctica occupied by its nationals; and

(c) any military personnel or equipment intended to be introduced by it into Antarctica subject to the conditions prescribed in paragraph 2 of Article I of the present Treaty.

ARTICLE VIII

1. In order to facilitate the exercise of their functions under the present Treaty, and without prejudice to the respective positions of the Contracting Parties relating to jurisdiction over all other persons in Antarctica, observers designated under paragraph I of Article VII and scientific personnel exchanged under subparagraph 1(b) of Article III of the Treaty, and members of the staffs accompanying any such persons, shall be subject only to the jurisdiction of the Contracting Party of which they are nationals in respect of all acts or omissions occurring while they are in Antarctica for the purpose of exercising their functions.

2. Without prejudice to the provisions of paragraph 1 of this Article, and pending the adoption of measures in pursuance of subparagraph 1(e) of Article IX, the Contracting Parties concerned in any case of dispute with regard to the exercise of jurisdiction in Antarctica shall immediately consult together with a view to reaching a mutually acceptable solution.

ARTICLE IX

1. Representatives of the Contracting Parties named in the preamble to the present Treaty shall meet at the City of Canberra within two months after the date of entry into force of the Treaty, and thereafter at suitable intervals and places, for the purpose of exchanging information, consulting together on matters of common interest petaining to Antarctica, and formulating and considering, and recommending to their Governments, measures in furtherance of the principles and objectives of the Treaty, including measures regarding:

(a) use of Antarctica for peaceful purposes only;
(b) facilitation of scientific research in Antarctica;

(c) facilitation of international scientific cooperation in Antarctica;
(d) facilitation of the exercise of the rights of inspection provided for in Article VII of the Treaty;
(e) questions relating to the exercise of jurisdiction in Antarctica;
(f) preservation and conservation of living resources in Antarctica.

2. Each Contracting Party which has become a party to the present Treaty by accession under Article XIII shall be entitled to appoint representatives to participate in the meetings referred to in paragraph 1 of the present Article, during such time as that Contracting Party demonstrates its interest in Antarctica by conducting substantial scientific research activity there, such as the establishment of a scientific station or the despatch of a scientific expedition.

3. Reports from the observers referred to in Article VII of the present Treaty shall be transmitted to the representatives of the Contracting Parties participating in the meetings referred to in paragraph 1 of the present Article.

4. The measures referred to in paragraph 1 of this Article shall become effective when approved by all the Contracting Parties whose representatives were entitled to participate in the meetings held to consider those measures.

5. Any or all of the rights established in the present Treaty may be exercised as from the date of entry into force of the Treaty whether or not any measures facilitating the exercise of such rights have been proposed, considered or approved as provided in this Article.

ARTICLE X

Each of the Contracting Parties undertakes to exert appropriate efforts, consistent with the Charter of the United Nations, to the end that no one engages in any activity in Antarctica contrary to the principles or purposes of the present Treaty.

ARTICLE XI

1. If any dispute arises between two or more of the Contracting Parties concerning the interpretation or application of the present Treaty, those Contracting Parties shall consult among themselves with a view to having the dispute resolved by negotiation, inquiry, mediation, conciliation, arbitration, judicial settlement or other peaceful means of their own choice.

2. Any dispute of this character not so resolved shall, with the consent, in each case, of all parties to the dispute, be referred to the International Court of Justice for settlement; but failure to reach agreement on reference to the International Court shall not absolve

parties to the dispute from the responsibility of continuing to seek to resolve it by any of the various peaceful means referred to in paragraph 1 of this Article.

ARTICLE XII

1. (a) The present Treaty may be modified or amended at any time by unanimous agreement of the Contracting Parties whose representatives are entitled to participate in the meetings provided for under Article IX. Any such modification or amendment shall enter into force when the depositary Government has received notice from all such Contracting Parties that they have ratified it.

(b) Such modification or amendment shall thereafter enter into force as to any other Contracting Party when notice of ratification by it has been received by the depositary Government. Any such Contracting Party from which no notice of ratification is received within a period of two years from the date of entry into force of the modification or amendment in accordance with the provisions of subparagraph 1(a) of this Article shall be deemed to have withdrawn from the present Treaty on the date of the expiration of such period.

2. (a) If after the expiration of thirty years from the date of entry into force of the present Treaty, any of the Contracting Parties whose representatives are entitled to participate in the meetings provided for under Article IX so requests by a communication addressed to the depositary Government, a Conference of all the Contracting Parties shall be held as soon as practicable to review the operation of the Treaty.

(b) Any modification or amendment to the present Treaty which is approved at such a Conference by a majority of the Contracting Parties there represented, including a majority of those whose representatives are entitled to participate in the meeting provided for under Article IX, shall be communicated by the depositary Government to all the Contracting Parties immediately after the termination of the Conference and shall enter into force in accordance with the provisions of paragraph 1 of the present Article.

(c) If any such modification or amendment has not entered into force in accordance with the provisions of subparagraph 1(a) of this Article within a period of two years after the date of its communication to all the Contracting Parties, any Contracting Party may at any time after the expiration of that period give notice to the depositary Government of its withdrawal from the present Treaty; and such withdrawal shall take effect two years after the receipt of the notice by the depositary Government.

ARTICLE XIII

1. The present Treaty shall be subject to ratification by the signatory States. It shall be open for accession by any State which is a Member of the United Nations, or by any other State which may be invited to accede to the Treaty with the consent of all the Contracting Parties whose representatives are entitled to participate in the meetings provided for under Article IX of the Treaty.

2. Ratification of or accession to the present Treaty shall be effected by each State in accordance with its constitutional processes.

3. Instruments of ratification and instruments of accession shall be deposited with the Government of the United States of America, hereby designated as the depositary Government.

4. The depositary Government shall inform all signatory and acceding States of the date of each deposit of an instrument of ratification or accession, and the date of entry into force of the Treaty and of any modification or amendment thereto.

5. Upon the deposit of instruments of ratification by all the signatory States, the present Treaty shall enter into force for those States and for States which have deposited instruments of accession. Thereafter the Treaty shall enter into force for any acceding State upon the deposit of its instrument of accession.

6. The present Treaty shall be registered by the depositary Government pursuant to Article 102 of the Charter of the United Nations.

ARTICLE XIV

The present Treaty, done in the English, French, Russian, and Spanish languages, each version being equally authentic, shall be deposited in the archives of the Government of the United States of America, which shall transmit duly certified copies thereof to the Governments of the signatory and acceding States.

IN WITNESS WHEREOF, the undersigned Plenipotentiaries, duly authorized, have signed the present Treaty.

DONE at Washington this first day of December, one thousand nine hundred and fifty-nine.

The Antarctic Conservation Act of 1978

PUBLIC LAW 95–541
95TH CONGRESS
AN ACT

Oct. 28, 1878

[H.R. 7749]

To implement the Agreed Measures for the Conservation of Antarctic Fauna and Flora, and for other purposes.

Antarctic
Conservation
Act
of 1978.
16 USC 2401
note.
16 USC 2401.
12 UST 794.
17 UST 991.

Be it enacted by the Senate and House of Representatives of the United States of America in Congress assembled. That this Act may be cited as the "Antarctic Conservation Act of 1978".

SEC. 2. FINDINGS AND PURPOSE.

(a) FINDINGS.—The Congress finds that—

(1) the Antarctic Treaty and the Agreed Measures for the Conservation of Antarctic Fauna and Flora, adopted at the Third Antarctic Treaty Consultative Meeting, have established a firm foundation for the continuation of international cooperation and the freedom of scientific investigation in Antarctica; and

(2) the study of Antarctic fauna and flora, their adaptation to their rigorous environment, and their interrelationships with that environment has special scientific importance for all mankind.

(b) PURPOSE.—The purpose of this Act is to provide for the conservation and protection of the fauna and flora of Antarctica, and of the ecosystem upon which such fauna and flora depend, consistent with the Antarctic Treaty, the Agreed Measures for the Conservation of Antarctic Fauna and Flora, and Recommendation VII-3 of the Eighth Antarctic Treaty Consultative Meeting.

SEC. 3. DEFINITIONS. 16 USC 2402.

For purposes of this Act—

(1) The term "Agreed Measures" means the Agreed Measures for the Conservation of Antarctic Fauna and Flora—

(A) as recommended to the Consultative Parties for approval at the Third Antarctic Treaty Consultative Meeting; and

(B) as amended from time to time in accordance with Article IX (1) of the Treaty.

(2) The term "Antarctica" means the area south of 60 degrees south latitude.

(3) The term "collect" means to cut, sever, or move, or to attempt to engage in any such conduct.

(4) The term "Director" means the Director of the National Science Foundation or an officer or employee of the Foundation designated by the Director.

(5) The term "foreign person" means—

(A) any individual who is a citizen or national of a foreign nation,

(B) any corporation, partnership, trust, association, or other legal entity existing or organized under the laws of any foreign nation, and

(C) any department, agency, or other instrumentality of any foreign nation and any officer, employee, or agent of any such instrumentality.

(6) The term "native bird" means any member, at any stage of its life cycle (including eggs), of any species of the class Aves which is designated as a native species by the Director under section 6(b) (1), and includes any part of any such member.

(7) The term "native mammal" means any member, at any stage of its life cycle, of any

species of the class Mammalia, other than any species regulated by the International Whaling Commission, which is designated as a native species by the Director under section 6(b) (1), and includes any part of such member.

(8) The term "native plant" means any member of any species of plant at any stage of its life cycle (including seeds) which is designated as such by the Director under section 6(b) (1), and includes any part of any such member.

(9) The term "pollutant" means any substance designated as such by the Director under section 6(b) (6).

(10) The term "site of special scientific interest" means any area designated as such by the Director under section 6(b) (3).

(11) The term "specially protected area" means any area designated as such by the Director under section 6(b) (4).

(12) The term "specially protected species" means any species of native mammal or native bird designated as such by the Director under section 6(b) (5).

(13) The term "take" means to harass, molest, harm, pursue, hunt, shoot, wound, kill, trap, or capture, or to attempt to engage in any such conduct.

12 UST 794. (14) The term "Treaty" means the Antarctic Treaty signed in Washington, D.C., on December 1, 1959.

(15) The term "United States" means the several States of the Union, the District of Columbia, the Commonwealth of Puerto Rico, American Samoa, the Virgin Islands, Guam, and the Trust Territory of the Pacific Islands, including the Government of the Northern Mariana Islands.

(16) The term "United States citizen" means—

(A) any individual who is a citizen or national of the United States;

(B) any corporation, partnership, trust, association, or other legal entity existing or organized under the laws of any of the United States; and

(C) any department, agency, or other instrumentality of the Federal Government or

of any State, and any officer, employee, or
agent of any such instrumentality.

SEC. 4. PROHIBITED ACTS.   16 USC 2403.
   (a) IN GENERAL.—It is unlawful—
      (1) for any United States citizen, unless au-
thorized by regulation pescribed under this Act or
a permit issued under section 5—
         (A) to take within Antarctica any native
mammal or native bird,
         (B) to collect within any specially pro-
tected area any native plant,
         (C) to introduce into Antarctica any ani-
mal or plant that is not indigenous to Antarctica,
         (D) to enter any specially protected area
or site of special scientific interest, or
         (E) to discharge, or othewise to dispose of,
any pollutant within Antarctica;
      (2) for any United States citizen wherever lo-
cated, or any foreign person while within the
United States, unless authorized by regulation
prescribed under this Act or a permit issued under
section 5—
         (A) to possess, sell, offer for sale, deliver,
receive, carry, transport, or ship by any
means whatsoever, or
         (B) to import into the United States, to
export from the United States, or attempt to
so import or export, any native mammal or
native bird taken in Antarctica or any native
plant collected in any specially protected
area;
      (3) for any United States citizen wherever lo-
cated, or any foreign person while within the
United States, to violate any regulation prescribed
under this Act; or
      (4) for any person, whether or not a United
States citizen, to violate any term or condition of
any permit issued under section 5.
No act described in paragraphs (1) through (4) shall be
unlawful if committed, under emergency circumstances, to prevent the loss of human life.
   (b) EXCEPTION.—Subsection (a) shall not apply
to—

The Antarctic Conservation Act of 1978   359

(1) any native mammal, native bird, or native plant which is held in captivity on the date of the enactment of this Act; or

(2) any offspring of any such mammal, bird, or plant.

With respect to any act prohibited by subsection (a) which occurs after the 180th day after such date of enactment, there shall be a rebuttable presumption that the native mammal, native bird, or native plant involved in such act was not held in captivity on such date or was not an offspring referred to in paragraph (2).

16 USC 2404.

SEC. 5. PERMITS.

(a) In General.—The Director may issue permits which authorize acts otherwise prohibited by section 4(a).

Regulation.

(b) Applications for Permits.—(1) Applications for permits under this section shall be made in such manner and form, and shall contain such information, as the Director shall by regulation prescribe.

Publication in Federal Register.

(2) The Director shall publish notice in the Federal Register of each application which is made for a permit under this section. The notice shall invite the submission by interested parties, within 30 days after the date of publication of the notice, of written data, comments, or views with respect to the application. Information received by the Director as a part of any application shall be available to the public as a matter of public record.

(c) Action by Appropriate Secretaries on Certain Permit Applications.—(1) If the Director receives an application for a permit under this section requesting authority to undertake any action with respect to—

(A) any native mammal which is a marine mammal within the meaning of section 3(5) of the Marine Mammal Protection Act of 1972 (16 U.S.C. 1362(5));

(B) any native mammal, native bird, or native plant which is an endangered species or threatened species under the Endangered Special Act of 1973 (16 U.S.C. 1531 et seq.); or

(C) any native bird which is protected under the Migratory Bird Treaty Act (16 U.S.C. 701 et seq.);

the Director shall submit a copy of the application to the Secretary of Commerce or to the Secretary of the Interior, as appropriate (hereinafter in this subsection referred to respectively as the "appropriate Secretary").

(2) After receiving a copy of any application from the Director under paragraph (1) the appropriate Secretary shall promptly determine, and notify the Director, whether or not any action proposed in the application also requires a permit or other authorization under any law administered by the appropriate Secretary.

(3) If the appropriate Secretary notifies the Director that any action proposed in the application requires a permit or other authorization under any law administered by the appropriate Secretary, the Director may not issue a permit under this section with respect to such action unless such other required permit or authorization is issued by the appropriate Secretary and a copy thereof is submitted to the Director. The issuance of any permit or other authorization by the appropriate Secretary for the carrying out of any action with respect to any native mammal, native bird, or native plant shall not be deemed to entitle the applicant concerned to the issuance by the Director of a permit under this section.

(d) ISSUANCE OF PERMITS.—As soon as practicable after receiving any application for a permit under this section, or, in the case of any application to which subsection (c) applies, as soon as practicable after the applicable requirements of such subsection are complied with, the Director shall issue, or deny the issuance of, the permit. Within 10 days after the date of the issuance or denial of a permit under this subsection, the Director shall publish notice of the issuance or denial in the Federal Register.

Publication in Federal Register.

(e) TERMS AND CONDITIONS OF PERMITS.—(1) Each permit issued under this section shall—

    (A) if applicable, specify—

        (i) the number and species of native mammals, native birds, or native plants to which the permit applies.

        (ii) if any such mammal or bird is authorized to be taken, transported, carried, or shipped, the manner (which manner must be determined by the Director to be humane) in which such action must be accomplished and the area in which such taking must occur, and

(iii) if any such plant is authorized to be collected, the location and manner in which it must be collected;

(B) the period during which the permit is valid; and

(C) such other terms and conditions as the Director deems necessary and appropriate to ensure that any act authorized under the permit is carried out in a manner consistent with the purpose of this Act, the criteria set forth in paragraph (2), if applicable, and the regulations prescribed under this Act.

Criteria. (2) The terms and conditions imposed by the Director in any permit issued under this section that authorizes any of the following acts shall be consistent with the following criteria:

(A) Permits authorizing the taking within Antarctica (other than within any specially protected area) of any native mammal or native bird (other than a specially protected species of any such mammal or bird)—

(i) may be issued only for the purpose of providing—

(I) specimens for scientific study or scientific information, or

(II) specimens for museums, zoological gardens, or other cultural institutions or uses; and

(ii) shall ensure, as far as possible, that—

(I) no more native mammals and native birds are taken in any year than can normally be replaced by net natural reproduction in the following breeding season, and

(II) the variety of species and the balance of the natural ecological systems with Antarctica are maintained.

(B) Permits authorizing the taking of specially protected species may be issued only if—

(i) there is a compelling scientific purpose for such taking; and

(ii) the actions allowed under any such permit will not jeopardize any existing natural ecological system, or the survival, of such species.

(C) Permits authorizing the entry into any specially protected area—

(i) may be issued only if—

(I) there is a compelling scientific purpose for such entry which cannot be served elsewhere, and

(II) the actions allowed under any such permit will not jeopardize the natural ecological system existing in such area; and

(ii) shall not allow the operation of any surface vehicle within such area.

(D) Permits authorizing the entry into any site of special scientific interest shall be consistent with the management plan prescribed under section 6(b)(3) for such site.

(e) JUDICIAL REVIEW.—Any applicant for a permit may obtain judicial review of the terms and conditions of any permit issued by the Director under this section or of the refusal of the Director to issue such a permit. Such review, which shall be pursuant to chapter 7 of title 5, United States Code, may be initiated by filing a petition for review in the United States district court for the district wherein the applicant for a permit resides, or has his principal place of business, or in the United States District Court for the District of Columbia, within 60 days after the date on which such permit is issued or denied.

5 USC 701 *et seq.*

(f) (1) MODIFICATION, SUSPENSION, AND REVOCATION.—The Director may modify, suspend, or revoke, in whole or part, any permit issued under this section—

(A) in order to make the permit consistent with any change made after the date of issuance of the permit, to any regulation prescribed under section 6;

(B) if there is any change in conditions which makes the permit inconsistent with the purpose of this Act; or

(C) in any case in which there has been any

violation of any term or condition of the permit, any regulation prescribed under this Act, or any provision of this Act.

(2) Whenever the Director proposes any modification, suspension, or revocation of a permit under this subsection, the permittee shall be afforded opportunity, after due notice, for a hearing by the Director with respect to such proposed modification, suspension, or revocation. If a hearing is requested, the action proposed by the Director shall not take effect before a decision is issued by him after the hearing, unless the proposed action is taken by the Director to meet an emergency situation. Any action taken by the Director after such a hearing is subject to judicial review on the same basis as is provided for with respect to permit applications under subsection (e).

Notice, publication in Federal Register.
(3) Notice of the modification, suspension, or revocation of any permit by the Director shall be published in the Federal Register within 10 days from the date of the Director's decision.

(g) PERMIT FEES.—The Director may establish and charge fees for processing applications for permits under this section. The amount of such fees shall be commensurate with the administrative costs incurred by the Director in undertaking such processing.

16 USC 2405. Consultation.
SEC. 6. REGULATIONS.
(a) IN GENERAL.—The Director, after consultation with the Secretary of State and other appropriate Federal officials, shall prescribe such regulations as are necessary and appropriate to implement the provisions of this Act.

(b) SPECIFIC REGULATIONS.—The regulations required to be prescribed under subsection (a) shall include, but shall not be limited to, regulations which—

(1) designate, as native species—

(A) each species of the class Aves,

(B) each species of the class Mammalia, and

(C) each species of plant,

which is indigenous to Antarctica or occurs in Antarctica through natural agencies of dispersal;

(2) specify those actions which must, and those actions which must not, be taken within Antarctica in order to protect, in accordance with the

applicable provisions of the Agreed Measures, 17 UST 991. members of each native species designated under paragraph (1):

(3) identify, as a site of special scientific interest, each area approved by the United States in accordance with Recommendation VIII-3 of the Eighth Antarctic Treaty Consultative Meeting as having unique value for scientific investigation and needing protection from interference, and prescribe a management plan for such site which is consistent with any management plan approved by the United States for such site in accordance with such Recommendation;

(4) identify, as a specially protected area, each area designated for special protection under the Agreed Measures because of its outstanding scientific or ecological interest;

(5) designate, as a specially protected species, any native species of mammal or bird which is approved by the United States for special protection under the Agreed Measures;

(6) designate as a pollutant any substance which the Director finds liable, if the substance is introduced into Antarctica, to create hazards to human health, to harm living resources or marine life, to damage amenities, or to interfere with other legitimate uses of Antarctica;

(7) specify those actions which must, and those actions which must not, be taken in order to prevent or control the discharge or other disposal of pollutants, from any source within Antarctica;

(8) designate those animals and plants, not indigenous to Antarctica, which either may, or may not, be introduced into Antarctica, and specify those control measures which must be observed with respect to any such animals or plants which are allowed to be so introduced;

(9) specify the emergency circumstances with respect to which the exclusion set forth in the last sentence of section 4(a) applies; and

(10) set forth the form, content, and manner of filing, if applicable, of all notices, reports, declarations, or other documentation which may be required incident to the carrying out of any act for which a permit is required under section 5.

The Antarctic Conservation Act of 1978

Regulations.
16 USC 2406.

12 UST 794.

"United States
citizen."

16 USC 2407.

SEC. 7. NOTIFICATION OF TRAVEL TO ANT-ARCTICA.

The Secretary of State shall p*r*escribe such regulations as may be necessary and appropriate to implement, with respect to United States citizens, paragraph 5 of Article VII of the Treaty pertaining to the filing of advance notifications of expeditions to, and within, Antarctica. For purposes of this section, the term "United States citizen" shall include any foreign person who organizes within the United States any expedition which will proceed to Antarctica from the United States.

SEC. 8. CIVIL PENALTIES.

(a) ASSESSMENT OF PENALTIES.—Any person who is found by the Director, after notice and opportunity for a hearing in accordance with subsection (b), to have committed any act prohibited by section 4(a) or to have violated any regulation prescribed under section 7 shall be liable to the United States for a civil penalty. The amount of the civil penalty shall not exceed $5,000 for each violation unless the prohibited act was knowingly committed, in which case the amount of the civil penalty shall not exceed $10,000 for each violation. Each day of a continuing violation shall constitute a separate offense. The amount of any civil penalty shall be assessed by the Director by written notice. Any civil penalty assessed under this subsection may be remitted or mitigated by the Director.

(b) HEARINGS.—Hearings for the assessment of civil penalties under subsection (a) shall be conducted in accordance with section 554 of title 5, United States Code. For the purposes of conducting any such hearing, the Director may issue subpenas for the attendance and testimony of witnesses and the production of relevant papers, books, and documents, and may administer oaths. Witnesses summoned shall be paid the same fees and mileage that are paid to witnesses in the courts of the United States. In case of contumacy or refusal to obey a subpena served upon any person pursuant to this subsection, the district court of the United States for any district in which such person is found, resides, or transacts business, upon application by the United States and after notice to such person, shall have jurisdiction to issue an order requiring such person to appear and give testimony before the Director or to appear and produce documents before the Director, or both, and any failure to obey such order of the court may be punished by such court as contempt thereof.

(c) REVIEW.—Upon the failure of any person against whom a civil penalty is assessed under subsection (a) to pay such penalty, the Director may request the Attorney General to institute a civil action in a district court of the United States for any district in which such person is found, resides, or transacts business to collect the penalty and such court shall have jurisdiction to hear and decide any such action. The court shall hear such action on the record made before the Director and shall sustain the decision of the Director if it is supported by substantial evidence on the record considered as a whole.

(d) PENALTIES UNDER OTHER LAWS.—The assessment of a civil penalty under subsection (a) for any act shall not be deemed to preclude the assessment of a civil penalty for such act under any other law, including, but not limited to, the Marine Mammal Protection Act of 1972, the Endangered Species Act of 1973, and the Migratory Bird Treaty Act.

SEC. 9. CRIMINAL OFFENSES.

(a) OFFENSES.—A person is guilty of an offense if he willfully commits any act prohibited by section 4(a).

(b) PUNISHMENT.—Any offense described in subsection (a) is punishable by a fine of $10,000, or imprisonment for not more than one year, or both.

(c) OFFENSES UNDER OTHER LAWS.—A conviction under subsection (a) for any act shall not be deemed to preclude a conviction for such act under any other law, including, but not limited to, the Marine Mammal Protection Act of 1972, the Endangered Species Act of 1973, and the Migratory Bird Treaty Act.

SEC. 10. ENFORCEMENT.

(a) RESPONSIBILITY.—The provisions of this Act and of any regulation prescribed, or permit issued, under this Act shall be enforced by the Director, the Secretary of the Treasury, the Secretary of Commerce, the Secretary of Interior, and the Secretary of the department in which the Coast Guard is operating. The

16 USC 1361 note, 1531 note. 16 USC 710. 16 USC 2408.

16 USC 1361 note, 1531 note. 16 USC 710. 16 USC 2409.

Cooperation.

Director and such Secretaries may utilize by agreement, on a reimbursable basis or otherwise, the personnel, services, and facilities of any other Federal agency or any State agency in the performance of such duties.

(d) POWERS OF AUTHORIZED OFFICERS.—Any officer who is authorized (by the Director, the Secretary of the Treasury, the Secretary of Commerce, the Secretary of the Interior, the Secretary of the department in which the Coast Guard is operating, or the head of any Federal or State agency which has entered into an agreement with the Director or any such Secretary under subsection (a)) to enforce the provisions of this Act and of any regulation or permit issued under this Act may—

(1) secure, execute, and serve any order, warrant, subpena, or other process, which is issued under the authority of the United States;

(2) search without warrant any person, place, or conveyance where there is reasonable grounds to believe that a person has committed or is attempting to commit an act prohibited by section 4(a);

(3) seize without warrant any evidentiary item where there is reasonable grounds to believe that a person has committed or is attempting to commit any such act;

(4) offer and pay rewards for services or information which may lead to the apprehension of violators of such provisions;

(5) make inquiries, and administer to, or take from, any person an oath, affirmation, or affidavit, concerning any matter which is related to the enforcement of such provisions;

(6) detain for inspection and inspect any package, crate, or other container, including its contents, and all accompanying documents, upon importation into, or exportation from, the United States; and

(7) make an arrest with or without a warrant with respect to any act prohibited by section 4(a) if such officer has reasonable grounds to believe that the person to be arrested is committing such

act in his presence or view, or has committed such act.

(c) SEIZURE.—Any property or item seized pursuant to subsection (b) shall be held by any person authorized by the Director, the Secretary of the Treasury, the Secretary of Commerce, the Secretary of the Interior, or the Secretary of the department in which the Coast Guard is operating pending the disposition of civil or criminal proceedings, or the institution of an action in rem for forfeiture of such property or item; except that such authorized person may, in lieu of holding such property or item, permit the owner or consignee thereof to post a bond or other satisfactory surety.

(d) FORFEITURE.—(1) Any animal or plant with respect to which an act prohibited by section 4(a) is committed shall be subject to forfeiture to the United States.

(2) All guns, traps, nets, and other equipment, vessels, vehicles, aircraft, and other means of transportation used in the commission of any act prohibited by section 4(a) shall be subject to forfeiture to the United States.

(3) Upon the forfeiture to the United States of any property or item described in paragraph (1) or (2), or upon the abandonment or waiver of any claim to any such property or item, it shall be disposed of by the Director, the Secretary of the Treasury, the Secretary of Commerce, the Secretary of the Interior, or the Secretary of the department in which the Coast Guard is operating, as the case may be, in such a manner, consistent with the purposes of the Act, as may be prescribed by regulation; except that no native mammal, native bird, or native plant may be disposed of by sale to the public.

Property disposal, regulation.

(e) APPLICATION OF CUSTOMS LAWS.—All provisions of law relating to the seizure, forfeiture, and condemnation of a vessel for violation of the customs laws, the disposition of such vessel or the proceeds from the sale thereof, and the remission or mitigation of such forfeiture, shall apply to the seizures and forfeitures incurred, or alleged to have been incurred, under the provision of this Act, insofar as such provisions of law are applicable and not inconsistent with the provisions of this Act; except that all powers, rights, and duties conferred or imposed by the customs laws upon any officer or employee of the Customs Service may, for the purposes of this Act, also be exercised or performed by the Director, the Secretary of Commerce, the Secretary of the Interior, or the Secretary of the department in which the Coast Guard is operating, or by such persons as each may designate.

Regulations.

(f) REGULATIONS.—The Director, the Secretary of the Treasury, the Secretary of Commerce, the Secretary of the Interior, and the Secretary of the department in which the Coast Guard is operating may prescribe such regulations as may be appropriate to enforce the provisions of this Act and of any regulation prescribed or permit issued under this Act, and charge reasonable fees for the expenses of the United States incurred in carrying out inspections and in transferring, boarding, handling, or storing native mammals, native birds, native plants, animals and plants not indigenous to Antarctica, and other evidentiary items seized or forfeited under this Act.

16 USC 2410.

SEC. 11. JURISDICTION OF COURTS.

The district courts of the United States shall have exclusive jurisdiction over any case or controversy arising under the provisions of this Act or of any regulation prescribed, or permit issued, under this Act.

16 USC 2411.

SEC. 12. FEDERAL AGENCY COOPERATION.

Each Federal department or agency whose activities affect Antarctica shall utilize, to the maximum extent practicable, its authorities in furtherance of the purposes of this Act, and shall cooperate with the Director in carrying out the purposes of this Act.

16 USC 2412.

SEC. 13. RELATIONSHIP TO EXISTING TREATIES.

Nothing in this Act shall be construed as contravening or superseding the provisions of any international treaty, convention, or agreement, if such treaty, convention, or agreement is in force with respect to the United States on the date of the enactment of this Act, or of any statute which implements any such treaty, convention, or agreement.

SEC. 14.

(a) The first section of the Fisherman's Protective Act of 1967 (22 U.S.C. 1971) is amended by adding at the end thereof the following new sentence: "Notwithstanding any other law, the documentation or certification of any such vessel shall not be considered to be affected, for the purposes of this Act, in any manner or to any extent if at any time during any voyage for the purpose of fishing beyond the fishery conservation zone (as defined in section 3(8) of the Fishery Conservation and Management Act of 1976 (16 U.S.C. 1802(8)), the vessel is commanded by other than a citizen of the United States."

(b) The amendment made by subsection (a) shall take effect January 1, 1978.

Effective date. 22 USC 1971 note.

Approved October 28, 1978.

LEGISLATIVE HISTORY:

HOUSE REPORTS: No. 95-1031, Parts I and II
(Comm. on Merchant Marine and Fisheries, and Comm. on Science and Technology)

CONGRESSIONAL RECORD, Vol. 124 (1978):

Sept. 25, considered and passed House.

Oct. 13, considered and passed Senate, amended.

Oct. 14, House concurred in certain Senate amendment.

Glossary

ablation: surface waste of ice or snow by melting or evaporation.
Adélie: Adélie penguin.
Air Ops: Air Operations.
aneroid barometer; aneroid: an instrument used for measuring atmospheric pressure, in which the pressure moves a pointer by distorting a metallic surface.
annual or *sea ice:* ice that breaks up during the austral summer, as distinguished from the so-called permanent ice of glaciers, ice shelves and the ice cap of the inland Antarctic plateau.
anorak: a form of parka; a parka-like windbreaker.
Argies: Argentines.
ASA: Antarctic Support Activities.
autorotation: emergency unpowered descending helicopter flight in which the spin of the rotors, due partially to momentum and partially to the passage of air across the blades, decreases the speed of the descent. The rotors act as a sort of parachute. Under certain conditions of autorotation the pilot has a limited control over his craft.
balaclava: heavy woolen masklike headgear that covers the neck and most of the face.
Barrier: see Great Ice Barrier.
BAS (pronounced as in the fish): British Antarctic Survey.
bear paws: large gauntleted fur-back leather mittens.
Beaufort Scale: see wind forces.
berg: iceberg.
bergy bit: a small piece of floating, usually glacier, ice.
bogs: a head, toilet area, including the toilets.

372

BOQ: Bachelor Officers' Quarters.

brash: small fragments and nodules of ice, resulting from a floe breaking up.

bunny boots: large, heavy thermal boots capable of providing protection against extremely low temperatures.

Buno: bureau number. Each aircraft has a number as it comes off the assembly line.

calving: natural breaking off of part of an ice shelf, glacier, glacier tongue or iceberg, resulting in the formation of a berg.

canvas tank: a canvas "hold-all" containing food bags and strapped to a sledge.

cat: Sno-cat, an American-made, tracked, oversnow vehicle.

Centigrade: the conversion of a Centigrade temperature into a Fahrenheit one is accomplished by multiplying the Centigrade figure by 9/5 and adding 32.

CG: Coast Guard.

Cheechee: Christchurch, New Zealand.

chopper: helicopter.

Clements building: a modular building with 4 × 8-foot panels for both top and sides, developed especially for Antarctic use by the United States Navy and prefabricated by the Clements Company.

Connie: the C-121 Super Constellation four-engine propeller aircraft.

CPO: Chief Petty Officer.

crabeater: a type of seal.

crevasse: a crack in a glacier or ice shelf. It can vary greatly in width and depth and can be either exposed or deceptively snowbridged.

DFA: Diesel Fuel Arctic.

DV: distinguished visitor.

emergency Oxo: Shackleton was probably referring to the original "Oxo," which was and still is a meat-extract fluid that, when mixed with hot water, provides a stimulating, beefy drink. I am informed by the manufacturers of the product, Brooke Bond Oxo Ltd., that although they have no record of Shackleton's having used the product, they do know that Scott used it in Antarctica.

erratics: rocks, usually ice-worn, that have been carried by a glacier from their original position.

F.: Fahrenheit.

fast ice: sea ice that is attached to land.

Fid: a young worker, generally in the field, of the British Antarctic Survey. Derived from the acronym FIDS (Falkland Islands Dependency Survey).

Fid deck: the deck of a BAS research ship assigned to the Fids.

Fiddery: the Fid equivalent of a wardroom.

FIDS: Falkland Islands Dependency Survey.

finneskoes: boots, including the soles, made of fur. The early explorers used "finnesko" for the plural form, as they also did "ski" for skis. Fineskoes provided warmth but little traction.

fumarole: a subsidiary vent in the side of a volcano, from which issue various gases and water vapor. Ice fumaroles are the result of condensation and freezing of the water vapor around and above fumaroles located in very cold places.

gash: food.

gashman: someone assigned to gash duty—in general cleaning up the interior of the Fid deck, the Fiddery, the gashroom, and serving food.

gashroom: messroom, mess hall, chow hall.

Gemini: a type of rubberized small water craft.

Gentle: the code name for aircraft of VXE-6. Each squadron has its own code name.

geographical mile: see knot.

glacier tongue: the part of a glacier, usually afloat, projecting out from the land.

Great Ice Barrier: early name for the Ross Ice Shelf.

growler: a piece of ice smaller than a bergy bit and floating low in the water.

head: U.S. Navy term for toilet facility.

helo: helicopter.

Herc or *Hercules:* the C-130 four-engine turboprop jet aircraft.

hold luggage: luggage carried in the "hold" of an aircraft.

hoosh: pemmican soup; that is, pemmican cooked with snow.

Huey: a twin-engine, turbine-powered helicopter.

hummock: a rough ridge or small hill of ice, usually formed by pressure.

hypsometer: an instrument used to estimate elevation in mountainous regions by measuring the boiling points of liquids.

the ice: a term used by Antarctic hands to designate the white continent.

Ice Barrier: see Great Ice Barrier.

icecap: a large dome-shaped glacier, in the present work used interchangeably with ice sheet.

icefalls: a crevassed part of a steeply descending glacier.

ice foot: fringes of ice skirting parts of Antarctic shores and often formed by sea spray.

ice piedmont: coastal land ice, usually backed by mountains.

ice shelf: a floating ice sheet attached to a coast.

IGY: International Geophysical Year (1957–58).

Jamesway hut: a green, tentlike, round-topped structure of prefabricated wood and insulated canvas, almost windowless, heated by two oil-fired units and containing several tiny semi-private cubicles.

katabatic wind: a strong, gravity-caused wind.

Kiwi: New Zealander.

knot: a knot is a unit of speed equal to one nautical or geographical mile per hour. A nautical mile (the international unit, used by the United States since 1959, is 6,076.115 feet or 1852 meters) is approximately the equivalent of 1.1 statute miles. A statute mile (5,280 feet) is approximately equal to 0.91 of a nautical mile. Differing from the international unit, the British nautical or geographical mile, known also as the Admiralty mile, is equal to 6,080 feet or 1853.2 meters.

lead (pronounced *leed*): a passage through floating ice.

MAC Center: McMurdo Center.

manhauling: hauling sledges by the sole use of manpower.

midrats: midnight rations.

mukluks: high, canvas, felt-lined boots with thick rubber soles, designed to afford protection at very low temperatures.

navaids: electronic aids to navigation.

nautical mile: see knot.

névé: the packed, hard-frozen snow of a snow field, containing minute ice crystals.

NSF: National Science Foundation.

nunatak: an island of bare land, in some cases the top of a high mountain, projecting through a snow field or ice sheet.

O Club or *O'Club:* officer's club.

Ob Hill: Observation Hill.

pack ice or *pack:* broken sea ice or broken ice of floes, caused by wind, temperature and current.

pancake ice: small circular pieces with raised edges.

pannikin: a small cup or pan.

pemmican: dried and powdered beef to which a relatively large percentage of fat has been added.

permanent ice: a term used relatively, as distinguished from annual or sea ice; the ice of glaciers, ice shelves and the ice cap of the inland plateau.

phone patch: a form of voice communication based on a combination of ham radio and telephone.

plasmon: a milk-protein health food, carried in powdered form during sledging traverses by the Scott and Shackleton expeditions; also used as a food supplement, for example in the manufacture of sledging biscuits.

P.O.: Petty Officer.

pram: a Norwegian-type skiff. Pram Point on Ross Island was so named by the Discovery Expedition when it was necessary to use a pram while traveling in open water between the point and Winter Quarters Bay.

pressure ice or pressure: ridges, hummocks and upthrust sharp masses of ice caused by the collision of slowly moving permanent ice with a land mass.

primus or Primus: an oil-burning stove, often used for cooking during sledging traverses in polar regions.

PSF: Point of Safe Return.

rack: bunk.

red ration: pea meal and bacon powder.

rep: representative.

rotten berg: an iceberg that has been wasted by winds, ablation, sublimation and the action of waves. Usually it no longer has the typical tabular form of the Antarctic berg.

rpm: revolutions per minute.

SAR Condition: Search and Rescue Condition.

sastrugi (singular: *sastrugus*): irregularities, often wavelike, formed by the wind on a snow plain or ice field.

scurvy: the dreaded vitamin-C deficiency disease, whose cause was not known at the time of Scott's two Antarctic expeditions and Shackleton's Nimrod Expedition.

Seabees: members of construction battalion units of the United States Navy.

sennegrass: a type of Norwegian hay used as a moisture-absorbing packing in finneskoes.

serac: a pointed ice ridge in a crevassed area.

skua: a large, gull-like, fearless bipolar bird with flight characteristics that have been described as being similar to those of a small eagle. The Antarctic skua preys on Adélie penguins, eating their eggs and chicks.

snout (of a glacier): a glacier's lower extremity.

snow bridge: a bridge of snow across a crevasse.

statute mile: see knot.

st.: stone (as a unit of weight).

stone: a British unit of weight—fourteen pounds.

sublimation: direct passage from the solid to the gaseous state, used here to denote the change from ice to water vapor.

tank: see canvas tank.

TOQ: Temporary Officers' Quarters.

Twin Otter: a type of fixed-wing, twin-engine aircraft.

U.K.: United Kingdom.

USARP: United States Antarctic Research Program.

Usarp: a member of USARP.

USCGC: United States Coast Guard Cutter.

UV: ultraviolet.

venesta case: a strong and relatively light packing case made of cemented and pressed layers of wood and used by the Scott and Shackleton expeditions.

ventifact: a rock sculpted by winds.

VHF: Very High Frequency.

VIP: very important person.

VXE-6: the air arm of Task Force 199 (formerly 43), the latter also known as Operation Deep Freeze.

wanigan: a boxlike modern refuge shelter, usually made of plywood and containing survival foodstuffs and gear.

whiteout: a dangerous polar weather and optical phenomenon in which the sky and the snow or ice reflect each other so thoroughly that one seems to see only a two-dimensional white mass and consequently is disoriented.

Willy or *Willy Field:* Williams Field.

wind forces: they are logged according to the Beaufort Scale, which in the early days of Antarctic exploration ranged in number from 0 to 12, in description from Calm to Hurricane, and in miles per hour from 0 to 92. The scale now ranges from 0 to 17, with a maximum wind velocity of 136 miles per hour.

x.o.: executive officer.

Zodiac: a type of rubberized small water craft.

Zulu: phonetic for z, standing for zero meridian of longitude (the meridian of Greenwich, England).

Selected Bibliography

Roald Amundsen, *The South Pole,* two volumes, London and New York, 1913, translated from the Norwegian by A. G. Chater.

Antarctic Bibliography. An invaluable reference work sponsored by the Division of Polar Programs of the National Science Foundation and compiled by the Cold Regions Bibliography Project, Science and Technology Division, Library of Congress, Washington. Volume 9 (1977) contains the following descriptive note: "... A continuing series of compilations presenting abstracts and indexes of current Antarctic literature published since 1962. A companion volume to the series, *Antarctic Bibliography, 1951–1961,* extends the coverage retrospectively." As an example of its contents, the volume contains sections with the following titles: General; Biological Sciences; Cartography; Expeditions; Geological Sciences; Ice & Snow; Logistics, Equipment and Supplies; Medical Sciences; Meteorology; Oceanography; Atmospheric Physics; Terrestrial Physics; and Political Geography. There are author, subject, geographic and grantee indexes.

Antarctic Bibliography. An earlier and still valuable work, published by the U.S. Navy, Washington, 1951 (Code: NAVAER 10-35-591), summarizing much Antarctic knowledge up to the date of publication.

Antarctic Journal of the United States. Established in 1966, it is published quarterly (March, June, September and December) by the Division of Polar Programs of the National Science Foundation. A fifth annual review issue is also published, dated October but often appearing later. The journal "reports on U.S. activities in Antarctica and related activities elsewhere, and on trends in the U.S. Antarctic Program," according to a notice on its masthead. It is for the most part a highly technical scientific journal.

Antarctic Map Folio Series, published by the American Geographical

378

Society, New York, various years, beginning with 1964. Large format (17 × 11″), unstitched, with many loose maps, some of the latter on folded sheets 19¾ ×22″. A valiant, scholarly and at times highly technical attempt to sum up Antarctic knowledge but in some respects necessarily datable. Folio 19, 1975, is *History of Antarctic Exploration and Scientific Investigation.*

The Antarctic Pilot, 4th edition, London, 1974. Primarily for mariners but also informative and interesting for the general reader. A complex work, with navigational and operational information; general, scientific and environmental information; discussions of natural conditions and geographic matters; and containing many illustrations, diagrams and panoramic views. Supplements are also published, the latest of which is No. 3, 1978.

Terence Armstrong, Brian Roberts and Charles Swithinbank, *Illustrated Glossary of Snow and Ice,* Cambridge, England, 1973. With linguistic equivalents in Danish, Finnish, French (including French Canadian usage), German, Icelandic, Norwegian, Russian and Spanish (Argentine form).

Thaddeus Bellingshausen, *The Voyage of Captain Bellingshausen to the Antarctic Seas 1819–1821,* two volumes, London, 1945, translated from the Russian by several hands and edited by Frank Debenham.

Kenneth J. Bertrand, *Americans in Antarctica,* New York, 1971. A scholarly and authoritative work, with many citations of published and unpublished sources.

Richard E. Byrd, *Alone,* New York, 1938.

Richard E. Byrd, *Little America,* New York, 1930. An account of his first Antarctic expedition, during which he made the first flight over the Pole. Laurence M. Gould was science leader and second in command of this expedition.

Apsley Cherry-Garrard, *The Worst Journey in the World,* two volumes, London, 1922. The photographs which Herbert Ponting took of Cherry-Garrard (1886–1959) during Scott's second expedition seem to be of a frail and sensitive young man. Cherry-Garrard's activities in Antarctica, however, dramatically belie the impression of frailty. He was twenty-four when he joined the expedition. Together with Wilson and Bowers he took part in what is possibly the most extraordinary traverse in Antarctic history: the round-trip midwinter trek from Cape Evans down around Hut Point to Cape Crozier, Ross Island. The goal was three emperor penguin eggs, to be garnered from the Crozier rookery for scientific study. (The Crozier is the southernmost rookery of the emperor penguin, which lays and hatches its single annual egg on the ice in the austral winter under unbelievably inauspicious circumstances.) The trek was successful, although on more than one occasion the men came very close to dying. Wilson and Bowers perished with Scott on the polar journey. Scott, on seeing the startlingly haggard condition of the three men as they returned to Cape Evans after an absence of some five weeks (during which they had manhauled their sledges in the austral night and had shivered more than slept in their tent), gave Cherry-Garrard's narrative its title by remarking that, in his opinion, it was the worst journey in the world. Cherry-Garrard's complete narrative describes much more than the midwinter journey. In many ways it is a graphic report on Scott's second expedition. It is one of the finest tales ever told of man's behavior while pitted against nature. Cherry-Garrard was also a member of the party, led by Charles S. Wright, that went searching in November 1912 on the Ross Ice Shelf for the doomed Scott and his companions.

James Cook, *A Voyage Towards the South Pole, and Round the World,* two volumes, London, 1777.

George Forster, *A Voyage Round the World in his Britannic Majesty's Sloop, Resolution, Commanded by Capt. James Cook, During the Years 1772, 3, 4 and 5,* two volumes, London, 1777.

Vivian Fuchs, with some chapters by Edmund Hillary, *The Crossing of Antarctica,* London, 1958.

Laurence M. Gould, *Cold,* New York, 1931. The author's view of Byrd's first Antarctic expedition.

Trevor Hatherton, editor, *Antarctica,* London, 1965.

Edmund Hillary, *No Latitude for Error,* New York, 1961. The author's account of his part in the first surface crossing of Antarctica.

M. W. Holdgate, editor, *Antarctic Ecology,* London and New York, 1970.

Philip C. Jessup and Howard J. Taubenfeld, *Controls for Outer Space and the Antarctic Analogy,* New York, 1959. This is still in some respects a suggestive work despite the fact that it is dated because it precedes the establishment of the Antarctic Treaty.

Richard S. Lewis and Philip M. Smith, editors, *Frozen Future,* New York, 1973. An interesting book although carelessly proofread. There are several important errors in the reproduction of the text of the Antarctic Treaty.

George A. Llano, editor, *Adaptations Within Antarctic Ecosystems,* Washington, 1977.

Maps. American Geographical Society, New York; British Antarctic Survey, Cambridge, England; National Geographic Society, Washington; U.S. Geological Survey, Washington; U.S. Navy, Washington.

Douglas Mawson, *The Home of the Blizzard,* two volumes, London and Philadelphia, 1915. This has not been one of my favorite polar narratives but there is no doubt that Mawson was one of the great Antarctic explorers.

Mary A. McWhinnie, editor, *Polar Research: To the Present, and the Future,* Boulder, Colorado, 1978.

Charles Neider, editor, *Antarctica,* New York, 1972. Subtitled "Authentic Accounts of Life and Exploration in the World's Highest, Driest, Windiest, Coldest and Most Remote Continent," it contains excerpts from the narratives of Cook, Forster, Bellingshausen, Weddell, Wilkes, Ross, Amundsen, Scott, Shackleton, Ponting, Cherry-Garrard, Byrd, Siple and Hillary.

Charles Neider, *Edge of the World: Ross Island, Antarctica,* New York, 1974. Subtitled "A Personal and Historical Narrative." It contains color photographs by the author, black/white photographs (historical as well as modern) and two-color maps.

The Polar Record, Cambridge, England. Published three times a year by the Scott Polar Research Institute, Cambridge, it provides, according to SPRI, "an authoritative international record of Arctic and Antarctic exploration and research. Each issue contains a wide variety of illustrated articles and notes for the geographer, the historian, the economist, the traveller, and all others interested in the polar regions. There is also a comprehensive review of all significant publications dealing with expeditions, research, equipment, and conditions of living in cold climates."

Polar Regions Atlas, published by the Central Intelligence Agency, Washington, 1978. An excellent rather brief work in large format (15 × 9¾″), with illustrations and maps. Among other things, it provides useful comparisons of the Arctic and Antarctic regions and deals with Antarctic climate, ice, exploration, sovereignty problems, the Antarctic Treaty, science programs, environmental protection, sealing, whaling, krill and minerals.

Herbert G. Ponting, *The Great White South,* London, 1921. Ponting (1870–1935) was the official photographer of Scott's second and last expedition. During his life he was widely known in England as a world traveler, master photographer, travel writer and lecturer. Now he is mostly remembered by the handful of admirers of his illustrations of *Scott's Last Expedition.* He met Scott in the autumn of 1909, at the height of his fame. In his time he was by far the most gifted photographer of the Antarctic. Even from today's perspective he seems to be possibly the finest photographer so far to have worked in Antarctica, despite the limitations of his early equipment. He worked arduously, extensively, intensively and, above all, with great artistic effect. We are indebted to him for many famous photographs—for example those showing Scott in the Cape Evans hut. He was equally good at dealing with landscapes and with men and animals. Scott prized not only his camera work but his lantern-slide lectures about exotic places given to members of the expedition. Ponting had a willingness, almost an eagerness, to teach others the art of photography. In his book about his experiences with the expedition he reveals himself to be a sensitive and articulate writer.

Raymond Priestley, *Antarctic Adventure,* London, 1914. Priestley was a member of Scott's last expedition. Later he and Charles S. Wright became brothers-in-law. This narrative details the incredible experiences of a marooned group of men known as Scott's Northern Party, whose survival is one of the remarkable moments of Antarctic history.

Louis O. Quam, *Research in the Antarctic,* Washington, 1971.

James Clark Ross, *A Voyage of Discovery and Research in the Southern and Antarctic Regions, During the Years 1839—43,* London, 1847.

Sailing Directions for Antarctica, 2d edition, revised, Washington, 1976. Issued primarily for the mariner but valuable and interesting to the layman as well.

Robert Falcon Scott, *Scott's Last Expedition,* arranged by Leonard Huxley, two volumes, London, 1913.

Robert Falcon Scott, *The Voyage of the "Discovery,"* two volumes, London and New York, 1905. The narrative of his first expedition, in which he revealed his unusual talents as a writer.

Ernest Shackleton, *The Heart of the Antarctic,* two volumes, London and Philadelphia, 1909. The author's first expedition.

Ernest Shackleton, *South,* London and New York, 1920. An account of the Endurance Expedition.

Paul Siple, *90° South,* New York, 1959. In 1928 a nationwide search was conducted to select a Boy Scout to accompany Richard E. Byrd on the latter's first Antarctic expedition. Paul Siple (1908–1968) was chosen. The event was to be the turning point of his life. Not only did he prove his value to the expedition; after serving in several subsequent expeditions he became recognized as an Antarctic expert. He was chief biologist of Byrd's 1933–35 expedition. During the IGY, when the United States set up a permanent station at the Pole, he was named as the station's science leader. He was among the small group of men who first wintered at the Pole. During his active years he made important contributions to knowledge of the continent.

Walter Sullivan, *Quest for a Continent,* New York, 1957.

George E. Watson, *Birds of the Antarctic and Sub-Antarctic,* Washington, 1975.

James Weddell, *A Voyage Towards the South Pole,* London, 1825.

Charles Wilkes, *Narrative of the United States Exploring Expedition,* five volumes, Philadelphia, 1845.

Frank A. Worsley, *Endurance,* New York, 1931. An important participant's view of Shackleton's Endurance Expedition, this is also, in my opinion, one of the best Antarctic narratives. Unfortunately it is largely neglected.

Index

Index   385

Index

OTHER COOPER SQUARE PRESS TITLES OF INTEREST

EDGE OF THE WORLD:
ROSS ISLAND, ANTARCTICA
A Personal and Historical Narrative
of Exploration, Adventure, Tragedy,
and Survival
Charles Neider
with a new introduction
536 pp., 45 b/w photos,
15 maps
0-8154-1154-5
$19.95

ANTARCTICA
Firsthand Accounts of Exploration
and Endurance
Edited by Charles Neider
468 pp.
0-8154-1023-9
$18.95

ADAM'S BURDEN
Charles Neider
304 pp.
1-56833-239-4
$26.95 cloth

THE GROTTO BERG
Charles Neider
184 pp., 3 color photos
0-8154-1123-5
$22.95 cloth

THE FABULOUS INSECTS
Essays by the Foremost
Nature Writers
Edited by Charles Neider
288 pp.
0-8154-1100-6
$17.95

THE NORTH POLE
Robert E. Peary
Foreword by Theodore
Roosevelt
New introduction by Robert
M. Bryce
472 pp., 110 b/w
illustrations
0-8154-1138-3
$22.95

MY ATTAINMENT OF THE POLE
Dr. Frederick A. Cook
New introduction by
Robert M. Bryce
624 pp., 52 b/w illustrations
0-8154-1137-5
$22.95

ARCTIC EXPERIENCES
Aboard the Doomed Polaris
Expedition and Six Months Adrift on
an Ice-Floe
Captain George E. Tyson
New introduction by
Edward E. Leslie
504 pp., 78 b/w illustrations
0-8154-1189-8
$24.95 cloth

A NEGRO EXPLORER AT THE NORTH POLE
Matthew A. Henson
Preface by
Booker T. Washington
Foreword by Robert E. Peary
New introduction by
Robert M. Bryce
272 pp., 6 b/w photos
0-8154-1125-1
$15.95

THE *KARLUK'S* LAST VOYAGE
An Epic of Death and Survival in the Arctic
Captain Robert A. Bartlett
New introduction by
Edward E. Leslie
378 pp., 23 b/w photos,
3 maps
0-8154-1124-3
$18.95

THE VOYAGE OF THE DISCOVERY
Scott's First Antarctic Expedition, 1901–1904
Captain Robert F. Scott
Preface by Fridtjof Nansen
New introduction by
Ross MacPhee

Volume I
712 pp., 147 b/w
illustrations
0-8154-1079-4
$35.00 cloth

Volume II
656 pp., 123 b/w
illustrations
0-8154-1151-0
$35.00 cloth

THE SOUTH POLE
An Account of the Norwegian Antarctic Expedition in the *Fram*, 1910–1912
Captain Roald Amundsen
Foreword by Fridtjof Nansen
New introduction by
Roland Huntford
896 pp., 136 b/w photos,
20 maps & charts
0-8154-1127-8
$29.95

THE GREAT WHITE SOUTH
Traveling with Robert F. Scott's Doomed South Pole Expedition
Herbert G. Ponting
New introduction by
Roland Huntford
440 pp., 178 b/w
illustrations
0-8154-1161-8
$18.95

EDGE OF THE JUNGLE
William Beebe
New introduction by
Robert Finch
320 pp., 1 b/w photo
0-8154-1160-X
$17.95

THE LIFE AND AFRICAN EXPLORATIONS OF DAVID LIVINGSTONE
Dr. David Livingstone
648 pp., 53 b/w illustrations
0-8154-1208-8
$22.95

IN SEARCH OF ROBINSÓN CRUSOE
Daisuke Takahashi
256 pp., 24 b/w photos
0-8154-1200-2
$24.95 cloth

AFRICAN GAME TRAILS
An Account of the African Wanderings of an American Hunter-Naturalist
Theodore Roosevelt
New introduction by
H. W. Brands
583 pp., 210 b/w
illustrations
0-8154-1132-4
$22.95

AFRICA EXPLORED
Europeans on the Dark Continent, 1769–1889
Christopher Hibbert
344 pp., 54 b/w
illustrations, 16 maps
0-8154-1193-6
$18.95

THROUGH THE BRAZILIAN WILDERNESS
Theodore Roosevelt
New introduction by
H. W. Brands
448 pp., 9 b/w photos,
3 maps
0-8154-1095-6
$19.95

STANLEY
The Making of an African Explorer
Frank McLynn
424 pp., 19 b/w illustrations
0-8154-1167-7
$18.95

THE DESERT AND THE SOWN
The Syrian Adventures of the Female Lawrence of Arabia
Gertrude Bell
New introduction by
Rosemary O'Brien
368 pp., 162 b/w photos
0-8154-1135-9
$19.95

MAN AGAINST NATURE
Firsthand Accounts of Adventure and Exploration
Edited by Charles Neider
512 pp.
0-8154-1040-9
$18.95

GREAT SHIPWRECKS AND CASTAWAYS
Firsthand Accounts of Disasters at Sea
Edited by Charles Neider
252 pp.
0-8154-1094-8
$16.95

Available at bookstores
or call 1-800-462-6420

Cooper Square Press

200 Park Avenue South ♦ Suite 1109 ♦ New York, New York 10003
www.coopersquarepress.com

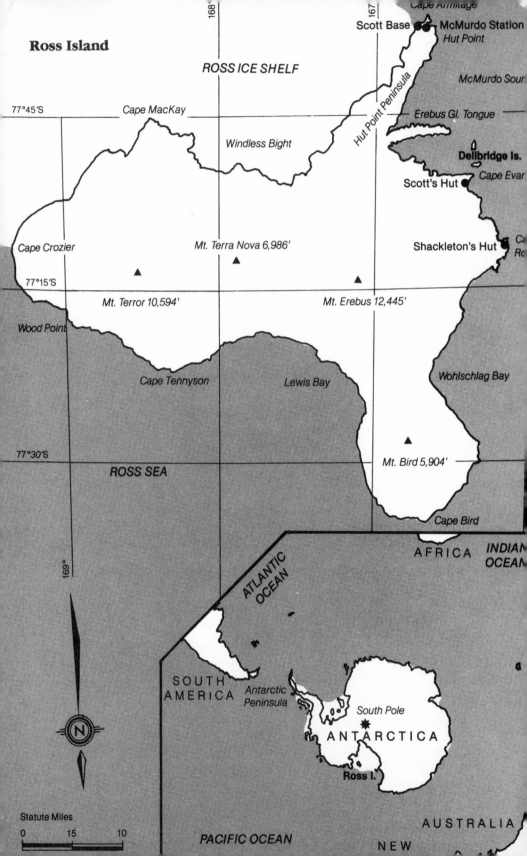

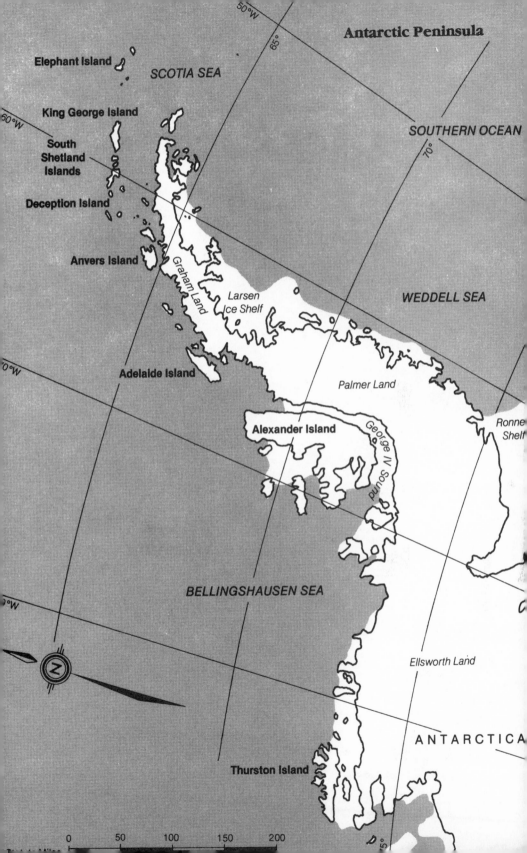

Antarctic Peninsula

SCOTIA SEA

Elephant Island

King George Island

South
Shetland
Islands

Deception Island

Anvers Island

Graham Land

Adelaide Island

SOUTHERN OCEAN

Larsen
Ice Shelf

WEDDELL SEA

Palmer Land

Alexander Island

George IV Sound

Ronne
Shelf

BELLINGSHAUSEN SEA

Ellsworth Land

ANTARCTICA

Thurston Island

50°W

65°

70°

60°W

70°W

0   50   100   150   200

N